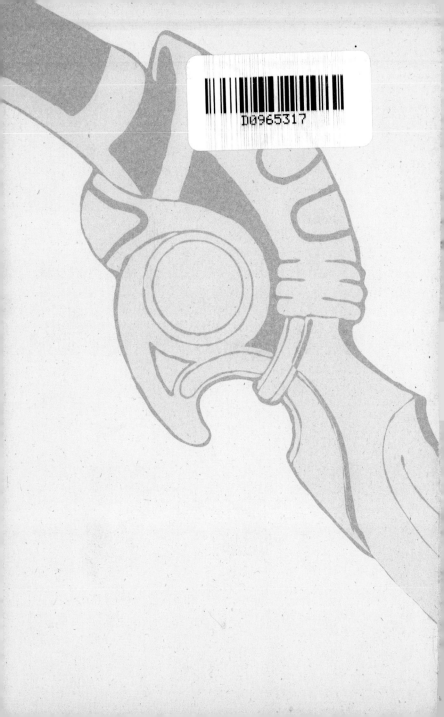

Arata
THE LEGEND
1

We are Man, born of Heaven and Earth,
Moon and Sun and everything under them.

Eyes, Ears, Nose, Tongue, Body, Mind...

Purity will pierce evil and
open up the world of darkness.

All life will be reborn and invigorated.

Appear now.

STORY & ART BY
Yuu Watase

Arata 1
THE LEGEND

CONTENTS

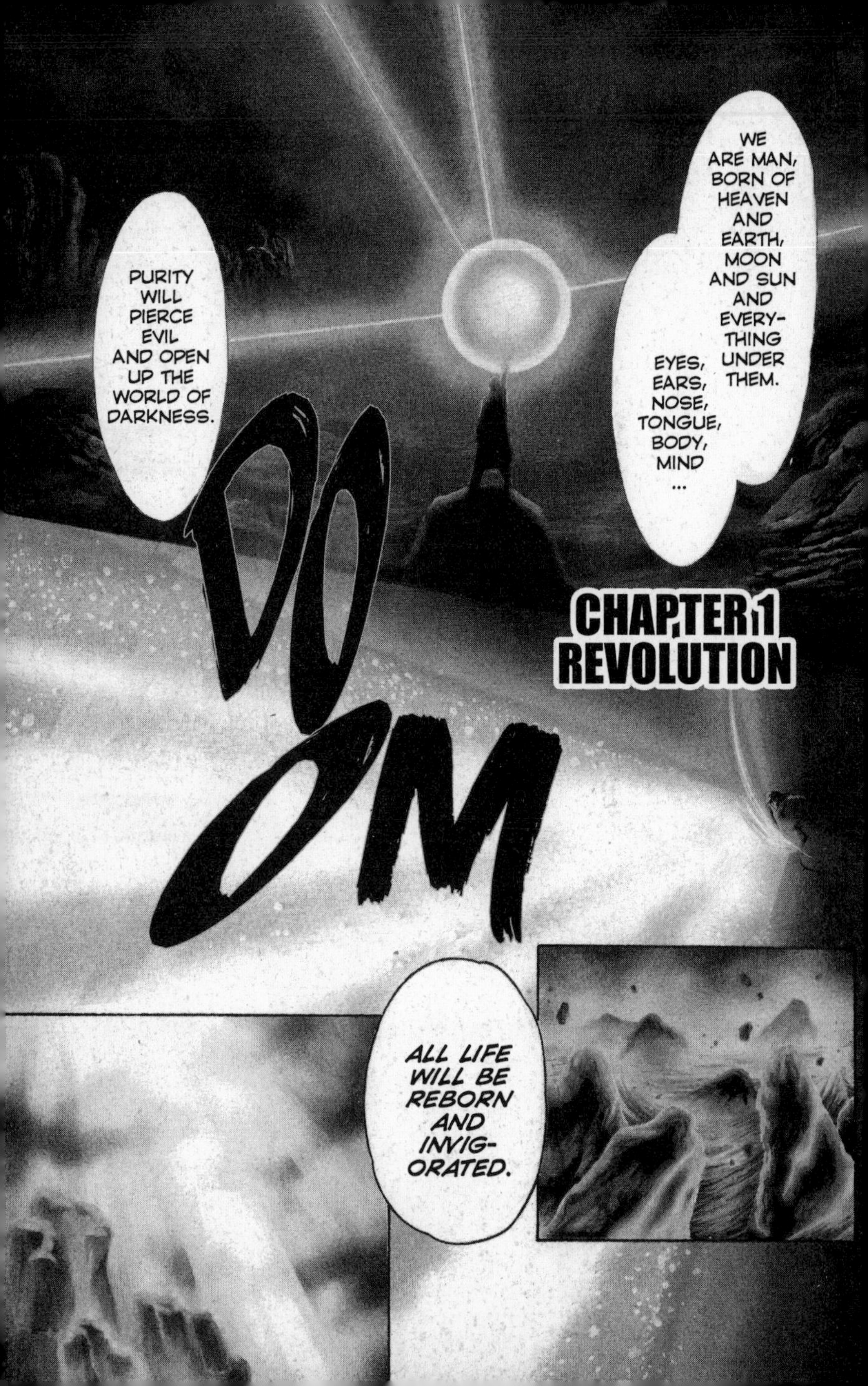
WE ARE MAN, BORN OF HEAVEN AND EARTH, MOON AND SUN AND EVERYTHING UNDER THEM.
EYES, EARS, NOSE, TONGUE, BODY, MIND ...
PURITY WILL PIERCE EVIL AND OPEN UP THE WORLD OF DARKNESS.
DOOM
CHAPTER 1 REVOLUTION
ALL LIFE WILL BE REBORN AND INVIGORATED.

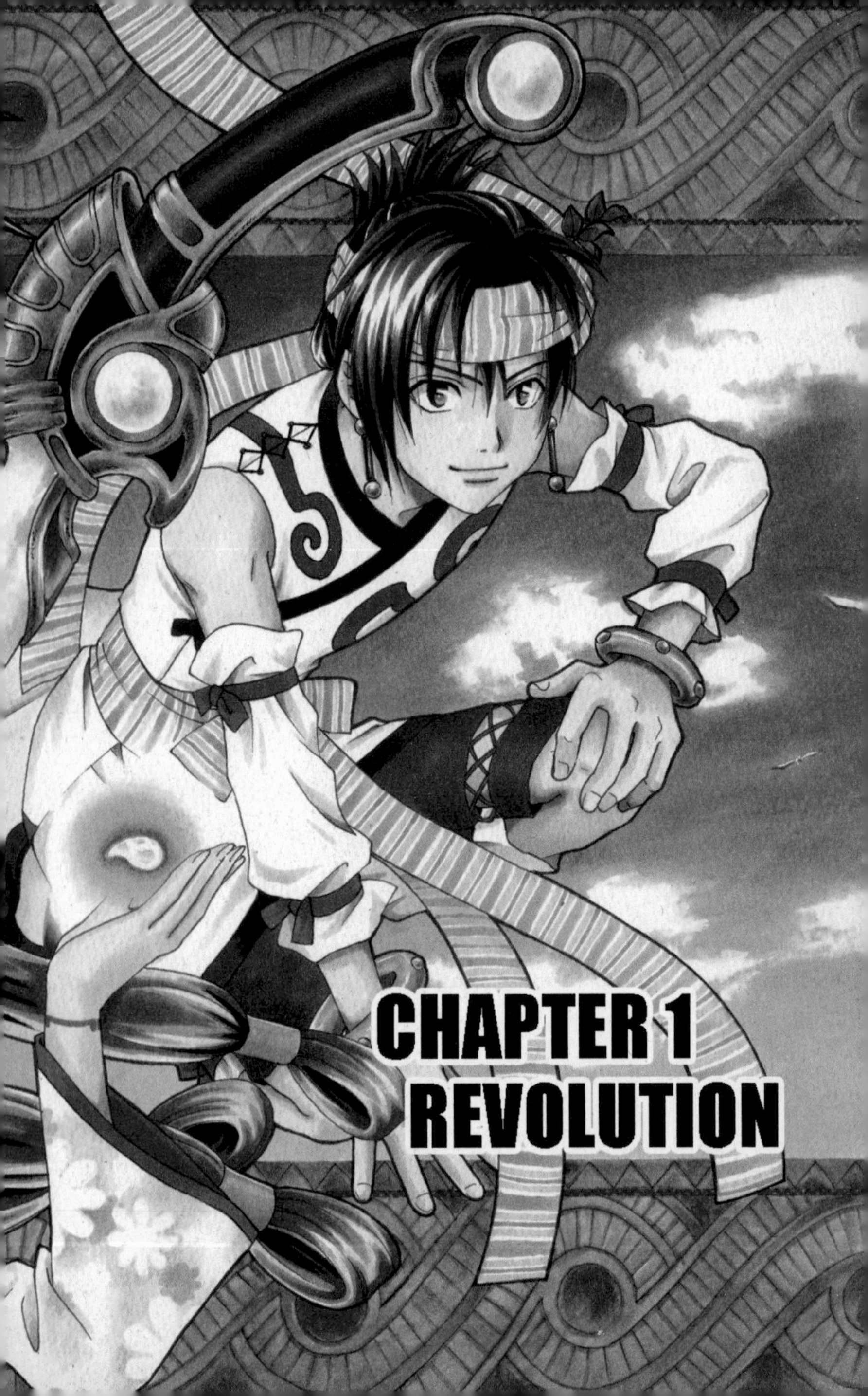
CHAPTER 1
REVOLUTION

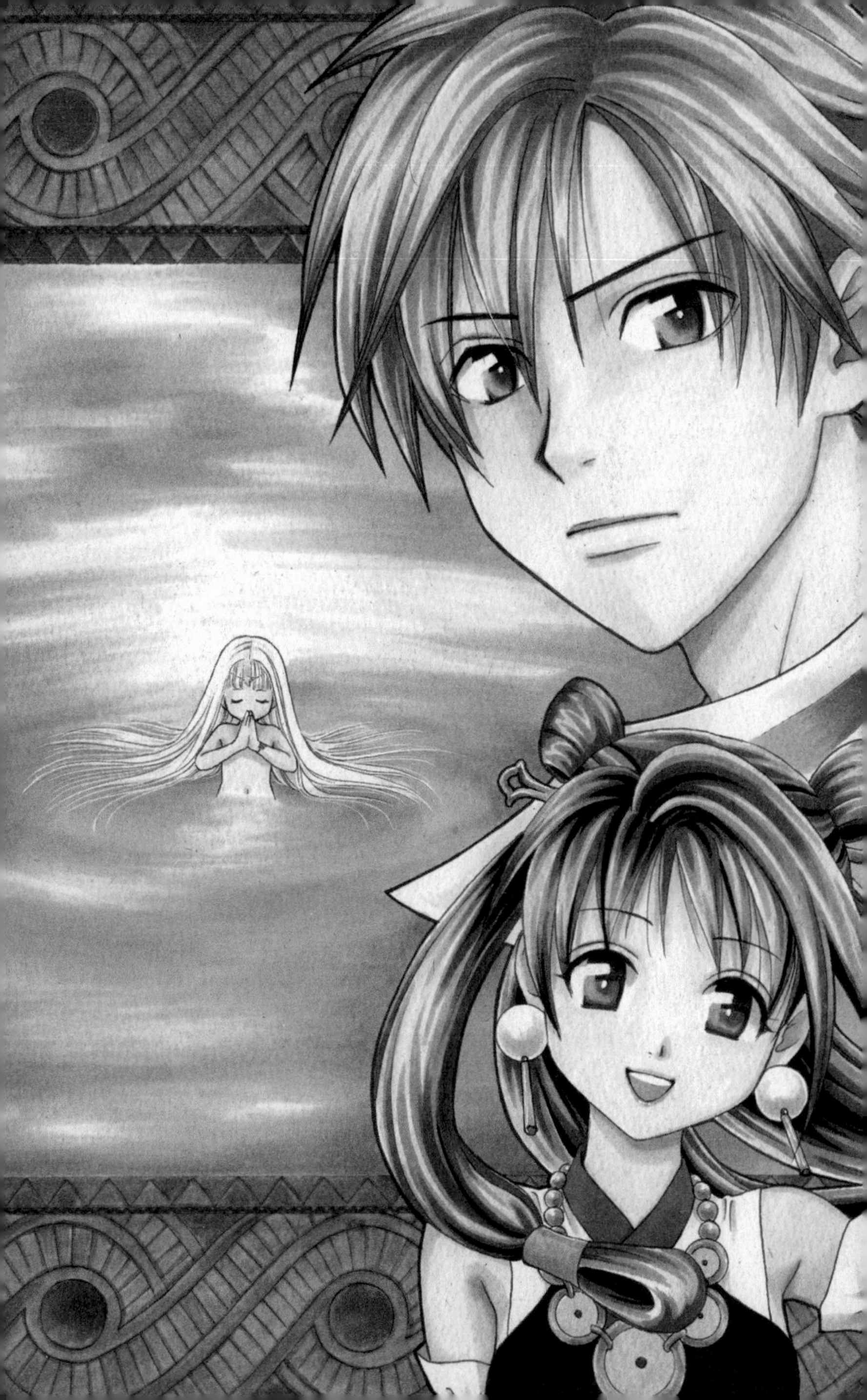

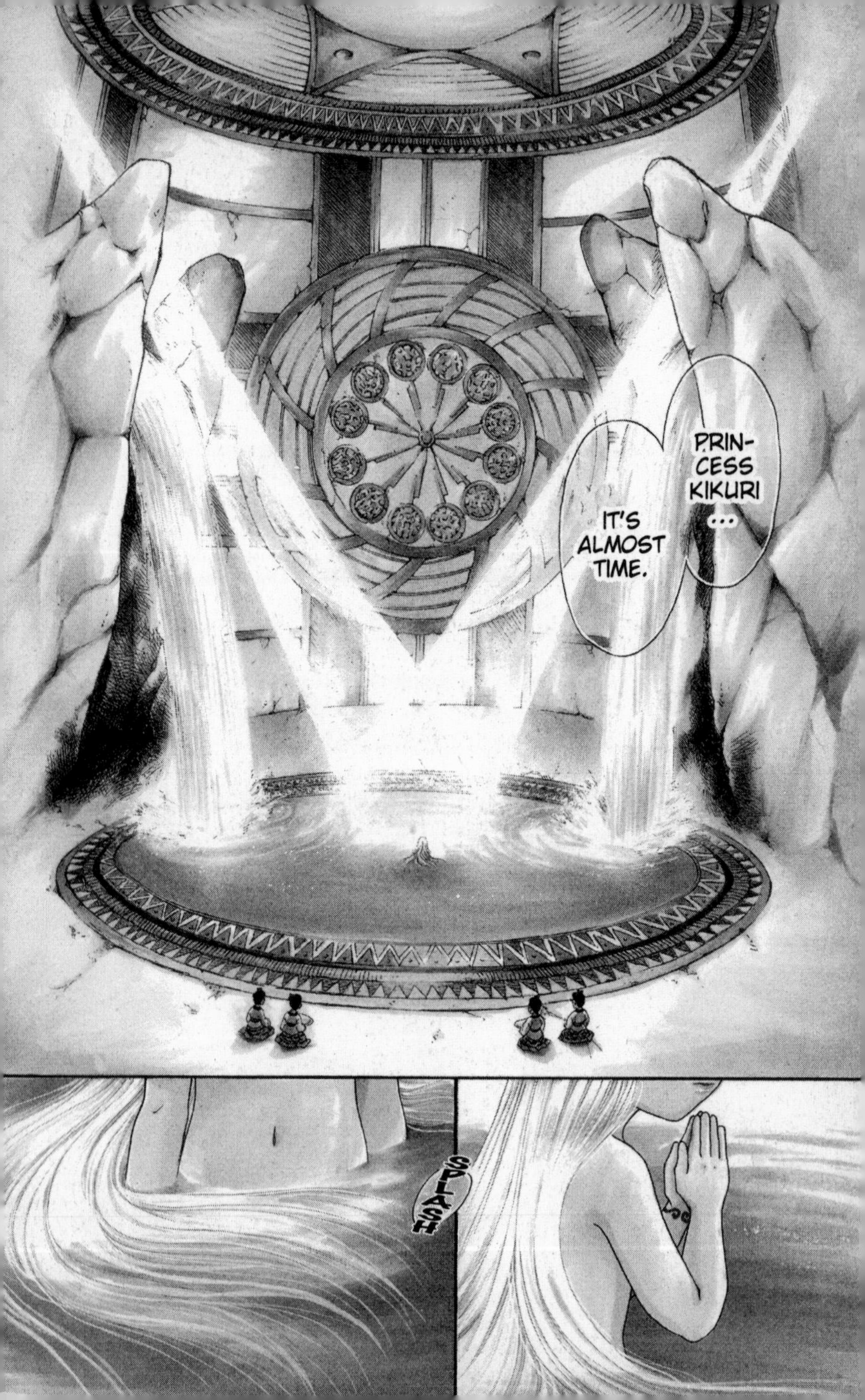
PRIN-CESS KIKURI ...
IT'S ALMOST TIME.
SPLASH

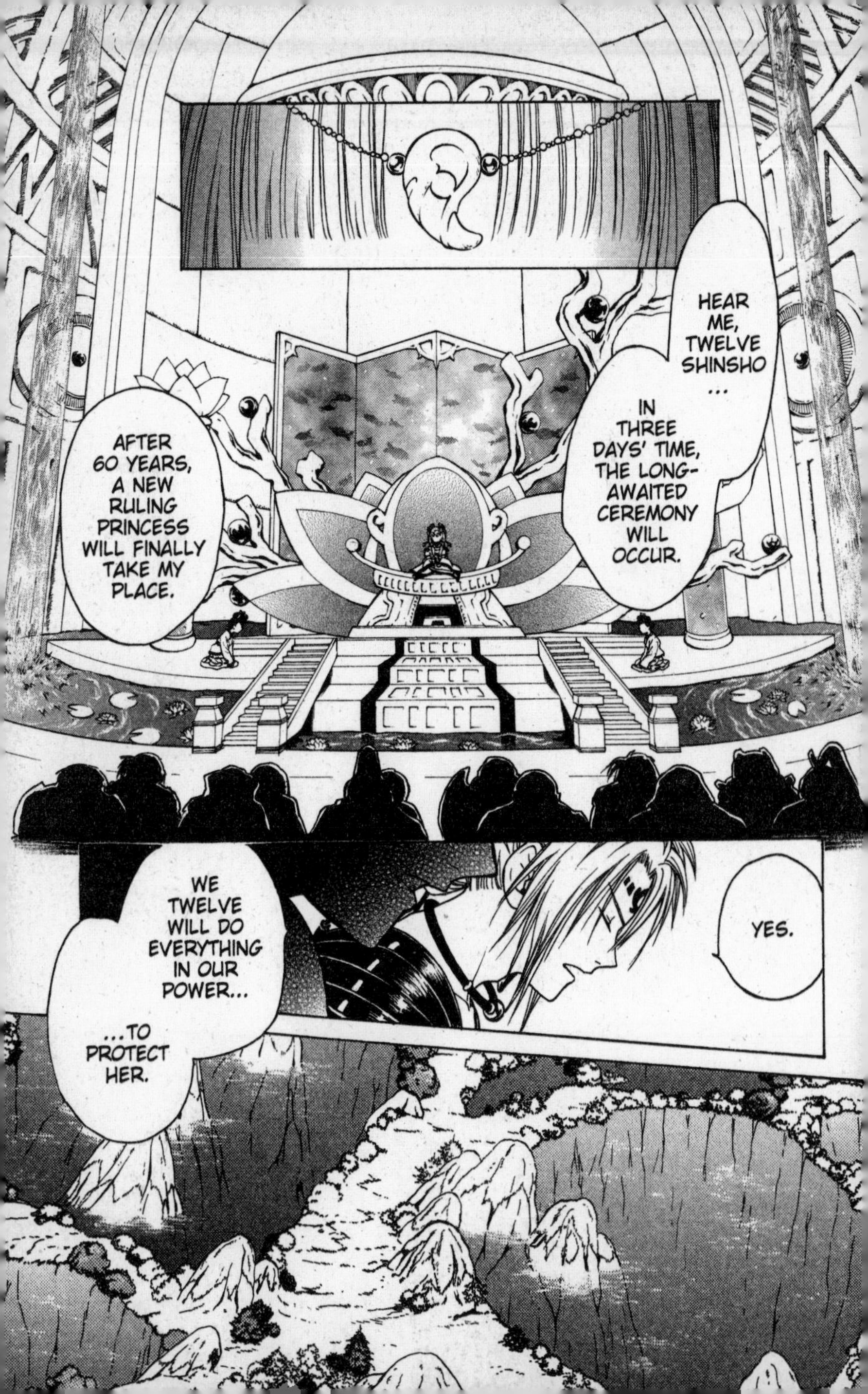
HEAR ME, TWELVE SHINSHO...
IN THREE DAYS' TIME, THE LONG-AWAITED CEREMONY WILL OCCUR.
AFTER 60 YEARS, A NEW RULING PRINCESS WILL FINALLY TAKE MY PLACE.
YES.
WE TWELVE WILL DO EVERYTHING IN OUR POWER...
...TO PROTECT HER.

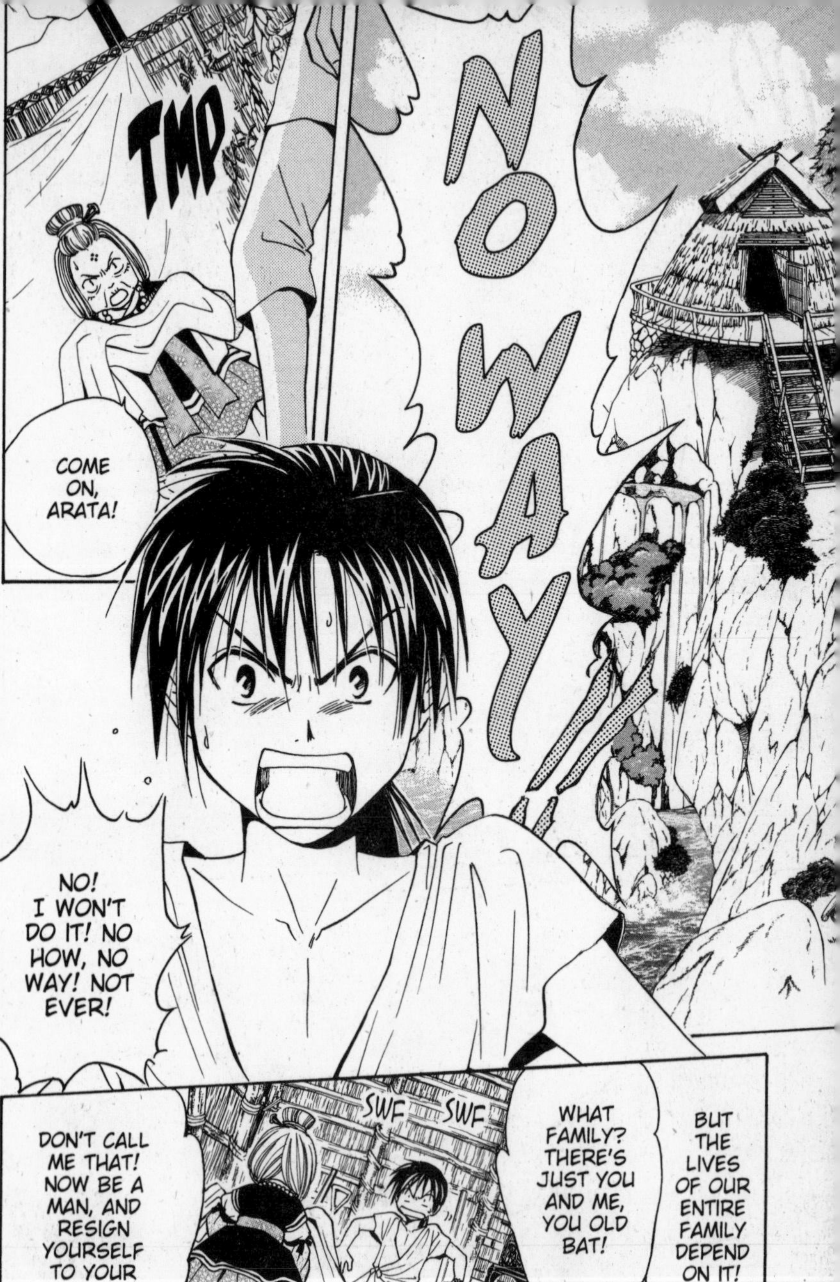
NO WAY!
NO! I WON'T DO IT! NO HOW, NO WAY! NOT EVER!
TMP
COME ON, ARATA!
BUT THE LIVES OF OUR ENTIRE FAMILY DEPEND ON IT!
WHAT FAMILY? THERE'S JUST YOU AND ME, YOU OLD BAT!
SWF SWF
DON'T CALL ME THAT! NOW BE A MAN, AND RESIGN YOURSELF TO YOUR DUTY!

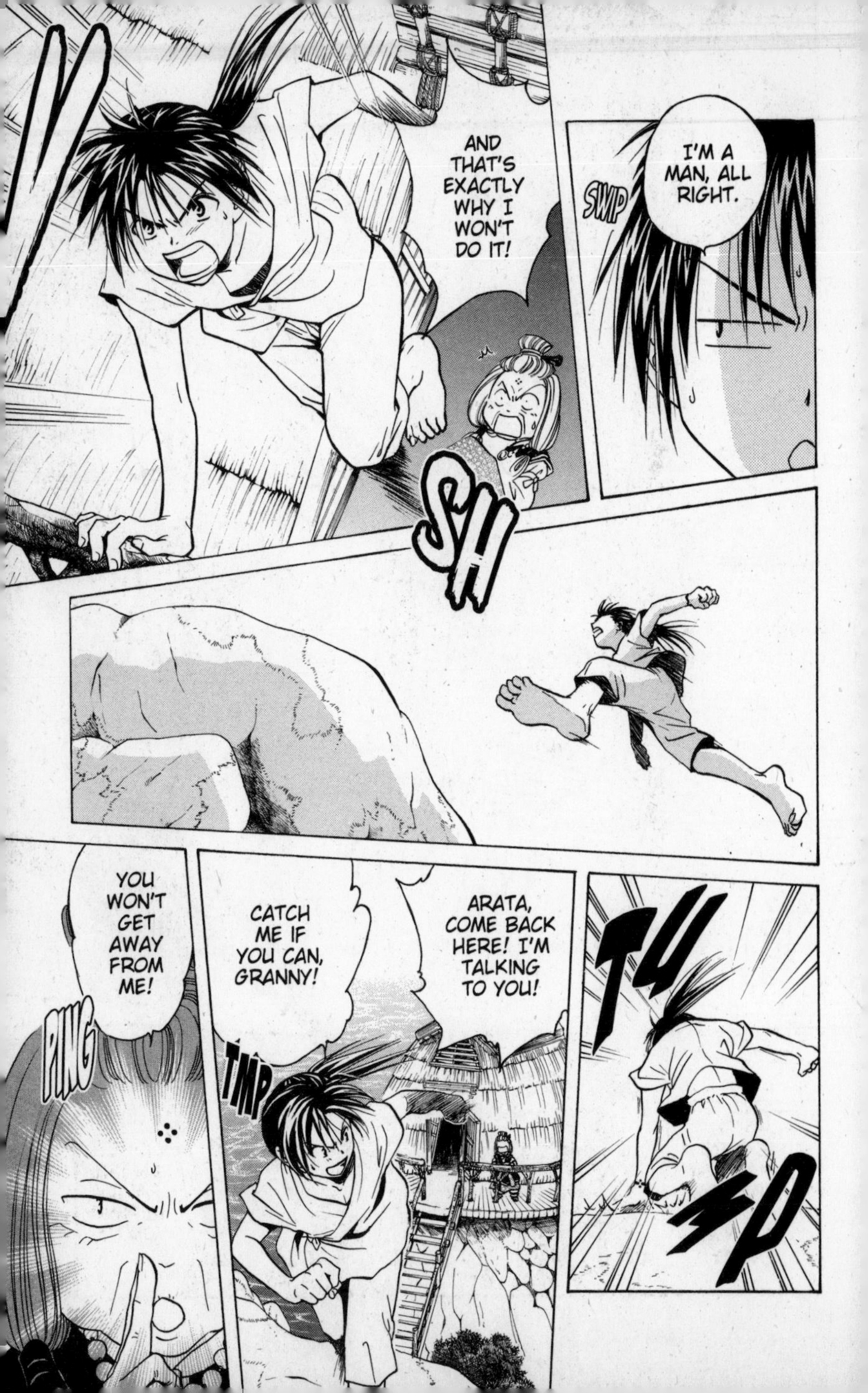
SWIP
I'M A MAN, ALL RIGHT.
AND THAT'S EXACTLY WHY I WON'T DO IT!
SH
TU
MP
ARATA, COME BACK HERE! I'M TALKING TO YOU!
CATCH ME IF YOU CAN, GRANNY!
TMP
YOU WON'T GET AWAY FROM ME!
PING

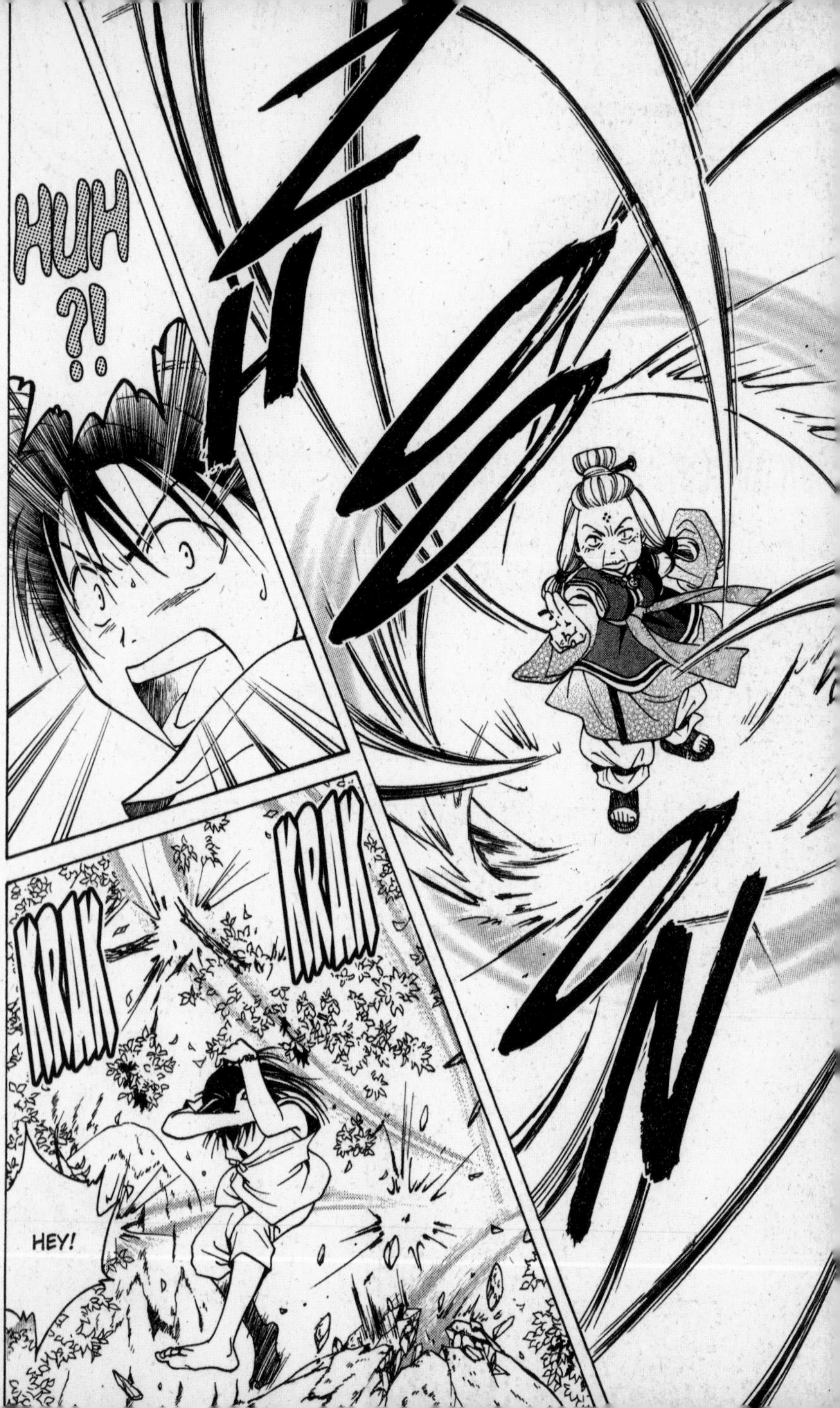
HUH ?!
KRAK
KRAK
HEY!

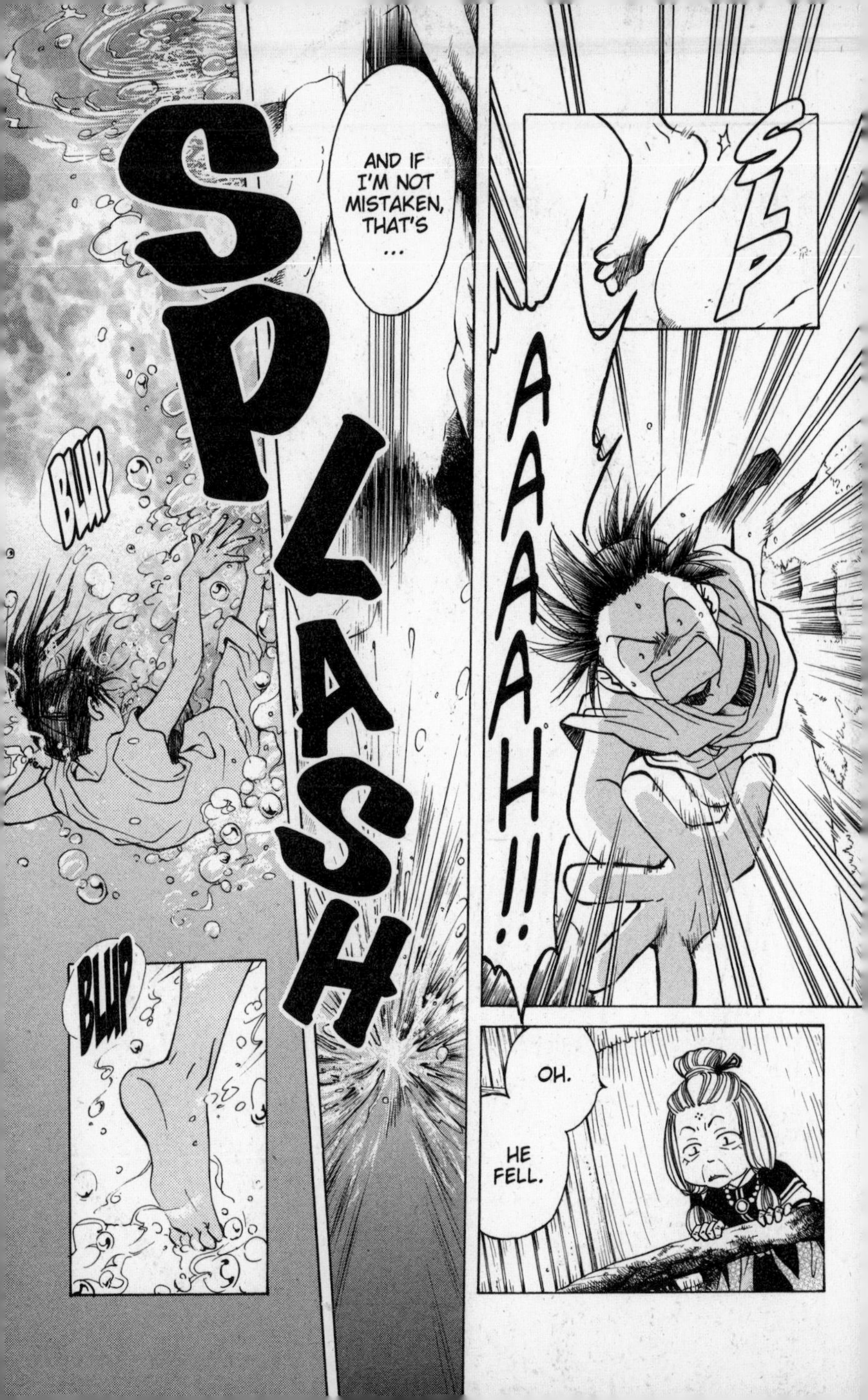
SLIP
AAAAH!!
OH.
HE FELL.
AND IF I'M NOT MISTAKEN, THAT'S ...
SPLASH
BLUP
BLUP

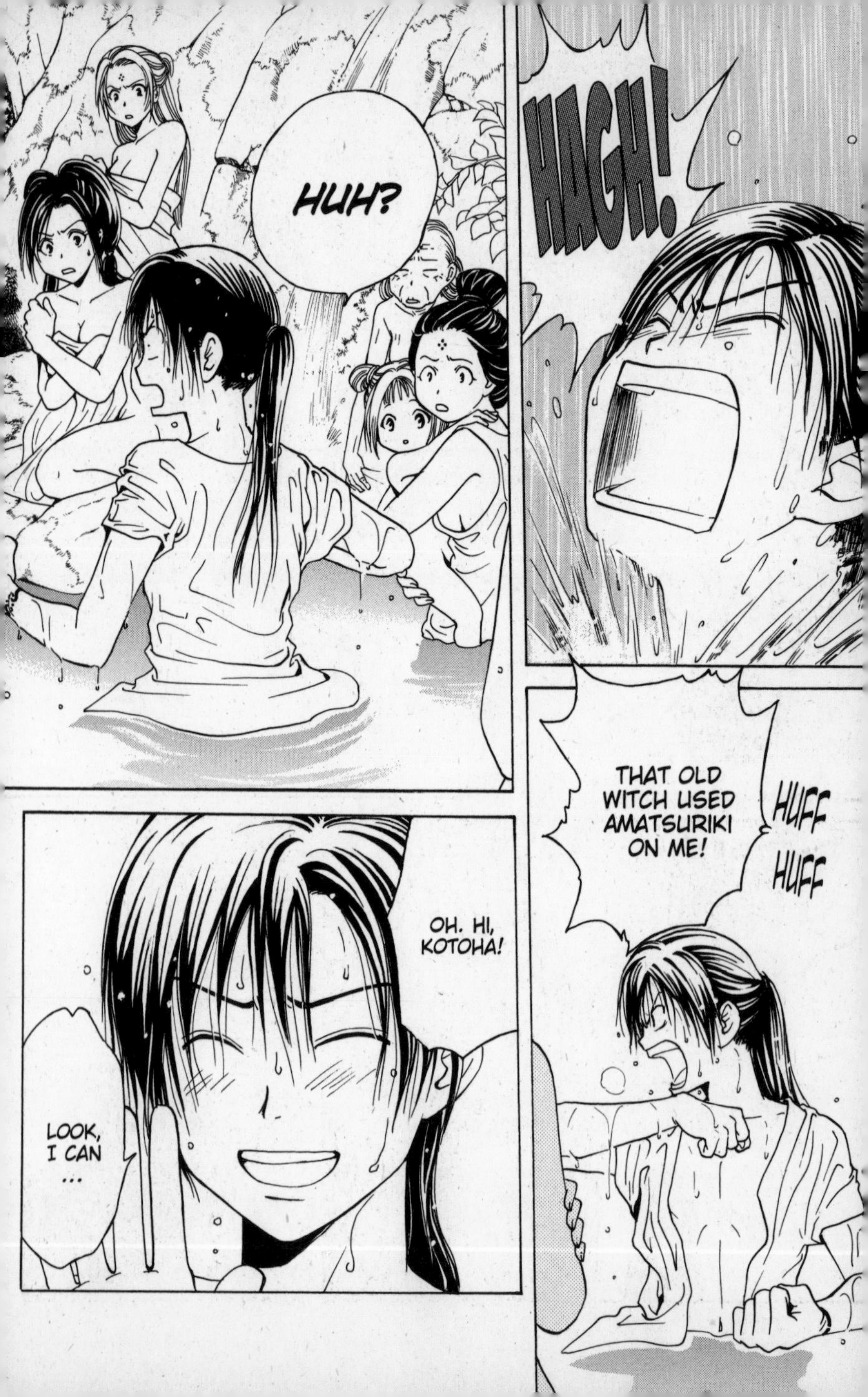
HAGH!
HUH?
THAT OLD WITCH USED AMATSURIKI ON ME!
HUFF HUFF
OH. HI, KOTOHA!
LOOK, I CAN ...

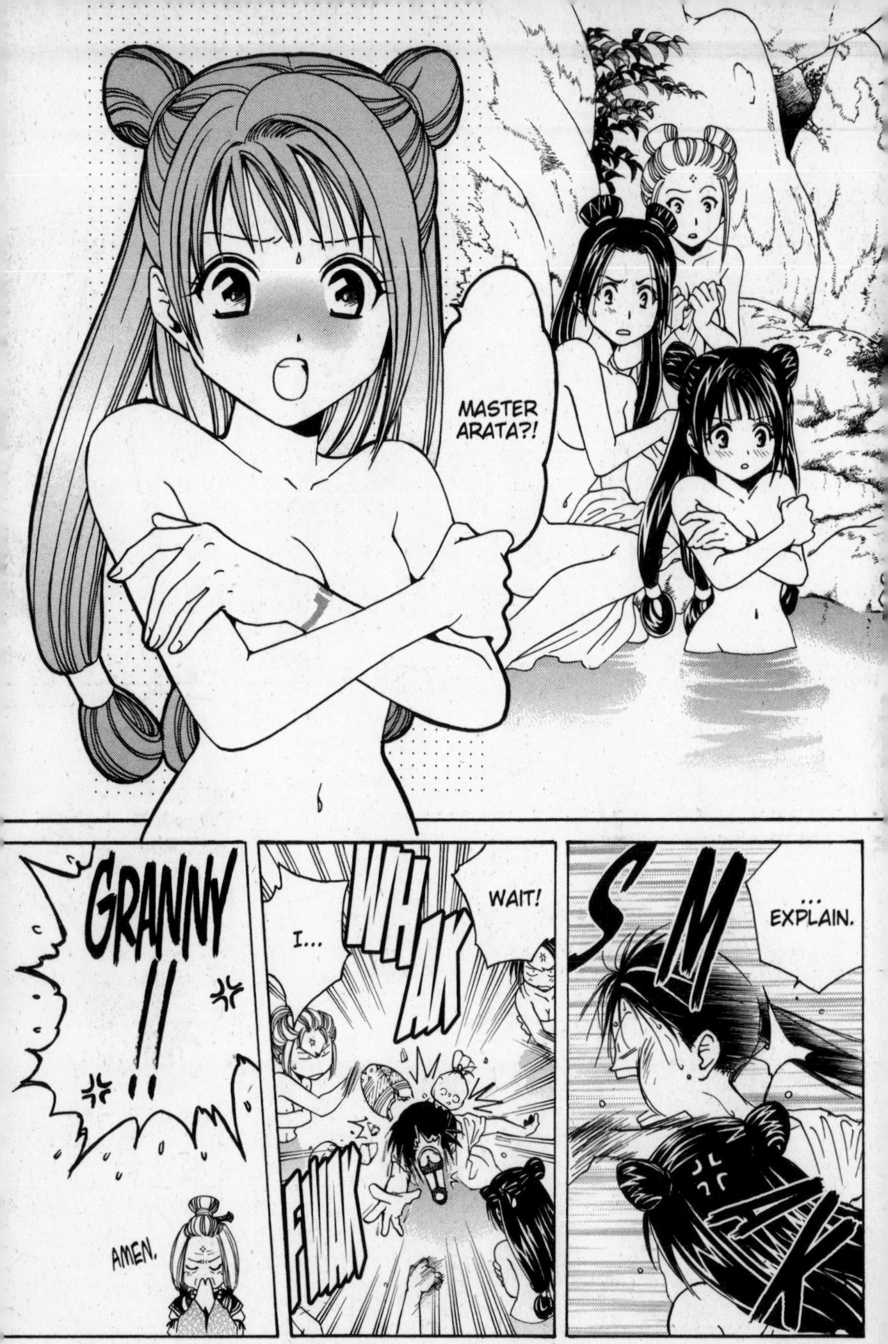
MASTER ARATA?!
...EXPLAIN.
WAIT!
I...
WHAK
GRANNY!!
AMEN.

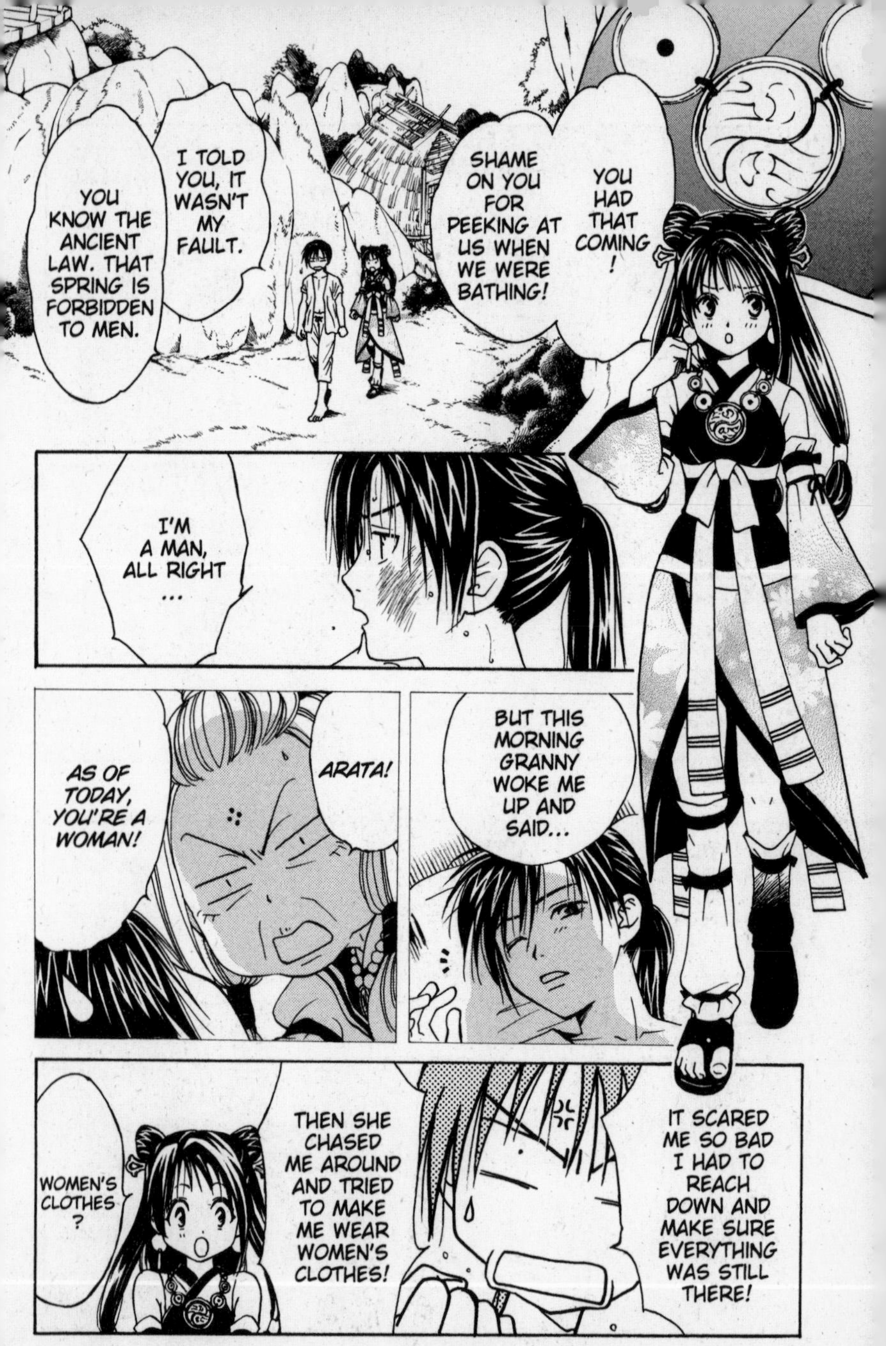
YOU HAD THAT COMING!
SHAME ON YOU FOR PEEKING AT US WHEN WE WERE BATHING!
I TOLD YOU, IT WASN'T MY FAULT.
YOU KNOW THE ANCIENT LAW. THAT SPRING IS FORBIDDEN TO MEN.
I'M A MAN, ALL RIGHT...
BUT THIS MORNING GRANNY WOKE ME UP AND SAID...
ARATA!
AS OF TODAY, YOU'RE A WOMAN!
IT SCARED ME SO BAD I HAD TO REACH DOWN AND MAKE SURE EVERYTHING WAS STILL THERE!
THEN SHE CHASED ME AROUND AND TRIED TO MAKE ME WEAR WOMEN'S CLOTHES!
WOMEN'S CLOTHES?

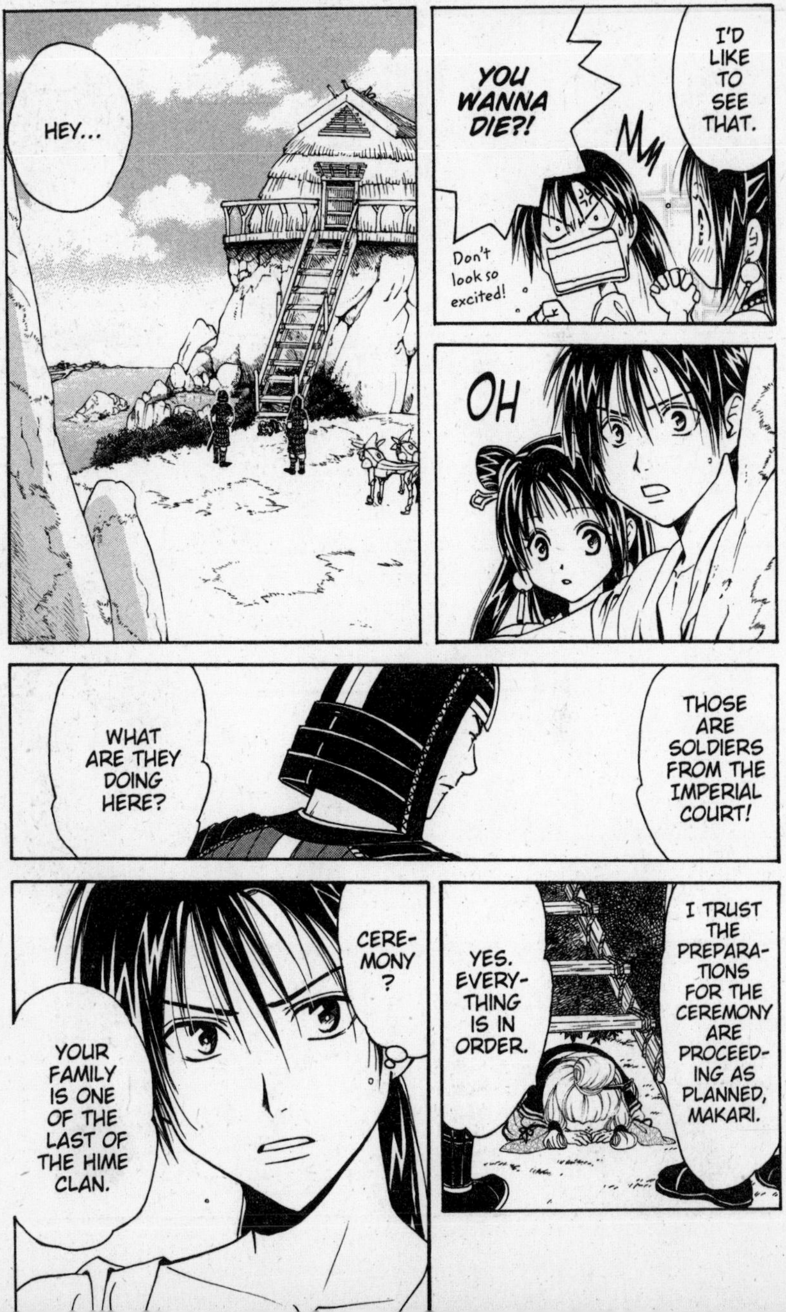
I'D LIKE TO SEE THAT.
YOU WANNA DIE?!
MM
Don't look so excited!
OH
HEY...
THOSE ARE SOLDIERS FROM THE IMPERIAL COURT!
WHAT ARE THEY DOING HERE?
I TRUST THE PREPARATIONS FOR THE CEREMONY ARE PROCEEDING AS PLANNED, MAKARI.
YES. EVERYTHING IS IN ORDER.
CEREMONY?
YOUR FAMILY IS ONE OF THE LAST OF THE HIME CLAN.

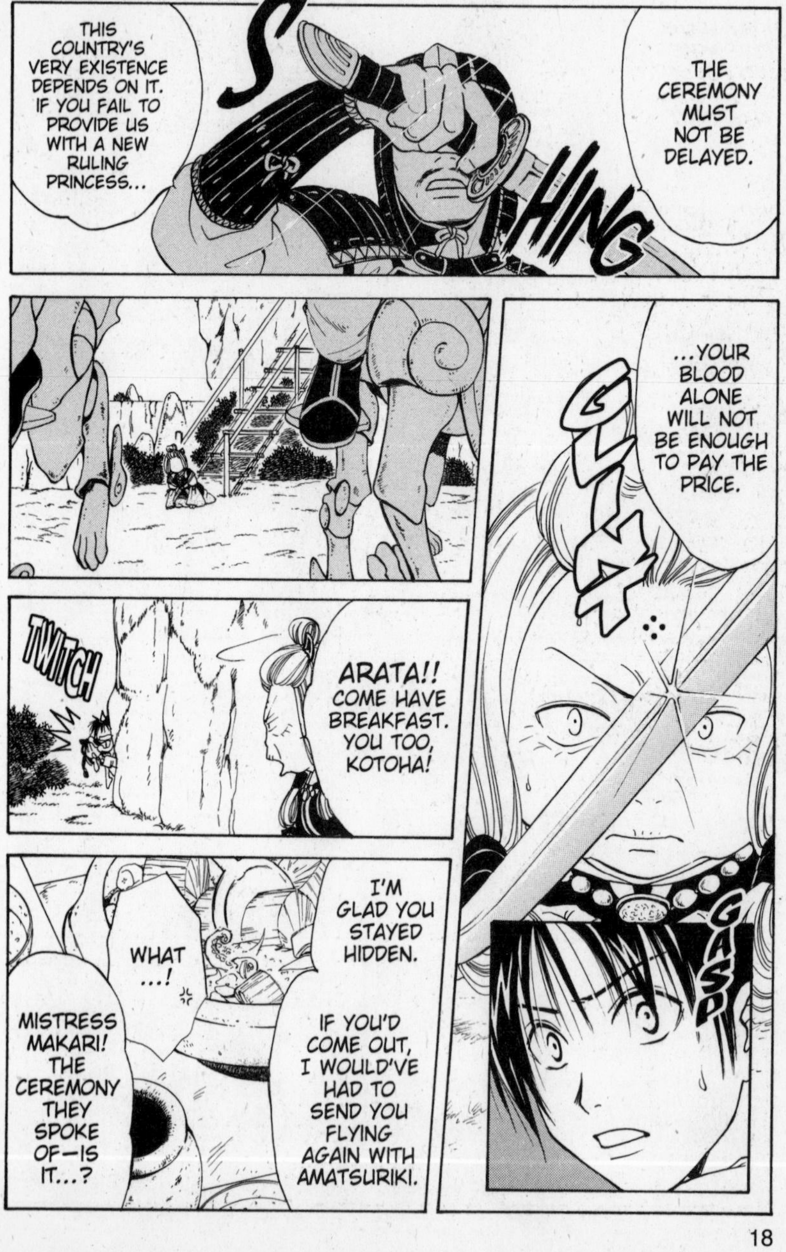
THE CEREMONY MUST NOT BE DELAYED.
SHING
THIS COUNTRY'S VERY EXISTENCE DEPENDS ON IT. IF YOU FAIL TO PROVIDE US WITH A NEW RULING PRINCESS...
GLINT
...YOUR BLOOD ALONE WILL NOT BE ENOUGH TO PAY THE PRICE.
GASP
ARATA!! COME HAVE BREAKFAST. YOU TOO, KOTOHA!
TWITCH
I'M GLAD YOU STAYED HIDDEN.
IF YOU'D COME OUT, I WOULD'VE HAD TO SEND YOU FLYING AGAIN WITH AMATSURIKI.
WHAT ...!
MISTRESS MAKARI! THE CEREMONY THEY SPOKE OF—IS IT...?

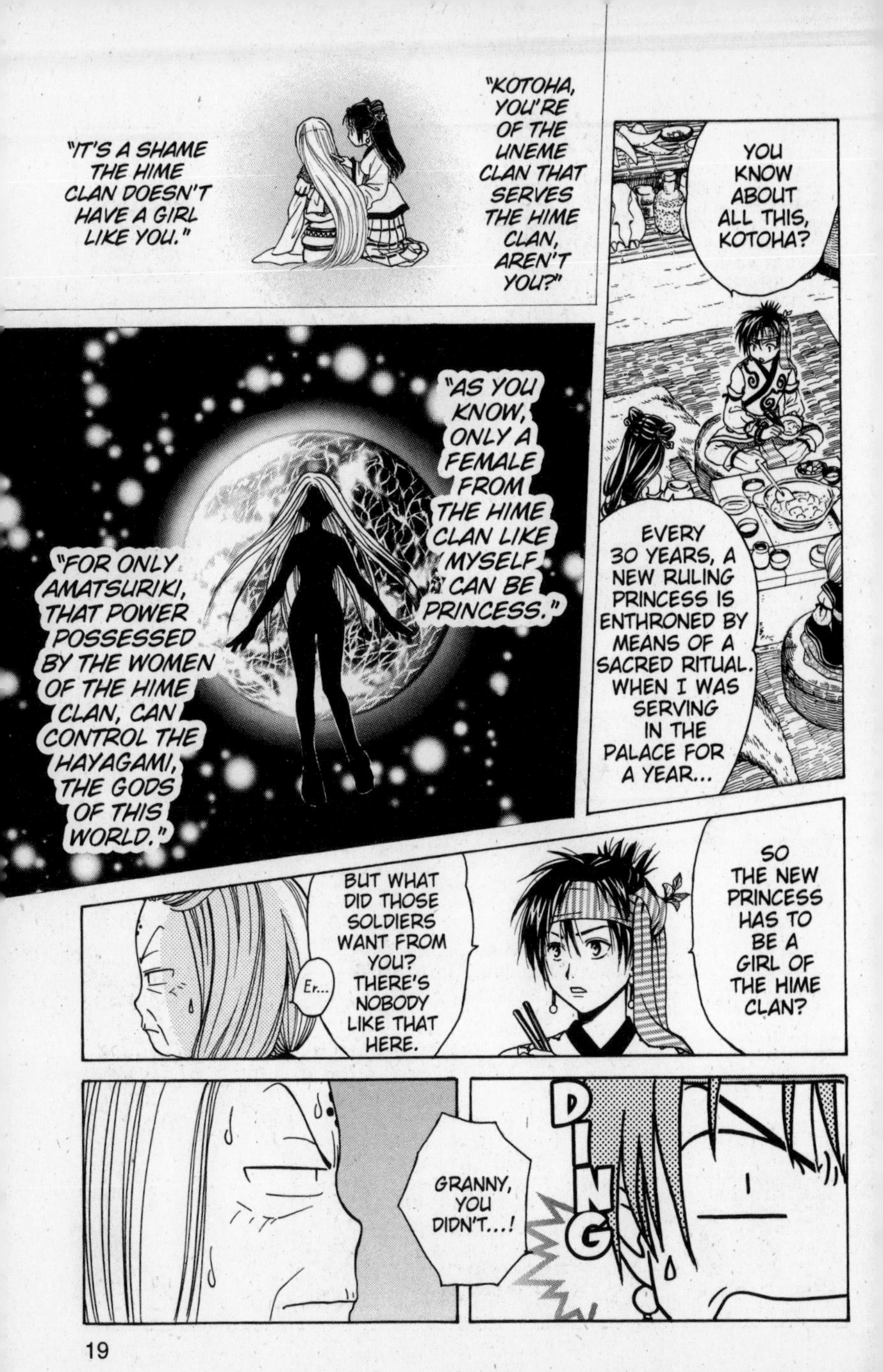
YOU KNOW ABOUT ALL THIS, KOTOHA?
EVERY 30 YEARS, A NEW RULING PRINCESS IS ENTHRONED BY MEANS OF A SACRED RITUAL. WHEN I WAS SERVING IN THE PALACE FOR A YEAR...
"KOTOHA, YOU'RE OF THE UNEME CLAN THAT SERVES THE HIME CLAN, AREN'T YOU?"
"IT'S A SHAME THE HIME CLAN DOESN'T HAVE A GIRL LIKE YOU."
"AS YOU KNOW, ONLY A FEMALE FROM THE HIME CLAN LIKE MYSELF CAN BE PRINCESS."
"FOR ONLY AMATSURIKI, THAT POWER POSSESSED BY THE WOMEN OF THE HIME CLAN, CAN CONTROL THE HAYAGAMI, THE GODS OF THIS WORLD."
SO THE NEW PRINCESS HAS TO BE A GIRL OF THE HIME CLAN?
BUT WHAT DID THOSE SOLDIERS WANT FROM YOU? THERE'S NOBODY LIKE THAT HERE.
Er...
DING
GRANNY, YOU DIDN'T...!

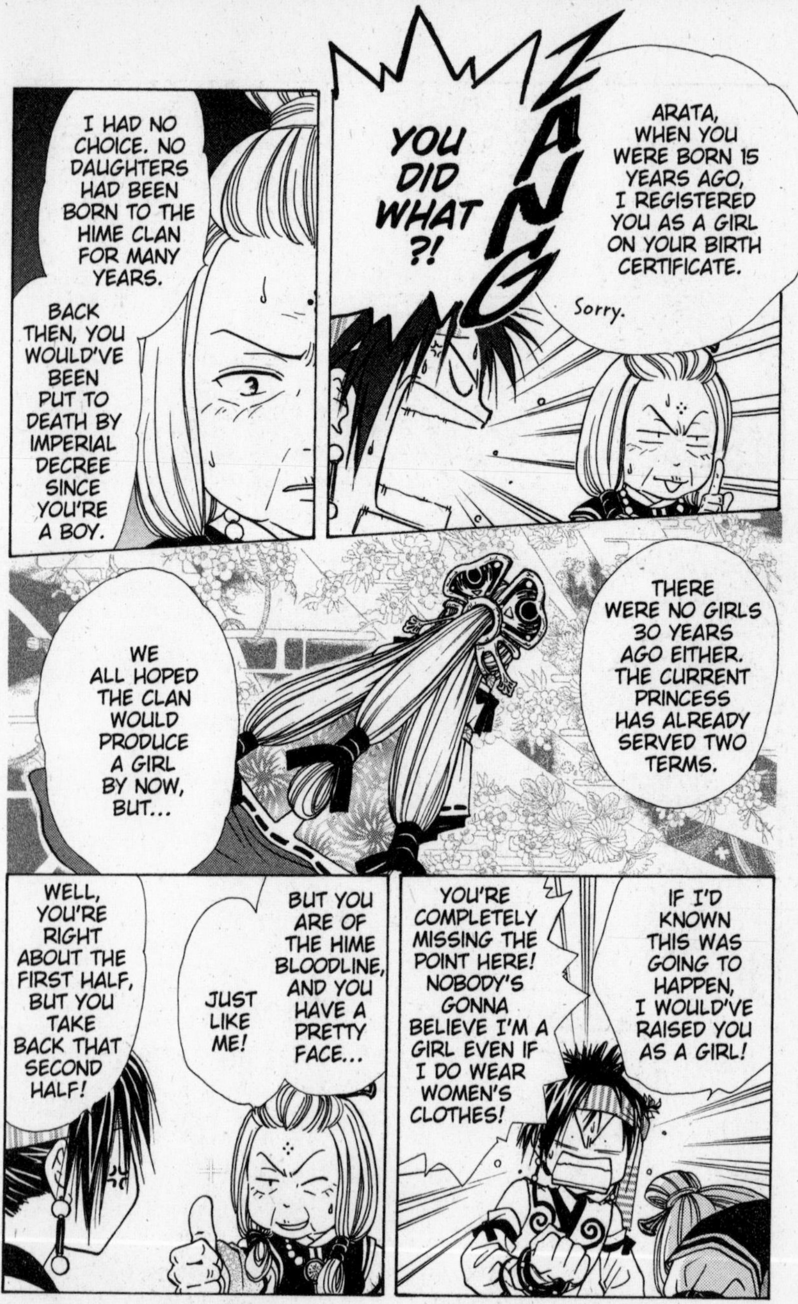
ARATA, WHEN YOU WERE BORN 15 YEARS AGO, I REGISTERED YOU AS A GIRL ON YOUR BIRTH CERTIFICATE.
Sorry.
YOU DID WHAT?!
ZANG
I HAD NO CHOICE. NO DAUGHTERS HAD BEEN BORN TO THE HIME CLAN FOR MANY YEARS.
BACK THEN, YOU WOULD'VE BEEN PUT TO DEATH BY IMPERIAL DECREE SINCE YOU'RE A BOY.
THERE WERE NO GIRLS 30 YEARS AGO EITHER. THE CURRENT PRINCESS HAS ALREADY SERVED TWO TERMS.
WE ALL HOPED THE CLAN WOULD PRODUCE A GIRL BY NOW, BUT...
IF I'D KNOWN THIS WAS GOING TO HAPPEN, I WOULD'VE RAISED YOU AS A GIRL!
YOU'RE COMPLETELY MISSING THE POINT HERE! NOBODY'S GONNA BELIEVE I'M A GIRL EVEN IF I DO WEAR WOMEN'S CLOTHES!
BUT YOU ARE OF THE HIME BLOODLINE, AND YOU HAVE A PRETTY FACE...
JUST LIKE ME!
WELL, YOU'RE RIGHT ABOUT THE FIRST HALF, BUT YOU TAKE BACK THAT SECOND HALF!

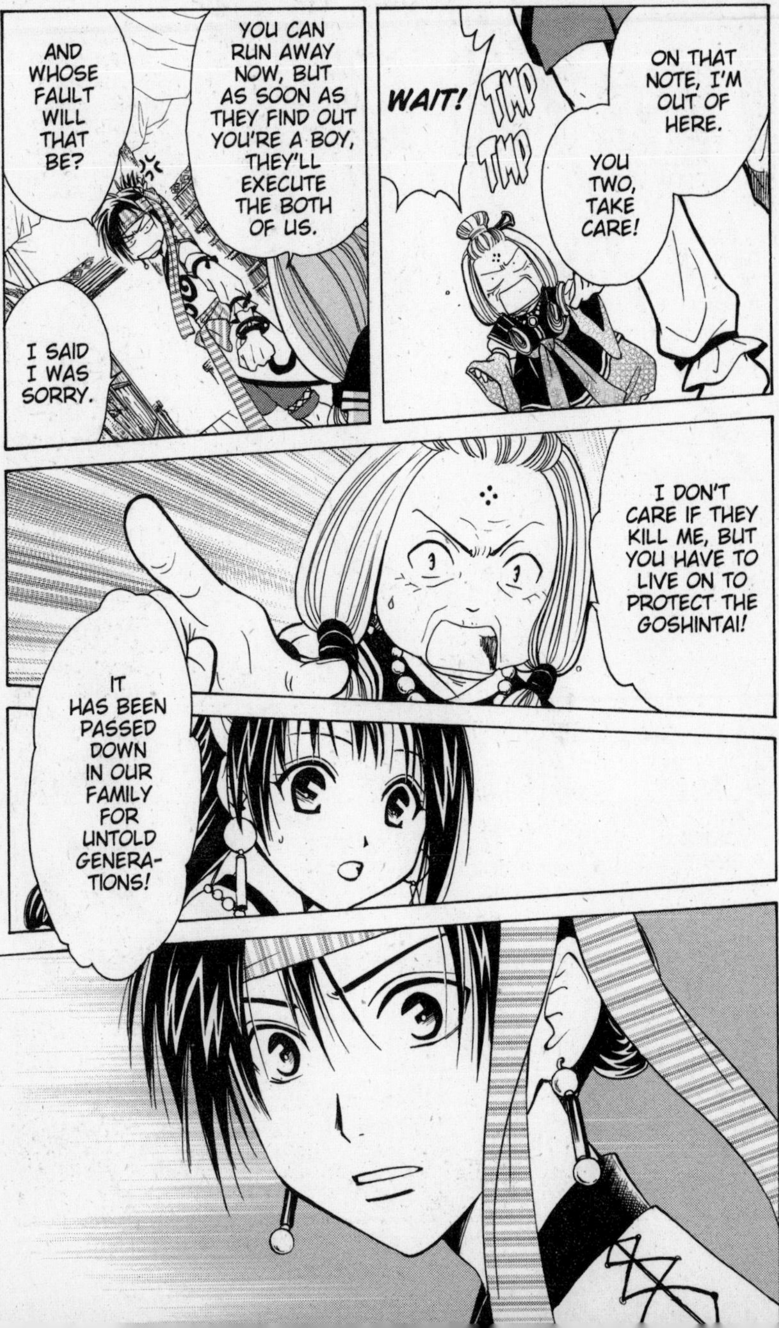
ON THAT NOTE, I'M OUT OF HERE.
YOU TWO, TAKE CARE!
WAIT!
TMP TMP
YOU CAN RUN AWAY NOW, BUT AS SOON AS THEY FIND OUT YOU'RE A BOY, THEY'LL EXECUTE THE BOTH OF US.
AND WHOSE FAULT WILL THAT BE?
I SAID I WAS SORRY.
I DON'T CARE IF THEY KILL ME, BUT YOU HAVE TO LIVE ON TO PROTECT THE GOSHINTAI!
IT HAS BEEN PASSED DOWN IN OUR FAMILY FOR UNTOLD GENERATIONS!

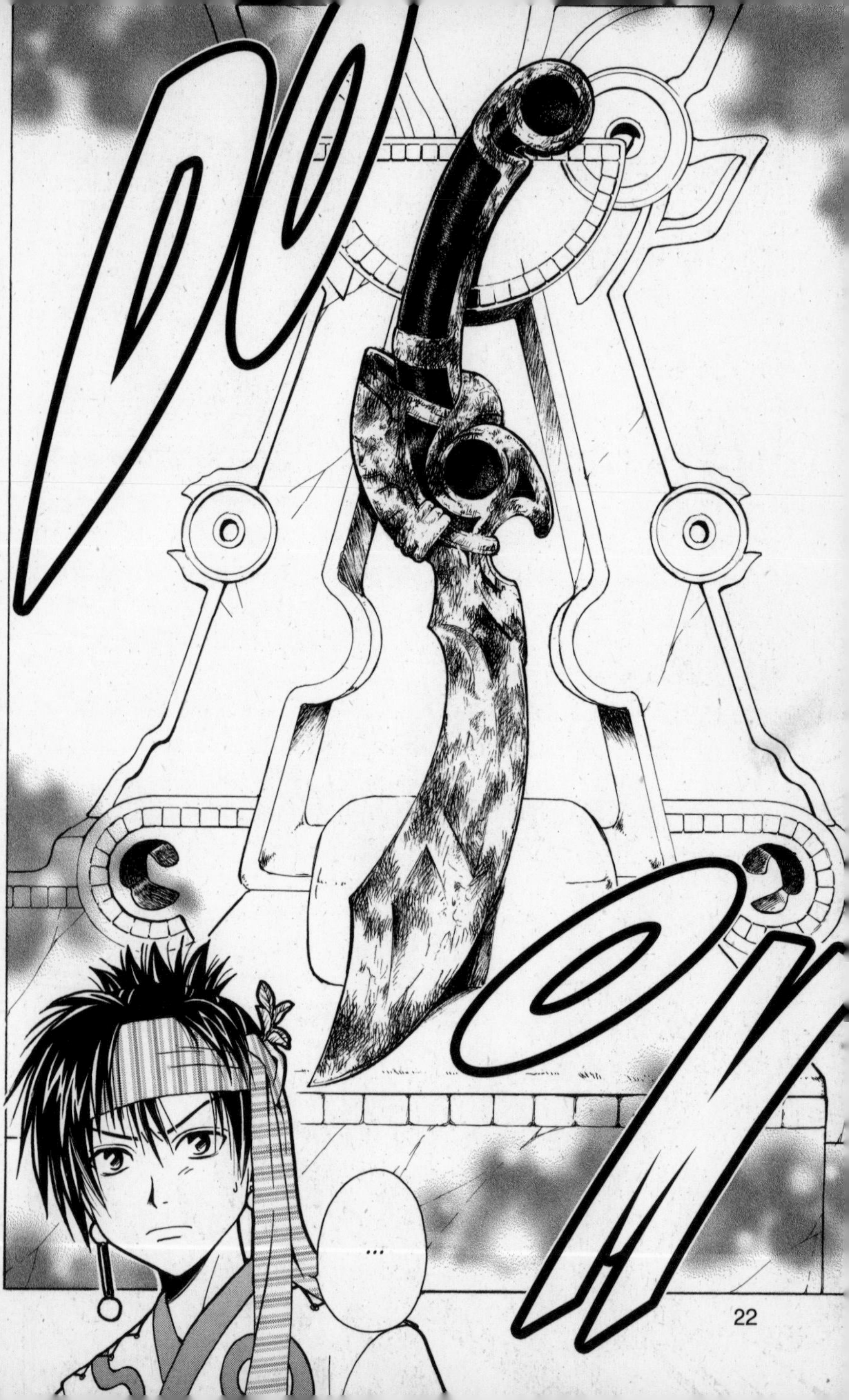
...

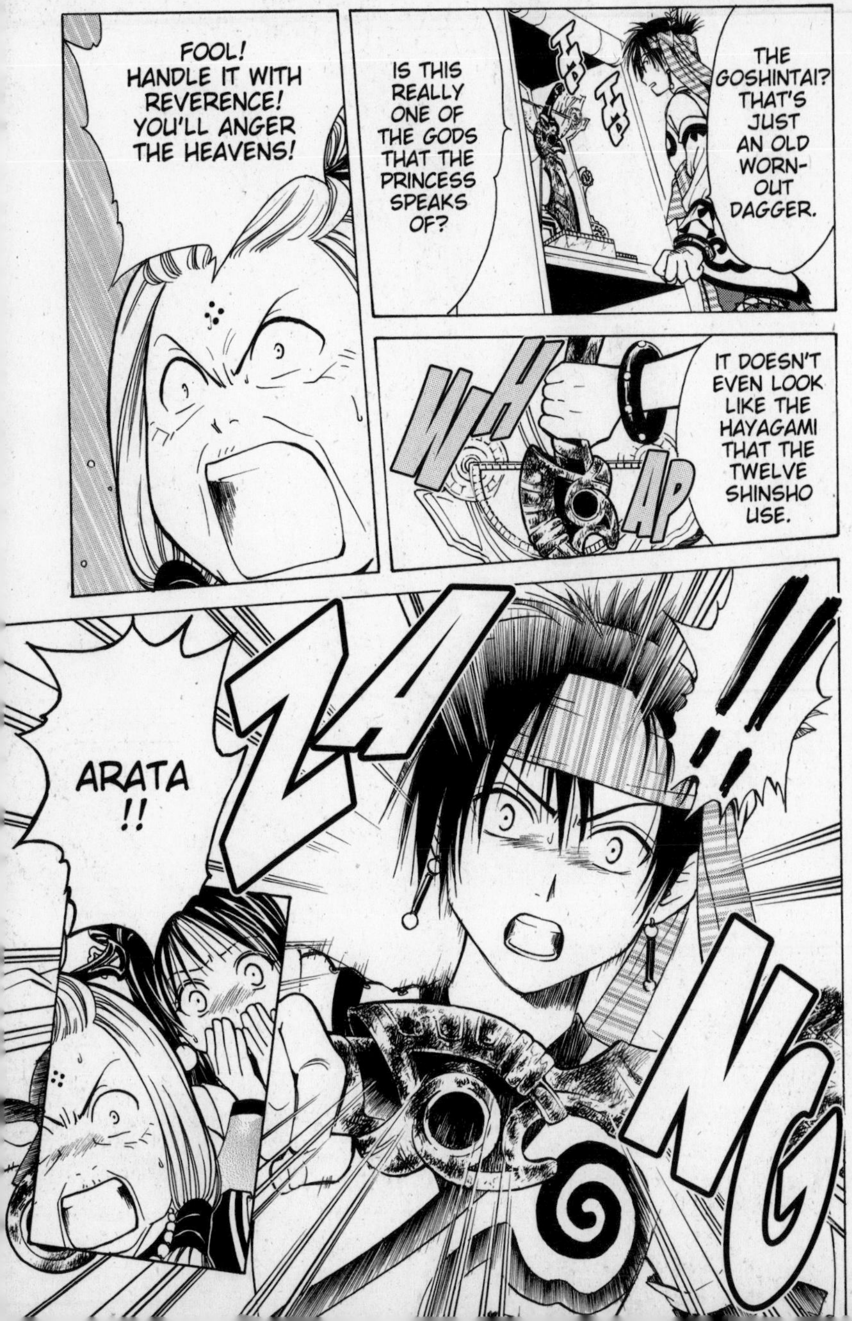
THE GOSHINTAI? THAT'S JUST AN OLD WORN-OUT DAGGER.
IS THIS REALLY ONE OF THE GODS THAT THE PRINCESS SPEAKS OF?
IT DOESN'T EVEN LOOK LIKE THE HAYAGAMI THAT THE TWELVE SHINSHO USE.
WHAP
FOOL! HANDLE IT WITH REVERENCE! YOU'LL ANGER THE HEAVENS!
!!
ARATA !!

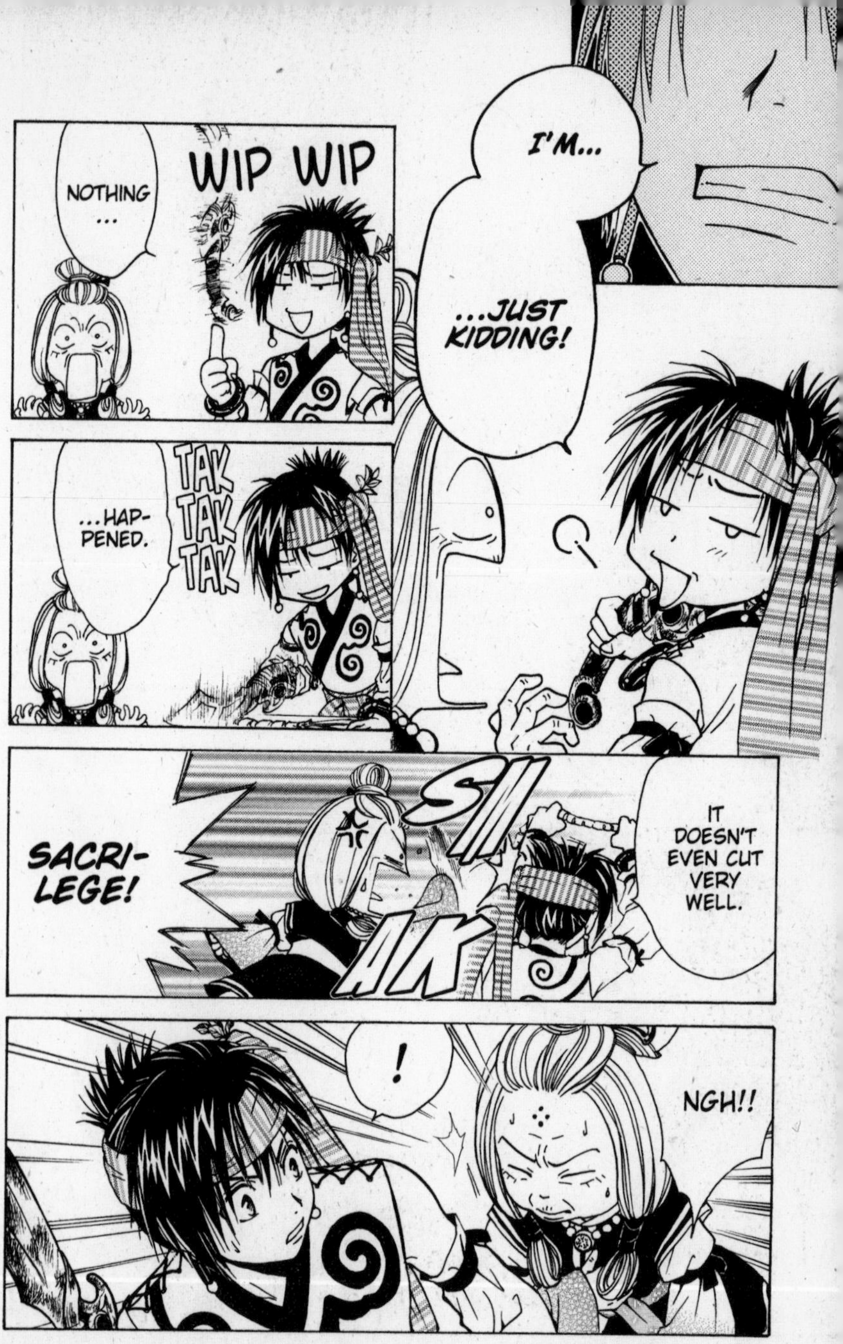
I'M...
...JUST KIDDING!
NOTHING ...
WIP WIP
...HAP-PENED.
TAK TAK TAK
IT DOESN'T EVEN CUT VERY WELL.
AK
SACRI-LEGE!
NGH!!
!

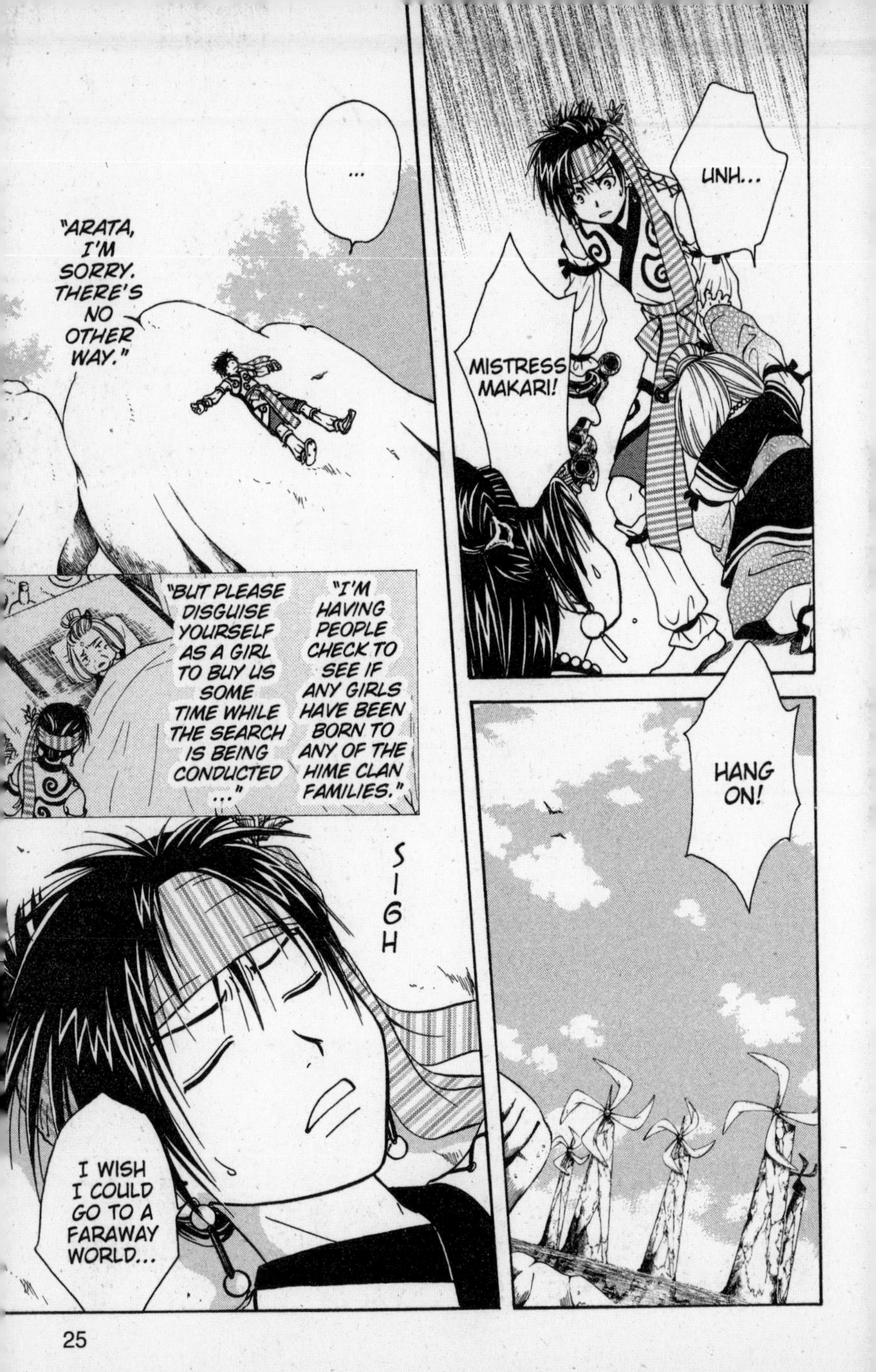
UNH...
MISTRESS MAKARI!
HANG ON!
...
"ARATA, I'M SORRY. THERE'S NO OTHER WAY."
"I'M HAVING PEOPLE CHECK TO SEE IF ANY GIRLS HAVE BEEN BORN TO ANY OF THE HIME CLAN FAMILIES."
"BUT PLEASE DISGUISE YOURSELF AS A GIRL TO BUY US SOME TIME WHILE THE SEARCH IS BEING CONDUCTED..."
SIGH
I WISH I COULD GO TO A FARAWAY WORLD...

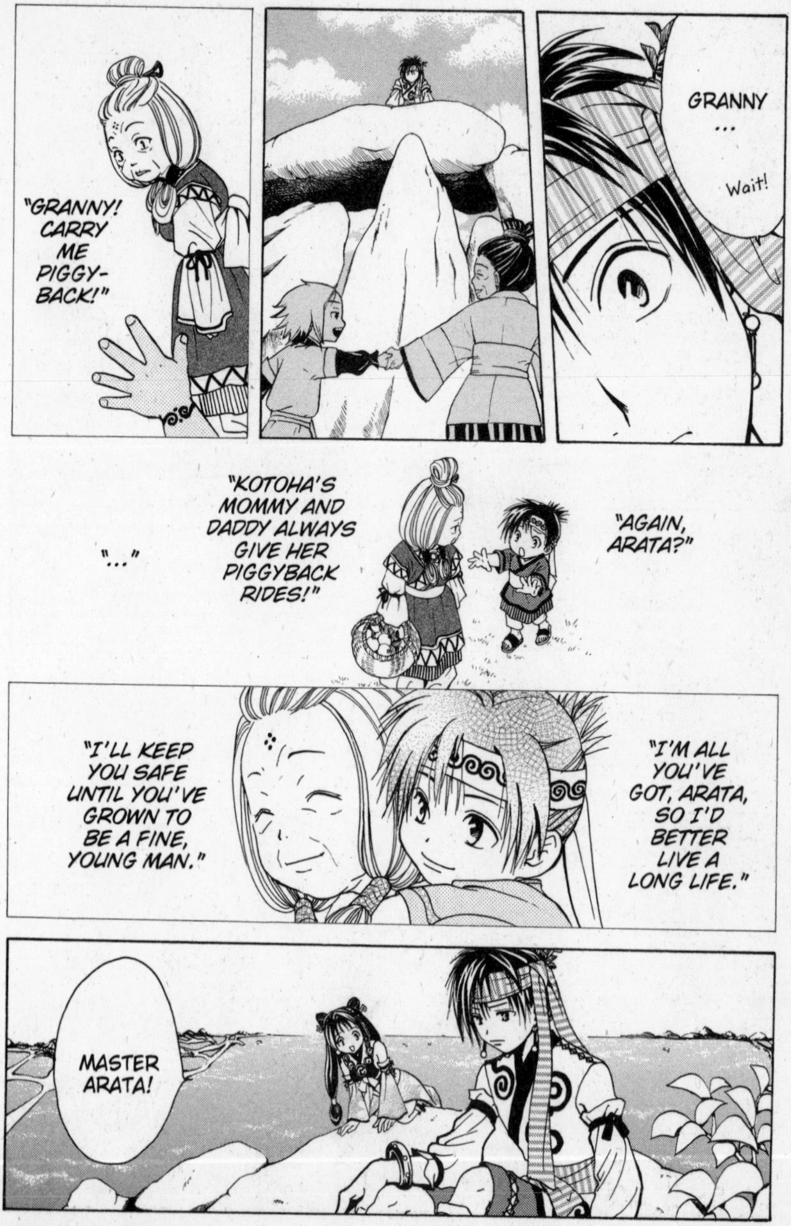
GRANNY ...
Wait!
"GRANNY! CARRY ME PIGGY-BACK!"
"AGAIN, ARATA?"
"KOTOHA'S MOMMY AND DADDY ALWAYS GIVE HER PIGGYBACK RIDES!"
"..."
"I'M ALL YOU'VE GOT, ARATA, SO I'D BETTER LIVE A LONG LIFE."
"I'LL KEEP YOU SAFE UNTIL YOU'VE GROWN TO BE A FINE, YOUNG MAN."
MASTER ARATA!

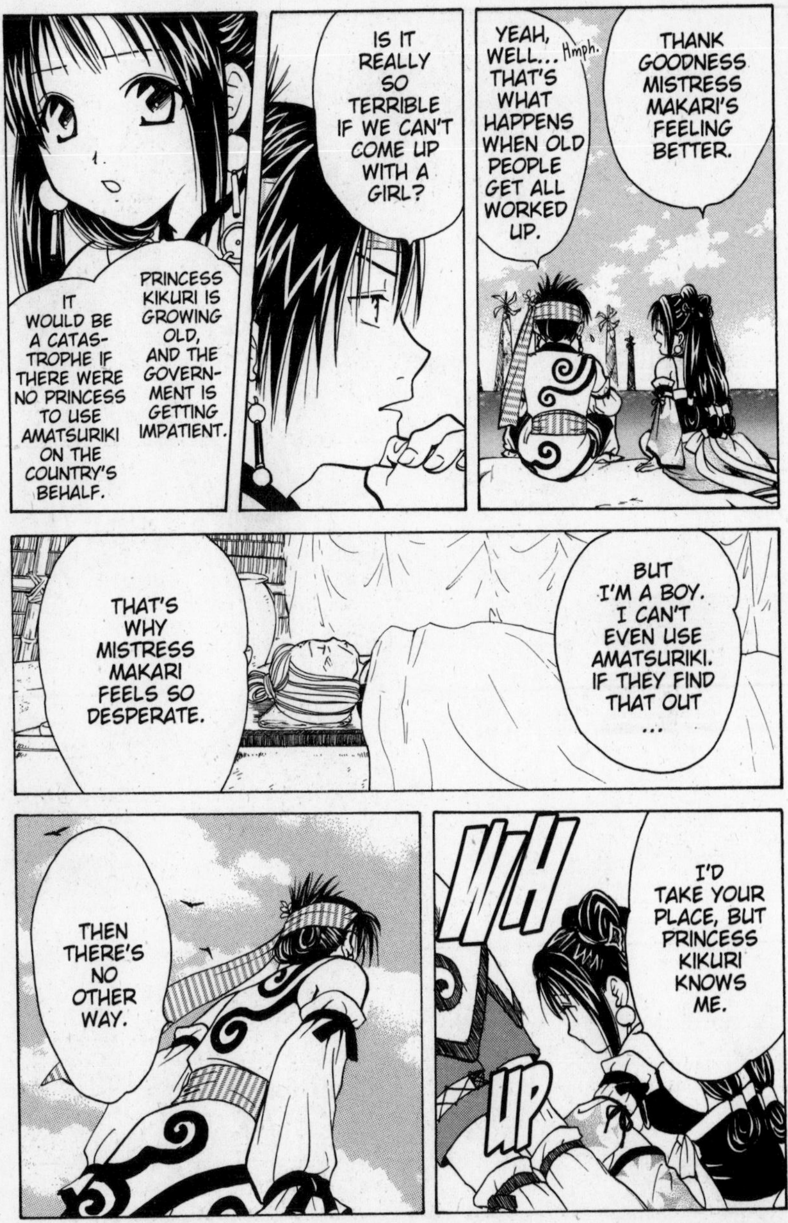
THANK GOODNESS MISTRESS MAKARI'S FEELING BETTER.
YEAH, WELL... THAT'S WHAT HAPPENS WHEN OLD PEOPLE GET ALL WORKED UP.
Hmph.
IS IT REALLY SO TERRIBLE IF WE CAN'T COME UP WITH A GIRL?
PRINCESS KIKURI IS GROWING OLD, AND THE GOVERNMENT IS GETTING IMPATIENT.
IT WOULD BE A CATASTROPHE IF THERE WERE NO PRINCESS TO USE AMATSURIKI ON THE COUNTRY'S BEHALF.
BUT I'M A BOY. I CAN'T EVEN USE AMATSURIKI. IF THEY FIND THAT OUT ...
THAT'S WHY MISTRESS MAKARI FEELS SO DESPERATE.
WHUP
I'D TAKE YOUR PLACE, BUT PRINCESS KIKURI KNOWS ME.
THEN THERE'S NO OTHER WAY.

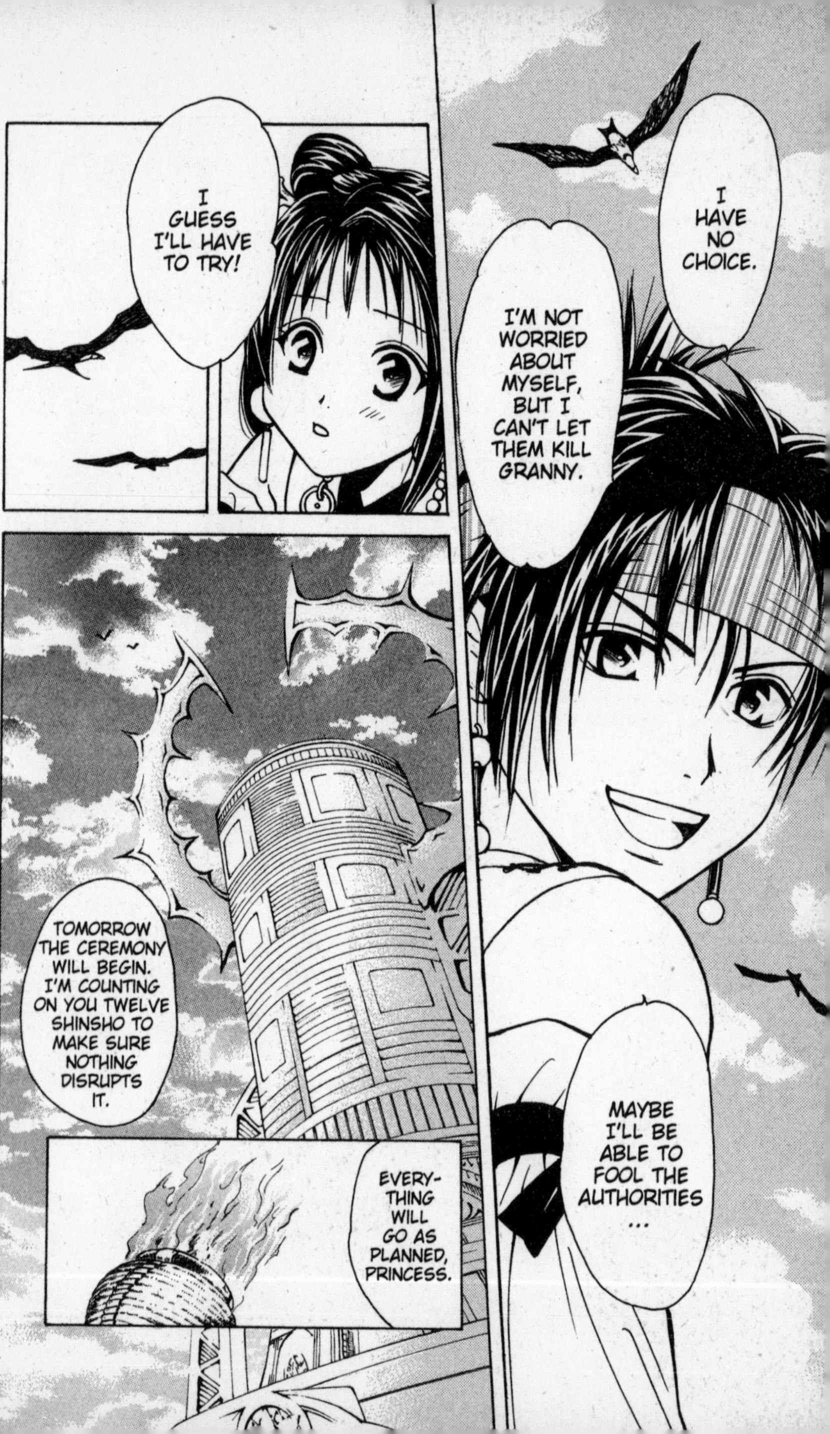
I HAVE NO CHOICE.
I'M NOT WORRIED ABOUT MYSELF, BUT I CAN'T LET THEM KILL GRANNY.
MAYBE I'LL BE ABLE TO FOOL THE AUTHORITIES...
I GUESS I'LL HAVE TO TRY!
TOMORROW THE CEREMONY WILL BEGIN. I'M COUNTING ON YOU TWELVE SHINSHO TO MAKE SURE NOTHING DISRUPTS IT.
EVERY-THING WILL GO AS PLANNED, PRINCESS.

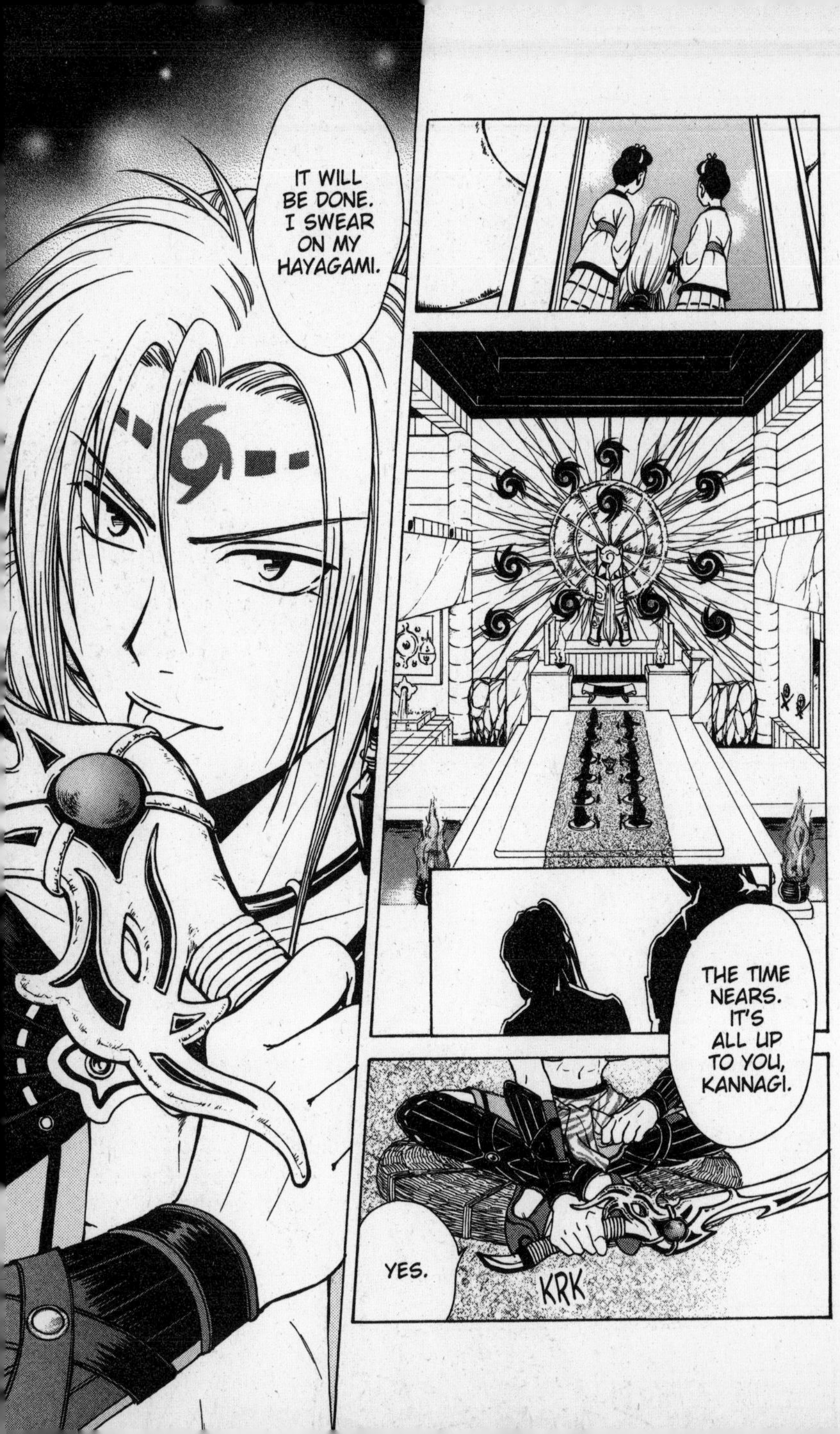
THE TIME NEARS. IT'S ALL UP TO YOU, KANNAGI.
YES.
KRK
IT WILL BE DONE. I SWEAR ON MY HAYAGAMI.

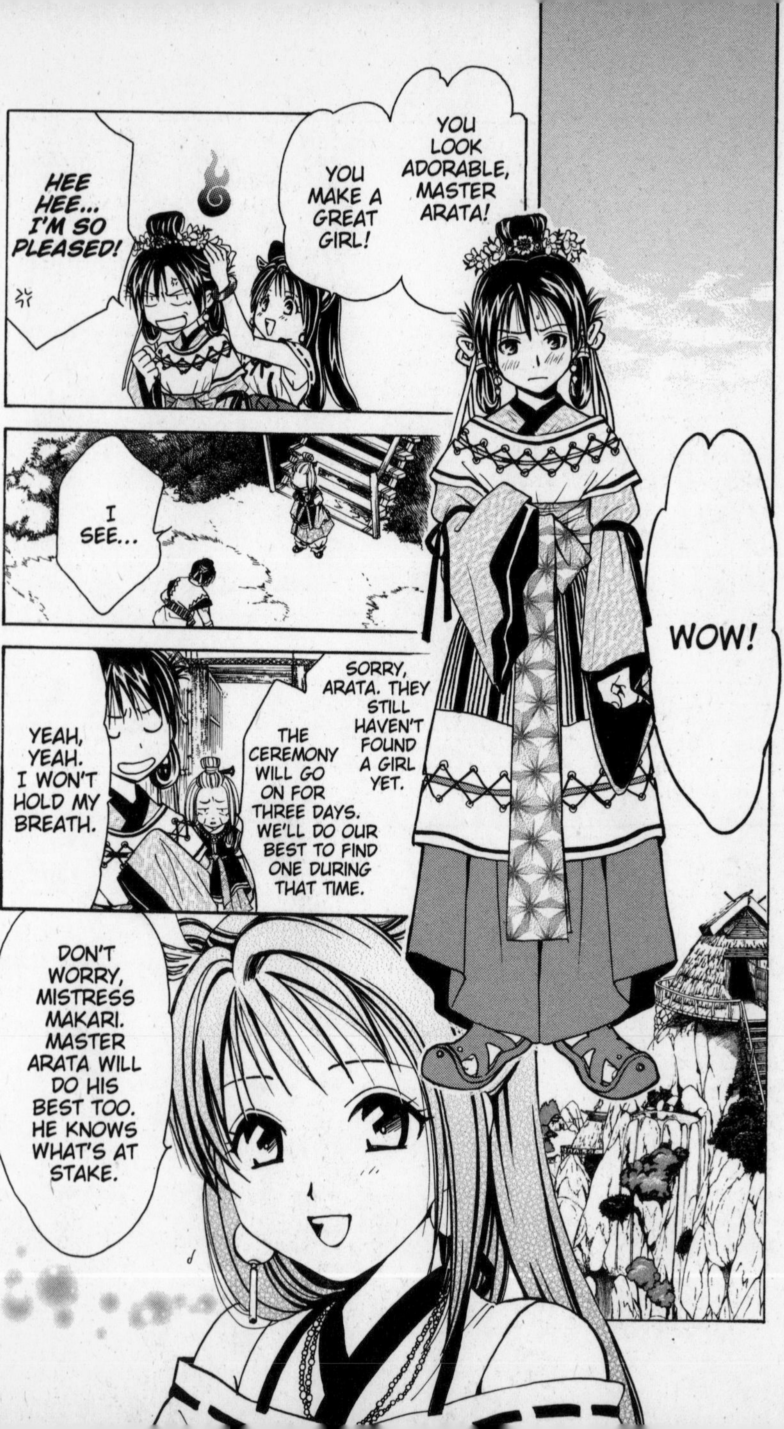
WOW!
YOU LOOK ADORABLE, MASTER ARATA!
YOU MAKE A GREAT GIRL!
HEE HEE... I'M SO PLEASED!
I SEE...
SORRY, ARATA. THEY STILL HAVEN'T FOUND A GIRL YET.
THE CEREMONY WILL GO ON FOR THREE DAYS. WE'LL DO OUR BEST TO FIND ONE DURING THAT TIME.
YEAH, YEAH. I WON'T HOLD MY BREATH.
DON'T WORRY, MISTRESS MAKARI. MASTER ARATA WILL DO HIS BEST TOO. HE KNOWS WHAT'S AT STAKE.

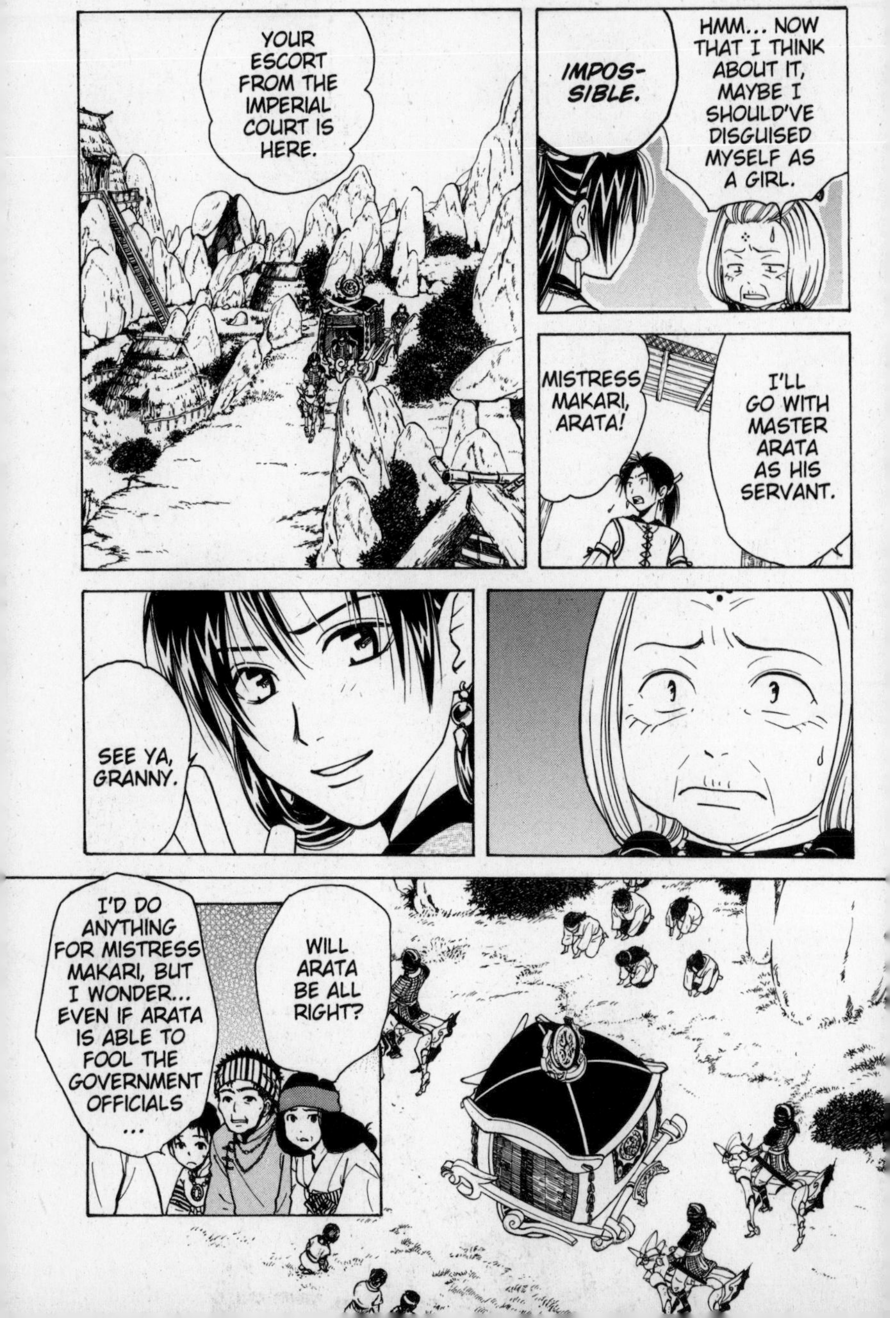
HMM... NOW THAT I THINK ABOUT IT, MAYBE I SHOULD'VE DISGUISED MYSELF AS A GIRL.
IMPOSSIBLE.
I'LL GO WITH MASTER ARATA AS HIS SERVANT.
MISTRESS MAKARI, ARATA!
YOUR ESCORT FROM THE IMPERIAL COURT IS HERE.
SEE YA, GRANNY.
WILL ARATA BE ALL RIGHT?
I'D DO ANYTHING FOR MISTRESS MAKARI, BUT I WONDER... EVEN IF ARATA IS ABLE TO FOOL THE GOVERNMENT OFFICIALS ...

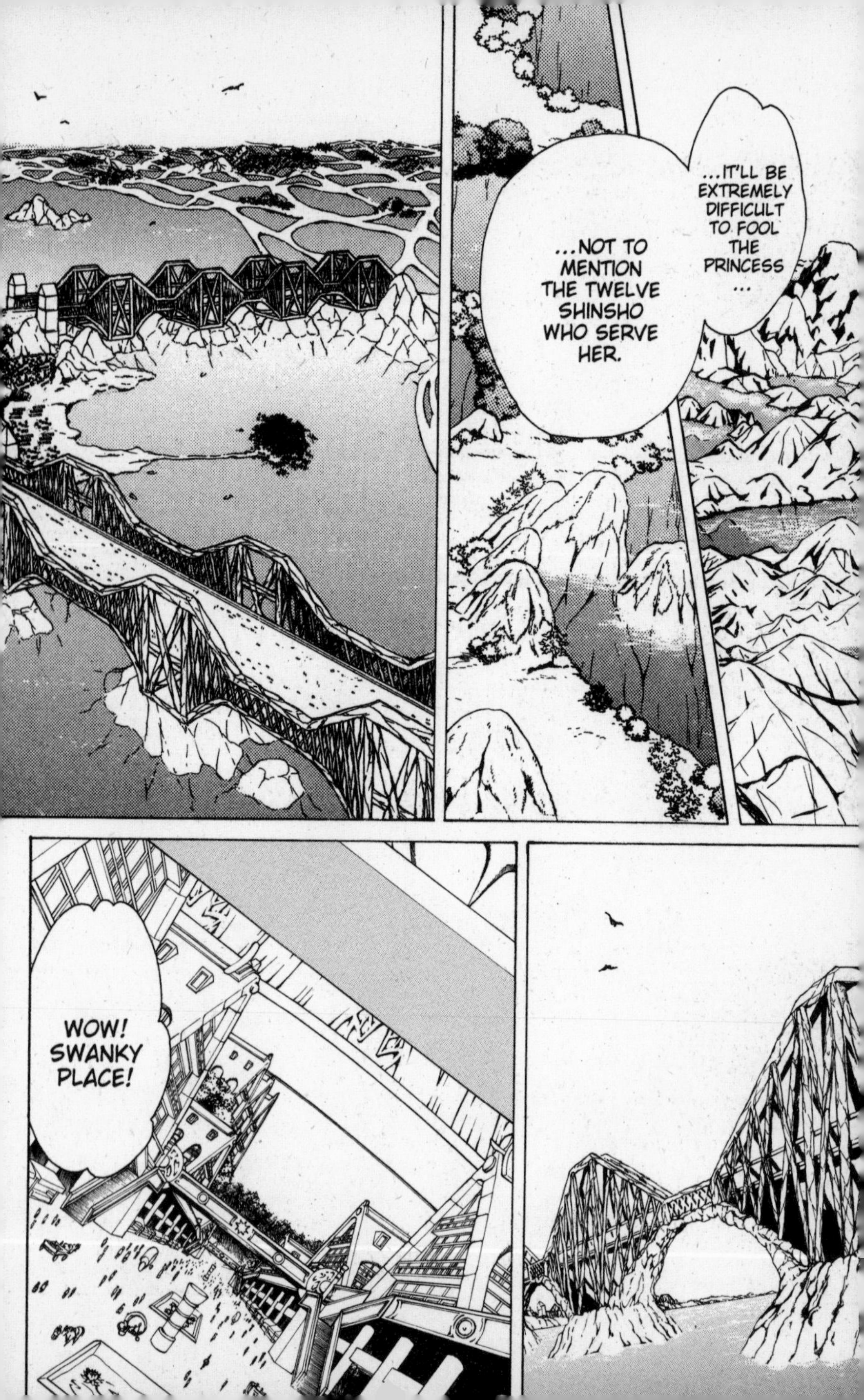
...IT'LL BE EXTREMELY DIFFICULT TO FOOL THE PRINCESS ...
...NOT TO MENTION THE TWELVE SHINSHO WHO SERVE HER.
WOW! SWANKY PLACE!

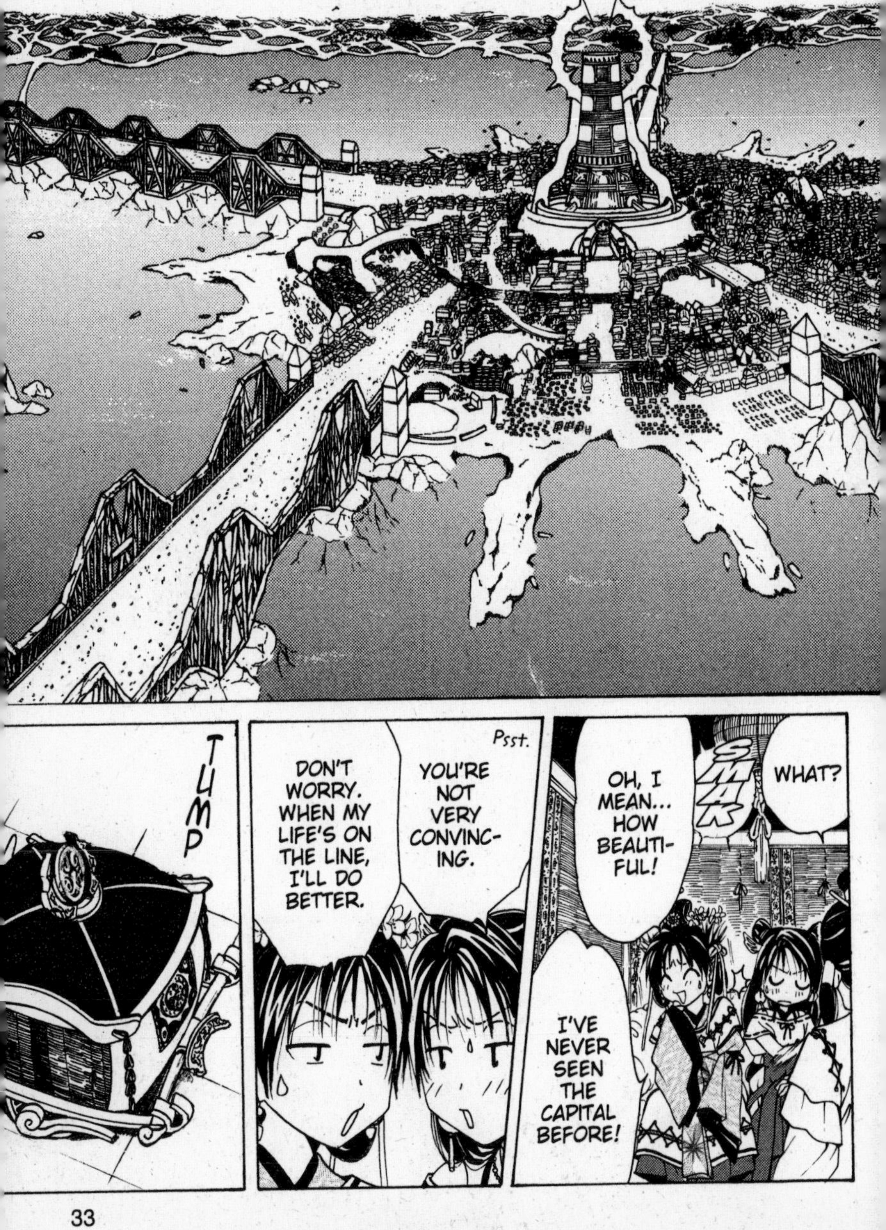
WHAT?
SMAK
OH, I MEAN... HOW BEAUTIFUL!
I'VE NEVER SEEN THE CAPITAL BEFORE!
Psst.
YOU'RE NOT VERY CONVINCING.
DON'T WORRY. WHEN MY LIFE'S ON THE LINE, I'LL DO BETTER.
TUMP

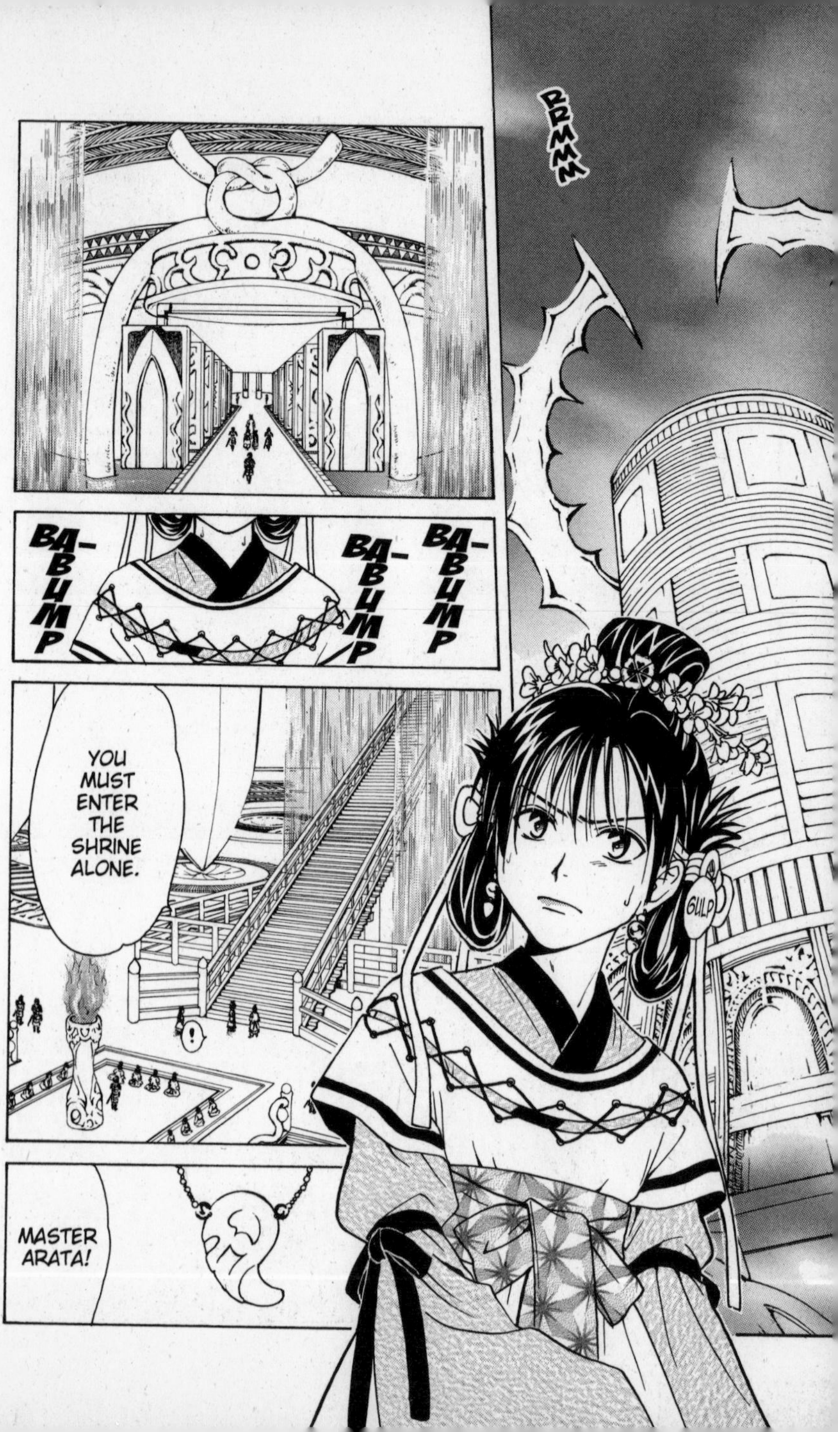
RRMMM
GULP
BA-BUMP
BA-BUMP
BA-BUMP
YOU MUST ENTER THE SHRINE ALONE.
MASTER ARATA!

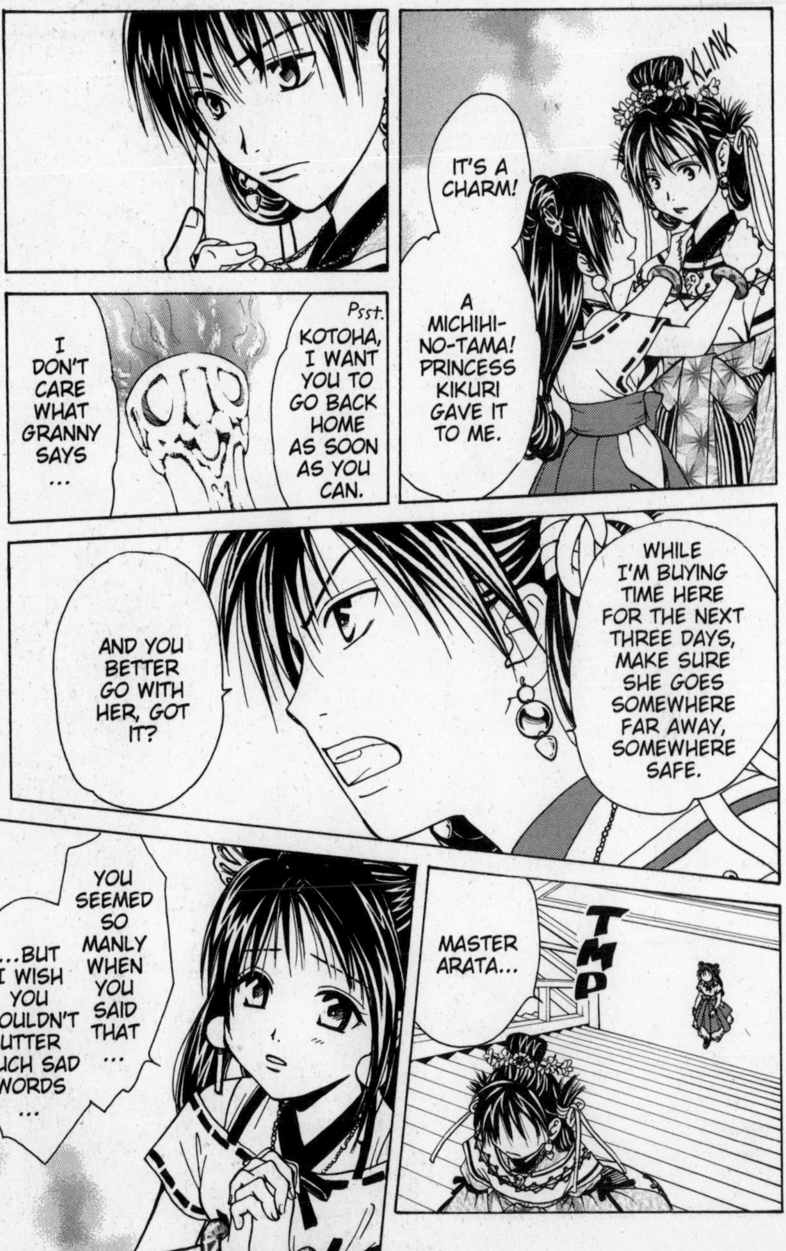
KLINK
IT'S A CHARM!
A MICHIHI-NO-TAMA! PRINCESS KIKURI GAVE IT TO ME.
Psst.
KOTOHA, I WANT YOU TO GO BACK HOME AS SOON AS YOU CAN.
I DON'T CARE WHAT GRANNY SAYS ...
WHILE I'M BUYING TIME HERE FOR THE NEXT THREE DAYS, MAKE SURE SHE GOES SOMEWHERE FAR AWAY, SOMEWHERE SAFE.
AND YOU BETTER GO WITH HER, GOT IT?
TMP
MASTER ARATA...
YOU SEEMED SO MANLY WHEN YOU SAID THAT ...
...BUT I WISH YOU WOULDN'T UTTER SUCH SAD WORDS ...

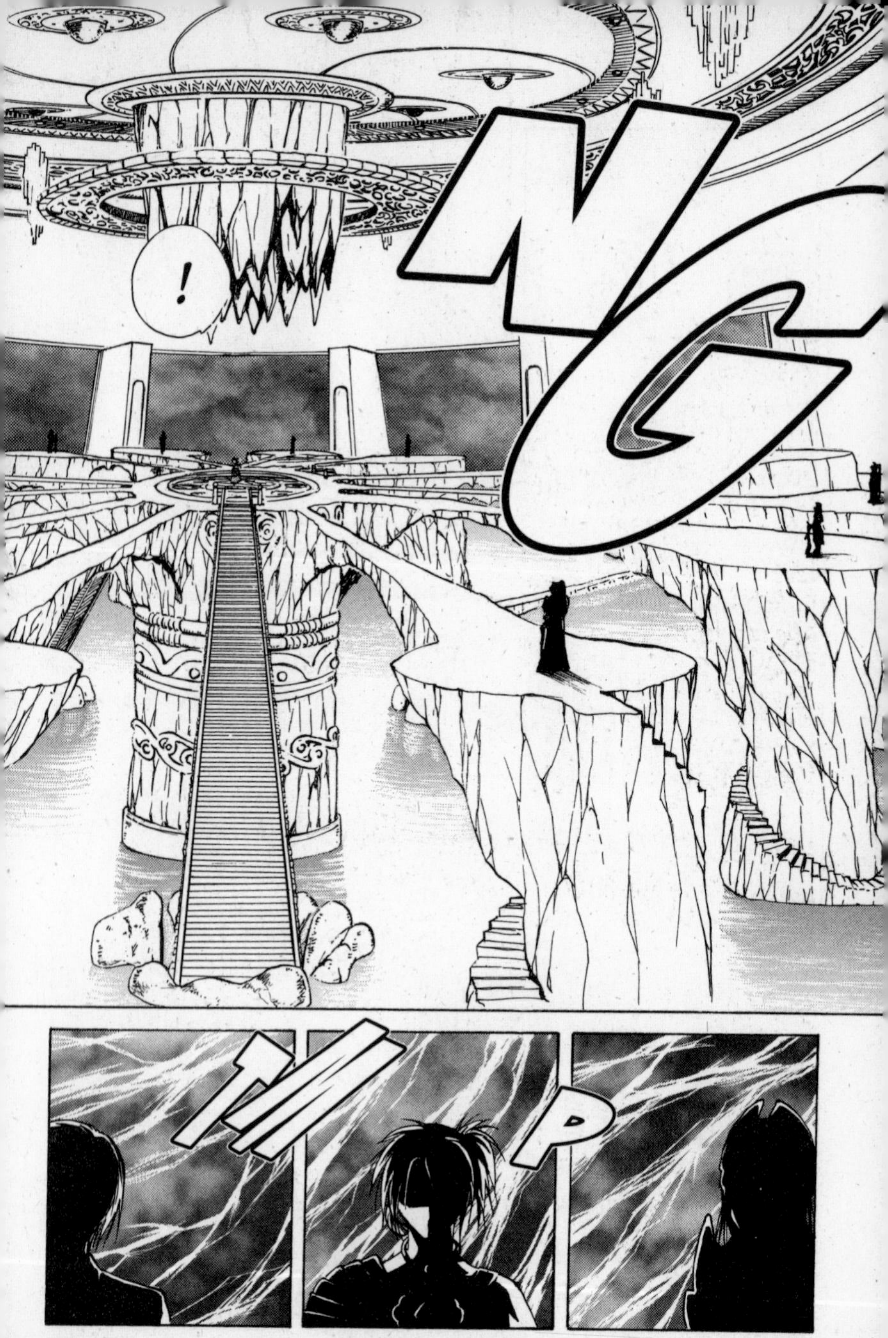
NG
!

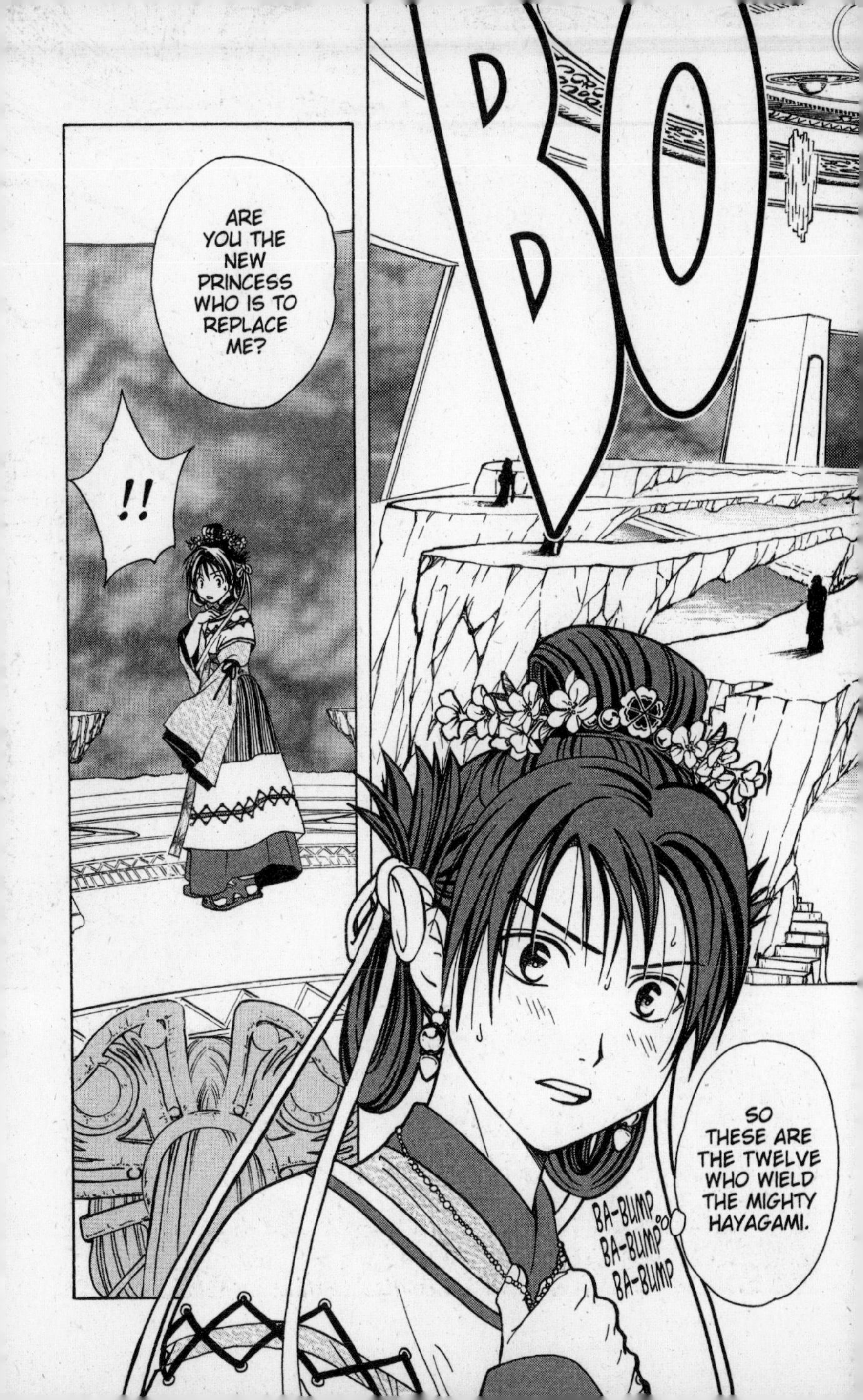
SO THESE ARE THE TWELVE WHO WIELD THE MIGHTY HAYAGAMI.
BA-BUMP BA-BUMP BA-BUMP
ARE YOU THE NEW PRINCESS WHO IS TO REPLACE ME?
!!

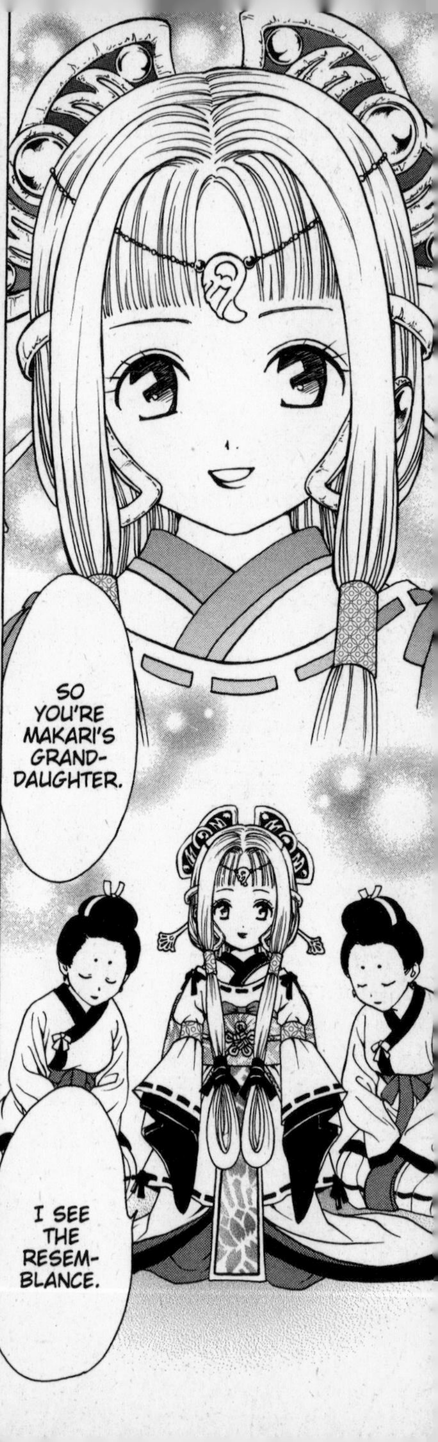
SO YOU'RE MAKARI'S GRAND-DAUGHTER.
I SEE THE RESEMBLANCE.

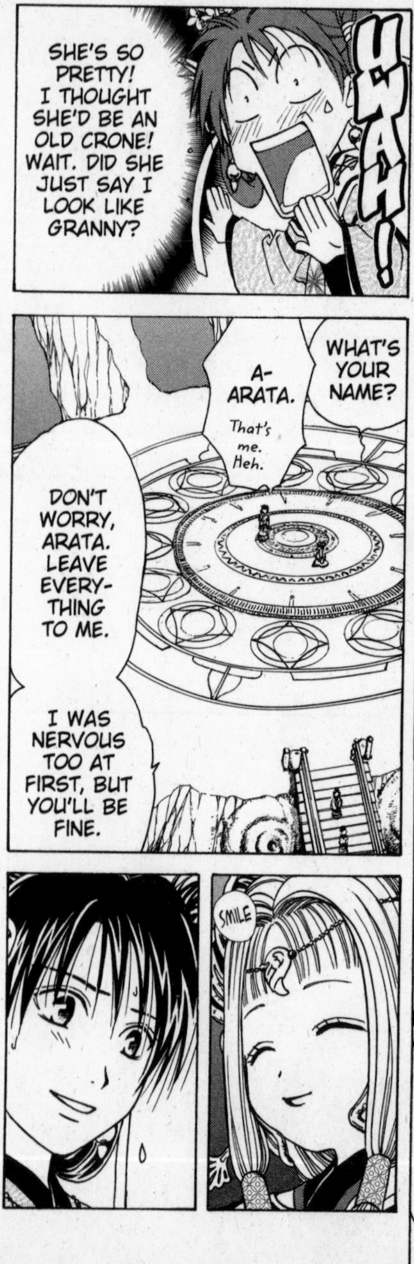
UWAH!
SHE'S SO PRETTY! I THOUGHT SHE'D BE AN OLD CRONE! WAIT. DID SHE JUST SAY I LOOK LIKE GRANNY?
WHAT'S YOUR NAME?
A-ARATA.
That's me. Heh.
DON'T WORRY, ARATA. LEAVE EVERY-THING TO ME.
I WAS NERVOUS TOO AT FIRST, BUT YOU'LL BE FINE.
SMILE

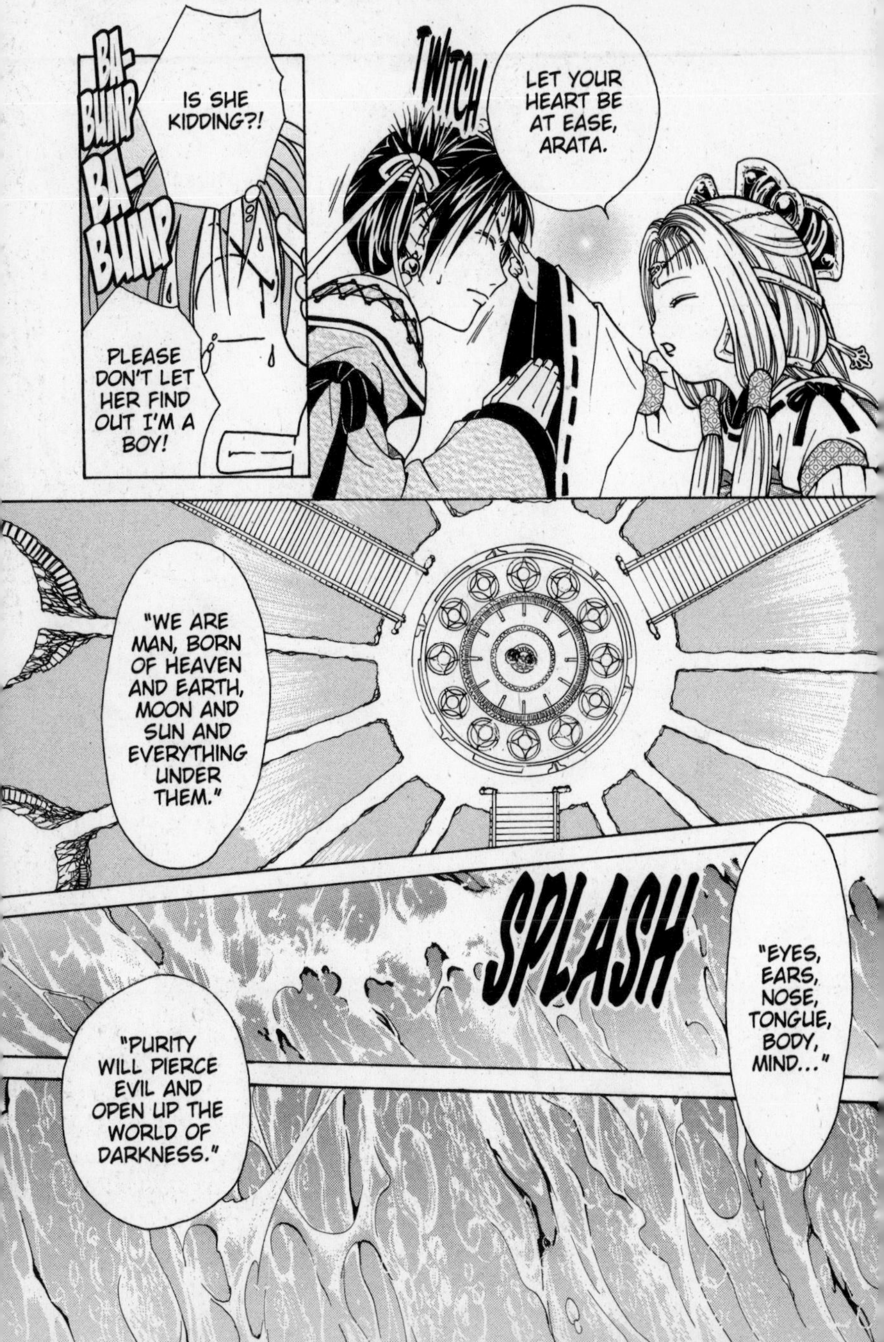
LET YOUR HEART BE AT EASE, ARATA.
TWITCH
BA-BUMP BA-BUMP
IS SHE KIDDING?!
PLEASE DON'T LET HER FIND OUT I'M A BOY!
"WE ARE MAN, BORN OF HEAVEN AND EARTH, MOON AND SUN AND EVERYTHING UNDER THEM."
SPLASH
"EYES, EARS, NOSE, TONGUE, BODY, MIND..."
"PURITY WILL PIERCE EVIL AND OPEN UP THE WORLD OF DARKNESS."

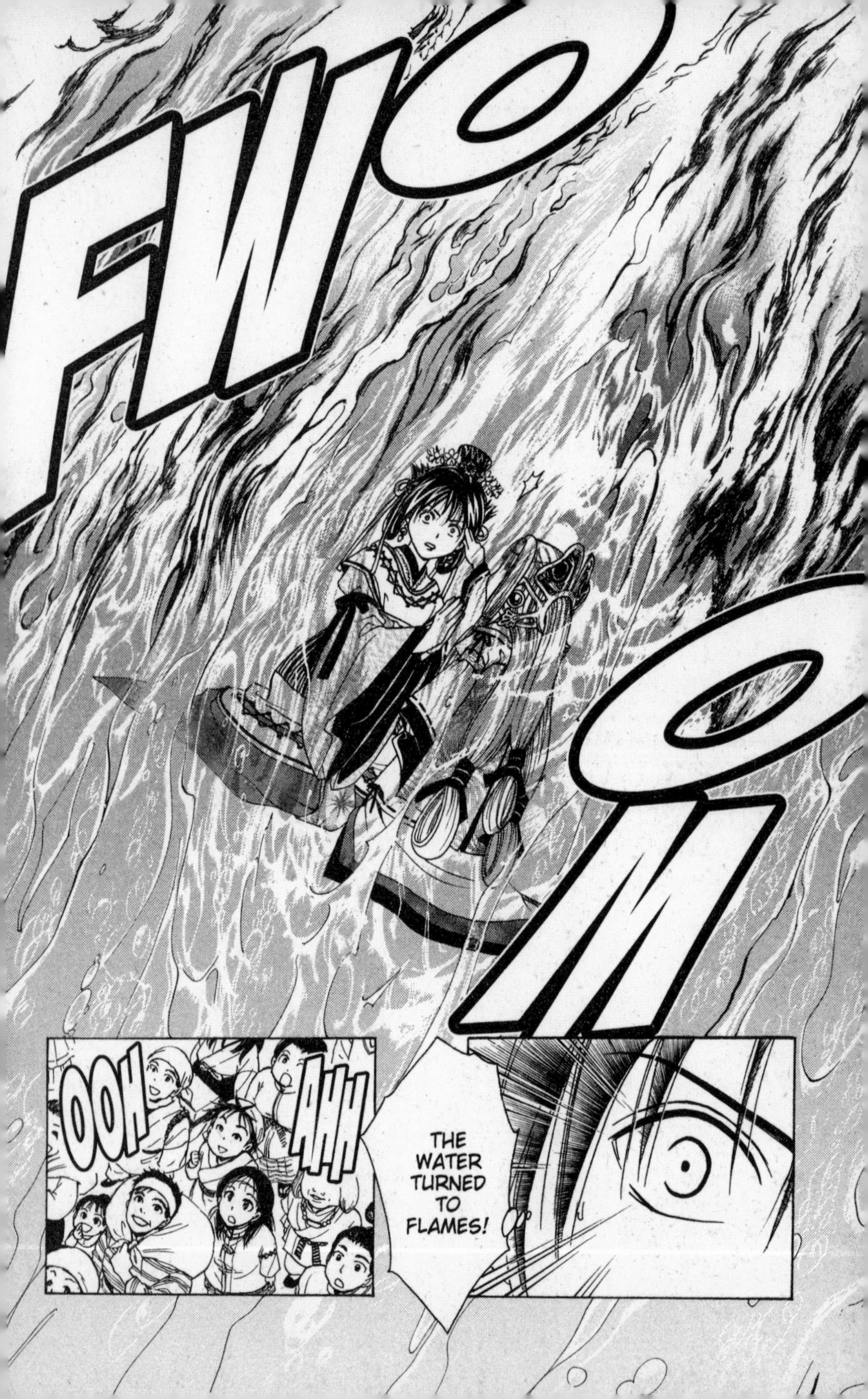
FWOOM
THE WATER TURNED TO FLAMES!
AHH
OOH

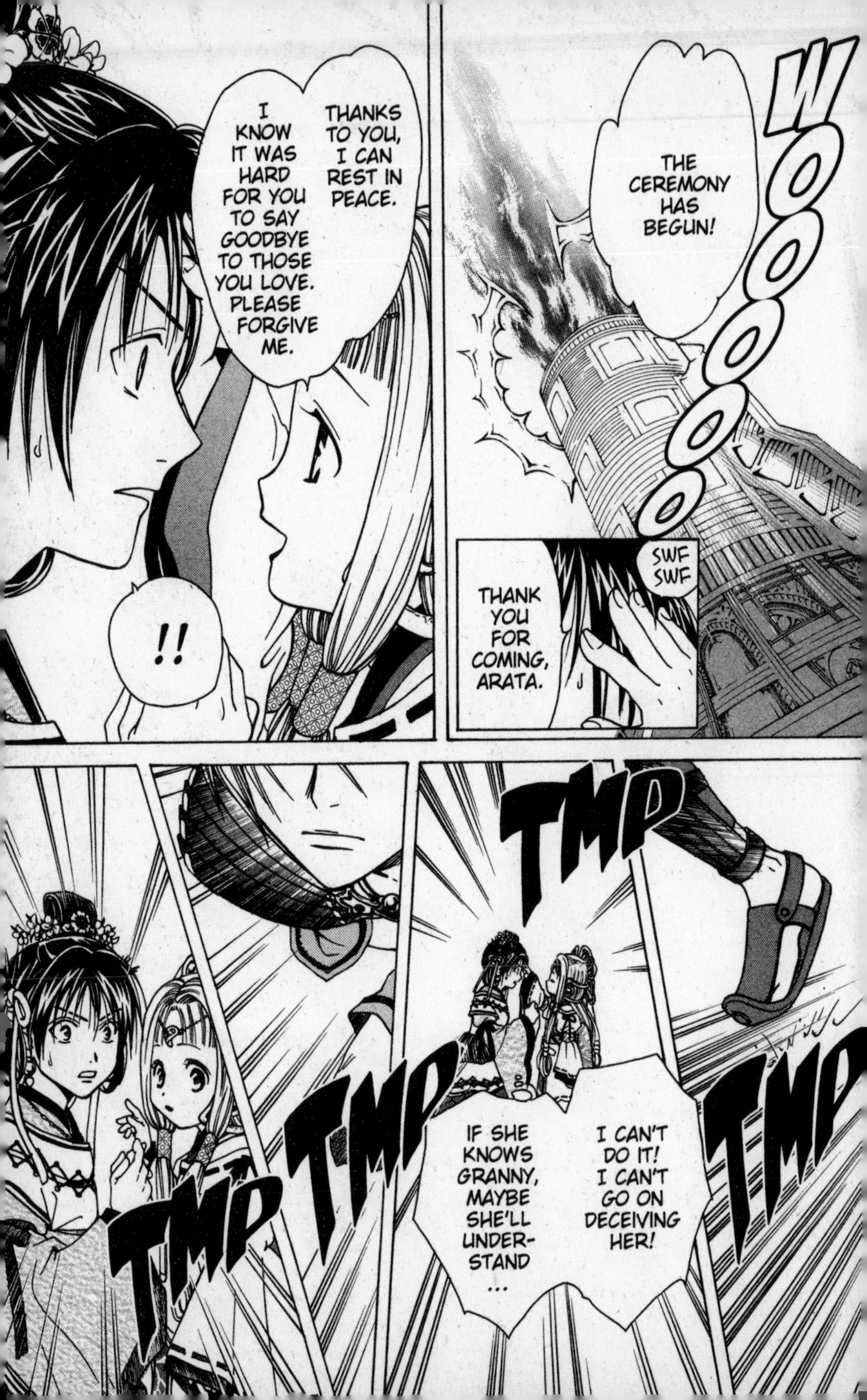
WOOOOOOOO
THE CEREMONY HAS BEGUN!
SWF SWF
THANK YOU FOR COMING, ARATA.
THANKS TO YOU, I CAN REST IN PEACE.
I KNOW IT WAS HARD FOR YOU TO SAY GOODBYE TO THOSE YOU LOVE. PLEASE FORGIVE ME.
!!
TMP
TMP
I CAN'T DO IT! I CAN'T GO ON DECEIVING HER!
IF SHE KNOWS GRANNY, MAYBE SHE'LL UNDER-STAND...
TMP
TMP
TMP

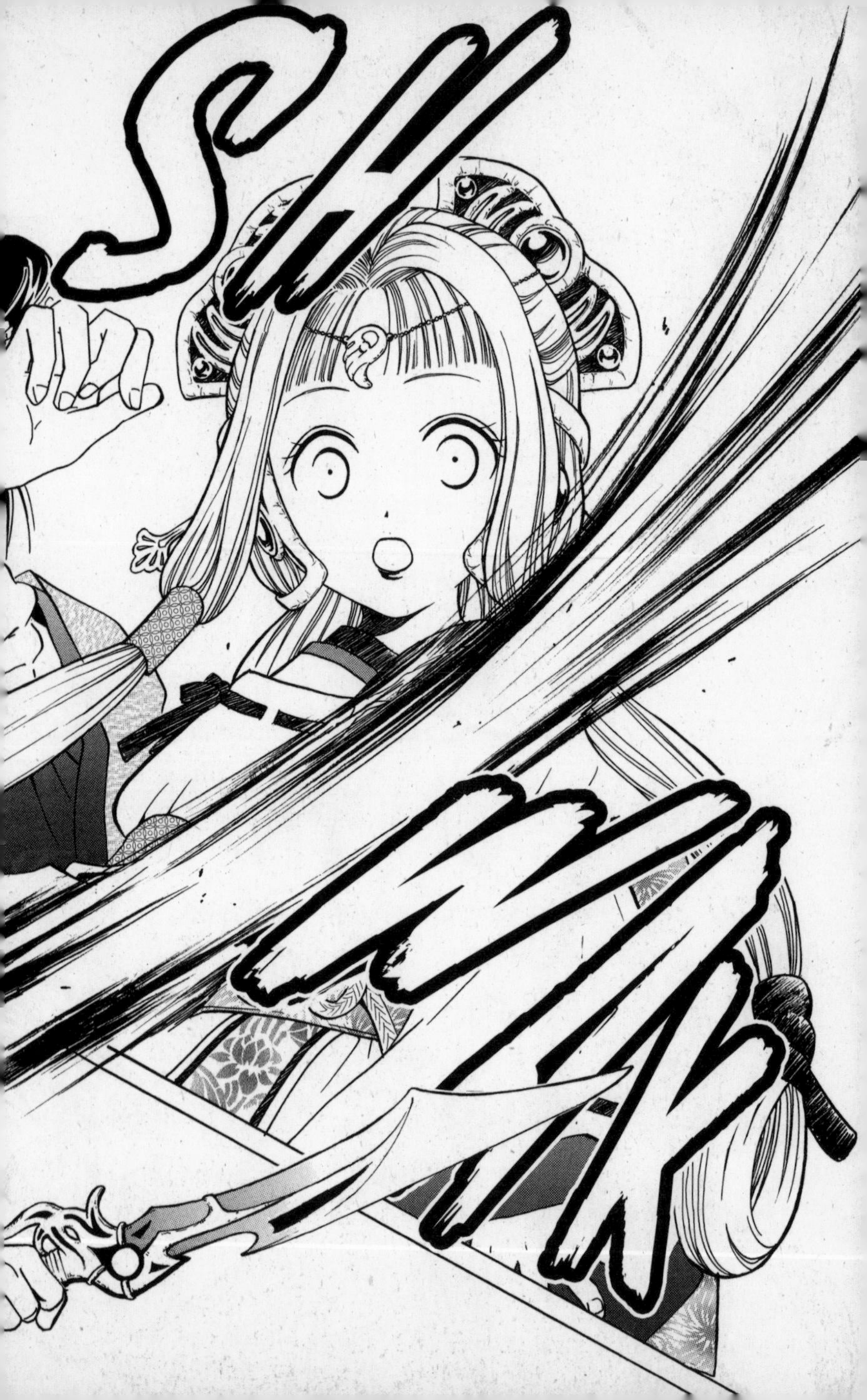

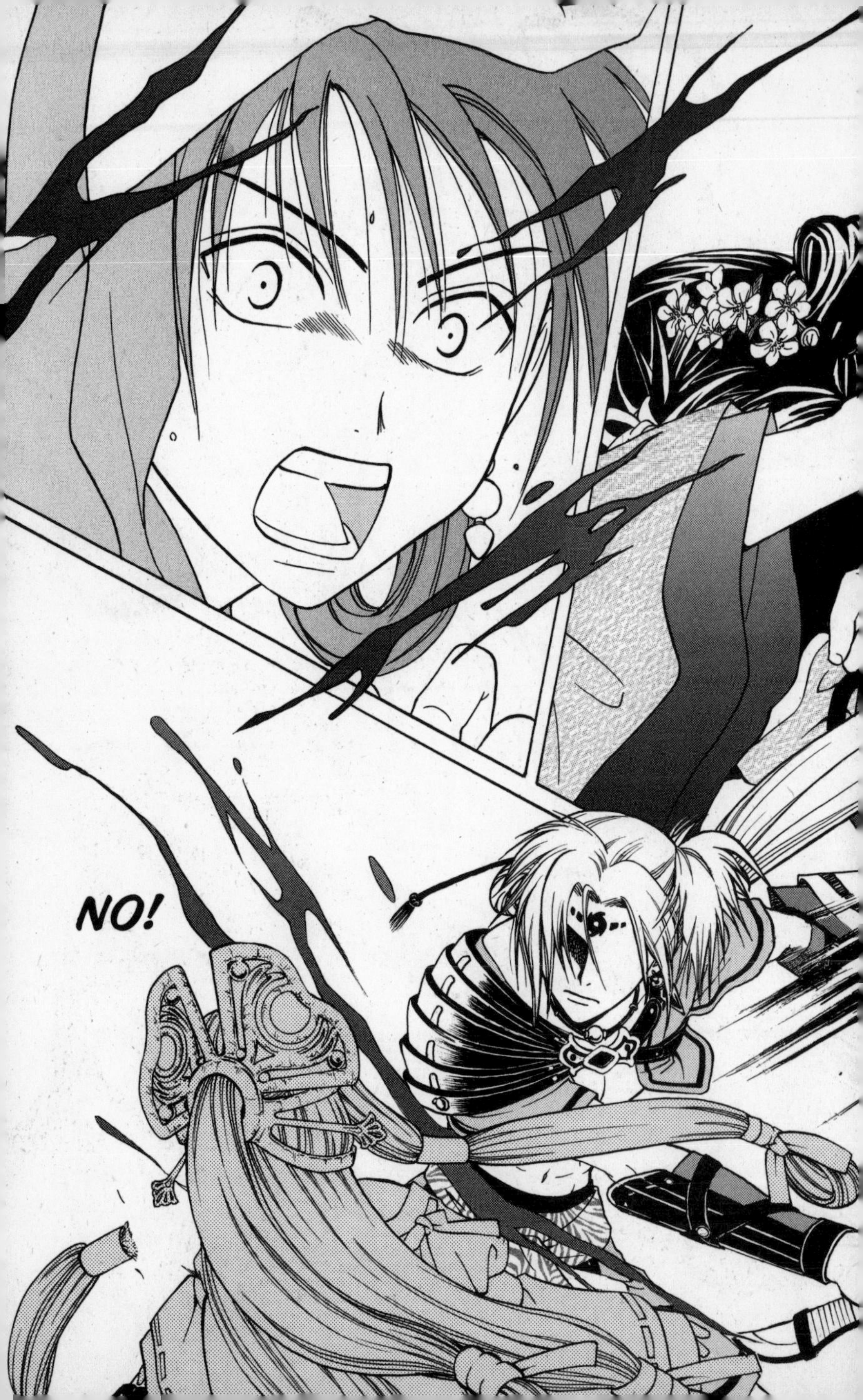
NO!

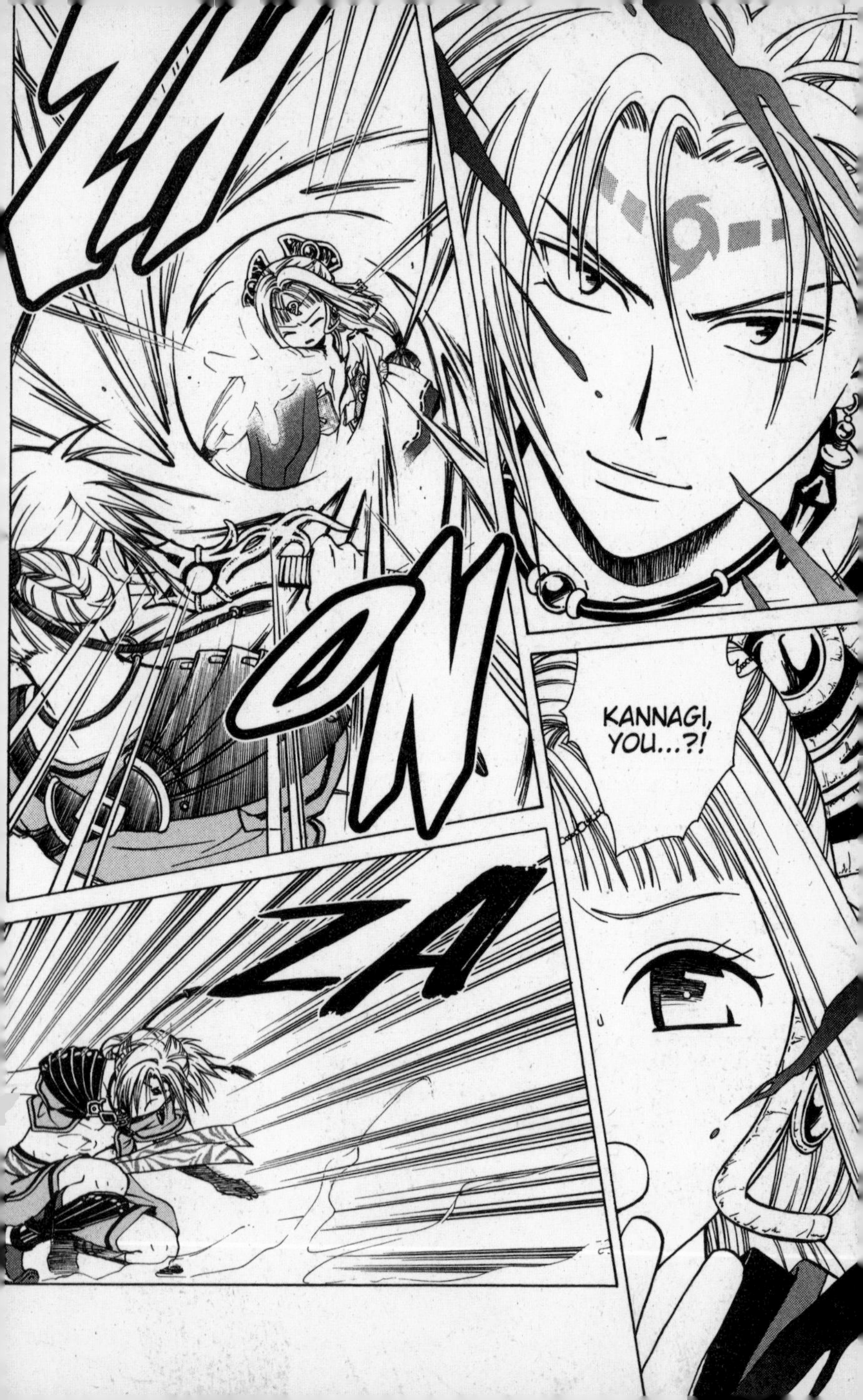
KANNAGI, YOU...?!
ZA

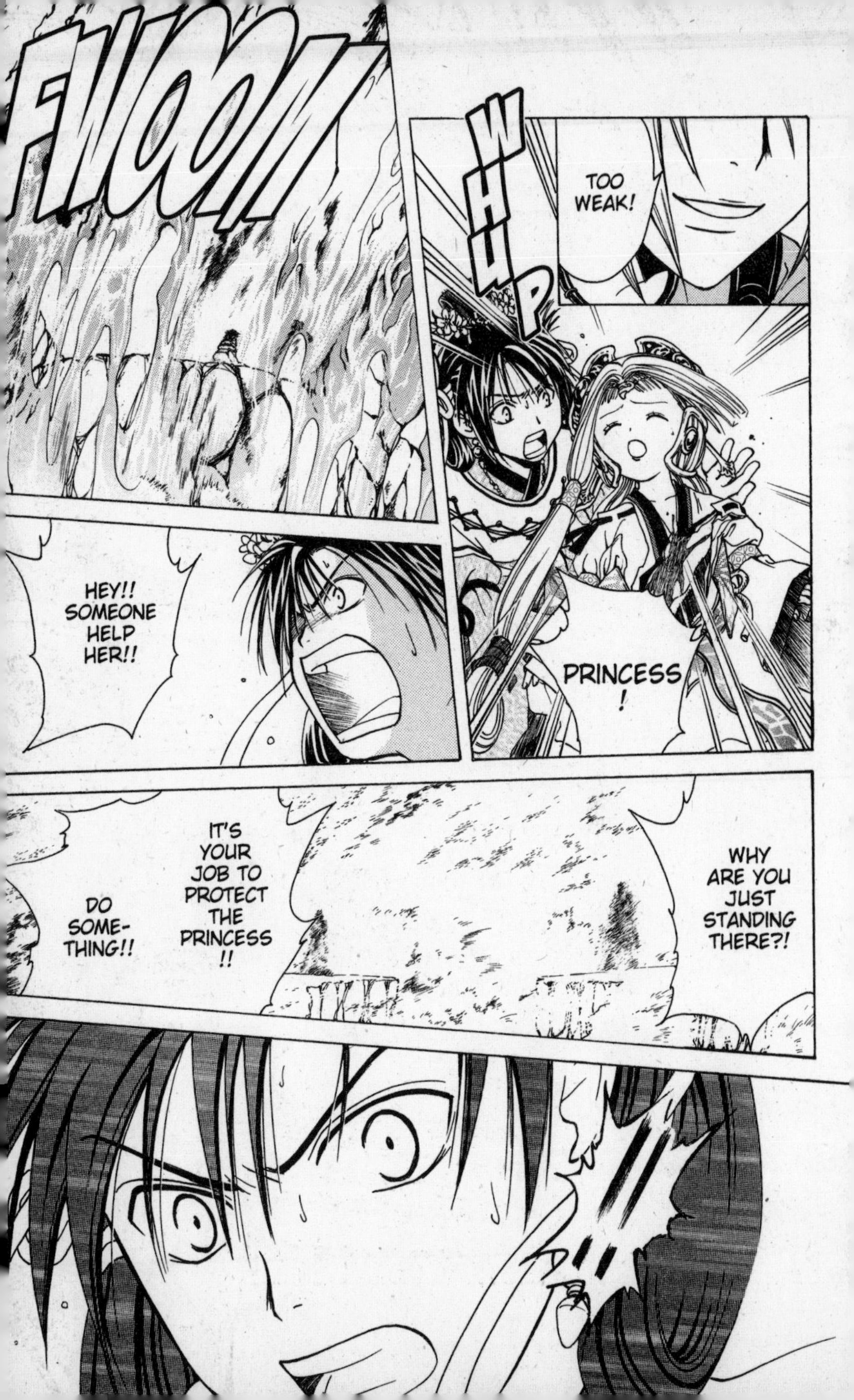
WHUP
TOO WEAK!
PRINCESS!
HEY!! SOMEONE HELP HER!!
WHY ARE YOU JUST STANDING THERE?!
IT'S YOUR JOB TO PROTECT THE PRINCESS!!
DO SOME-THING!!

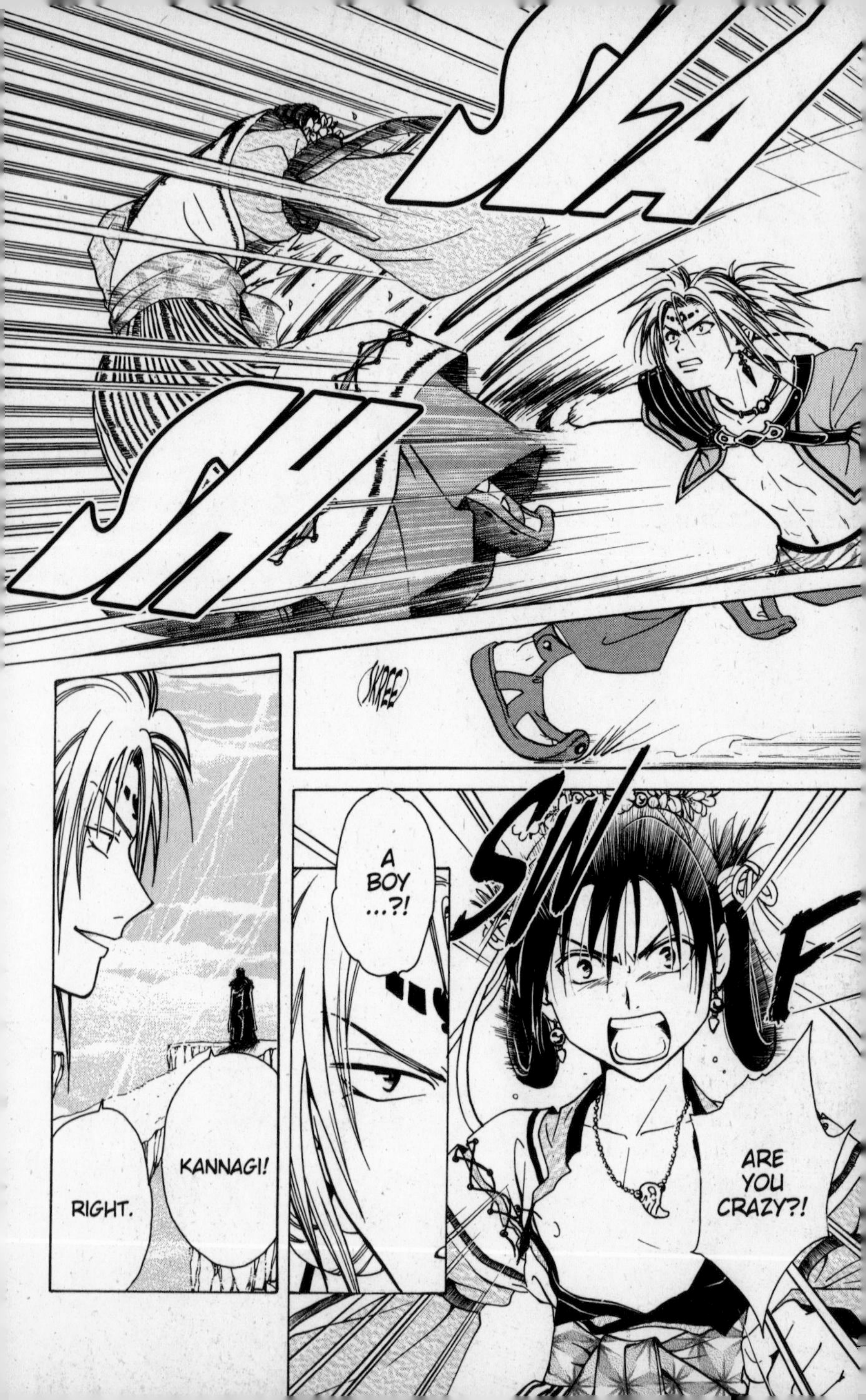
SHA
SHA
SKREE
SHF
ARE YOU CRAZY?!
A BOY ...?!
KANNAGI!
RIGHT.

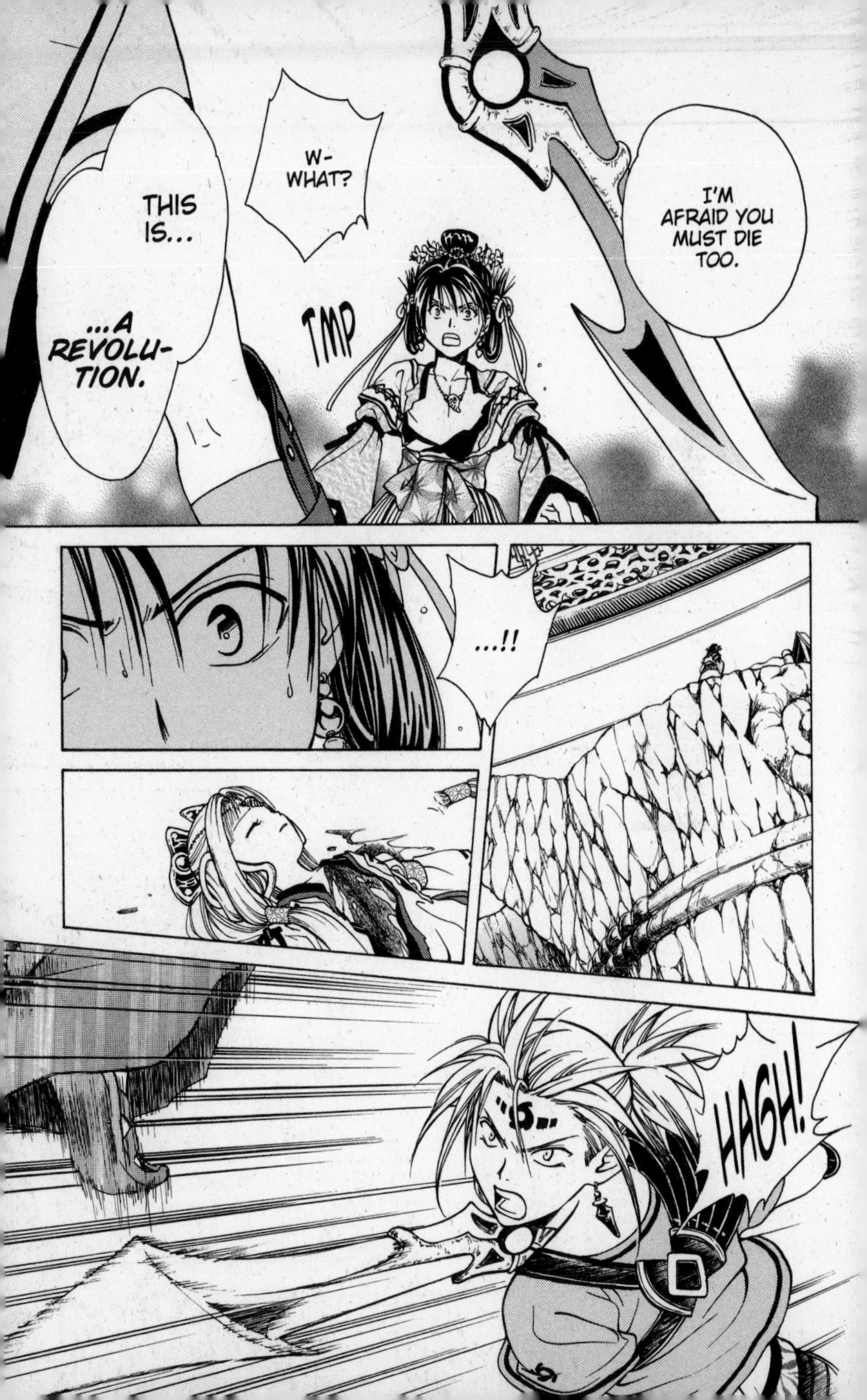
I'M AFRAID YOU MUST DIE TOO.
W- WHAT?
TMP
THIS IS...
...A REVOLUTION.
...!!
HAGH!

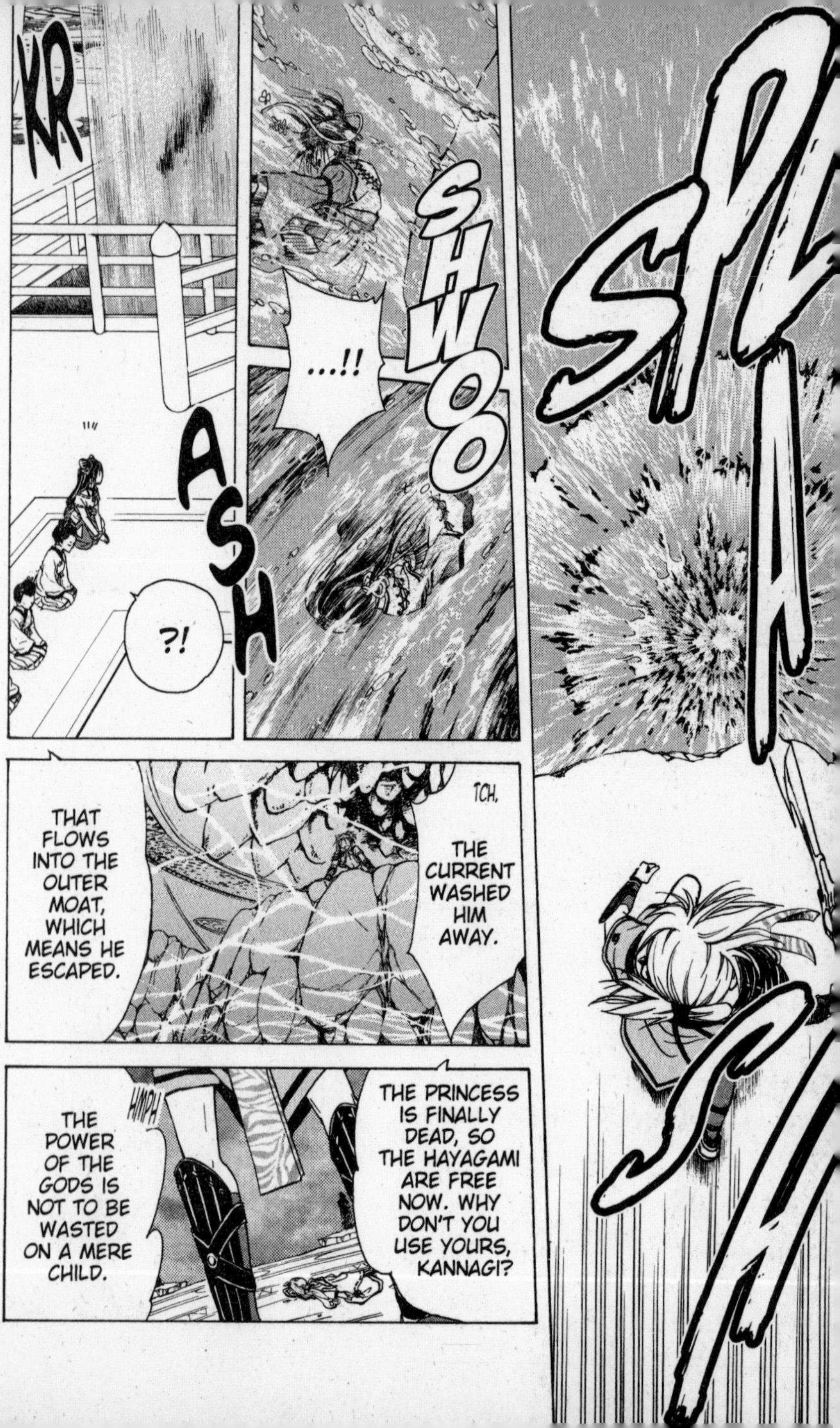
SHWOOO
...!!
KR
ASH
?!
TCH.
THE CURRENT WASHED HIM AWAY.
THAT FLOWS INTO THE OUTER MOAT, WHICH MEANS HE ESCAPED.
THE PRINCESS IS FINALLY DEAD, SO THE HAYAGAMI ARE FREE NOW. WHY DON'T YOU USE YOURS, KANNAGI?
HMPH
THE POWER OF THE GODS IS NOT TO BE WASTED ON A MERE CHILD.

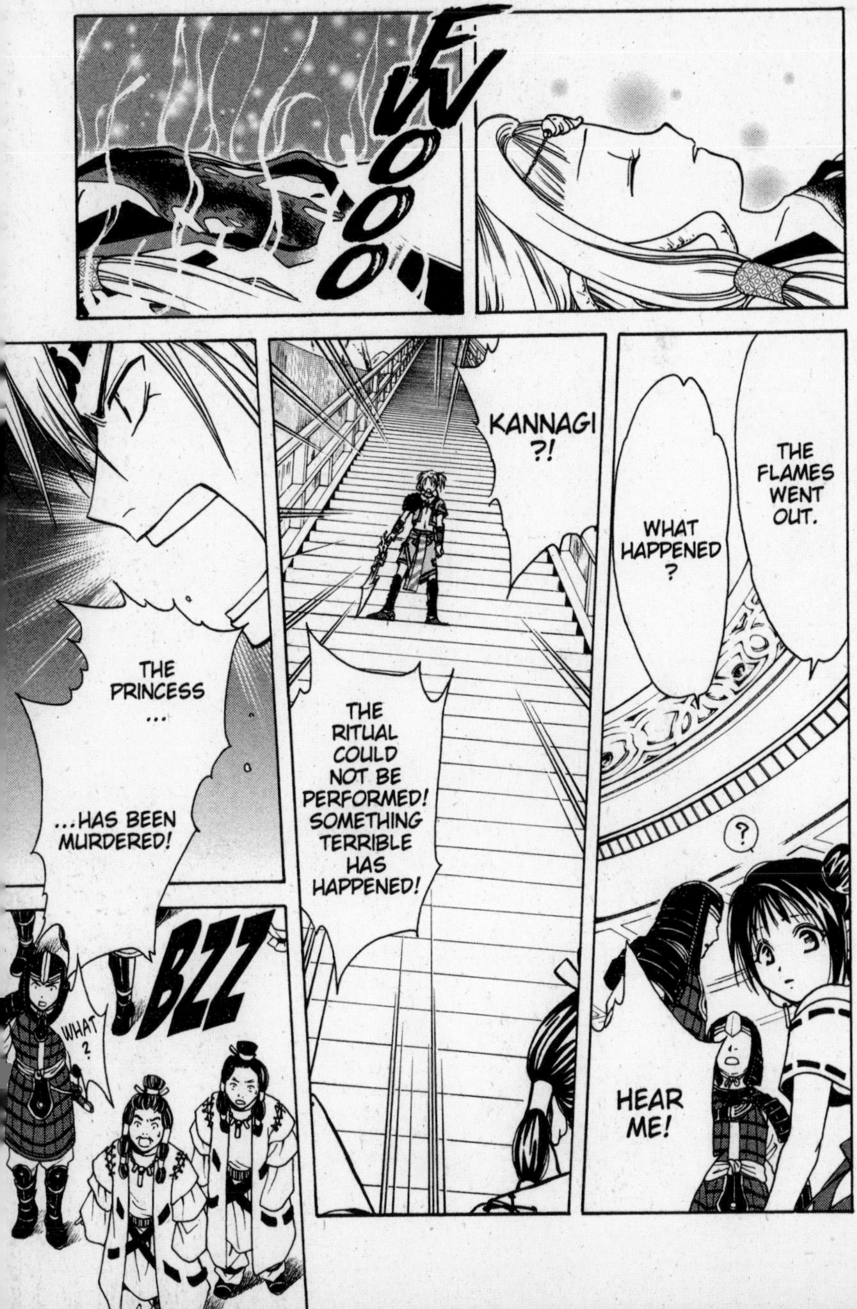
FWOOOOO
THE FLAMES WENT OUT.
WHAT HAPPENED?
?
HEAR ME!
KANNAGI?!
THE RITUAL COULD NOT BE PERFORMED! SOMETHING TERRIBLE HAS HAPPENED!
THE PRINCESS...
...HAS BEEN MURDERED!
BZZ
WHAT?

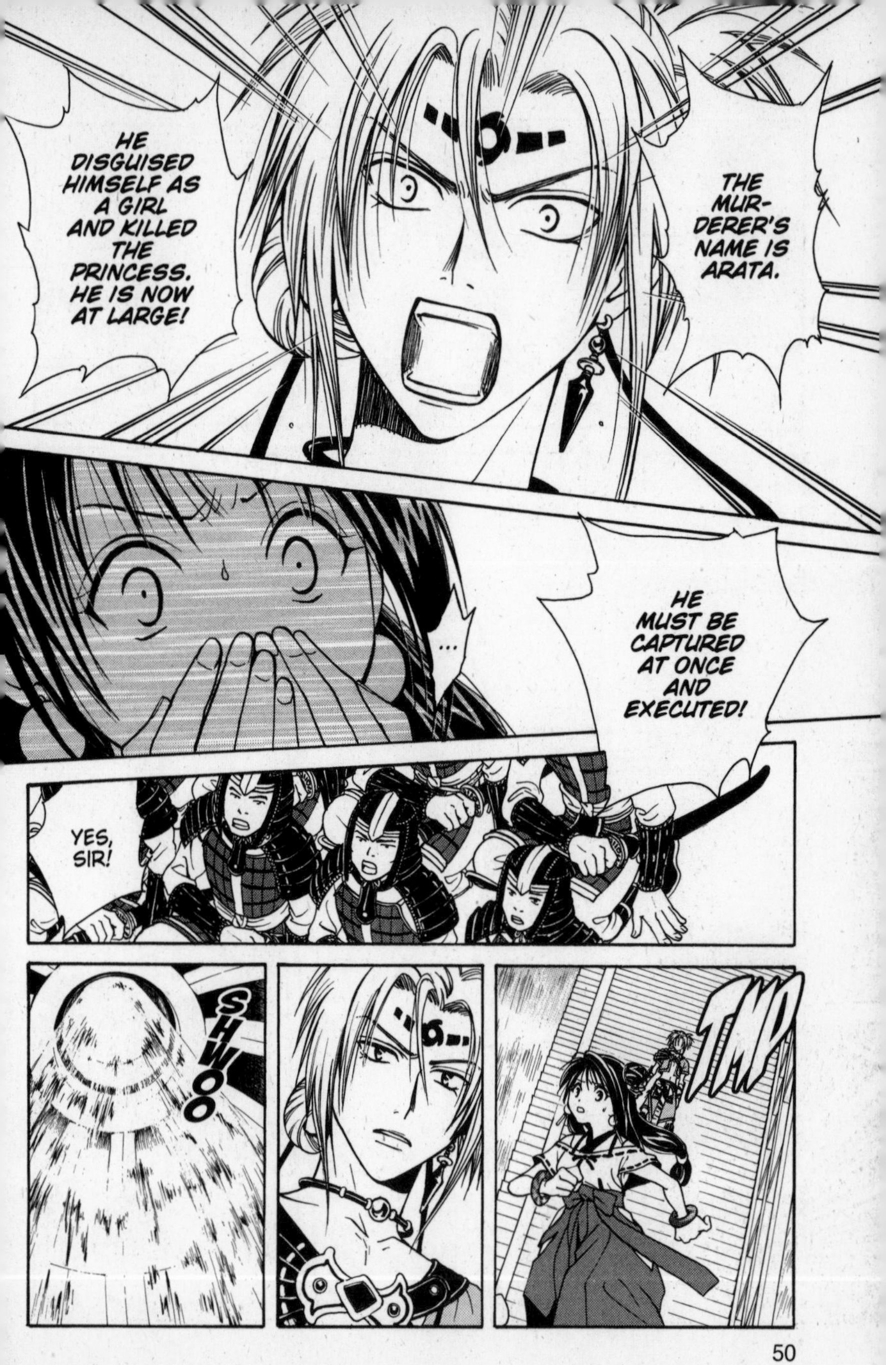
THE MUR-DERER'S NAME IS ARATA.
HE DISGUISED HIMSELF AS A GIRL AND KILLED THE PRINCESS. HE IS NOW AT LARGE!
HE MUST BE CAPTURED AT ONCE AND EXECUTED!
...
YES, SIR!
TMP
SHWOO

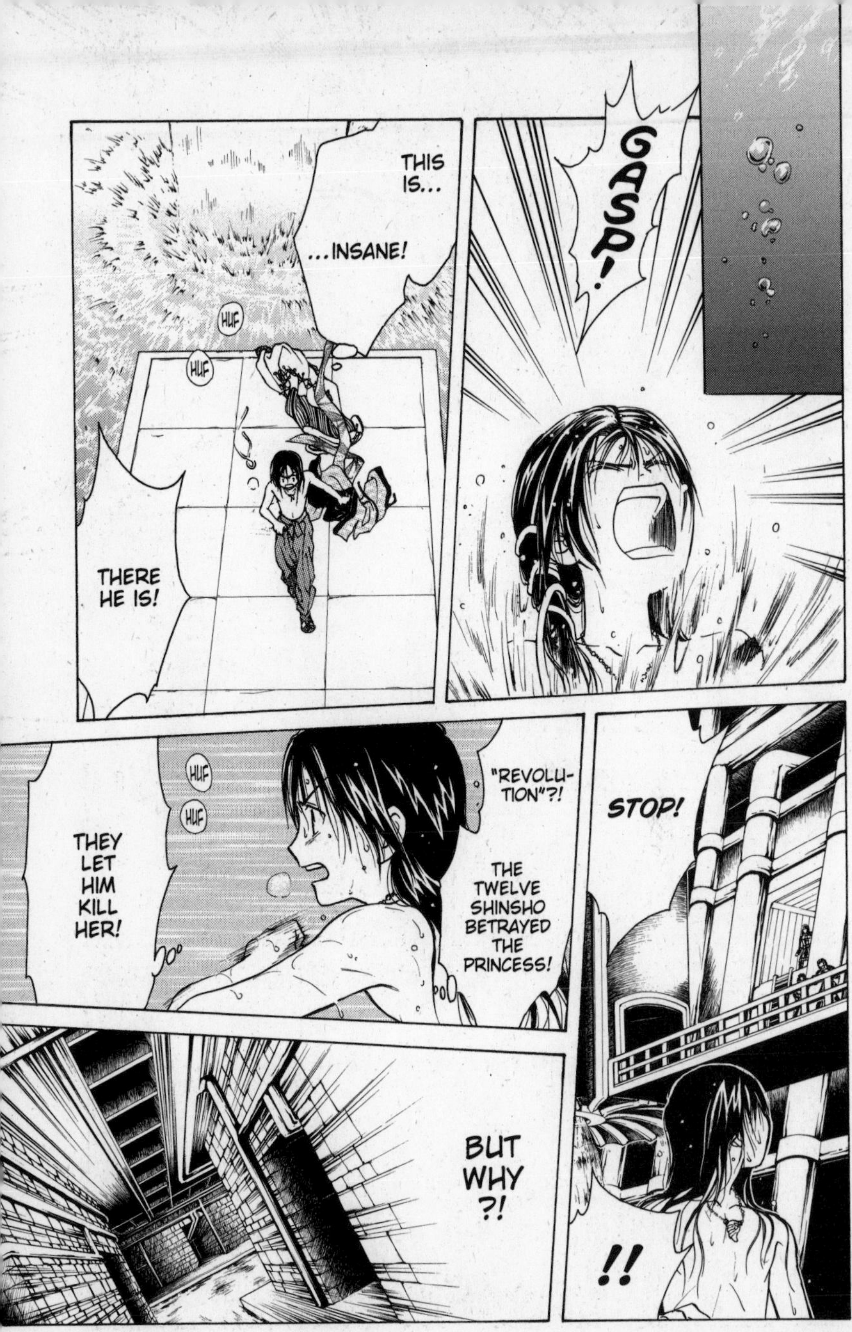
GASP!
THIS IS...
...INSANE!
HUF
HUF
THERE HE IS!
STOP!
!!
HUF
HUF
"REVOLUTION"?!
THE TWELVE SHINSHO BETRAYED THE PRINCESS!
THEY LET HIM KILL HER!
BUT WHY?!

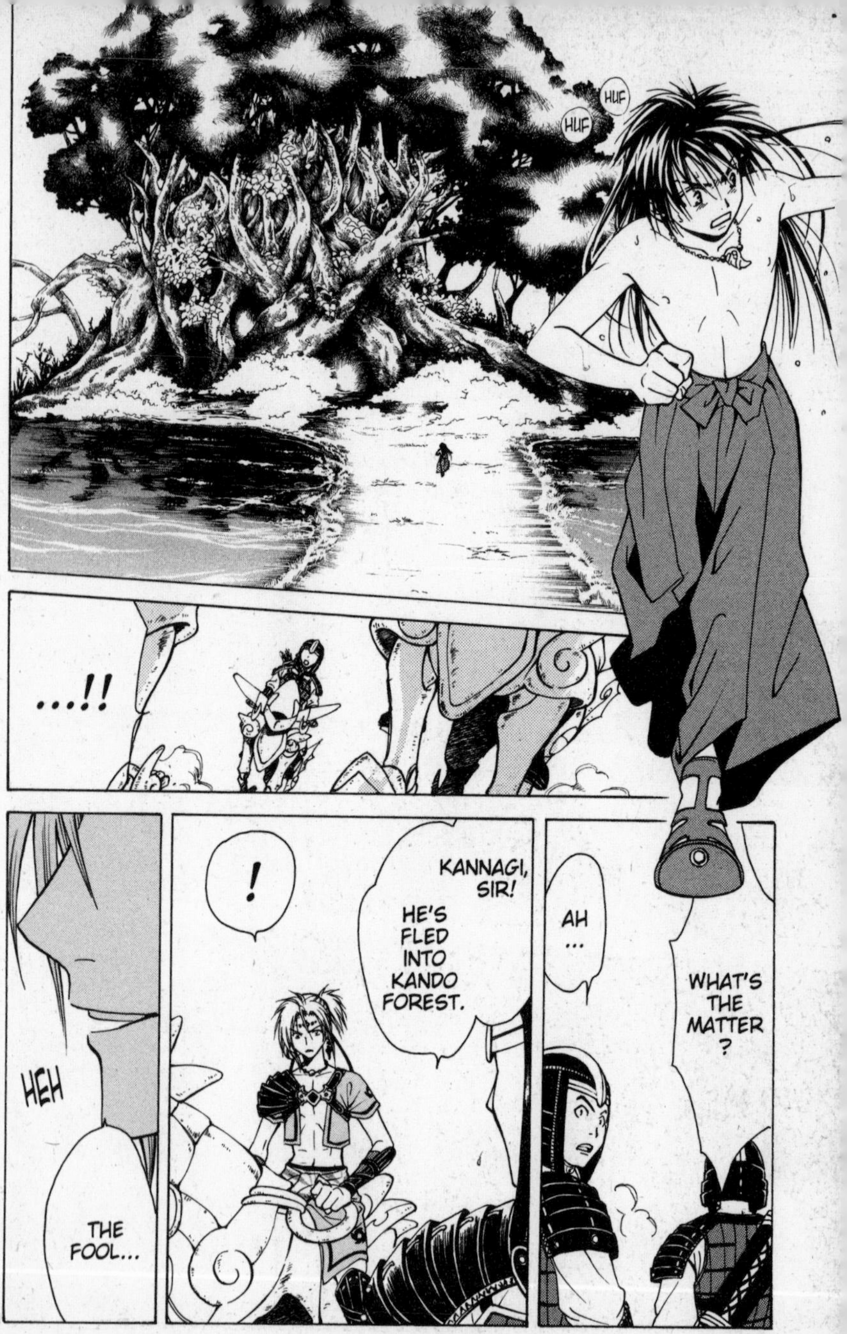
HUF
HUF
...!!
WHAT'S THE MATTER?
AH...
KANNAGI, SIR!
HE'S FLED INTO KANDO FOREST.
!
HEH
THE FOOL...

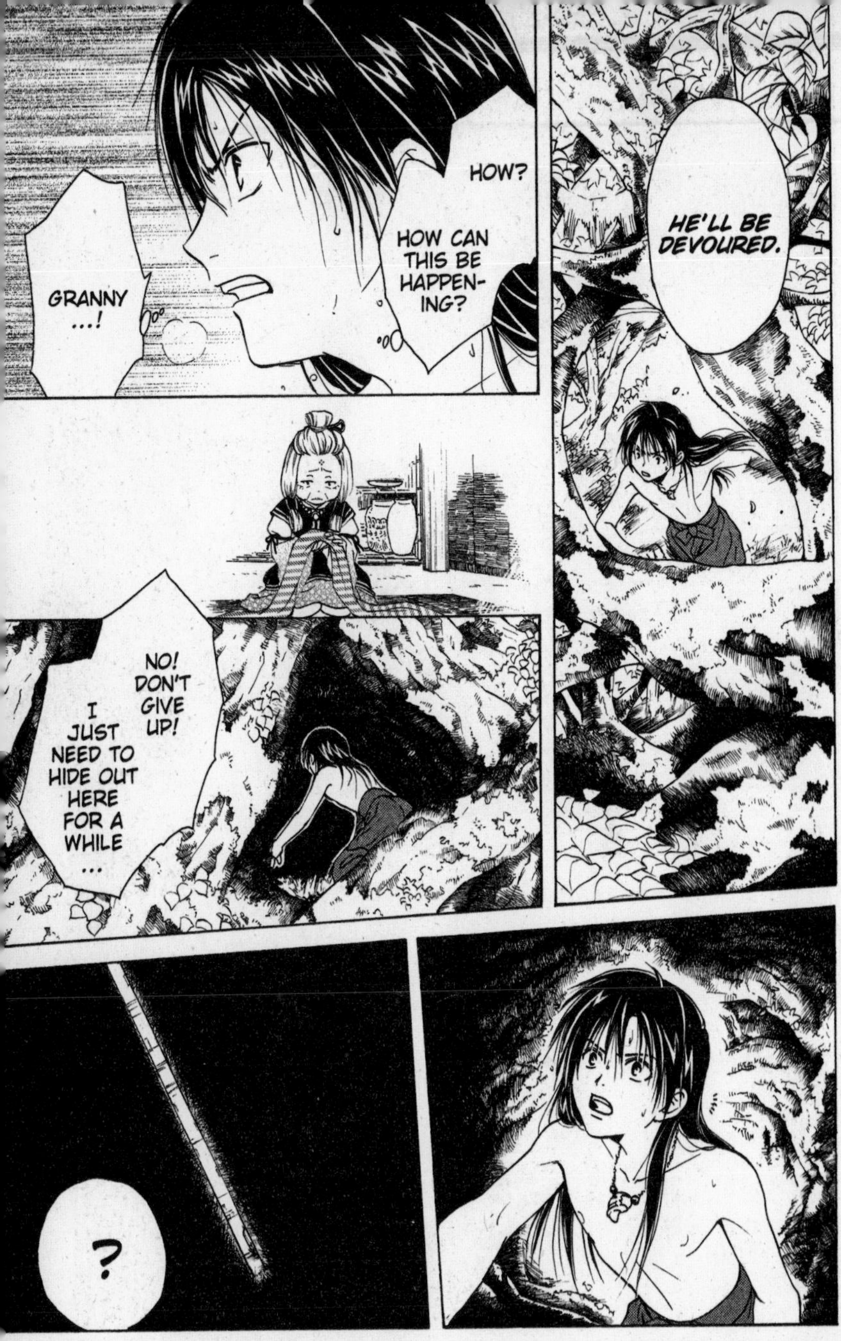
HE'LL BE DEVOURED.
HOW?
HOW CAN THIS BE HAPPEN-ING?
GRANNY ...!
NO! DON'T GIVE UP!
I JUST NEED TO HIDE OUT HERE FOR A WHILE ...
?

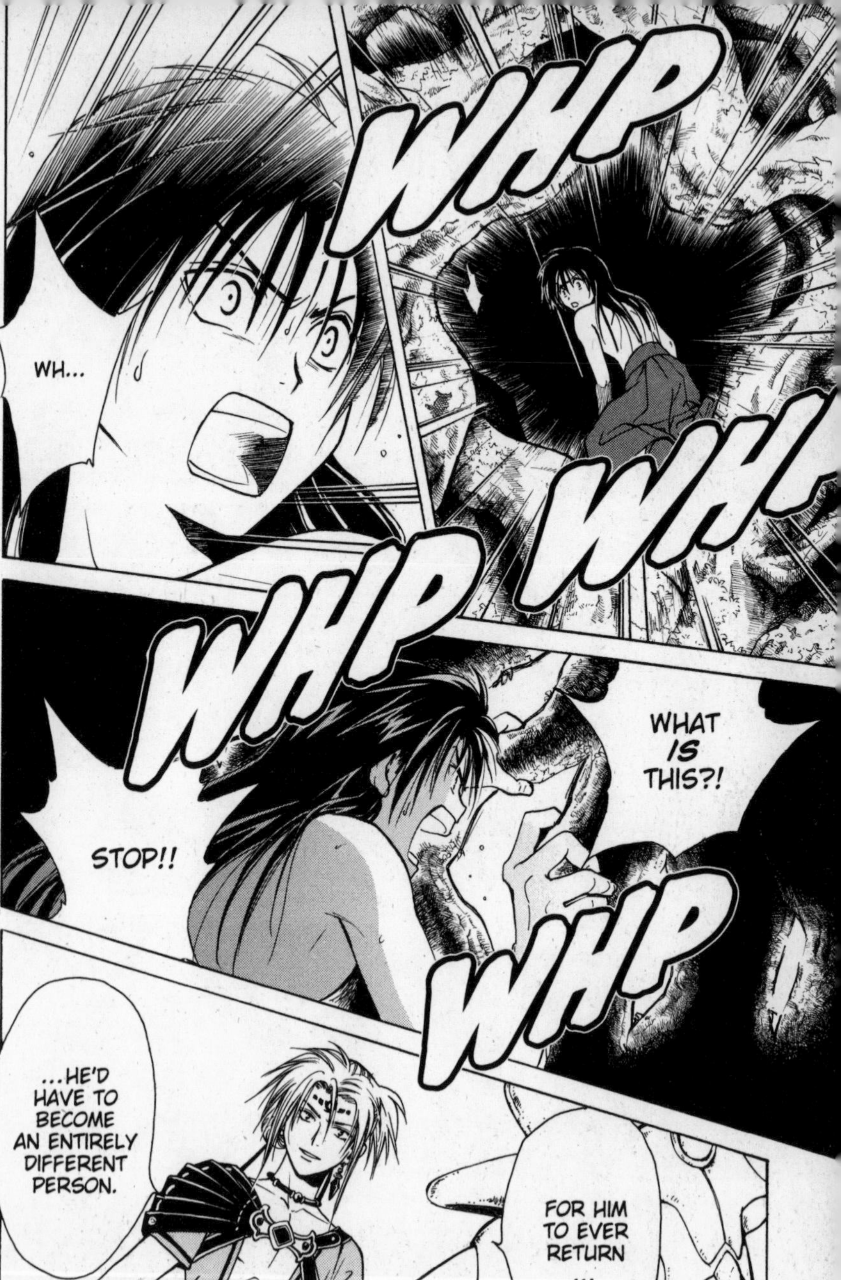
WHIP
WH...
WHIP
WHAT IS THIS?!
STOP!!
WHIP
FOR HIM TO EVER RETURN ...
...HE'D HAVE TO BECOME AN ENTIRELY DIFFERENT PERSON.

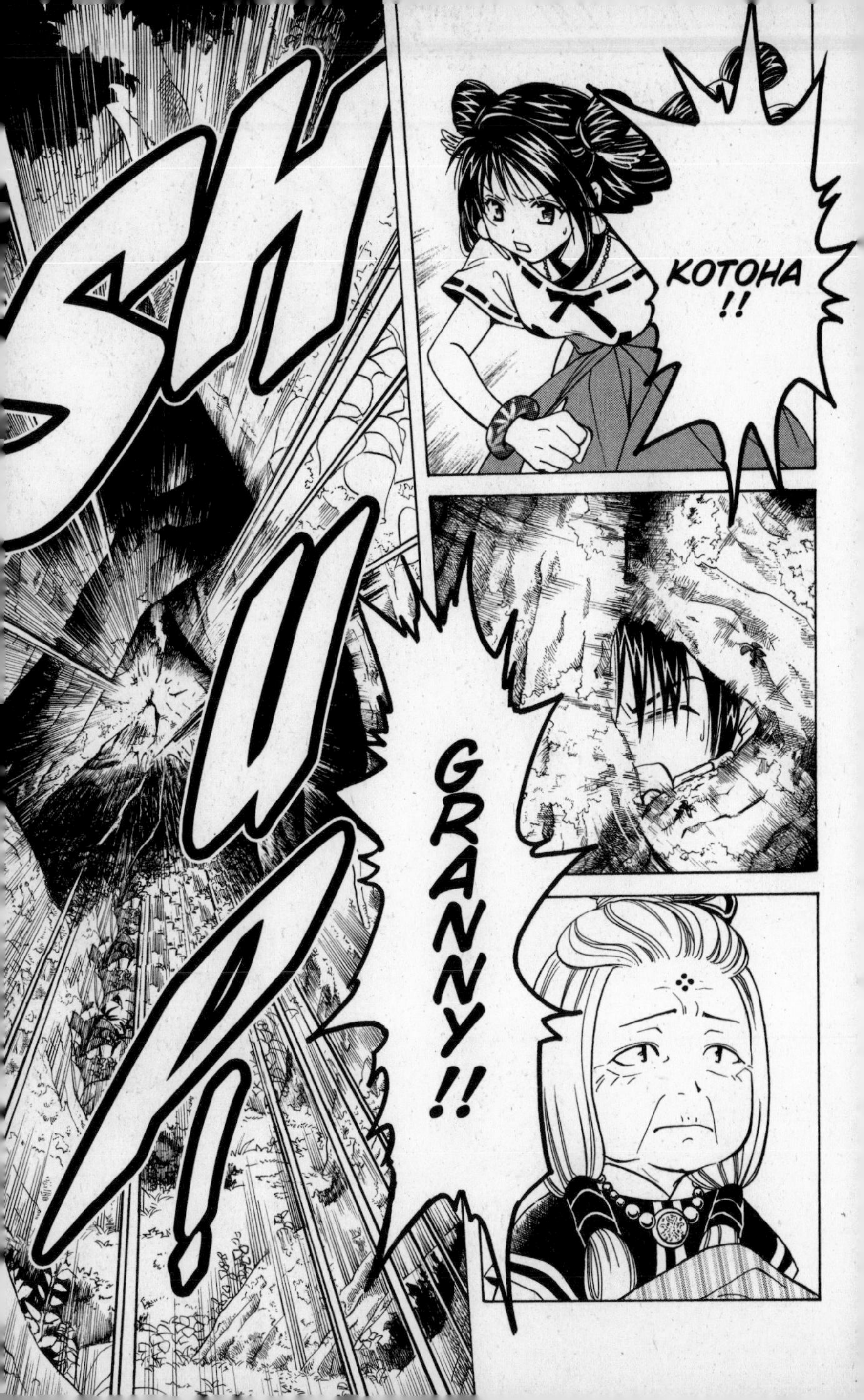
KOTOHA!!
GRANNY!!

Arata
THE LEGEND

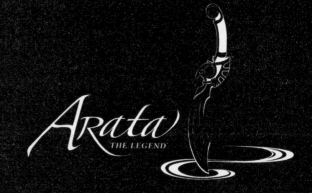

CHAPTER 2 FRIENDS

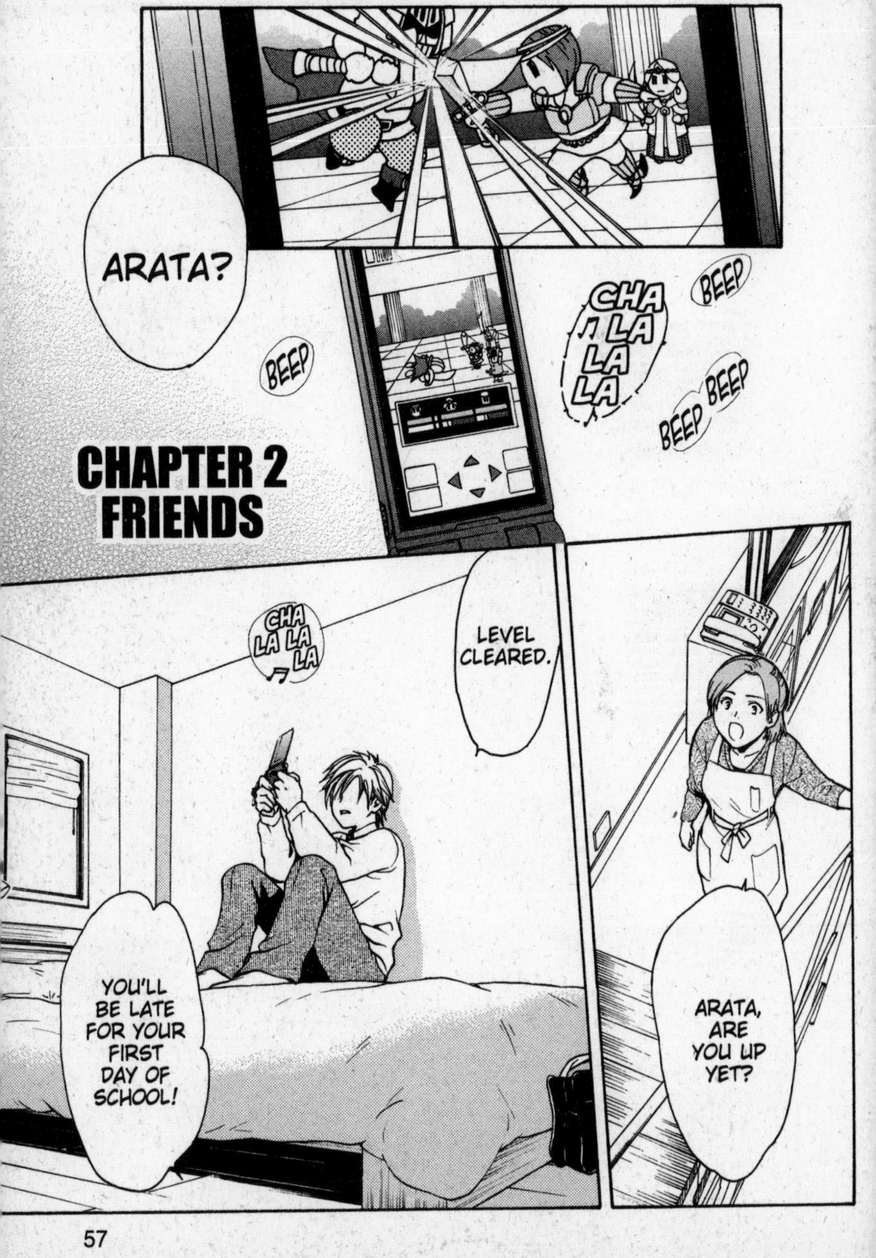
ARATA?
BEEP
CHA LA LA LA
BEEP BEEP
BEEP
ARATA, ARE YOU UP YET?
LEVEL CLEARED.
CHA LA LA LA
YOU'LL BE LATE FOR YOUR FIRST DAY OF SCHOOL!

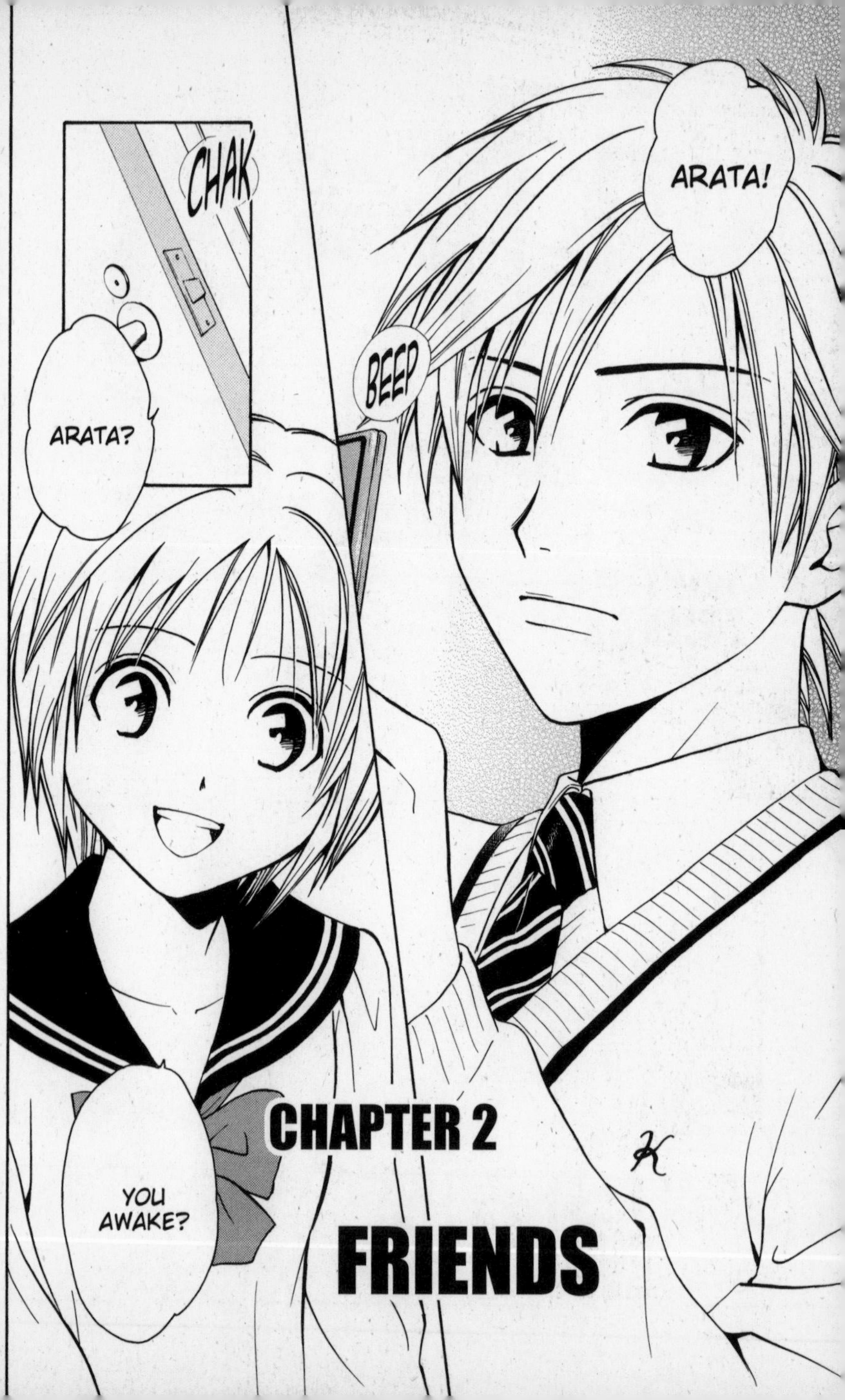
ARATA!
BEEP
CHAK
ARATA?
YOU AWAKE?
CHAPTER 2
FRIENDS

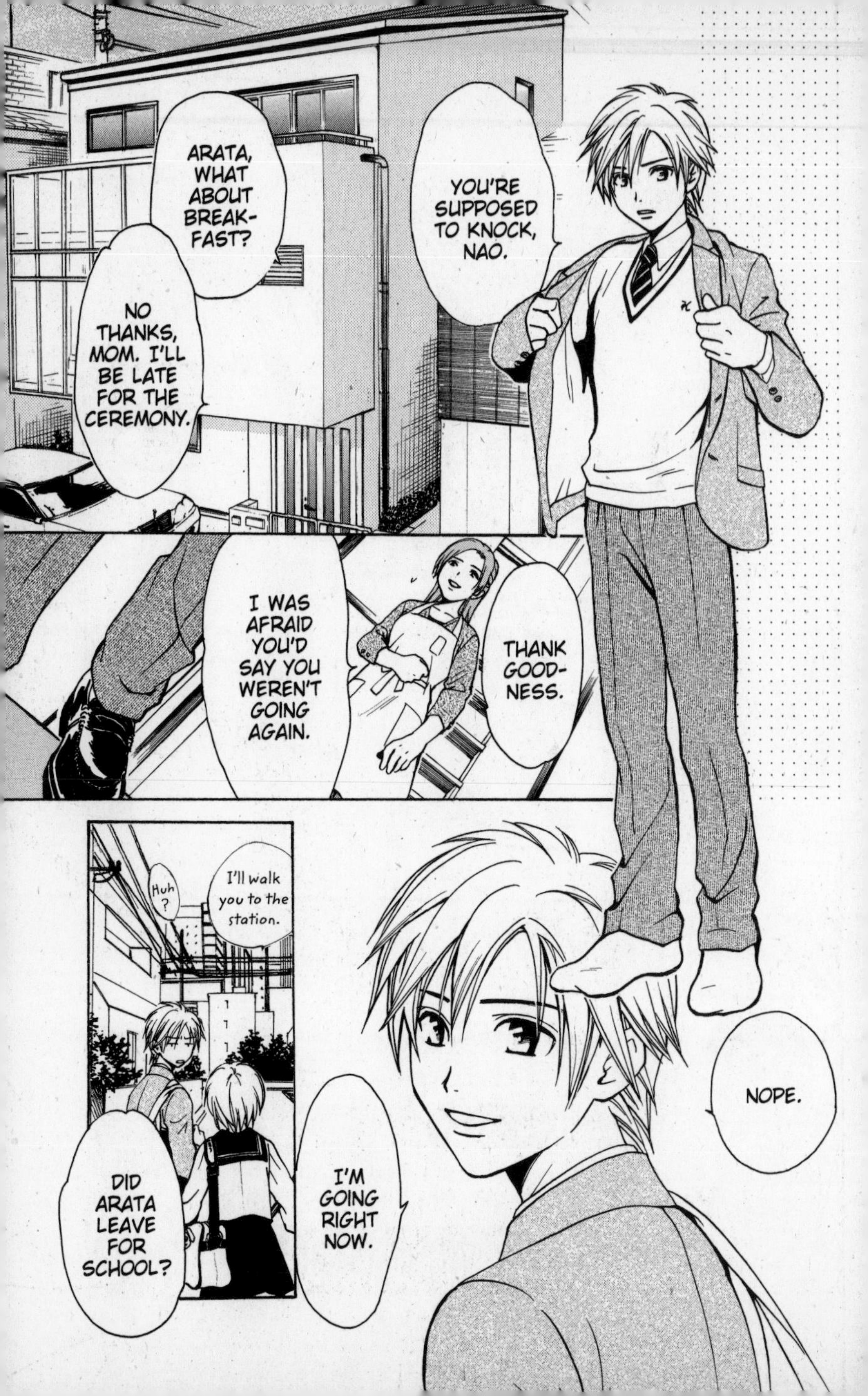
YOU'RE SUPPOSED TO KNOCK, NAO.
ARATA, WHAT ABOUT BREAK-FAST?
NO THANKS, MOM. I'LL BE LATE FOR THE CEREMONY.
THANK GOOD-NESS.
I WAS AFRAID YOU'D SAY YOU WEREN'T GOING AGAIN.
NOPE.
I'M GOING RIGHT NOW.
DID ARATA LEAVE FOR SCHOOL?
I'll walk you to the station.
Huh?

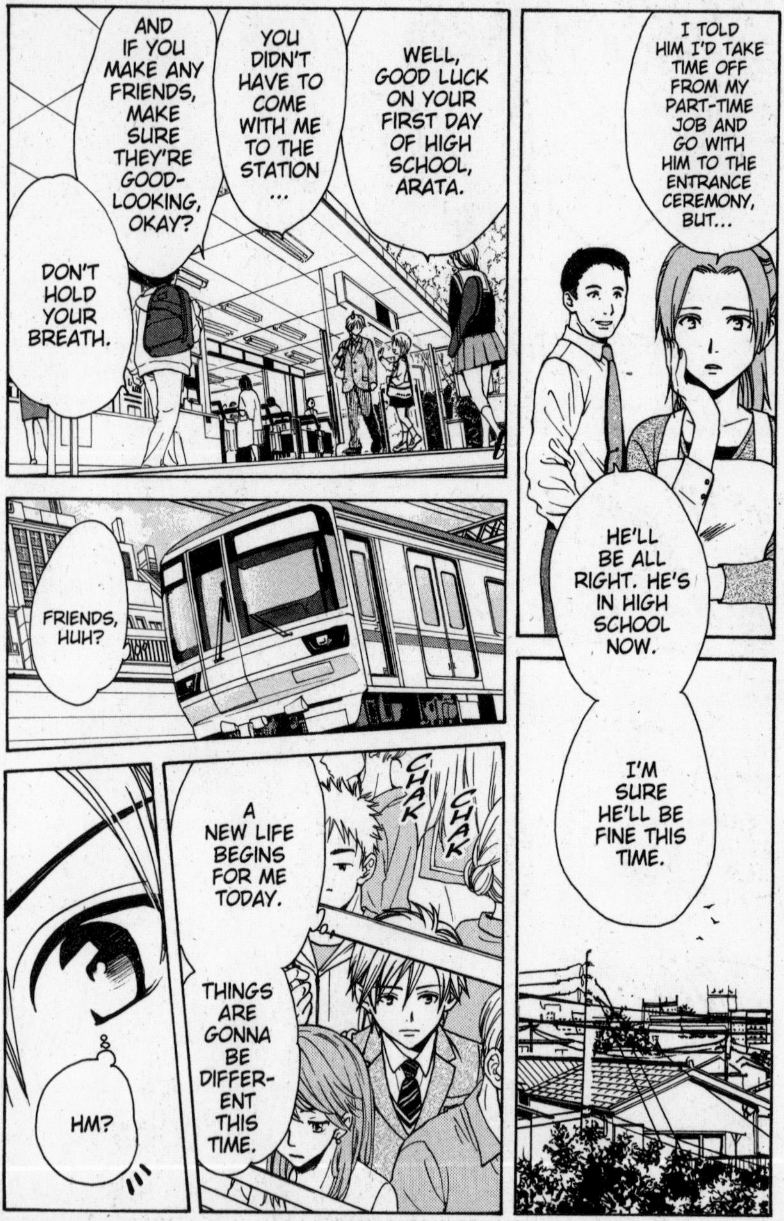
I TOLD HIM I'D TAKE TIME OFF FROM MY PART-TIME JOB AND GO WITH HIM TO THE ENTRANCE CEREMONY, BUT...
HE'LL BE ALL RIGHT. HE'S IN HIGH SCHOOL NOW.
I'M SURE HE'LL BE FINE THIS TIME.
WELL, GOOD LUCK ON YOUR FIRST DAY OF HIGH SCHOOL, ARATA.
YOU DIDN'T HAVE TO COME WITH ME TO THE STATION ...
AND IF YOU MAKE ANY FRIENDS, MAKE SURE THEY'RE GOOD-LOOKING, OKAY?
DON'T HOLD YOUR BREATH.
FRIENDS, HUH?
CHAK
CHAK
A NEW LIFE BEGINS FOR ME TODAY.
THINGS ARE GONNA BE DIFFERENT THIS TIME.
HM?

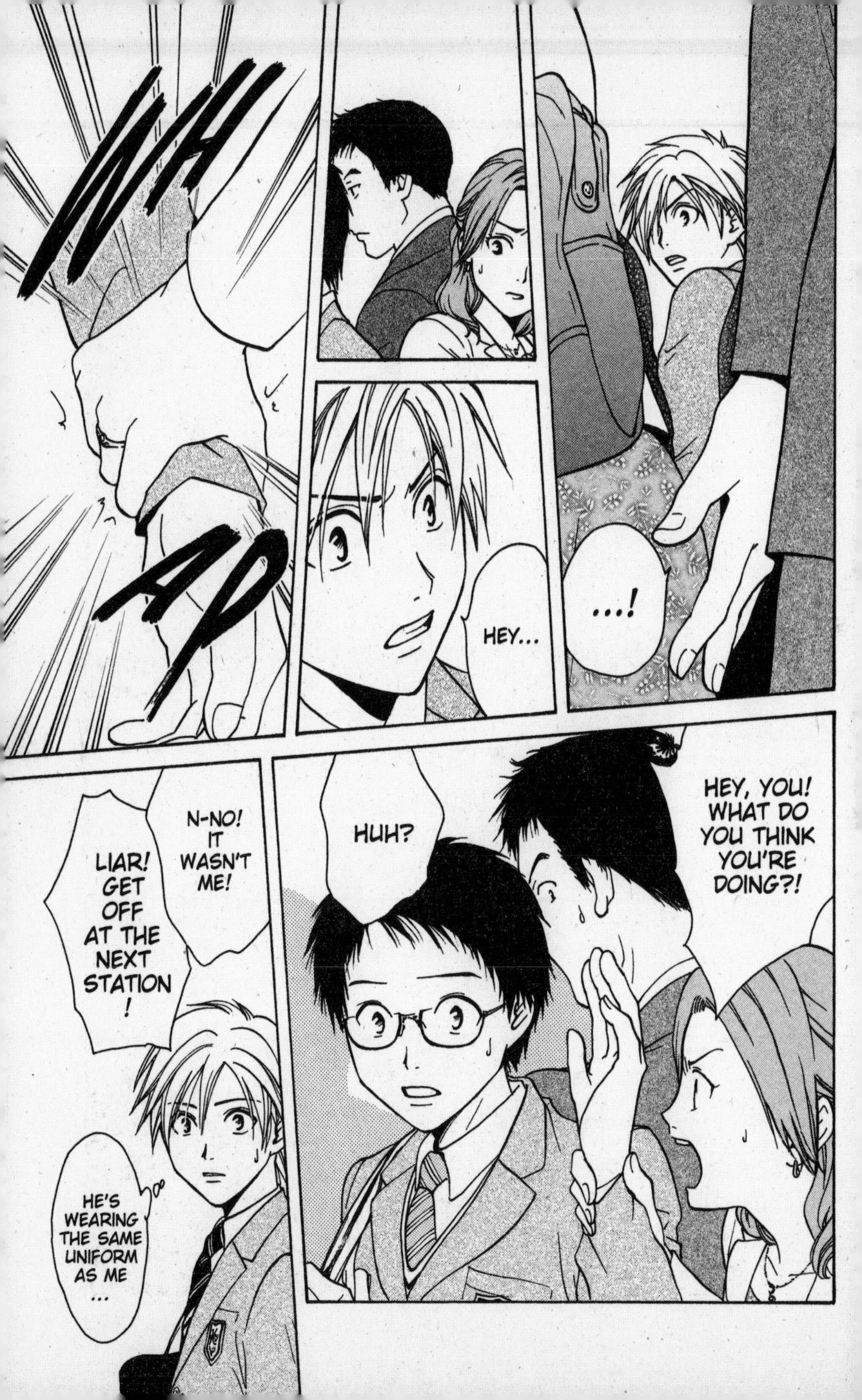
...!
HEY...
WHAP
HEY, YOU! WHAT DO YOU THINK YOU'RE DOING?!
HUH?
N-NO! IT WASN'T ME!
LIAR! GET OFF AT THE NEXT STATION!
HE'S WEARING THE SAME UNIFORM AS ME...

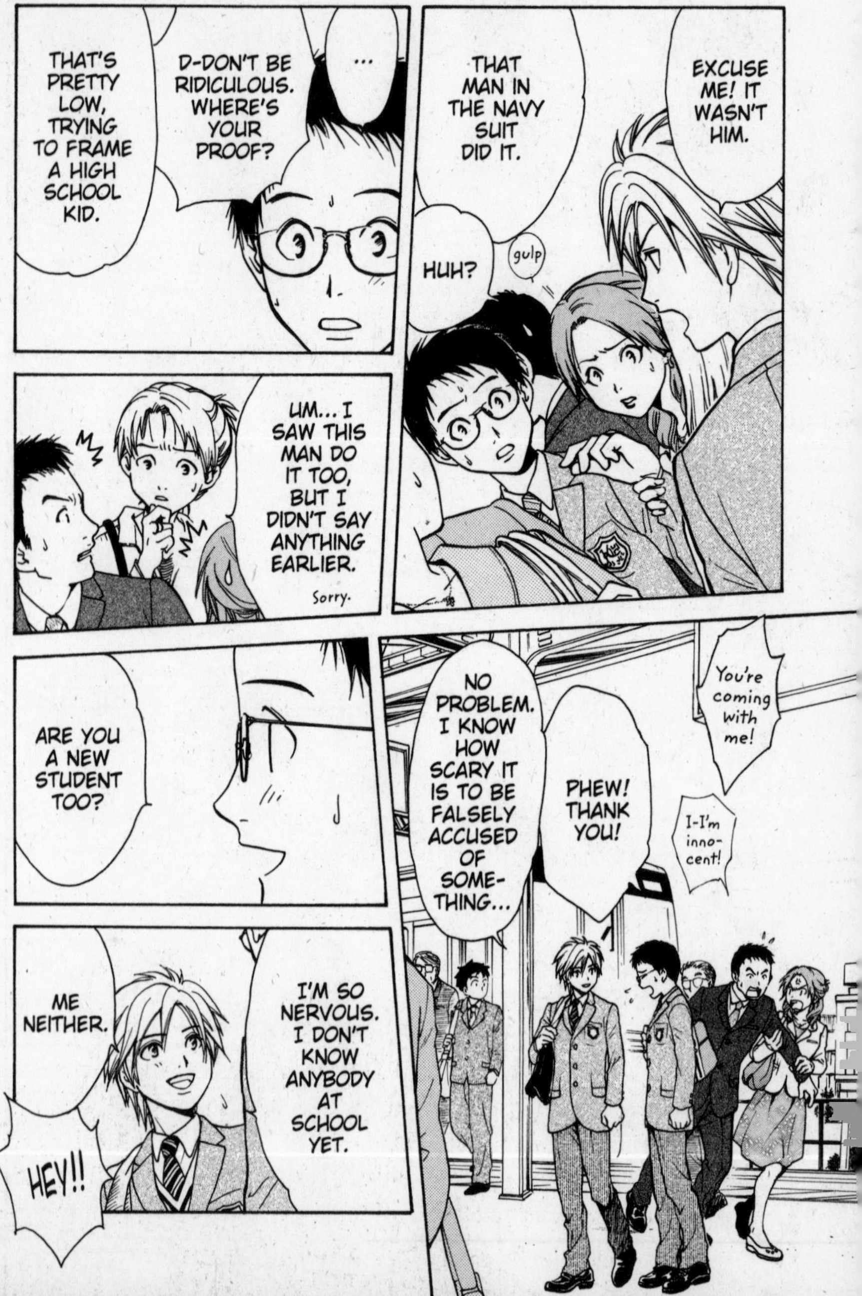
EXCUSE ME! IT WASN'T HIM.
THAT MAN IN THE NAVY SUIT DID IT.
gulp
HUH?
...
D-DON'T BE RIDICULOUS. WHERE'S YOUR PROOF?
THAT'S PRETTY LOW, TRYING TO FRAME A HIGH SCHOOL KID.
UM... I SAW THIS MAN DO IT TOO, BUT I DIDN'T SAY ANYTHING EARLIER.
Sorry.
You're coming with me!
I-I'm inno-cent!
PHEW! THANK YOU!
NO PROBLEM. I KNOW HOW SCARY IT IS TO BE FALSELY ACCUSED OF SOME-THING...
ARE YOU A NEW STUDENT TOO?
I'M SO NERVOUS. I DON'T KNOW ANYBODY AT SCHOOL YET.
ME NEITHER.
HEY!!

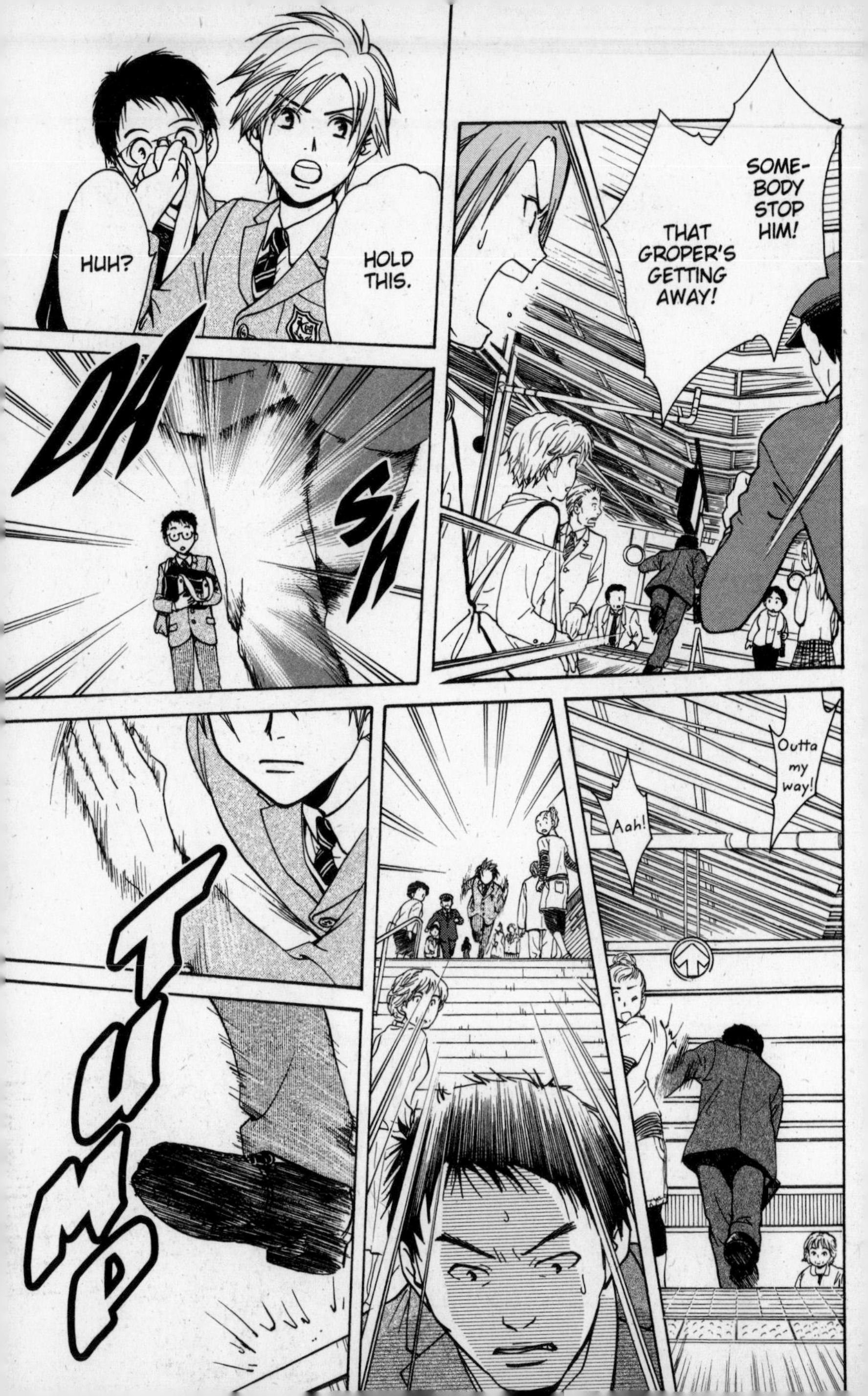
SOMEBODY STOP HIM!
THAT GROPER'S GETTING AWAY!
HOLD THIS.
HUH?
DASH
Outta my way!
Aah!
TUMP

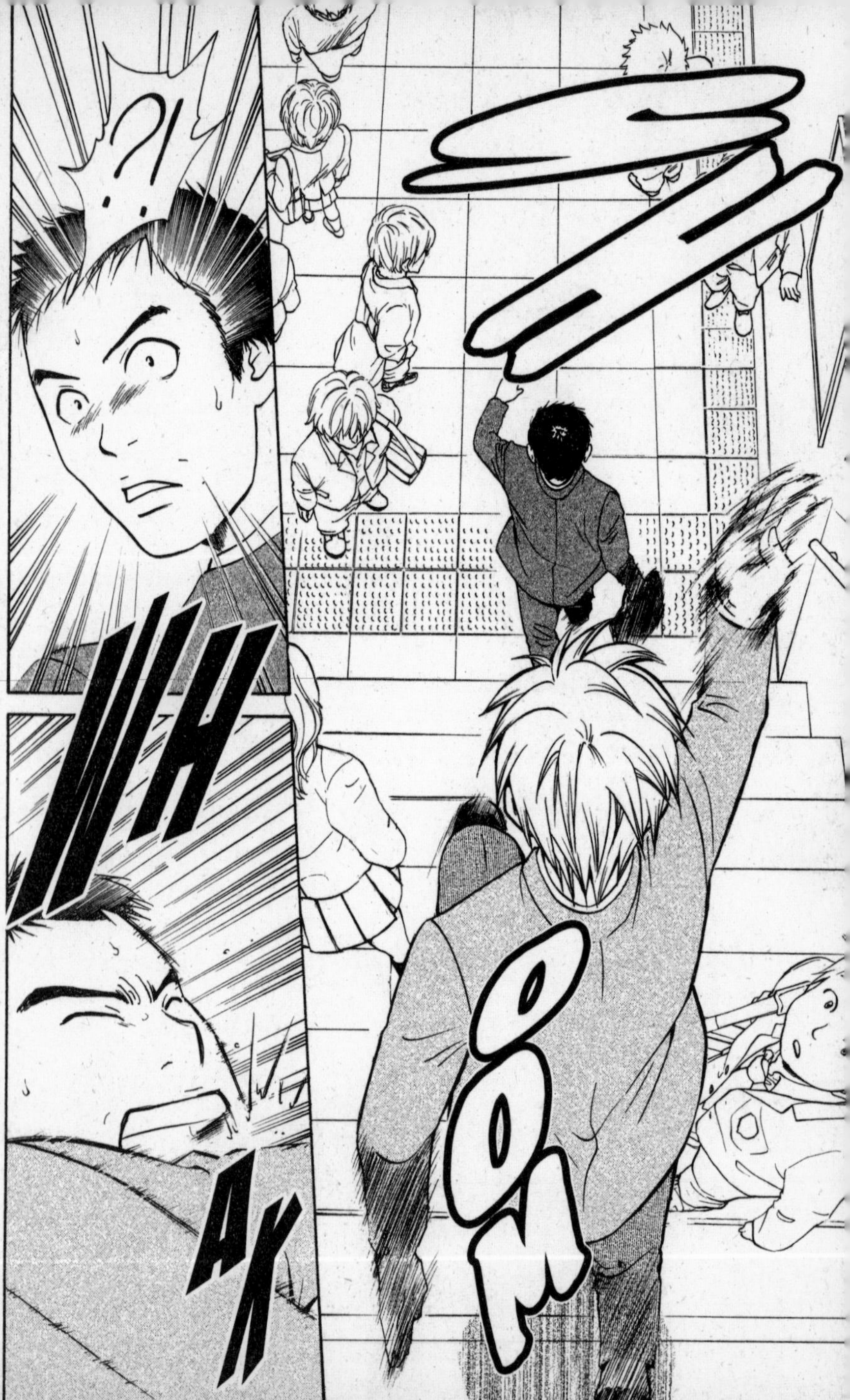
ZOOOM
?!
WHAK

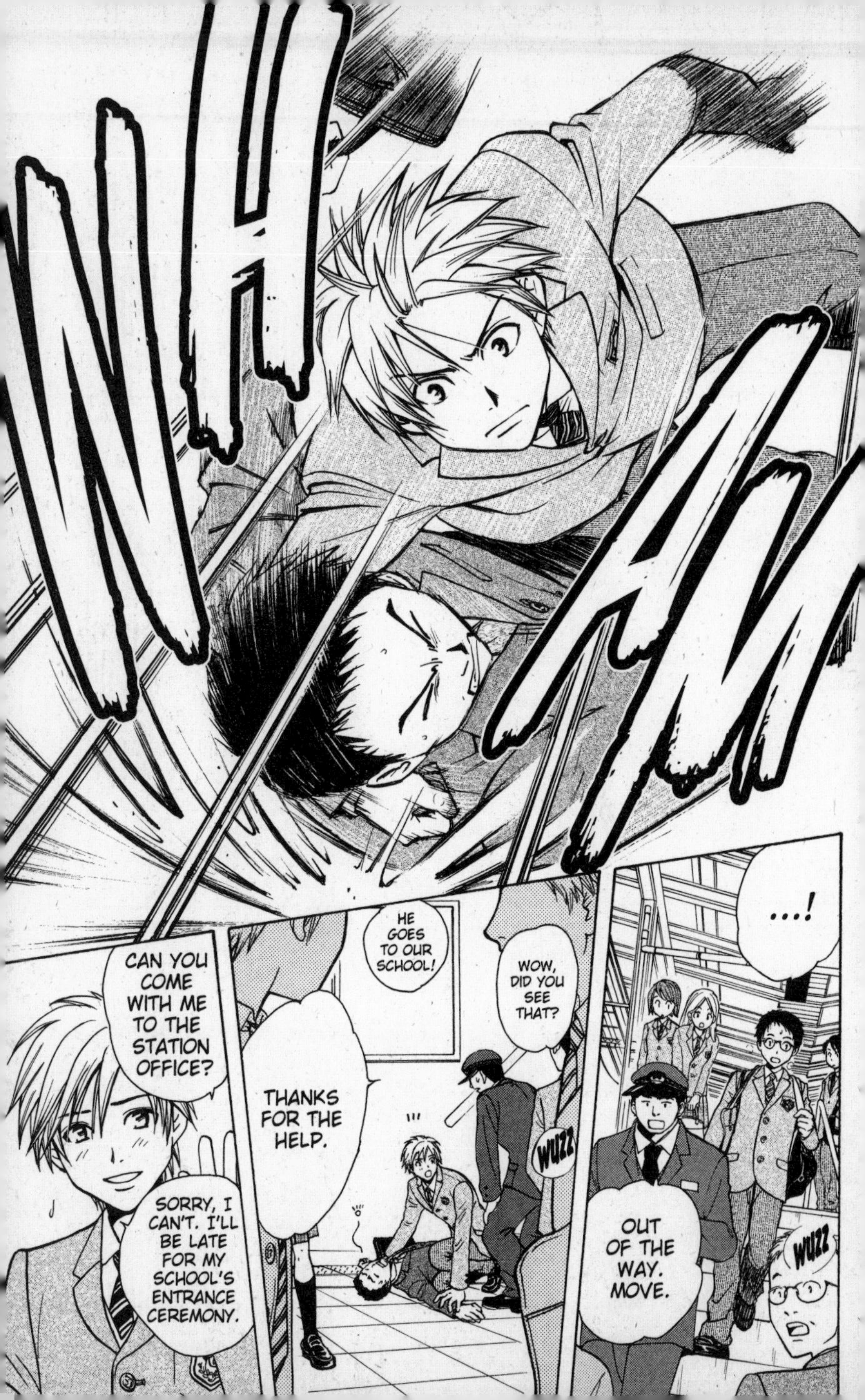

WHAM
...!
WUZZ
OUT OF THE WAY. MOVE.
WUZZ
WOW, DID YOU SEE THAT?
HE GOES TO OUR SCHOOL!
THANKS FOR THE HELP.
CAN YOU COME WITH ME TO THE STATION OFFICE?
SORRY, I CAN'T. I'LL BE LATE FOR MY SCHOOL'S ENTRANCE CEREMONY.

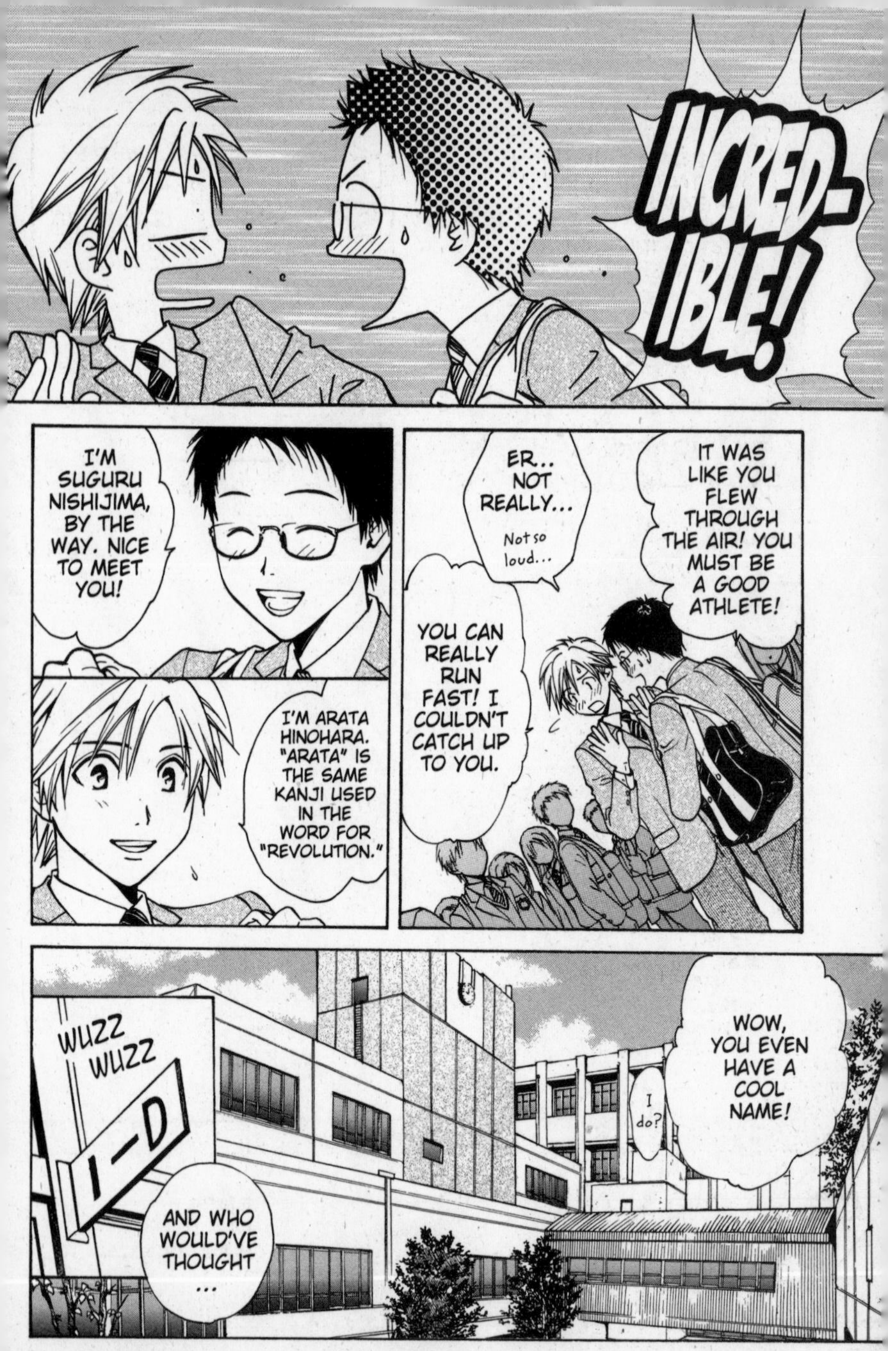
INCRED-IBLE!
IT WAS LIKE YOU FLEW THROUGH THE AIR! YOU MUST BE A GOOD ATHLETE!
ER.. NOT REALLY...
Not so loud...
YOU CAN REALLY RUN FAST! I COULDN'T CATCH UP TO YOU.
I'M SUGURU NISHIJIMA, BY THE WAY. NICE TO MEET YOU!
I'M ARATA HINOHARA. "ARATA" IS THE SAME KANJI USED IN THE WORD FOR "REVOLUTION."
WOW, YOU EVEN HAVE A COOL NAME!
I do?
WUZZ WUZZ
1-D
AND WHO WOULD'VE THOUGHT ...

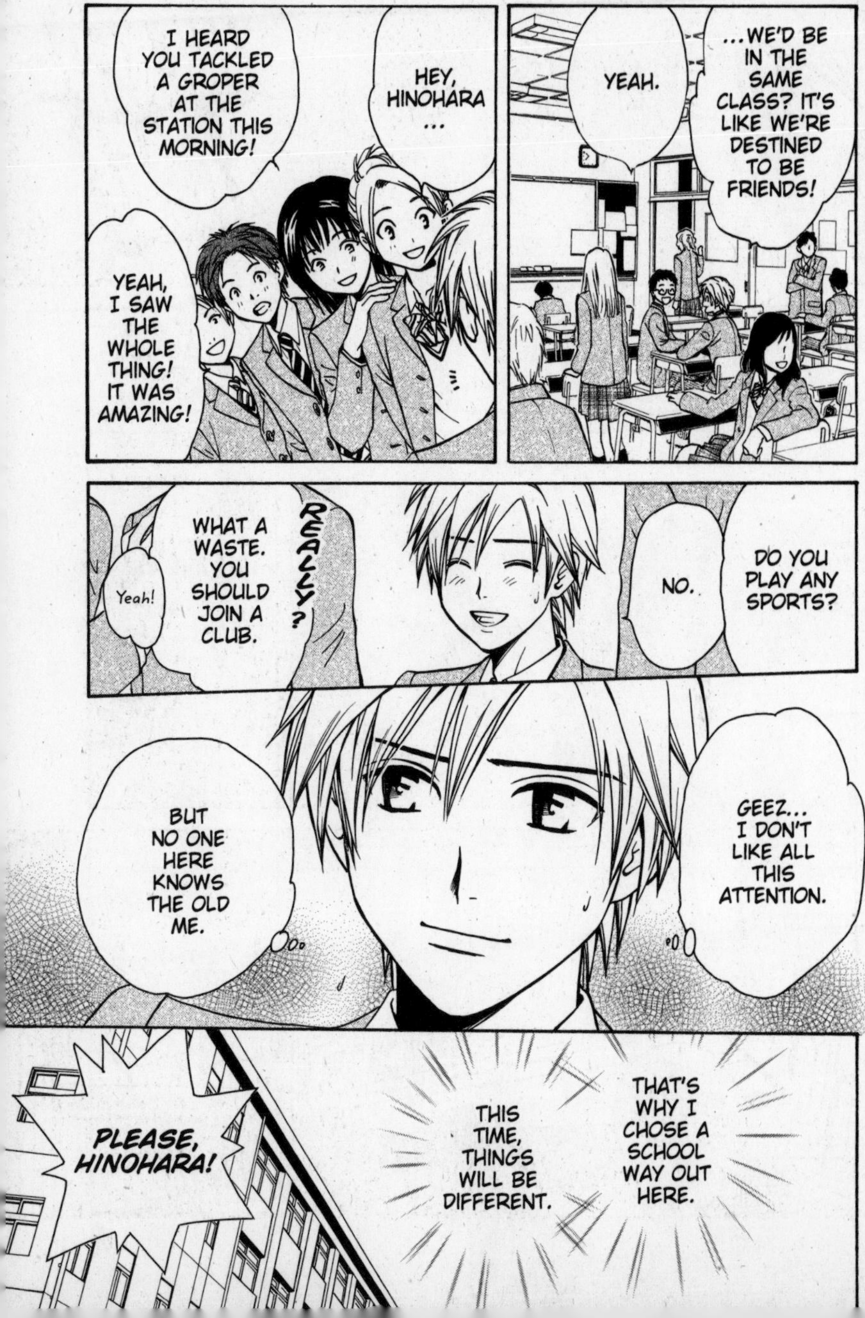
...WE'D BE IN THE SAME CLASS? IT'S LIKE WE'RE DESTINED TO BE FRIENDS!
YEAH.
HEY, HINOHARA...
I HEARD YOU TACKLED A GROPER AT THE STATION THIS MORNING!
YEAH, I SAW THE WHOLE THING! IT WAS AMAZING!
DO YOU PLAY ANY SPORTS?
NO.
REALLY?
WHAT A WASTE. YOU SHOULD JOIN A CLUB.
Yeah!
GEEZ... I DON'T LIKE ALL THIS ATTENTION.
BUT NO ONE HERE KNOWS THE OLD ME.
THAT'S WHY I CHOSE A SCHOOL WAY OUT HERE.
THIS TIME, THINGS WILL BE DIFFERENT.
PLEASE, HINOHARA!

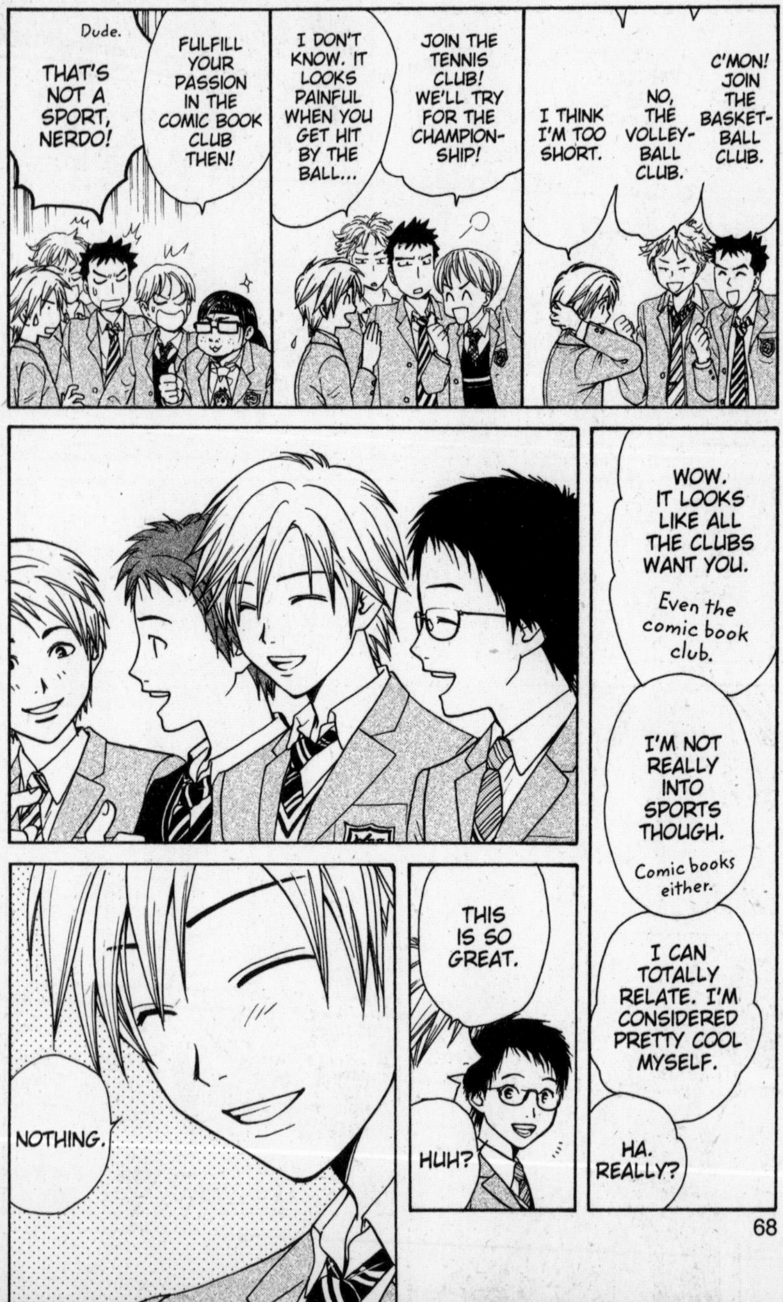
C'MON! JOIN THE BASKET-BALL CLUB.
NO, THE VOLLEY-BALL CLUB.
I THINK I'M TOO SHORT.
JOIN THE TENNIS CLUB! WE'LL TRY FOR THE CHAMPION-SHIP!
I DON'T KNOW. IT LOOKS PAINFUL WHEN YOU GET HIT BY THE BALL...
FULFILL YOUR PASSION IN THE COMIC BOOK CLUB THEN!
Dude.
THAT'S NOT A SPORT, NERDO!
WOW. IT LOOKS LIKE ALL THE CLUBS WANT YOU.
Even the comic book club.
I'M NOT REALLY INTO SPORTS THOUGH.
Comic books either.
I CAN TOTALLY RELATE. I'M CONSIDERED PRETTY COOL MYSELF.
HA. REALLY?
THIS IS SO GREAT.
HUH?
NOTHING.

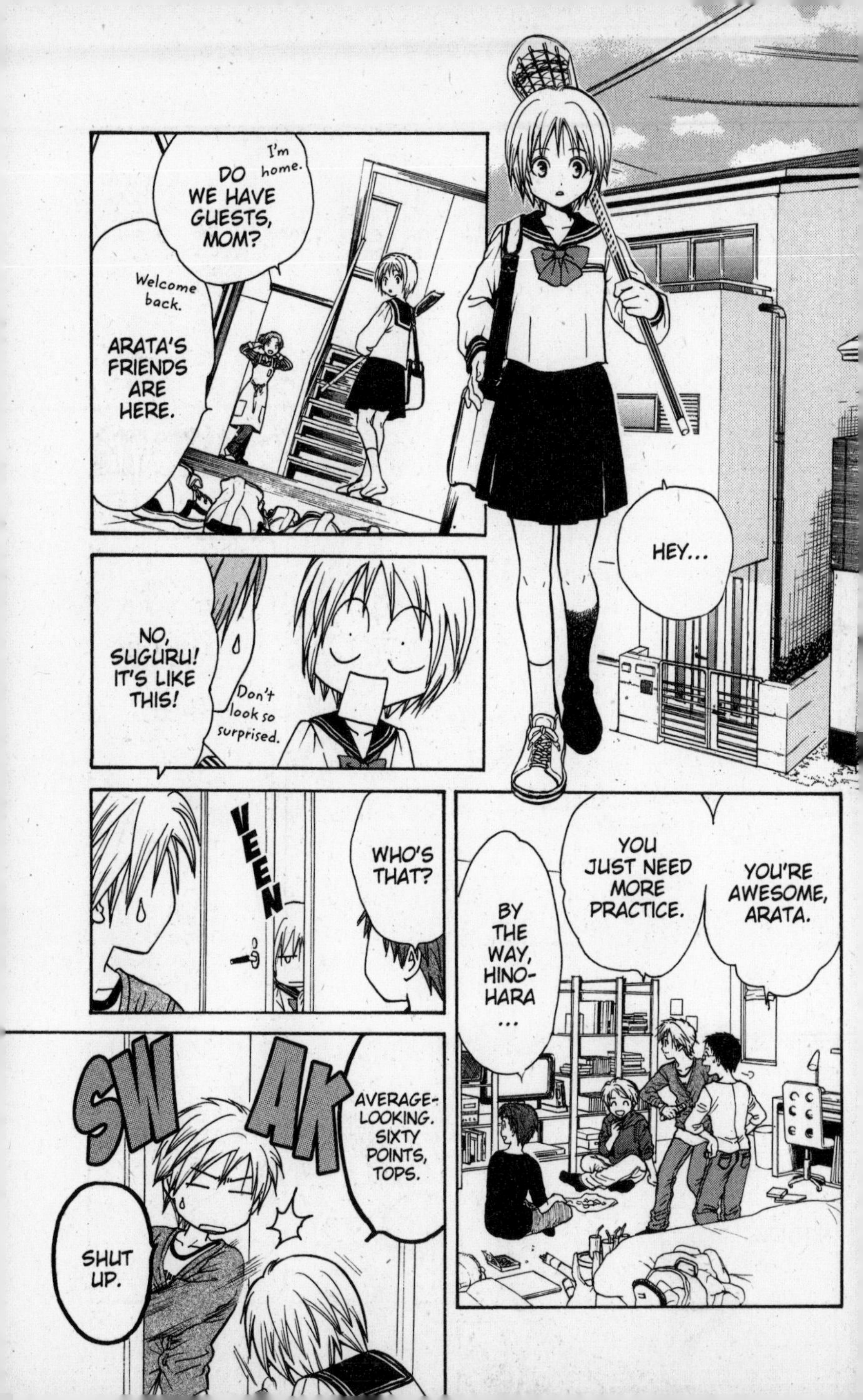
HEY...
I'm home.
DO WE HAVE GUESTS, MOM?
Welcome back.
ARATA'S FRIENDS ARE HERE.
NO, SUGURU! IT'S LIKE THIS!
Don't look so surprised.
YOU'RE AWESOME, ARATA.
YOU JUST NEED MORE PRACTICE.
BY THE WAY, HINOHARA...
WHO'S THAT?
VEEN
AVERAGE-LOOKING. SIXTY POINTS, TOPS.
SWAK
SHUT UP.

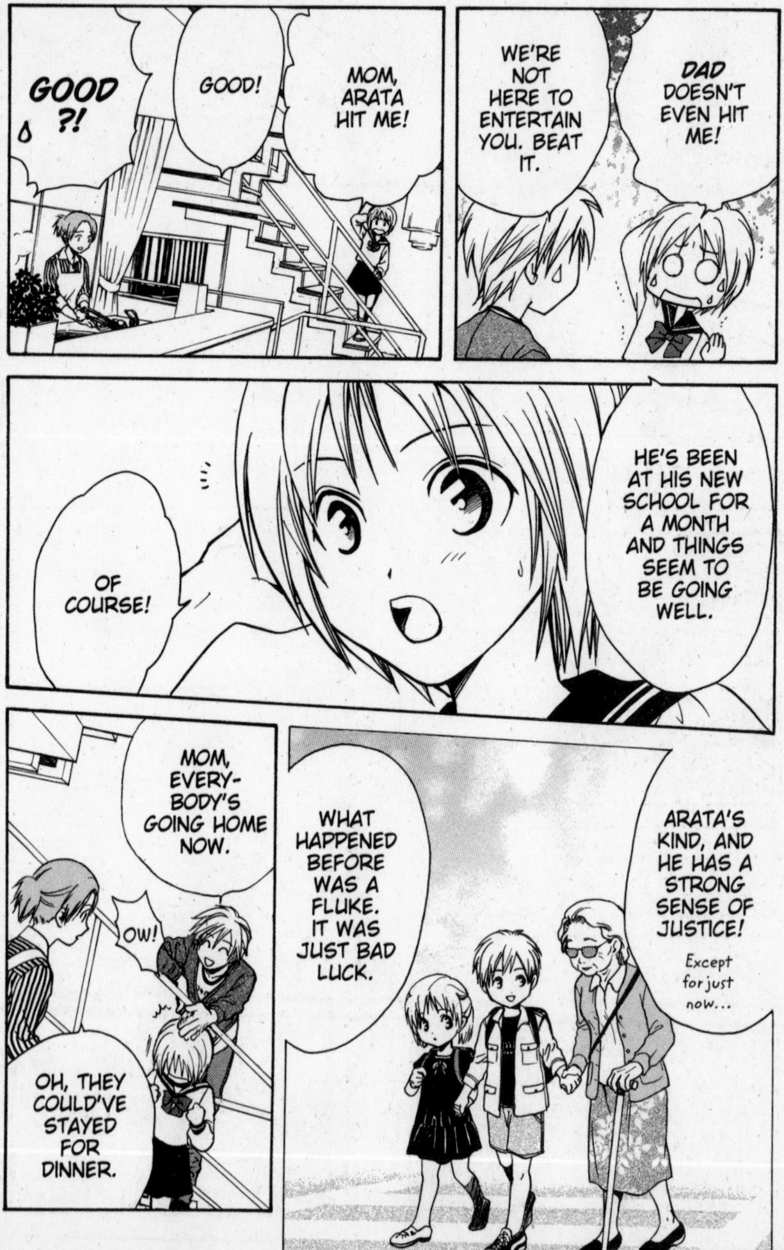
DAD DOESN'T EVEN HIT ME!
WE'RE NOT HERE TO ENTERTAIN YOU. BEAT IT.
MOM, ARATA HIT ME!
GOOD!
GOOD ?!
HE'S BEEN AT HIS NEW SCHOOL FOR A MONTH AND THINGS SEEM TO BE GOING WELL.
OF COURSE!
ARATA'S KIND, AND HE HAS A STRONG SENSE OF JUSTICE!
Except for just now...
WHAT HAPPENED BEFORE WAS A FLUKE. IT WAS JUST BAD LUCK.
MOM, EVERY-BODY'S GOING HOME NOW.
OW!
OH, THEY COULD'VE STAYED FOR DINNER.

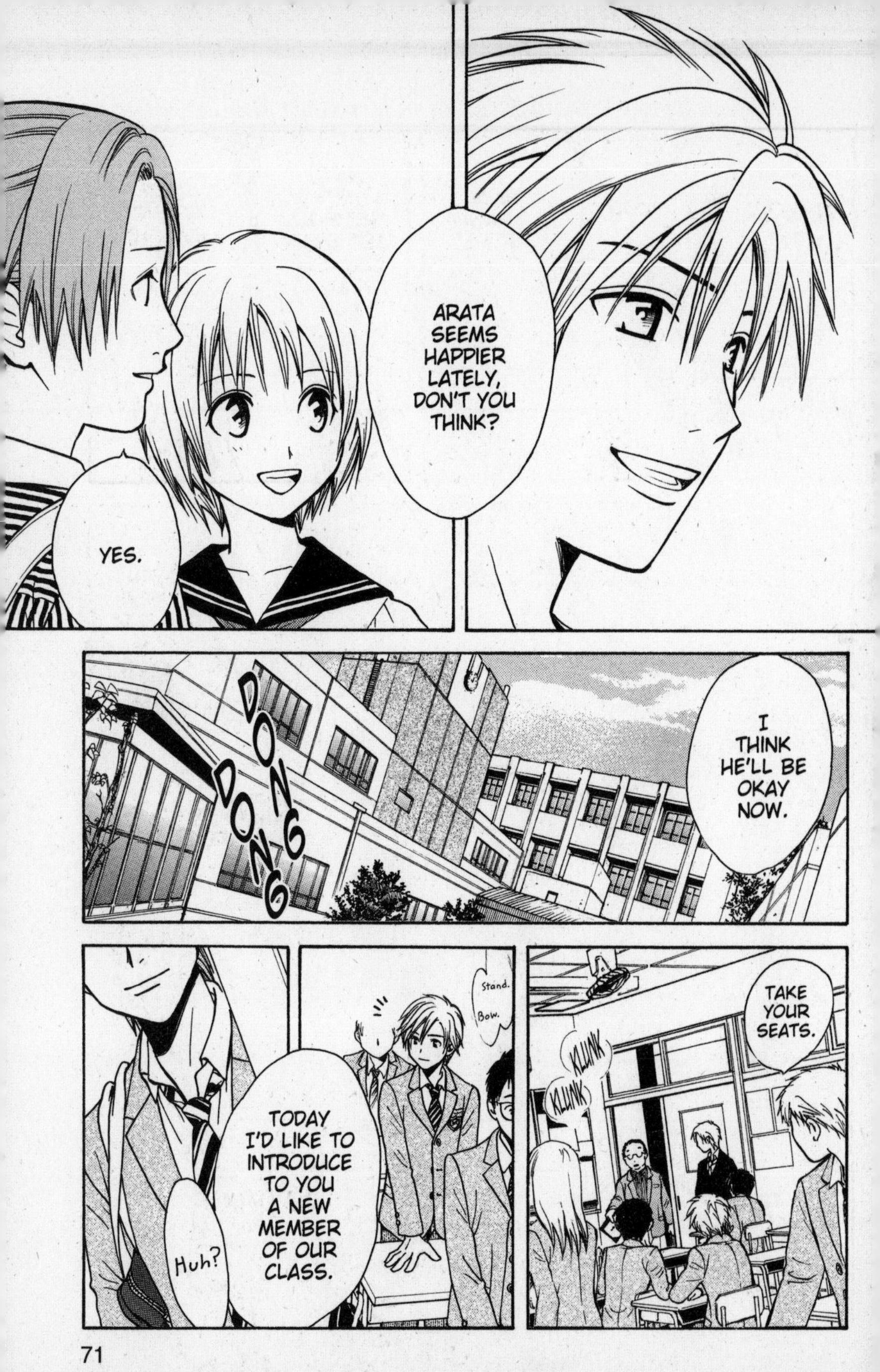
ARATA SEEMS HAPPIER LATELY, DON'T YOU THINK?
YES.
DONG DONG
I THINK HE'LL BE OKAY NOW.
TAKE YOUR SEATS.
KLUNK
KLUNK
Stand.
Bow.
TODAY I'D LIKE TO INTRODUCE TO YOU A NEW MEMBER OF OUR CLASS.
Huh?

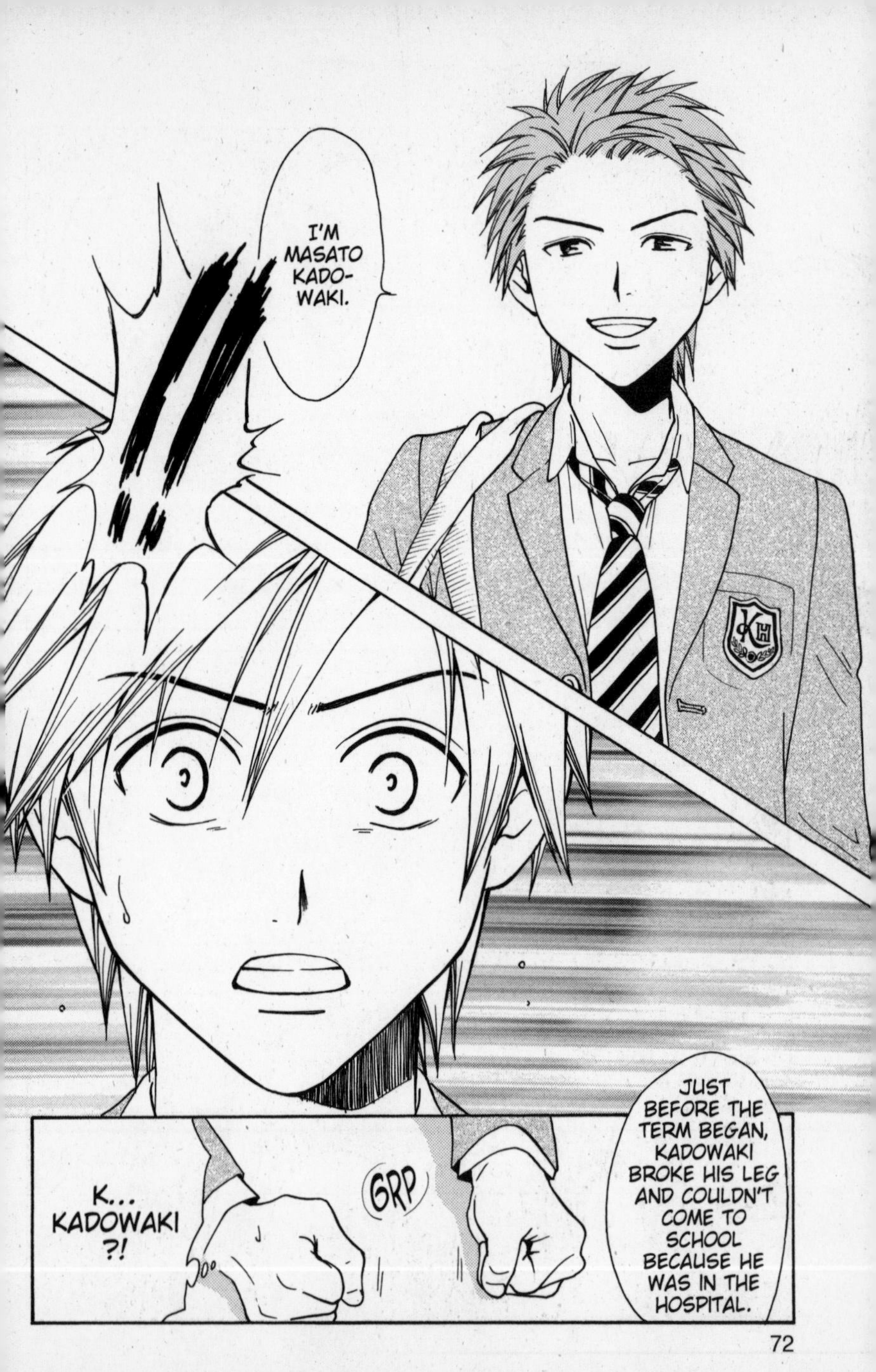
I'M MASATO KADOWAKI.
JUST BEFORE THE TERM BEGAN, KADOWAKI BROKE HIS LEG AND COULDN'T COME TO SCHOOL BECAUSE HE WAS IN THE HOSPITAL.
GRP
K... KADOWAKI ?!

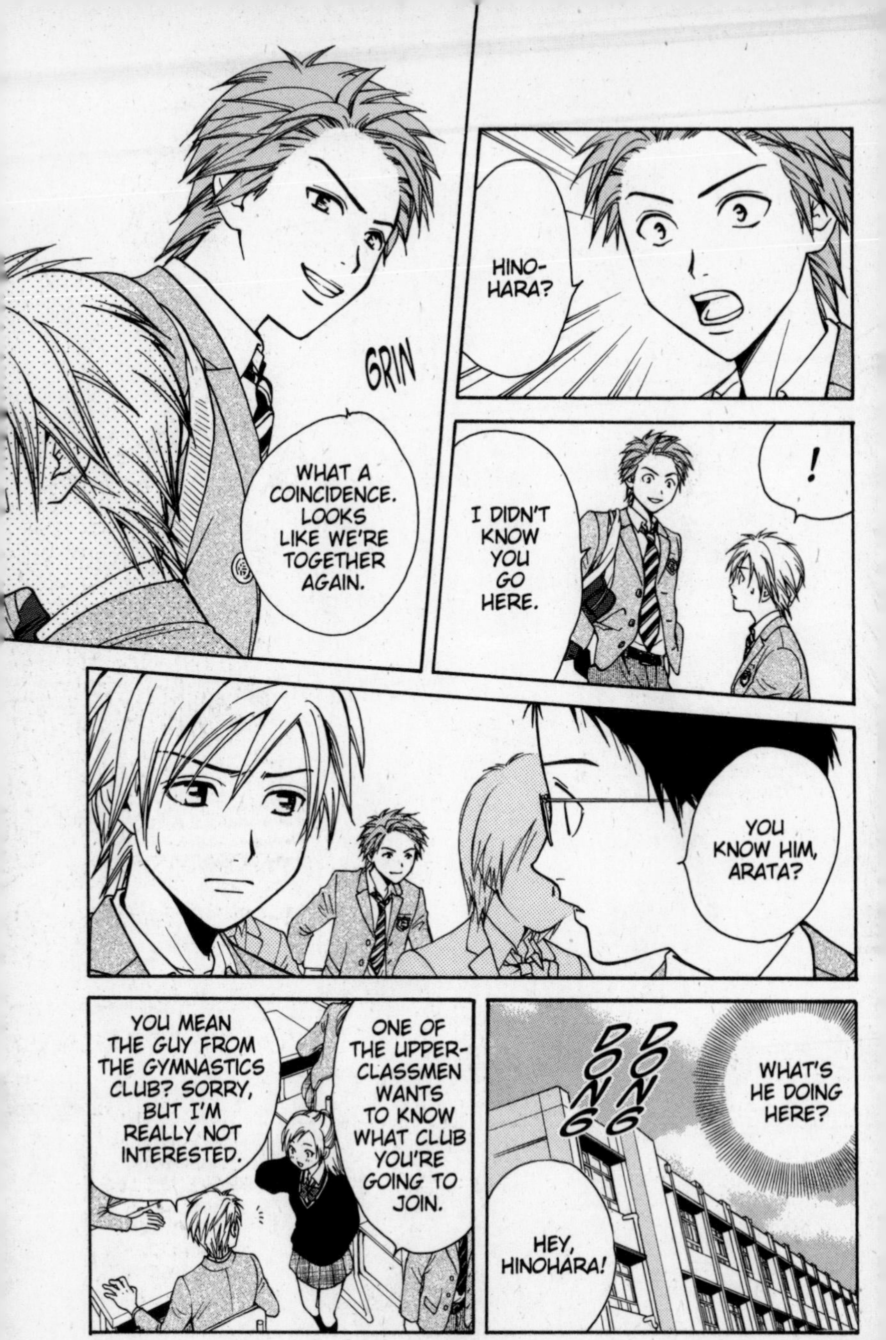
HINO-HARA?
!
I DIDN'T KNOW YOU GO HERE.
GRIN
WHAT A COINCIDENCE. LOOKS LIKE WE'RE TOGETHER AGAIN.
YOU KNOW HIM, ARATA?
DONG DONG
WHAT'S HE DOING HERE?
HEY, HINOHARA!
ONE OF THE UPPER-CLASSMEN WANTS TO KNOW WHAT CLUB YOU'RE GOING TO JOIN.
YOU MEAN THE GUY FROM THE GYMNASTICS CLUB? SORRY, BUT I'M REALLY NOT INTERESTED.

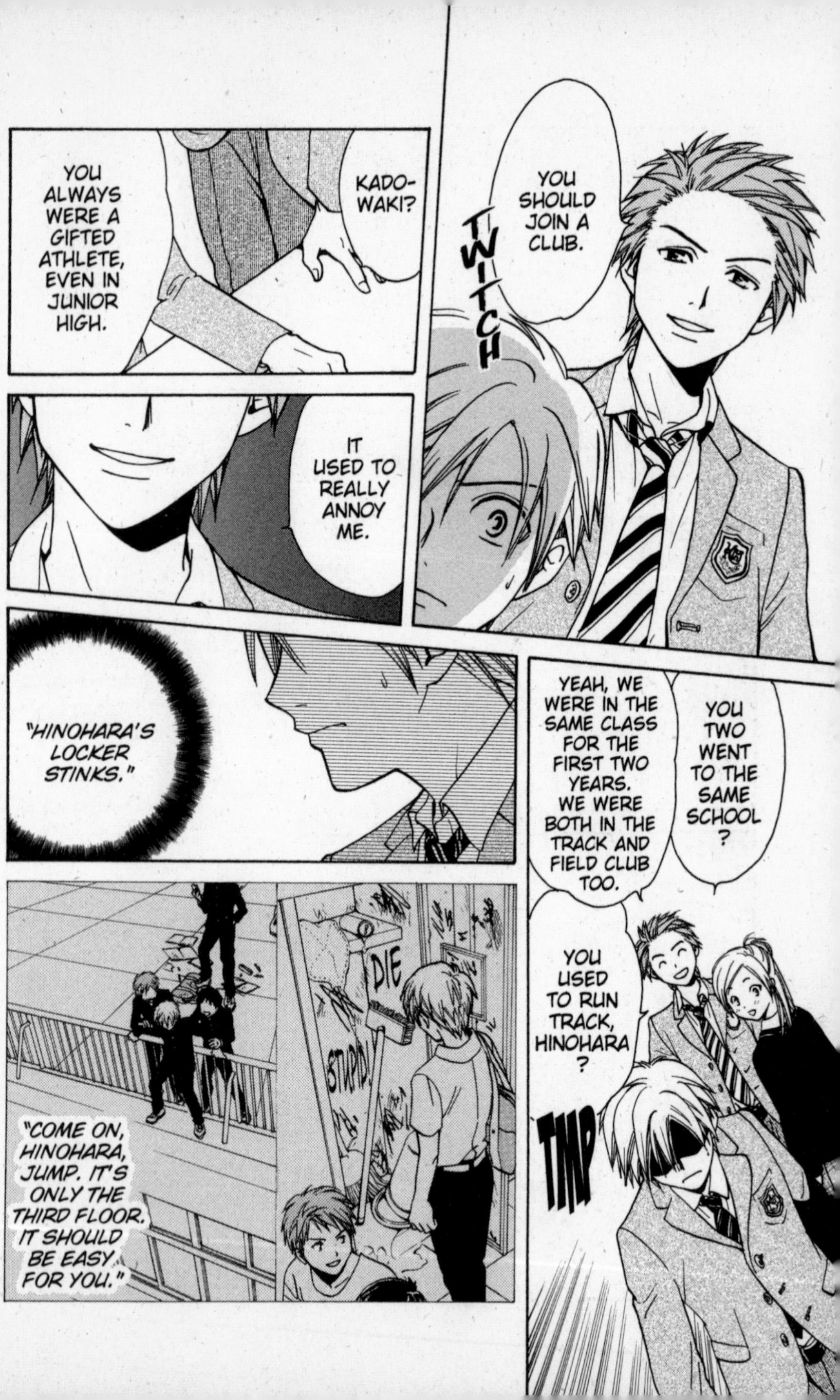
YOU SHOULD JOIN A CLUB.
TWITCH
KADO-WAKI?
YOU ALWAYS WERE A GIFTED ATHLETE, EVEN IN JUNIOR HIGH.
IT USED TO REALLY ANNOY ME.
YOU TWO WENT TO THE SAME SCHOOL?
YEAH, WE WERE IN THE SAME CLASS FOR THE FIRST TWO YEARS. WE WERE BOTH IN THE TRACK AND FIELD CLUB TOO.
YOU USED TO RUN TRACK, HINOHARA?
TMP
"HINOHARA'S LOCKER STINKS."
DIE
STUPID
"COME ON, HINOHARA, JUMP. IT'S ONLY THE THIRD FLOOR. IT SHOULD BE EASY FOR YOU."

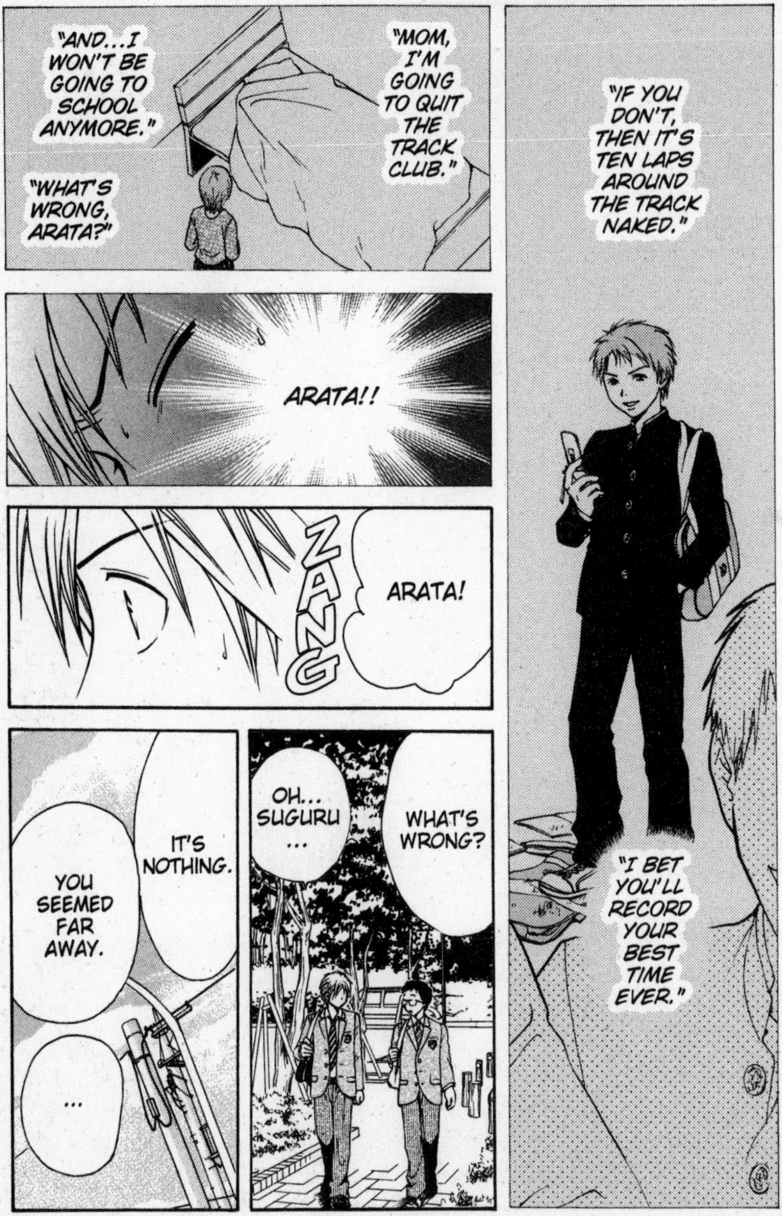
"IF YOU DON'T, THEN IT'S TEN LAPS AROUND THE TRACK NAKED."
"I BET YOU'LL RECORD YOUR BEST TIME EVER."
"MOM, I'M GOING TO QUIT THE TRACK CLUB."
"AND...I WON'T BE GOING TO SCHOOL ANYMORE."
"WHAT'S WRONG, ARATA?"
ARATA!!
ZANG
ARATA!
WHAT'S WRONG?
OH... SUGURU ...
IT'S NOTHING.
YOU SEEMED FAR AWAY.
...

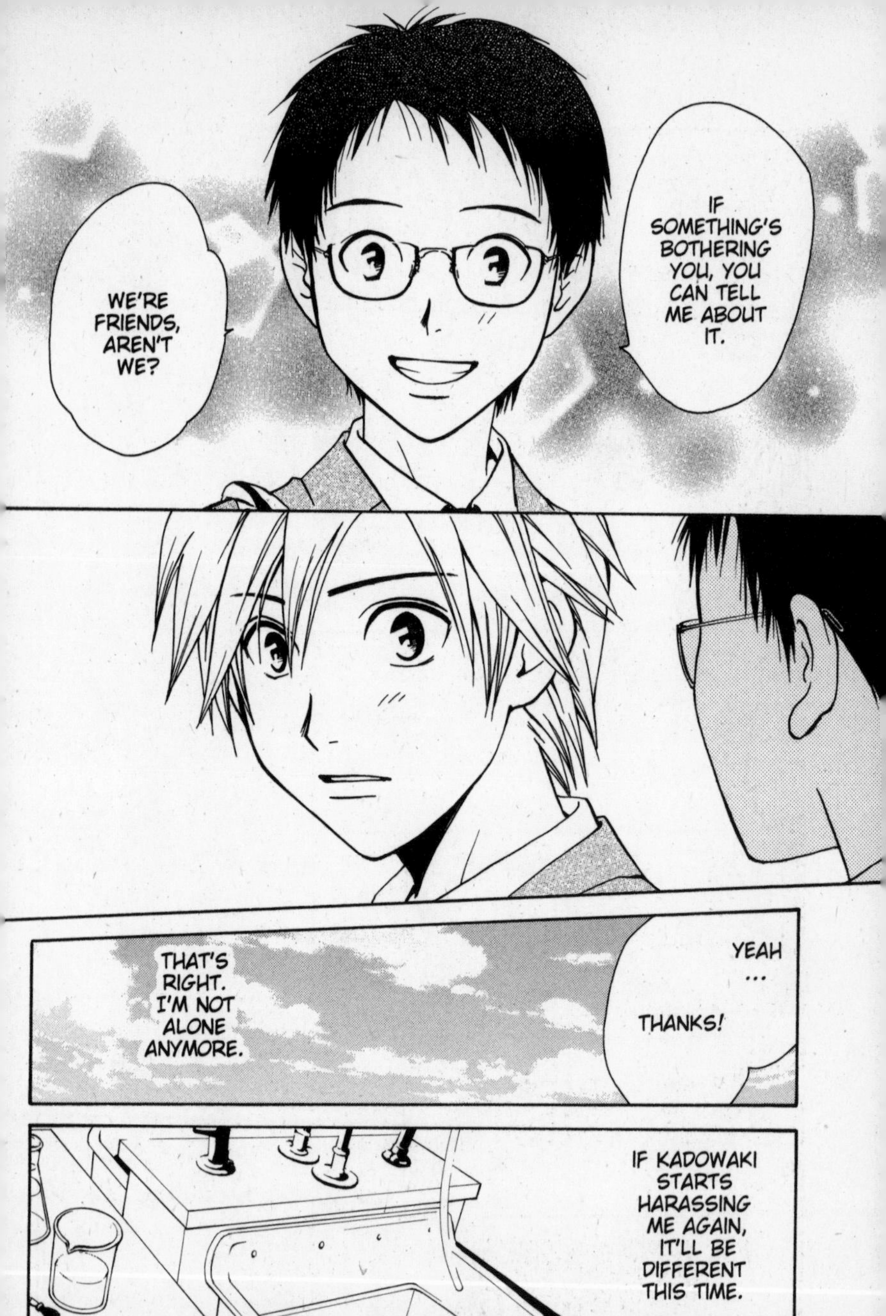
IF SOMETHING'S BOTHERING YOU, YOU CAN TELL ME ABOUT IT.
WE'RE FRIENDS, AREN'T WE?
YEAH... THANKS!
THAT'S RIGHT. I'M NOT ALONE ANYMORE.
IF KADOWAKI STARTS HARASSING ME AGAIN, IT'LL BE DIFFERENT THIS TIME.

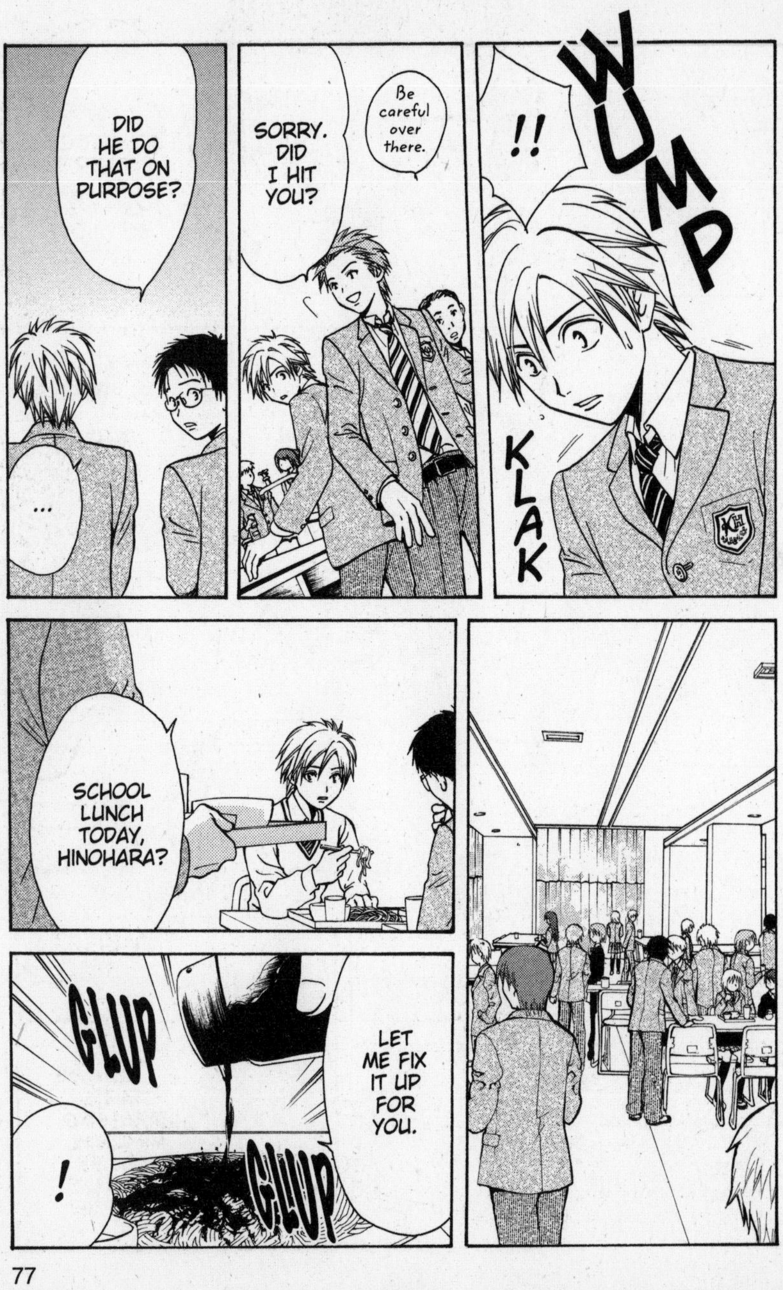
WUMP
!!
KLAK
Be careful over there.
SORRY. DID I HIT YOU?
DID HE DO THAT ON PURPOSE?
...
SCHOOL LUNCH TODAY, HINOHARA?
LET ME FIX IT UP FOR YOU.
GLUP
GLUP
!

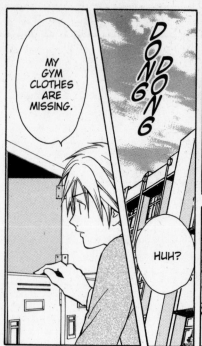

WHAT ...?
OOPS. GUESS I OVERDID IT.
HA HA HA
WHOA... YOU CAN'T EAT THAT NOW.
Want some of mine?
DONG DONG
HUH?
MY GYM CLOTHES ARE MISSING.
THOUGHT AS MUCH...
ARE YOU OKAY, ARATA?
AT LEAST THEY'RE NOT TORN UP. I CAN STILL GO TO CLASS.
WSP
WSP

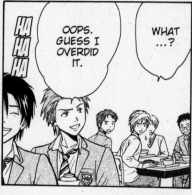

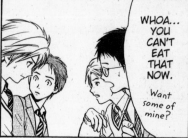

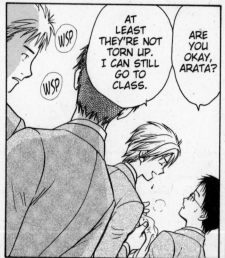

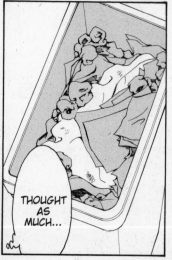

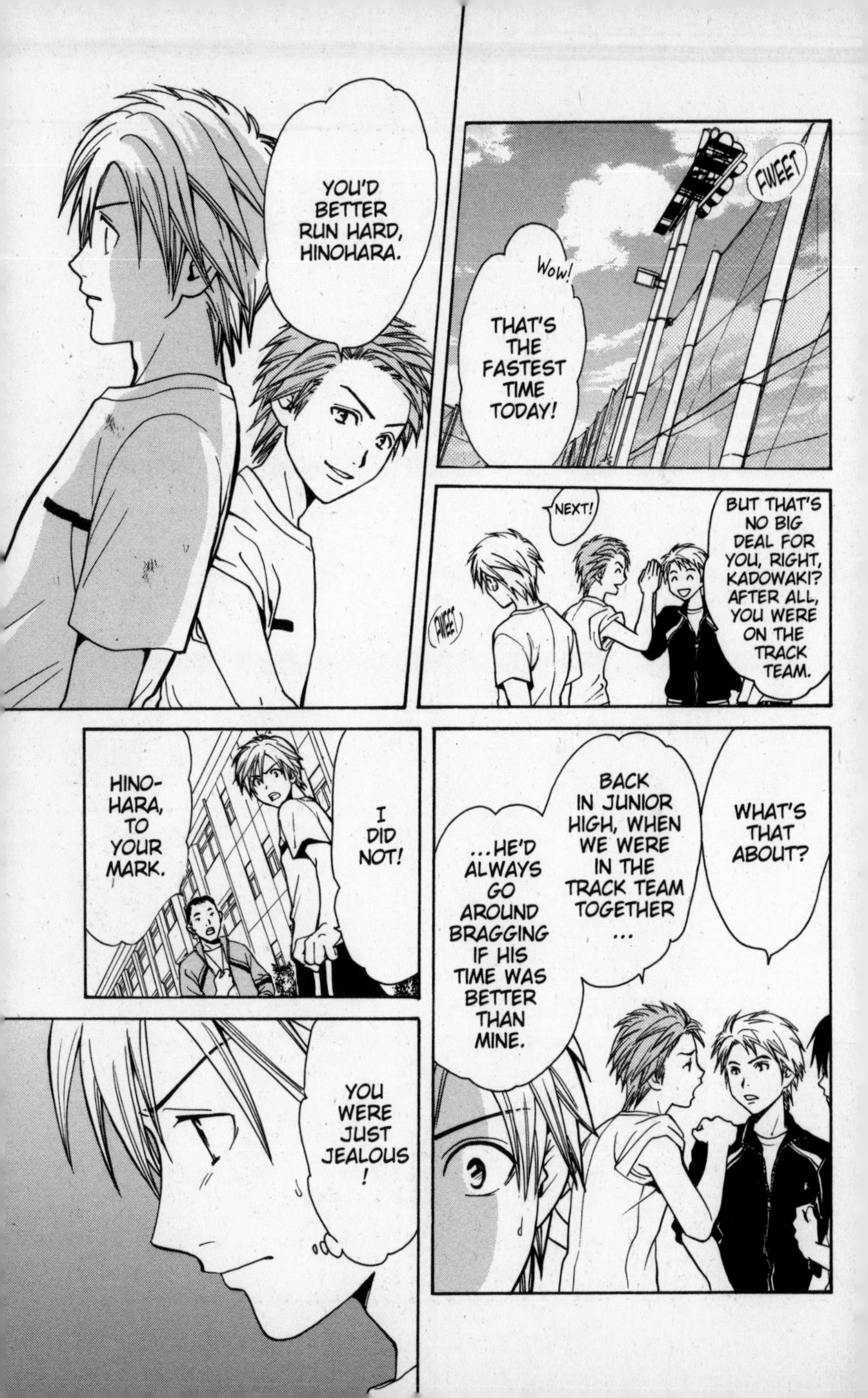
FWEET
Wow!
THAT'S THE FASTEST TIME TODAY!
BUT THAT'S NO BIG DEAL FOR YOU, RIGHT, KADOWAKI? AFTER ALL, YOU WERE ON THE TRACK TEAM.
NEXT!
FWEET
YOU'D BETTER RUN HARD, HINOHARA.
WHAT'S THAT ABOUT?
BACK IN JUNIOR HIGH, WHEN WE WERE IN THE TRACK TEAM TOGETHER...
...HE'D ALWAYS GO AROUND BRAGGING IF HIS TIME WAS BETTER THAN MINE.
I DID NOT!
HINO-HARA, TO YOUR MARK.
YOU WERE JUST JEALOUS!

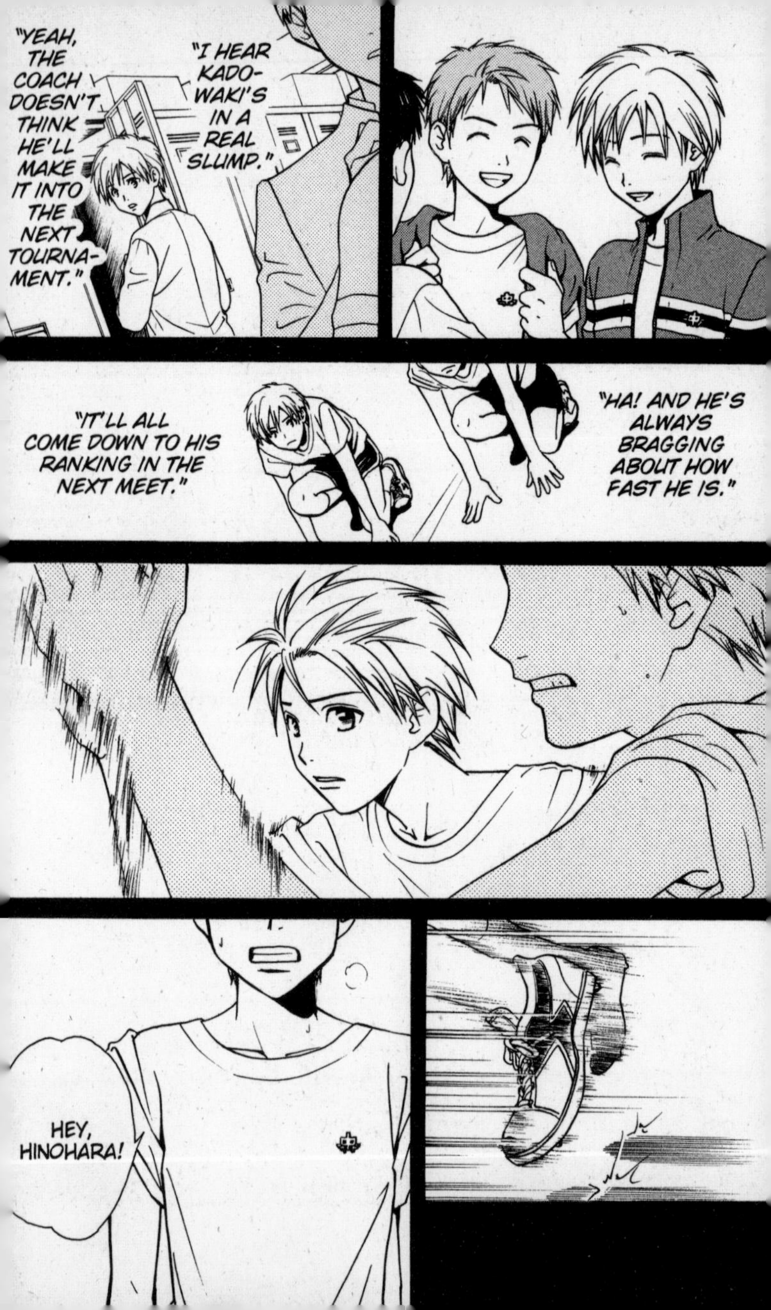
"I HEAR KADO-WAKI'S IN A REAL SLUMP."
"YEAH, THE COACH DOESN'T THINK HE'LL MAKE IT INTO THE NEXT TOURNA-MENT."
"HA! AND HE'S ALWAYS BRAGGING ABOUT HOW FAST HE IS."
"IT'LL ALL COME DOWN TO HIS RANKING IN THE NEXT MEET."
HEY, HINOHARA!

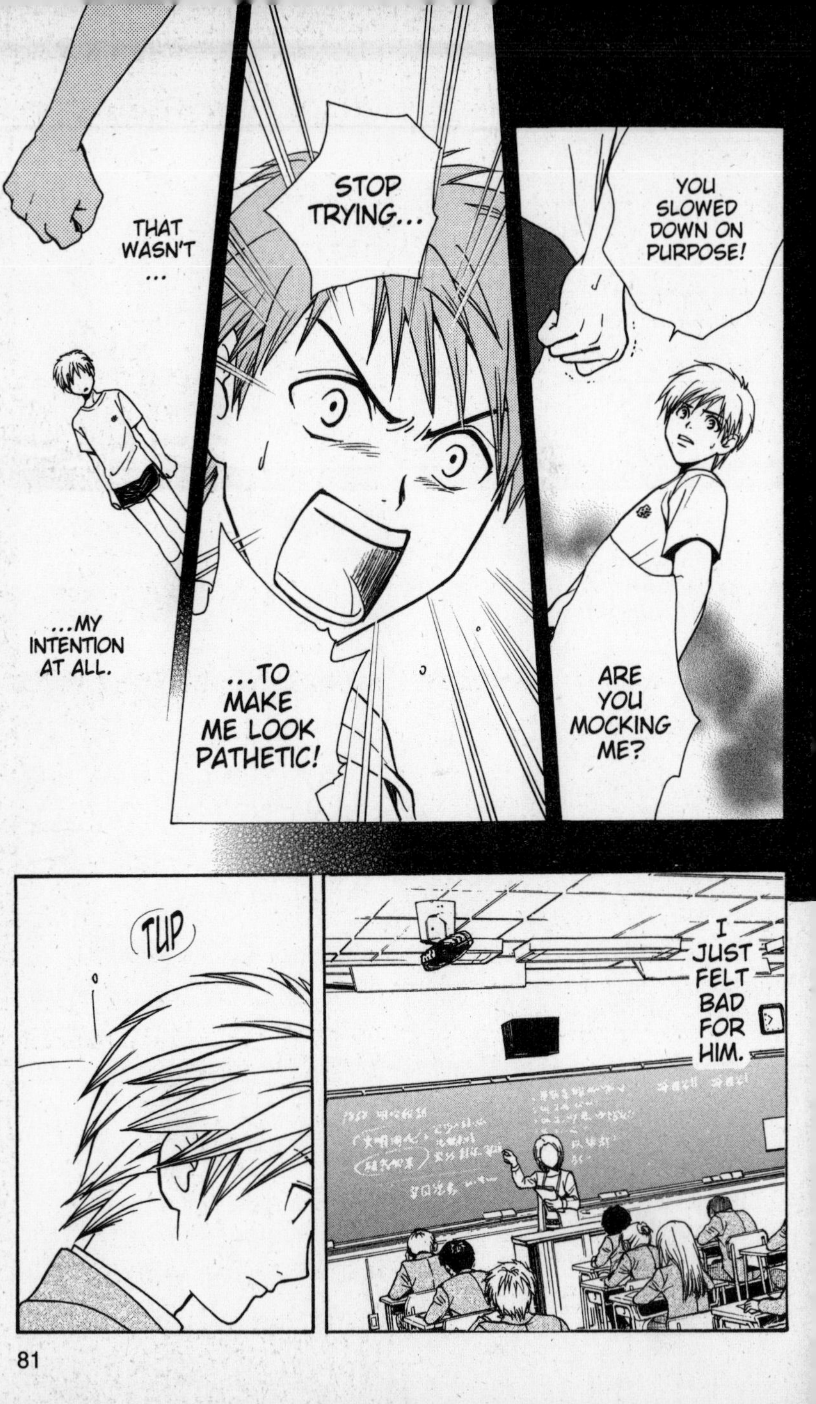
YOU SLOWED DOWN ON PURPOSE!
ARE YOU MOCKING ME?
STOP TRYING...
...TO MAKE ME LOOK PATHETIC!
THAT WASN'T ...
...MY INTENTION AT ALL.
I JUST FELT BAD FOR HIM.
TUP

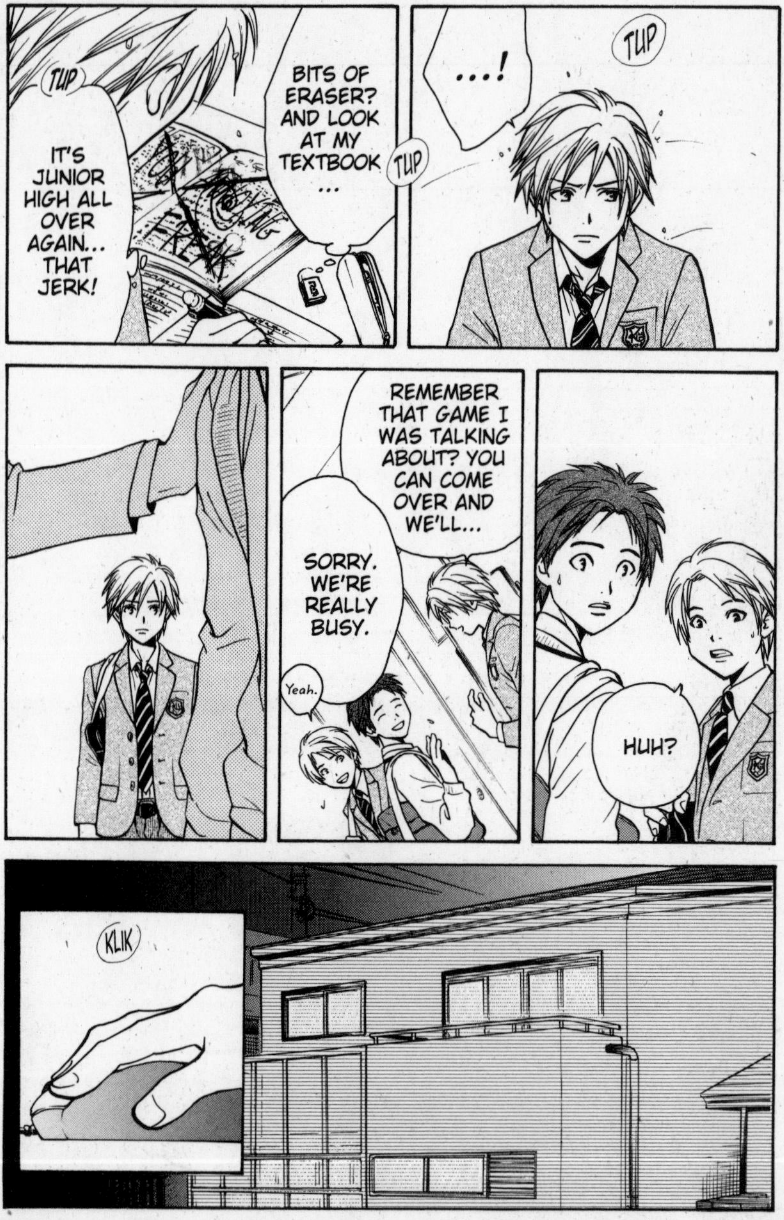
TUP
...!
TUP
BITS OF ERASER? AND LOOK AT MY TEXTBOOK ...
TUP
IT'S JUNIOR HIGH ALL OVER AGAIN... THAT JERK!
HUH?
REMEMBER THAT GAME I WAS TALKING ABOUT? YOU CAN COME OVER AND WE'LL...
SORRY. WE'RE REALLY BUSY.
Yeah.
KLIK

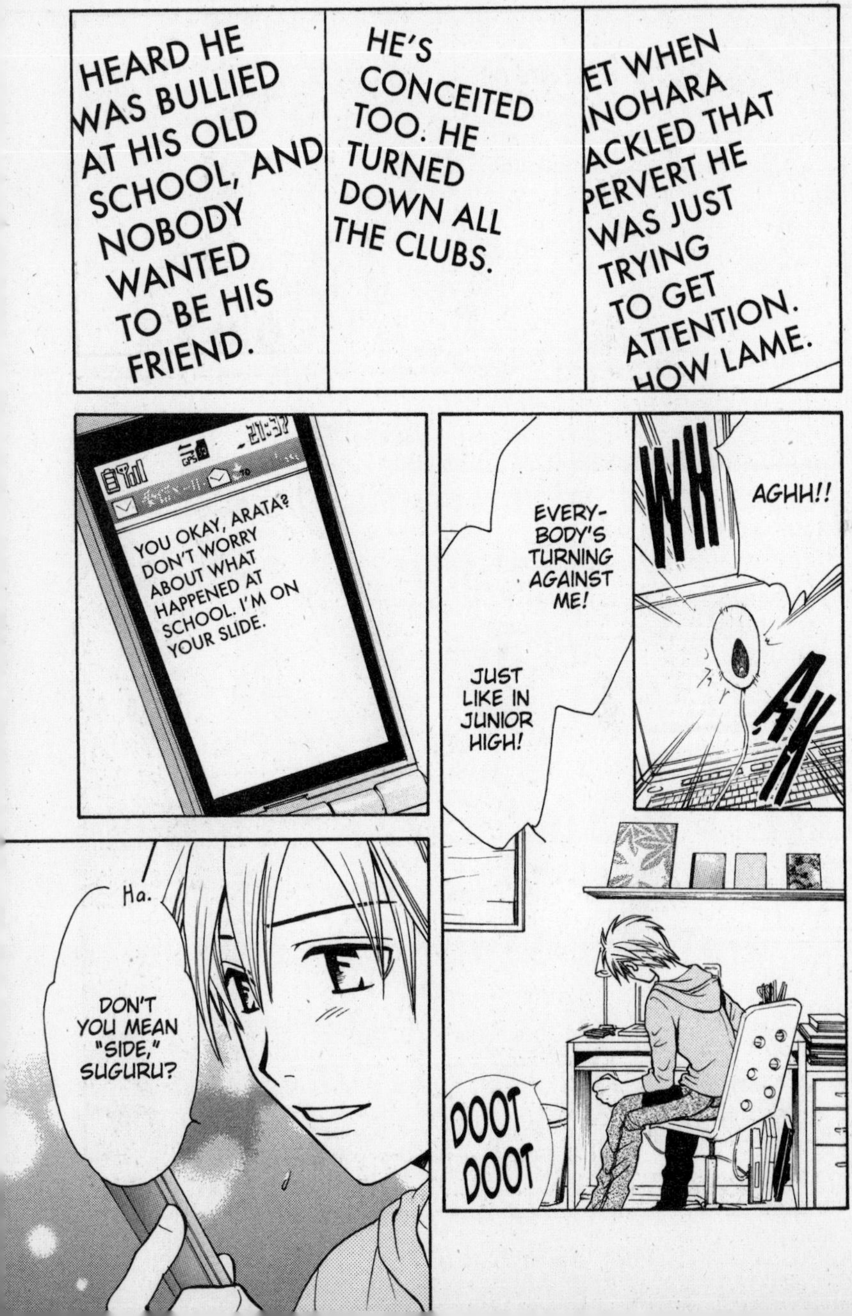
ET WHEN INOHARA ACKLED THAT PERVERT HE WAS JUST TRYING TO GET ATTENTION. HOW LAME.
HE'S CONCEITED TOO. HE TURNED DOWN ALL THE CLUBS.
HEARD HE WAS BULLIED AT HIS OLD SCHOOL, AND NOBODY WANTED TO BE HIS FRIEND.
WH
AGHH!!
AH
EVERY-BODY'S TURNING AGAINST ME!
JUST LIKE IN JUNIOR HIGH!
DOOT DOOT
YOU OKAY, ARATA? DON'T WORRY ABOUT WHAT HAPPENED AT SCHOOL. I'M ON YOUR SLIDE.
Ha.
DON'T YOU MEAN "SIDE," SUGURU?

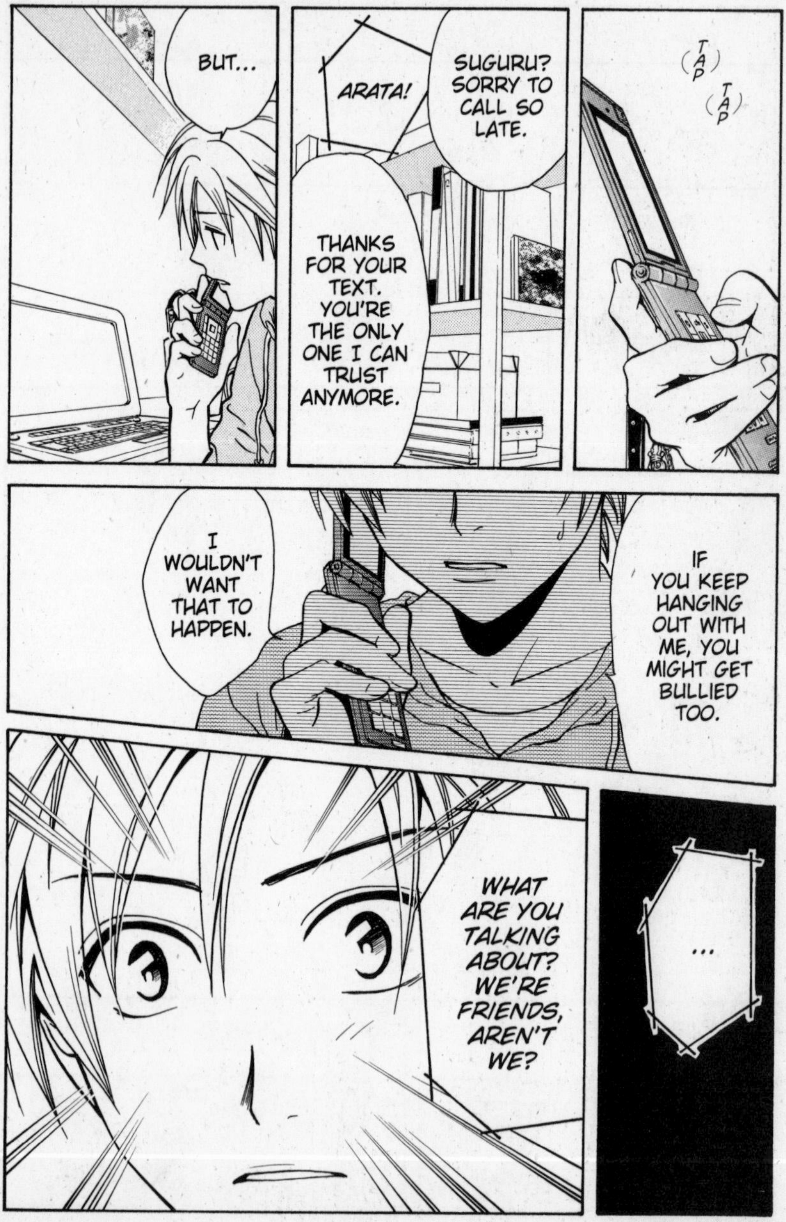
TAP
TAP
SUGURU? SORRY TO CALL SO LATE.
ARATA!
THANKS FOR YOUR TEXT. YOU'RE THE ONLY ONE I CAN TRUST ANYMORE.
BUT...
IF YOU KEEP HANGING OUT WITH ME, YOU MIGHT GET BULLIED TOO.
I WOULDN'T WANT THAT TO HAPPEN.
...
WHAT ARE YOU TALKING ABOUT? WE'RE FRIENDS, AREN'T WE?

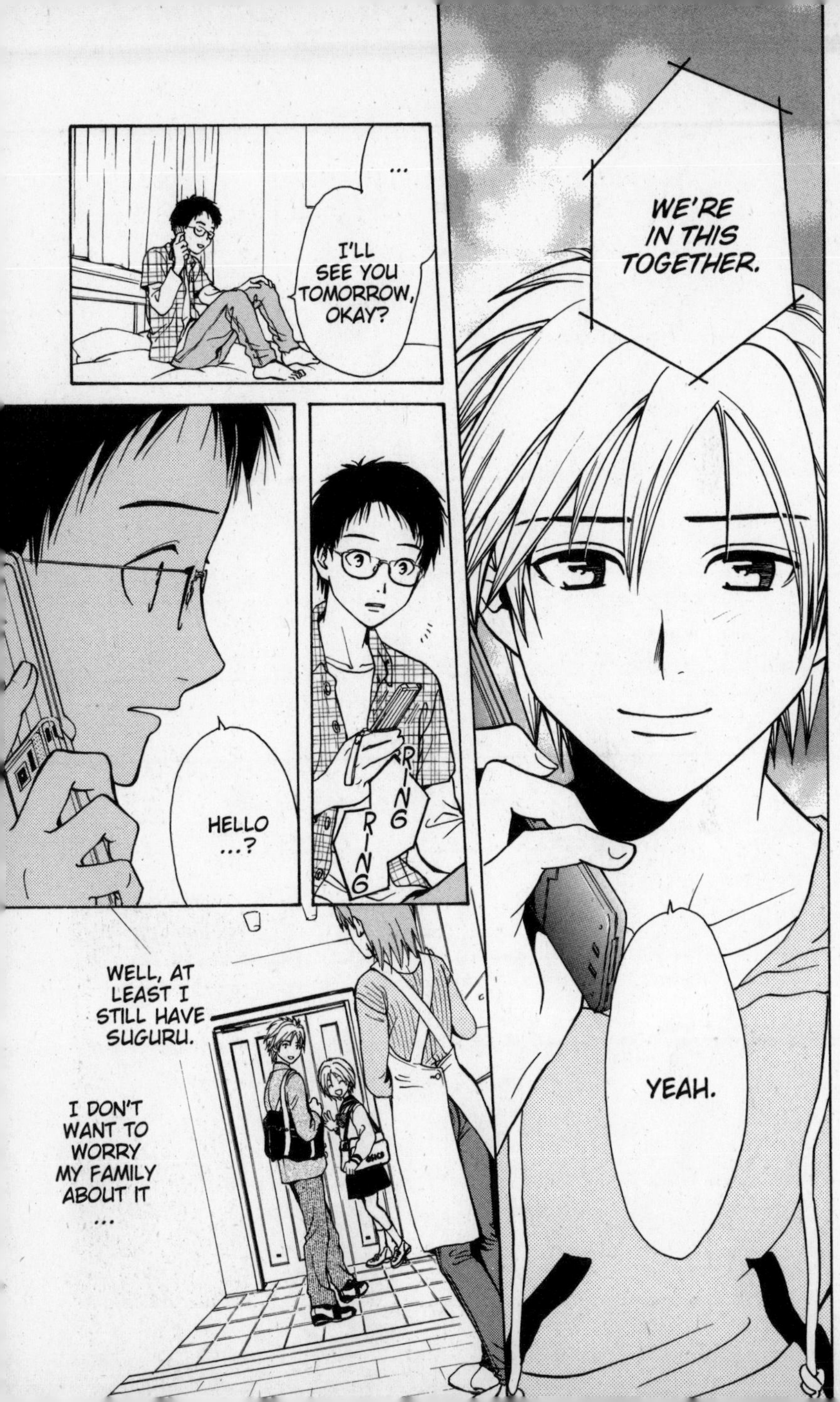
WE'RE IN THIS TOGETHER.
YEAH.
...
I'LL SEE YOU TOMORROW, OKAY?
RING RING
HELLO ...?
WELL, AT LEAST I STILL HAVE SUGURU.
I DON'T WANT TO WORRY MY FAMILY ABOUT IT ...

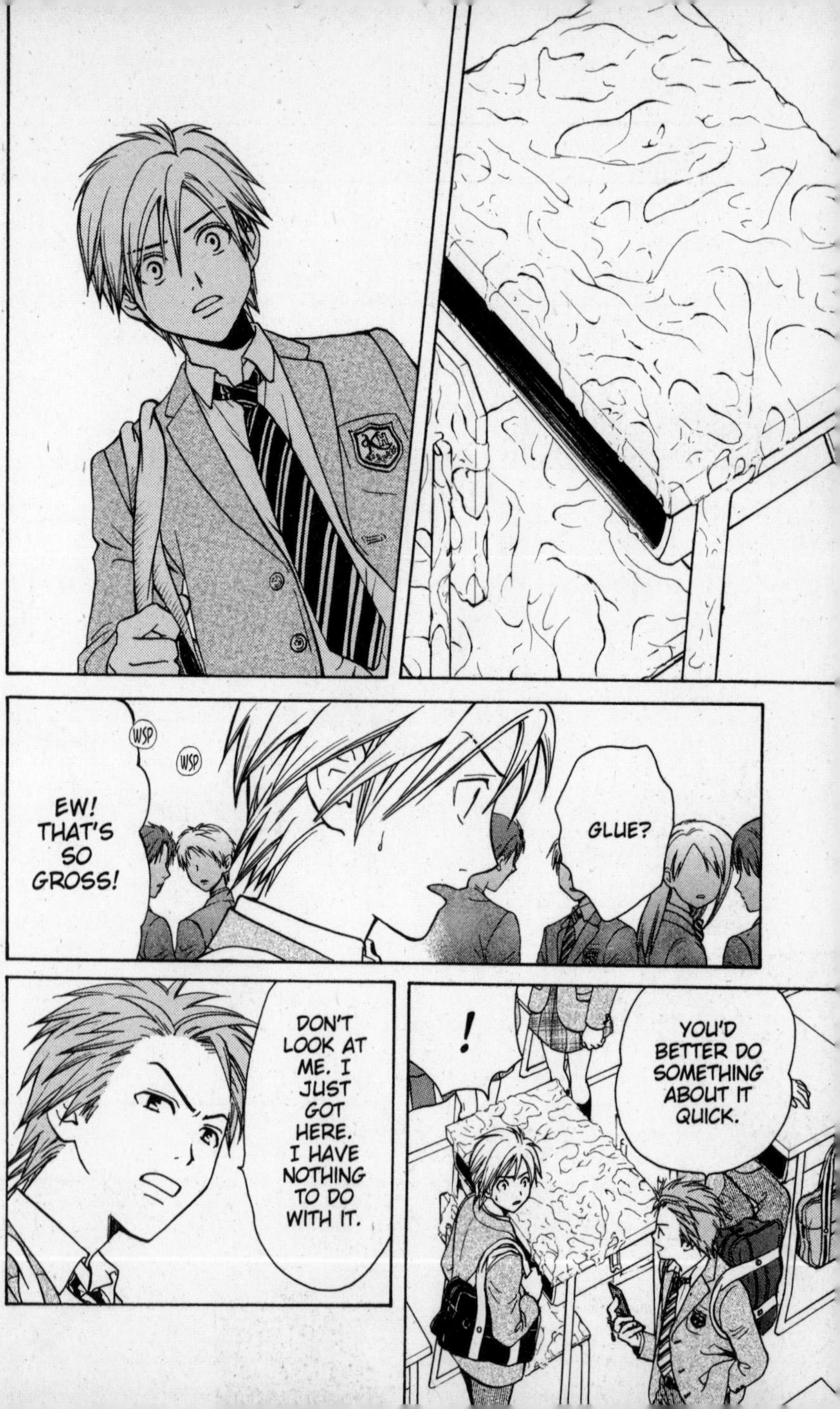
GLUE?
WSP
WSP
EW! THAT'S SO GROSS!
!
YOU'D BETTER DO SOMETHING ABOUT IT QUICK.
DON'T LOOK AT ME. I JUST GOT HERE. I HAVE NOTHING TO DO WITH IT.

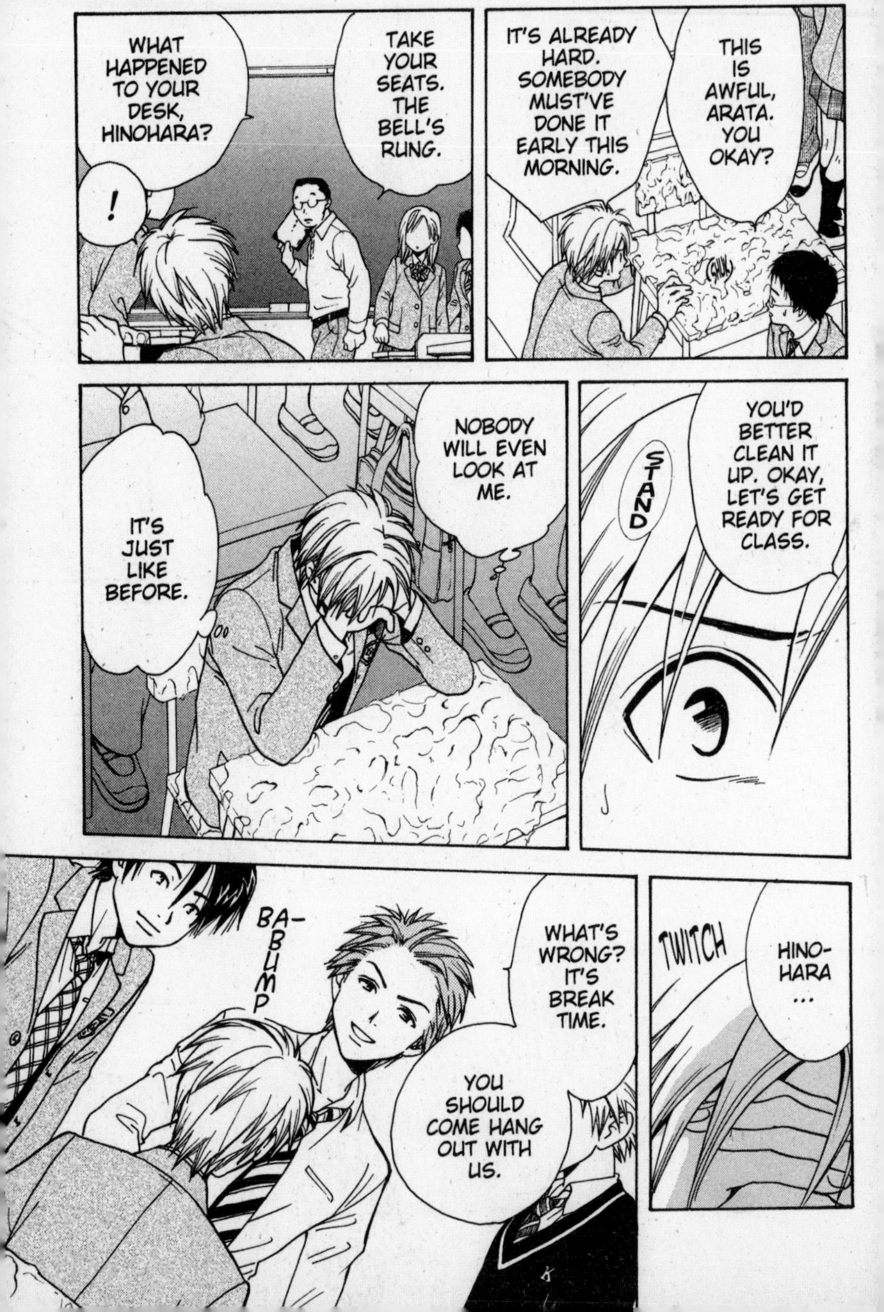
THIS IS AWFUL, ARATA. YOU OKAY?
IT'S ALREADY HARD. SOMEBODY MUST'VE DONE IT EARLY THIS MORNING.
SHUK
TAKE YOUR SEATS. THE BELL'S RUNG.
WHAT HAPPENED TO YOUR DESK, HINOHARA?
!
YOU'D BETTER CLEAN IT UP. OKAY, LET'S GET READY FOR CLASS.
STAND
NOBODY WILL EVEN LOOK AT ME.
IT'S JUST LIKE BEFORE.
HINO-HARA...
TWITCH
WHAT'S WRONG? IT'S BREAK TIME.
YOU SHOULD COME HANG OUT WITH US.
BA-BUMP

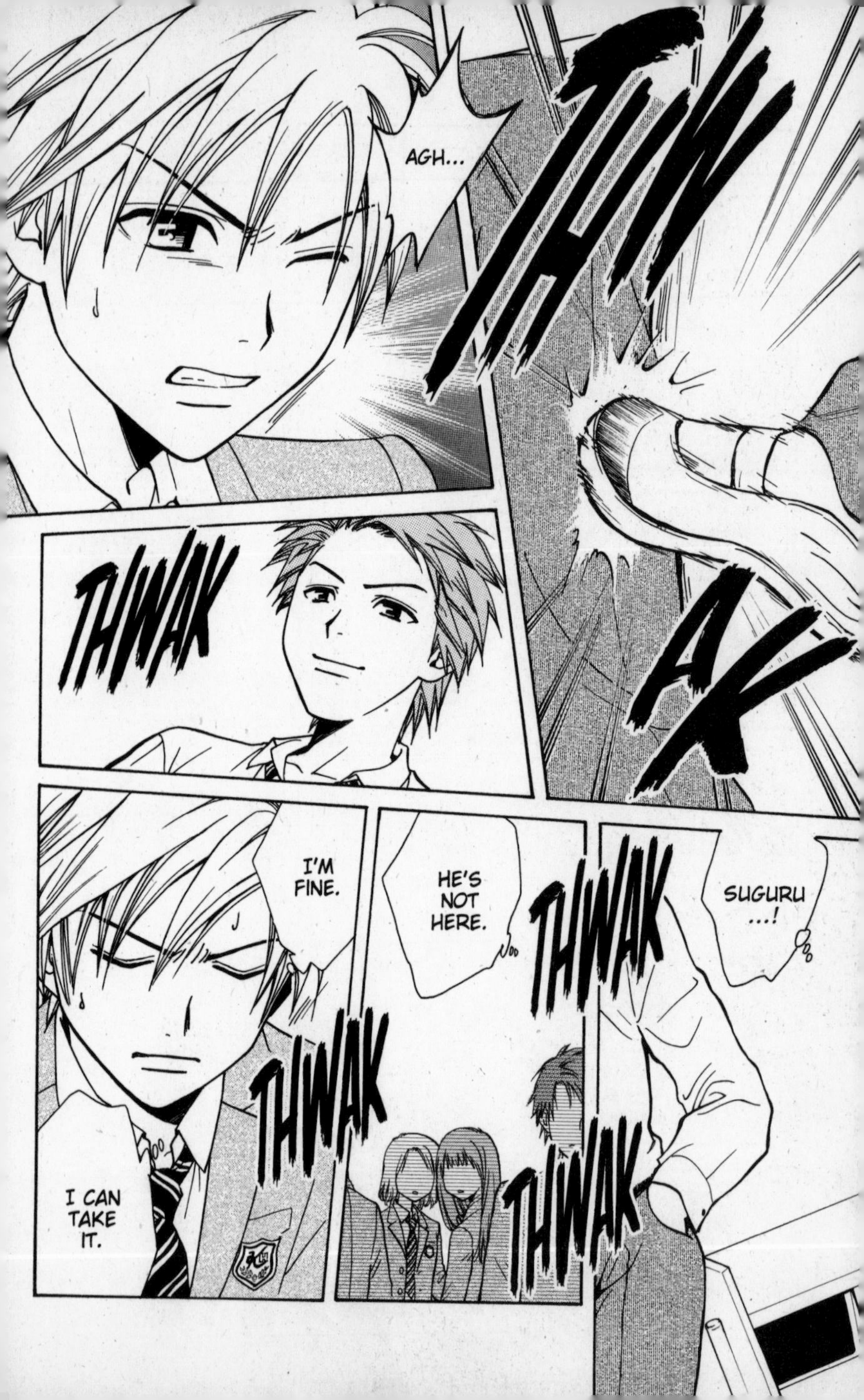
THWAK
AGH...
THWAK
SUGURU ...!
THWAK
THWAK
HE'S NOT HERE.
THWAK
I'M FINE.
I CAN TAKE IT.

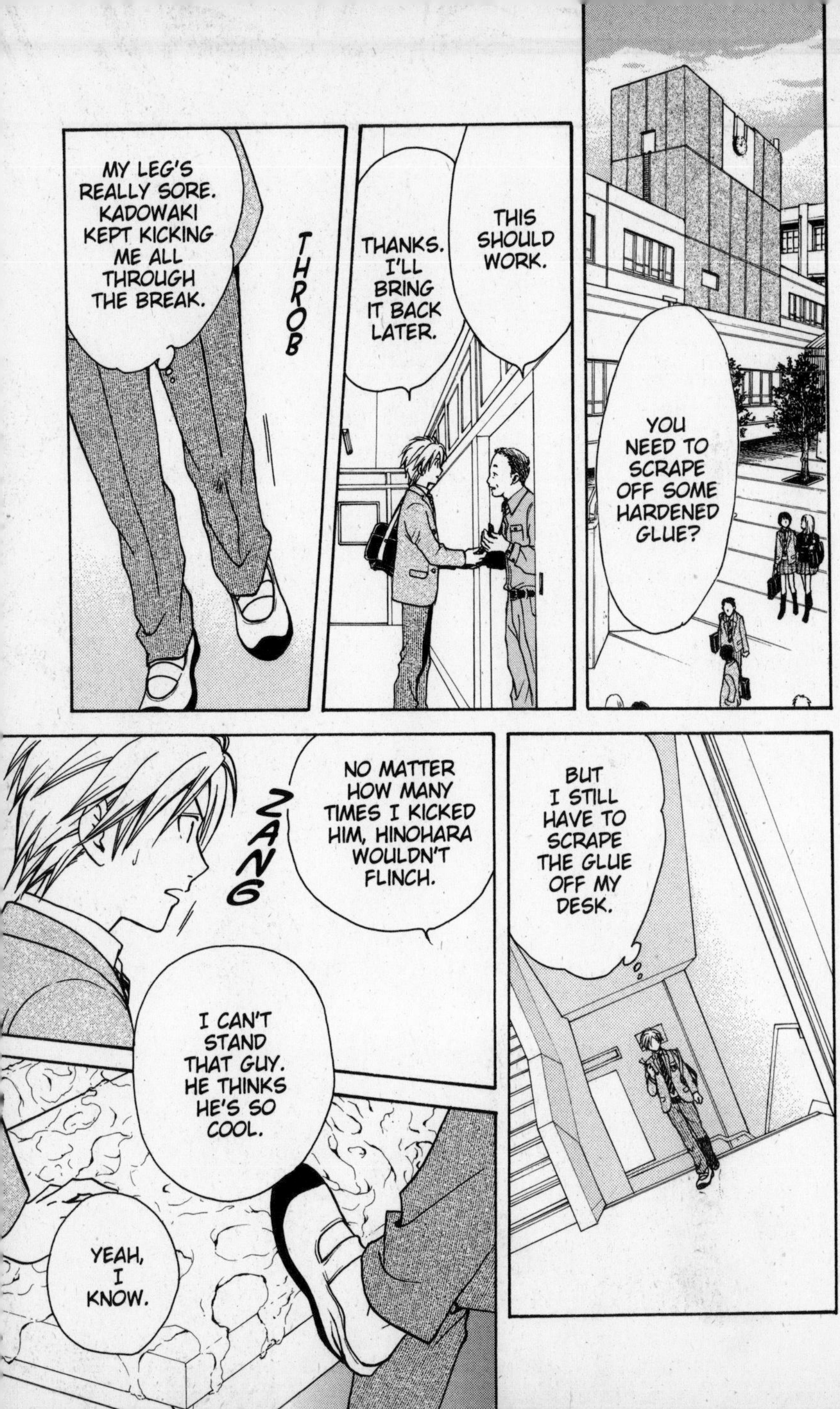
YOU NEED TO SCRAPE OFF SOME HARDENED GLUE?
THIS SHOULD WORK.
THANKS. I'LL BRING IT BACK LATER.
MY LEG'S REALLY SORE. KADOWAKI KEPT KICKING ME ALL THROUGH THE BREAK.
THROB
BUT I STILL HAVE TO SCRAPE THE GLUE OFF MY DESK.
NO MATTER HOW MANY TIMES I KICKED HIM, HINOHARA WOULDN'T FLINCH.
ZANG
I CAN'T STAND THAT GUY. HE THINKS HE'S SO COOL.
YEAH, I KNOW.

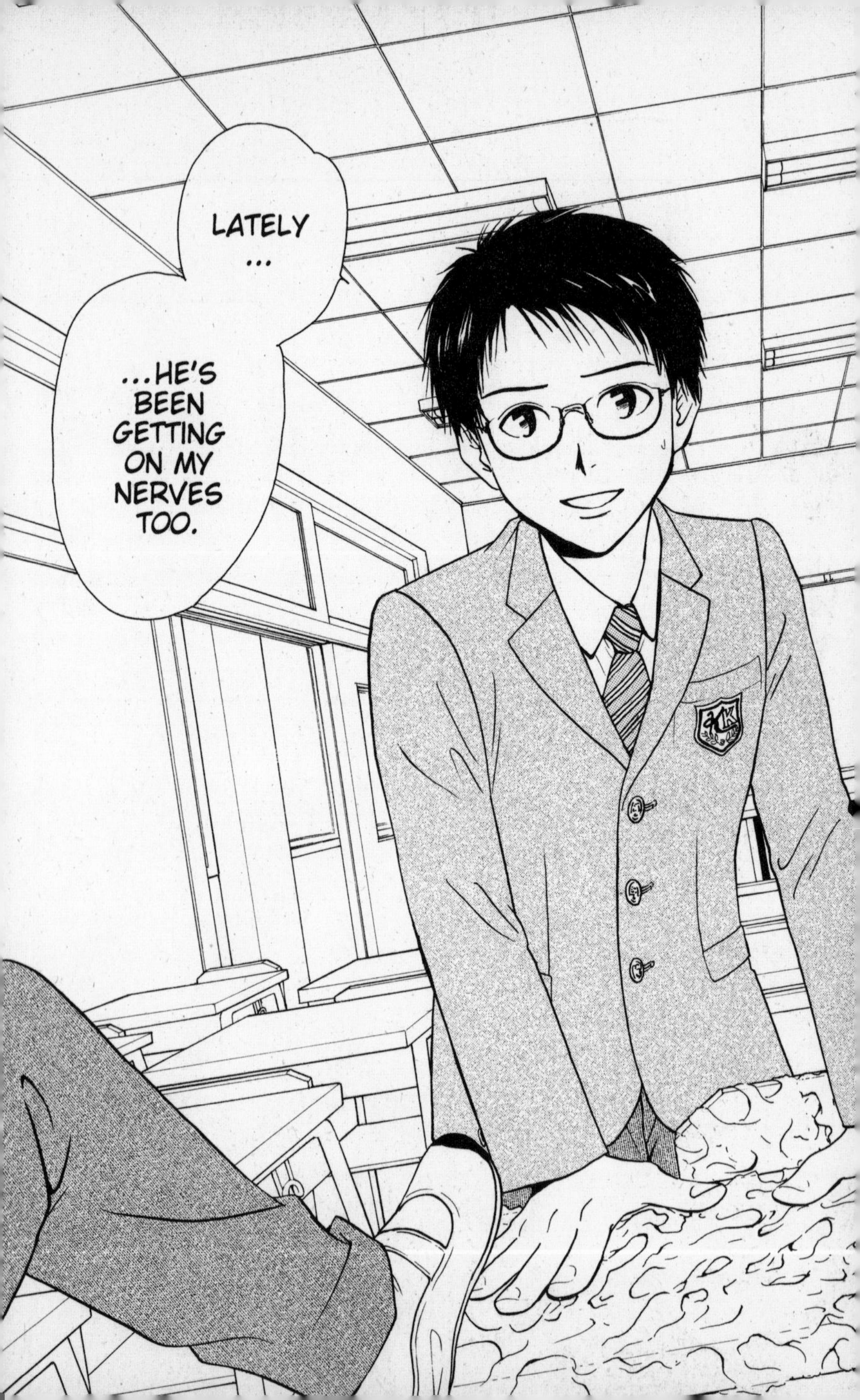
LATELY ...
...HE'S BEEN GETTING ON MY NERVES TOO.

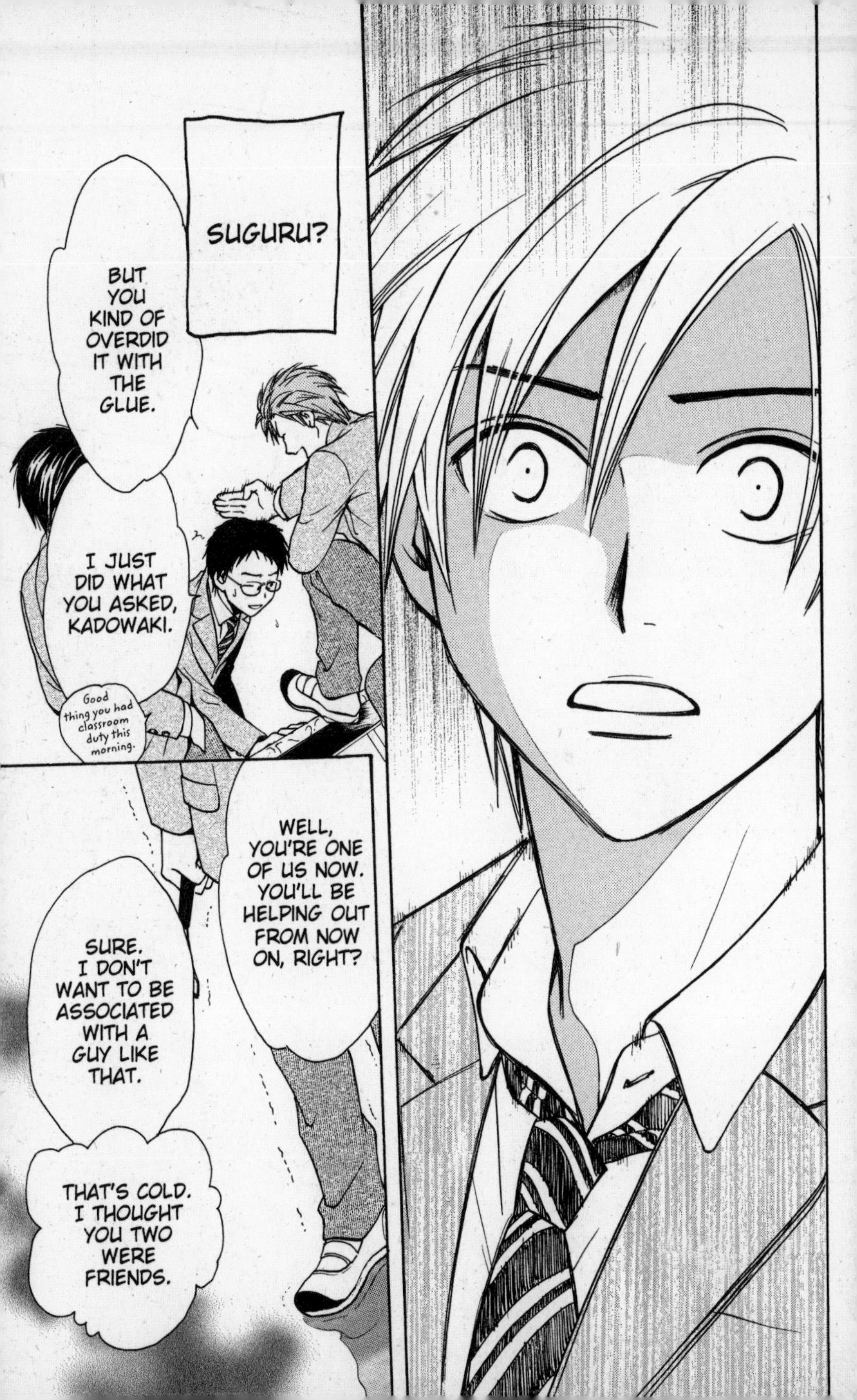

SUGURU?
BUT YOU KIND OF OVERDID IT WITH THE GLUE.
I JUST DID WHAT YOU ASKED, KADOWAKI.
Good thing you had classroom duty this morning.
WELL, YOU'RE ONE OF US NOW. YOU'LL BE HELPING OUT FROM NOW ON, RIGHT?
SURE. I DON'T WANT TO BE ASSOCIATED WITH A GUY LIKE THAT.
THAT'S COLD. I THOUGHT YOU TWO WERE FRIENDS.

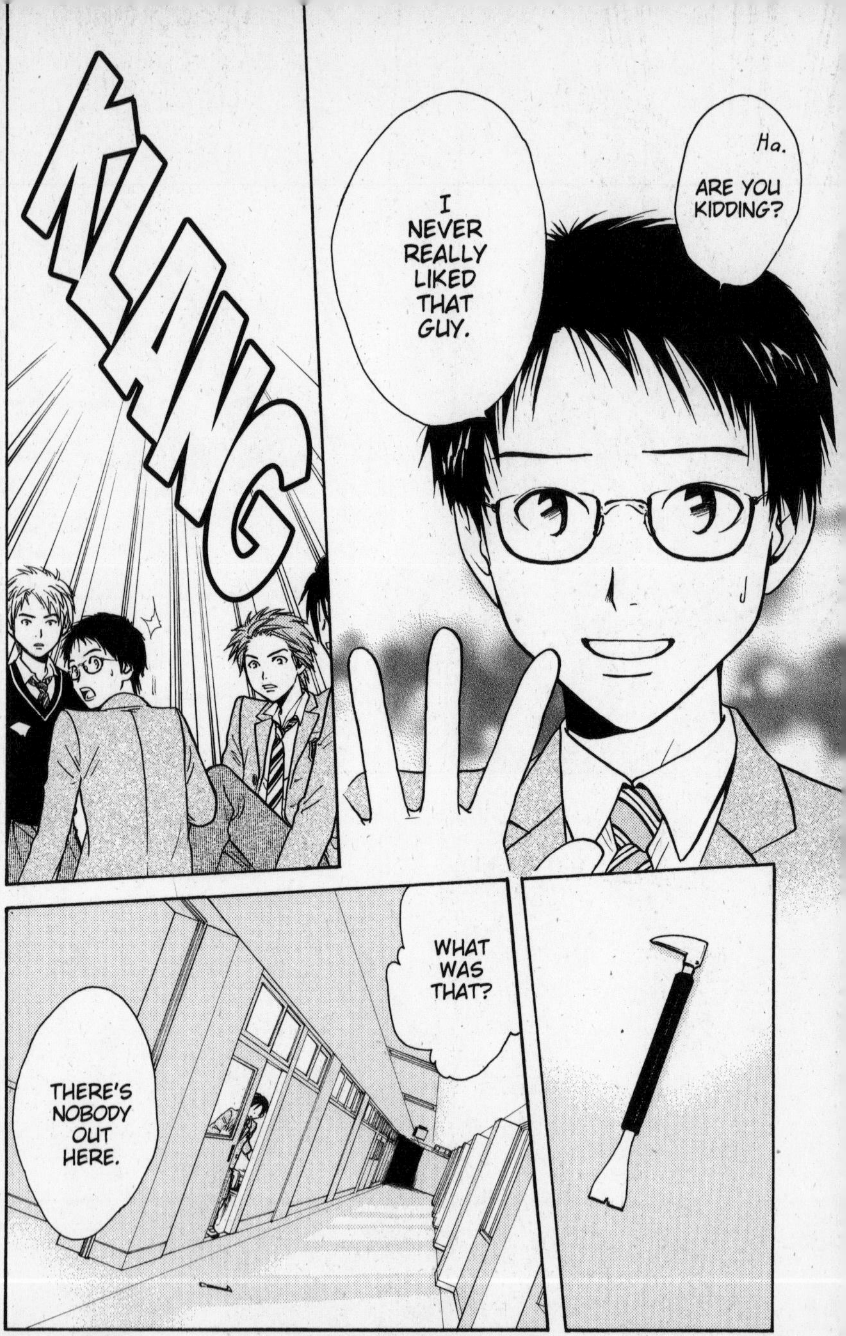
Ha.
ARE YOU KIDDING?
I NEVER REALLY LIKED THAT GUY.
KLANG
WHAT WAS THAT?
THERE'S NOBODY OUT HERE.

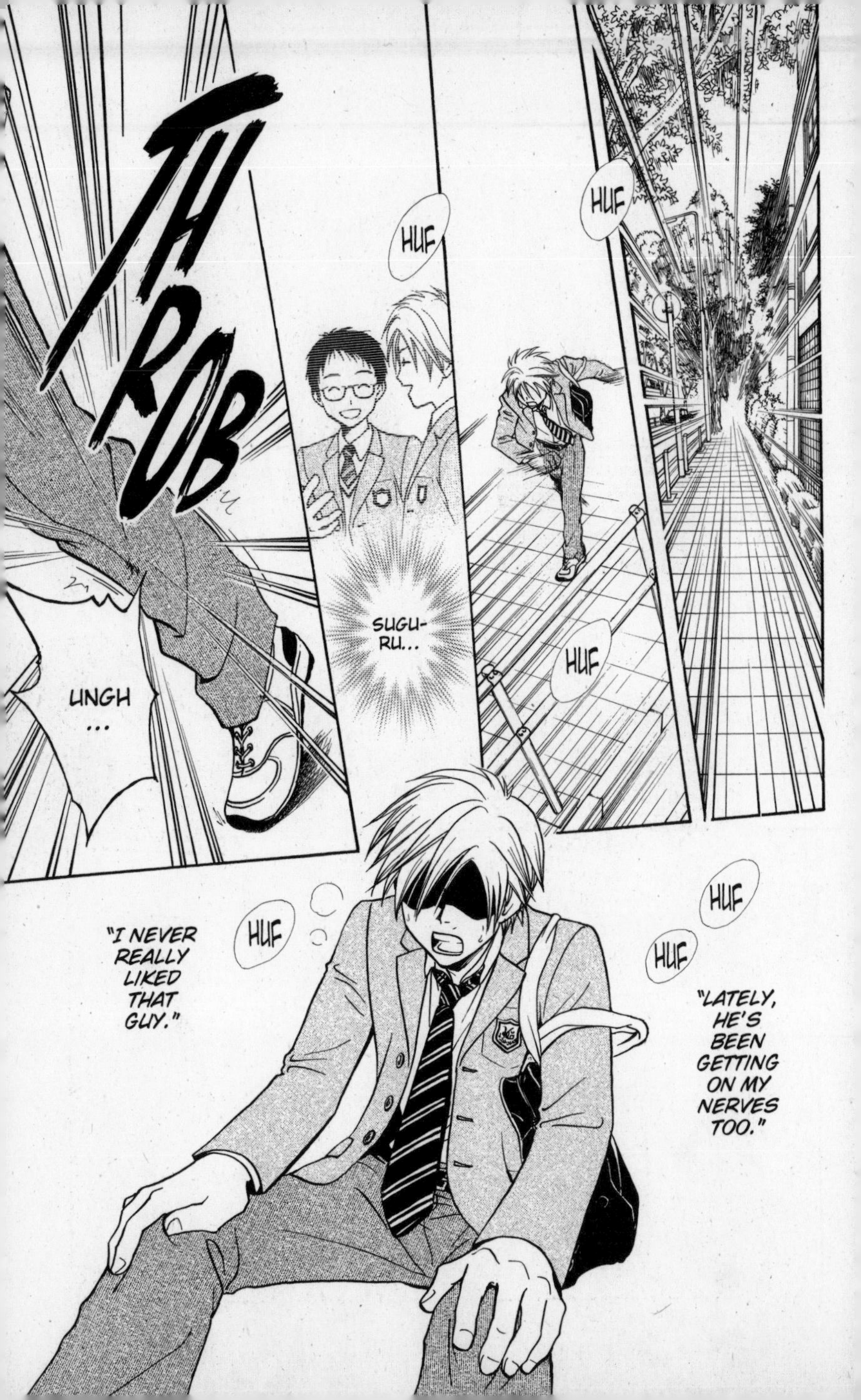
HUF
HUF
HUF
SUGU-RU...
THROB
UNGH ...
HUF
HUF
"LATELY, HE'S BEEN GETTING ON MY NERVES TOO."
HUF
"I NEVER REALLY LIKED THAT GUY."

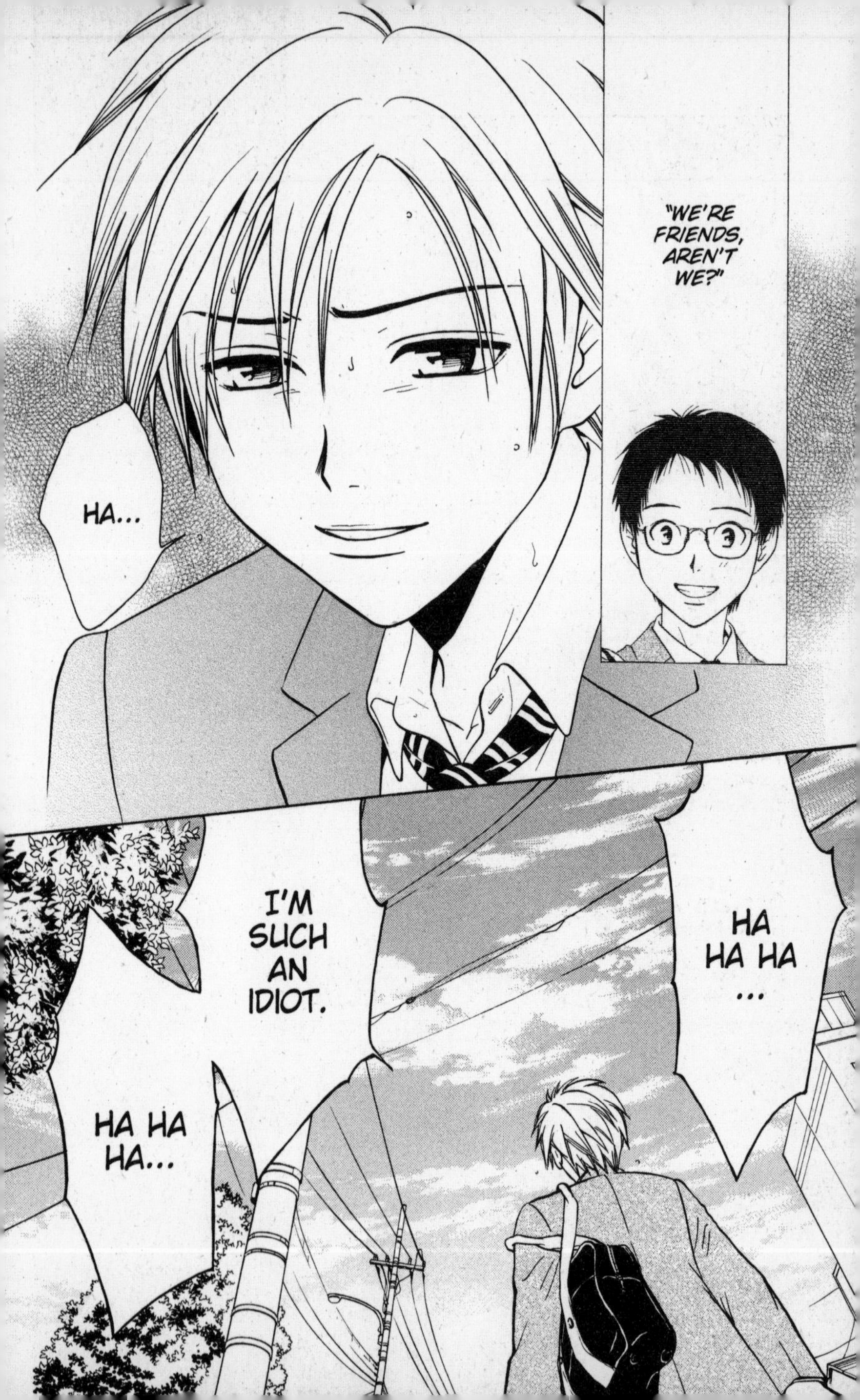
"WE'RE FRIENDS, AREN'T WE?"
HA...
HA HA HA ...
I'M SUCH AN IDIOT.
HA HA HA...

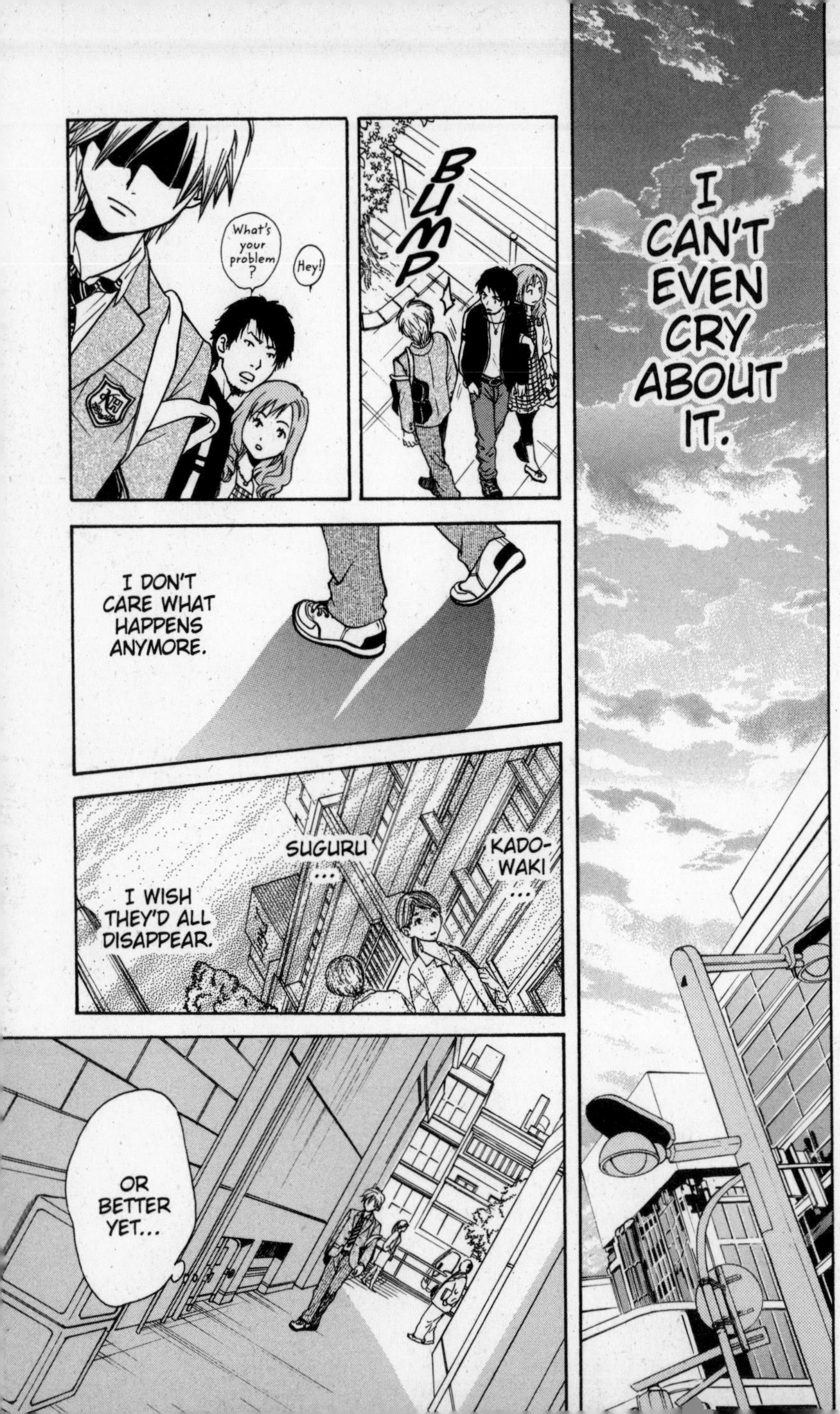
I CAN'T EVEN CRY ABOUT IT.
BUMP
Hey!
What's your problem?
I DON'T CARE WHAT HAPPENS ANYMORE.
KADO-WAKI...
SUGURU...
I WISH THEY'D ALL DISAPPEAR.
OR BETTER YET...

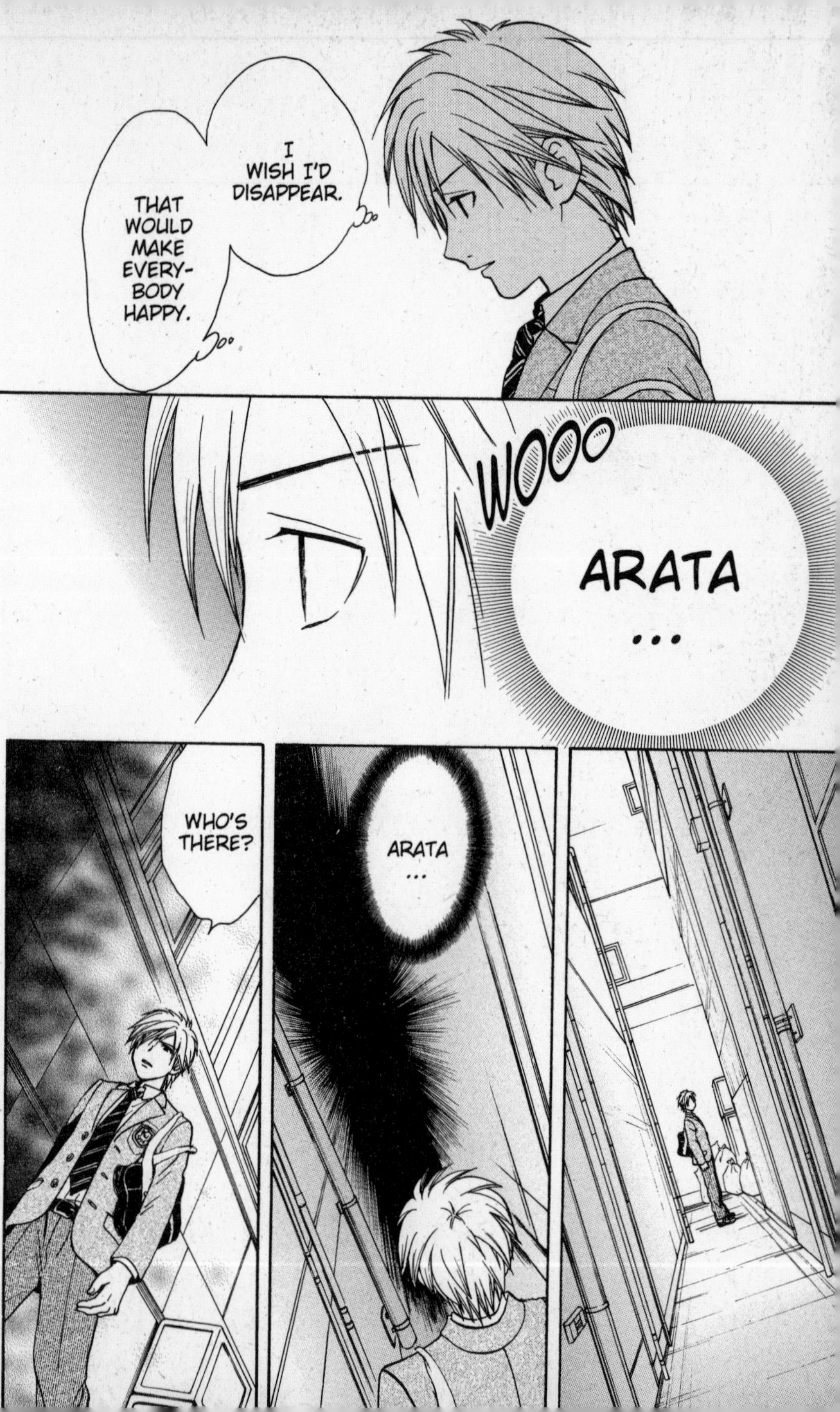
I WISH I'D DISAPPEAR.
THAT WOULD MAKE EVERY-BODY HAPPY.
WOOO
ARATA ...
ARATA ...
WHO'S THERE?

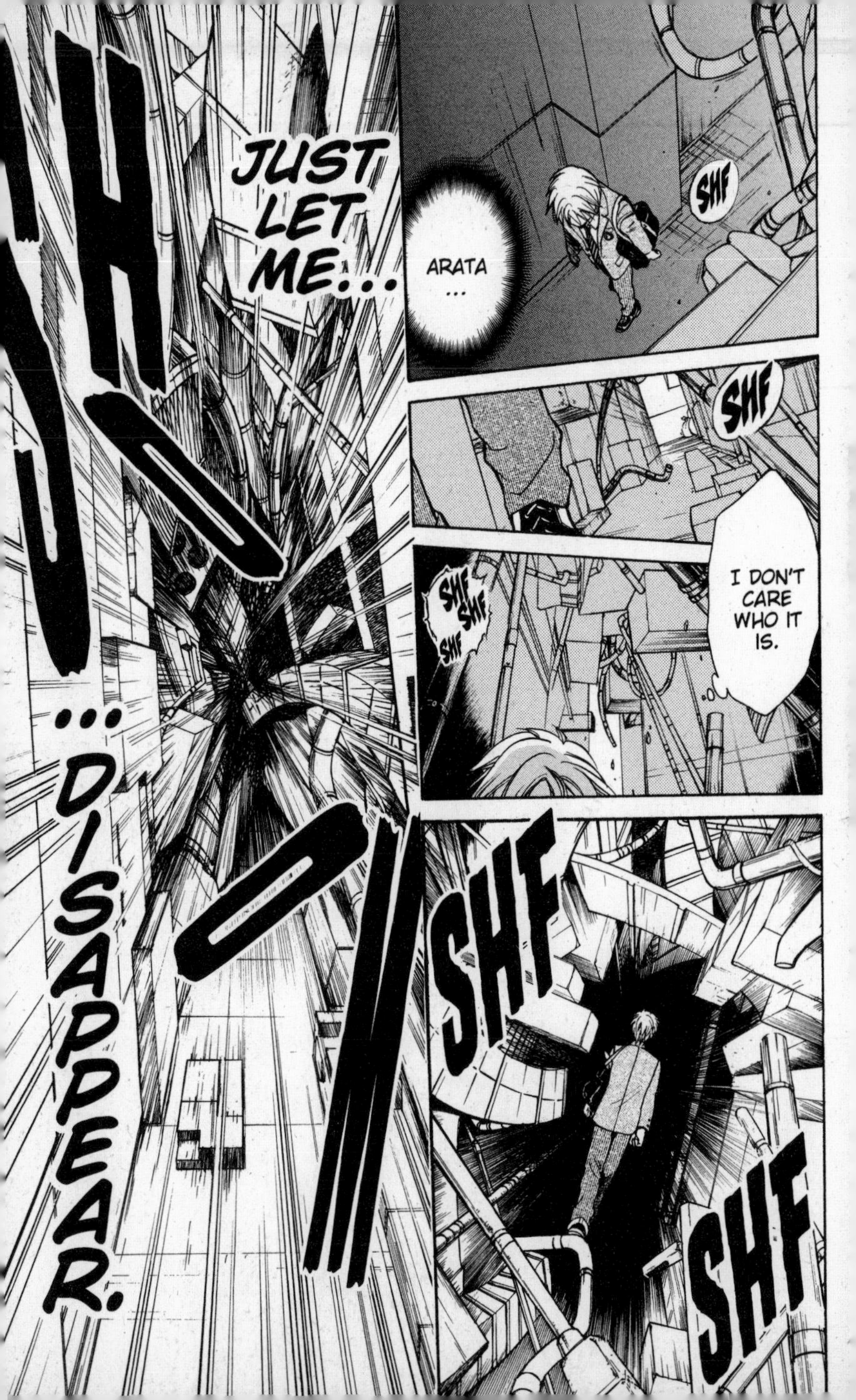

SHF
ARATA ...
SHF
I DON'T CARE WHO IT IS.
SHF SHF SHF
SHF
SHF
JUST LET ME...
...DISAPPEAR.

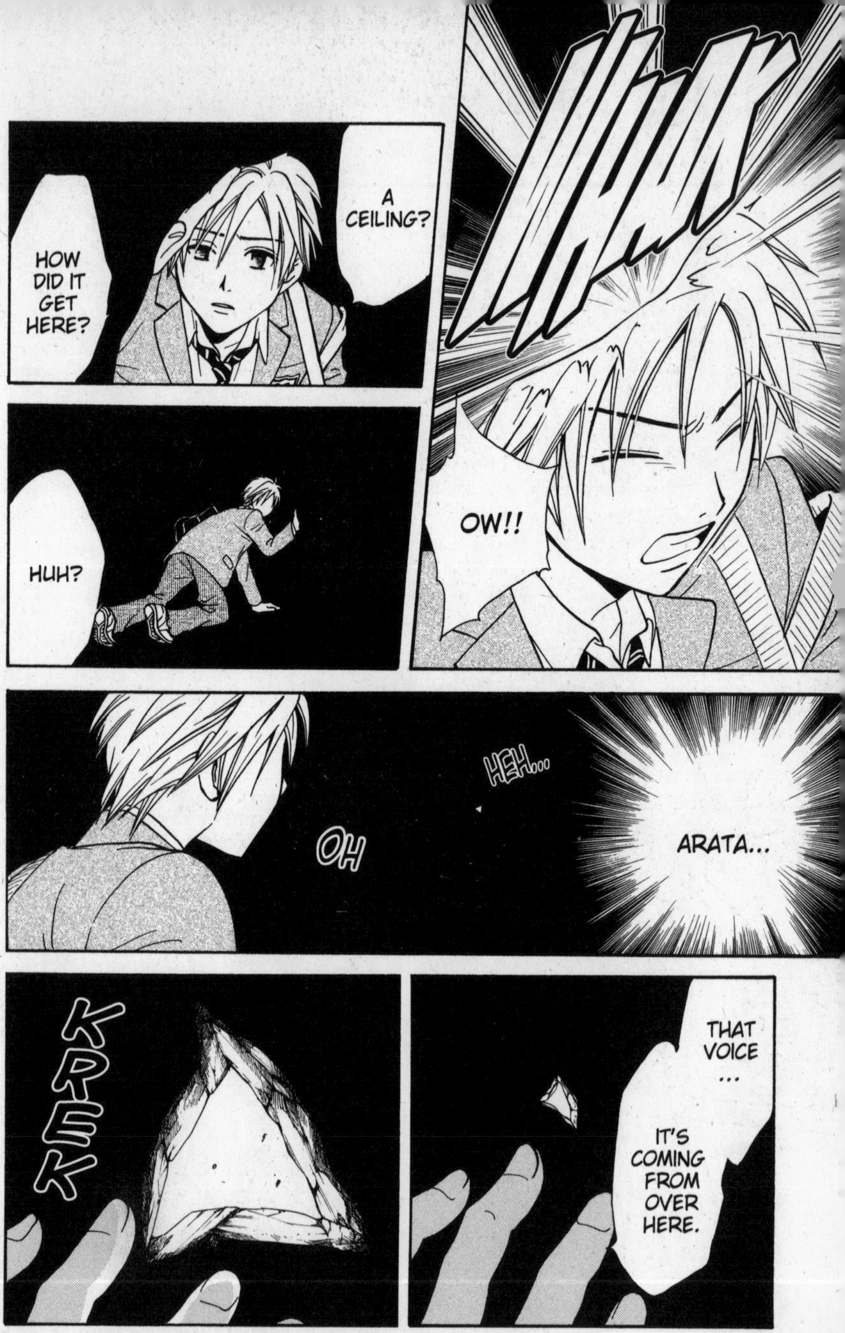
OW!!
A CEILING?
HOW DID IT GET HERE?
HUH?
ARATA...
HEH...
OH
THAT VOICE ...
IT'S COMING FROM OVER HERE.
KREK

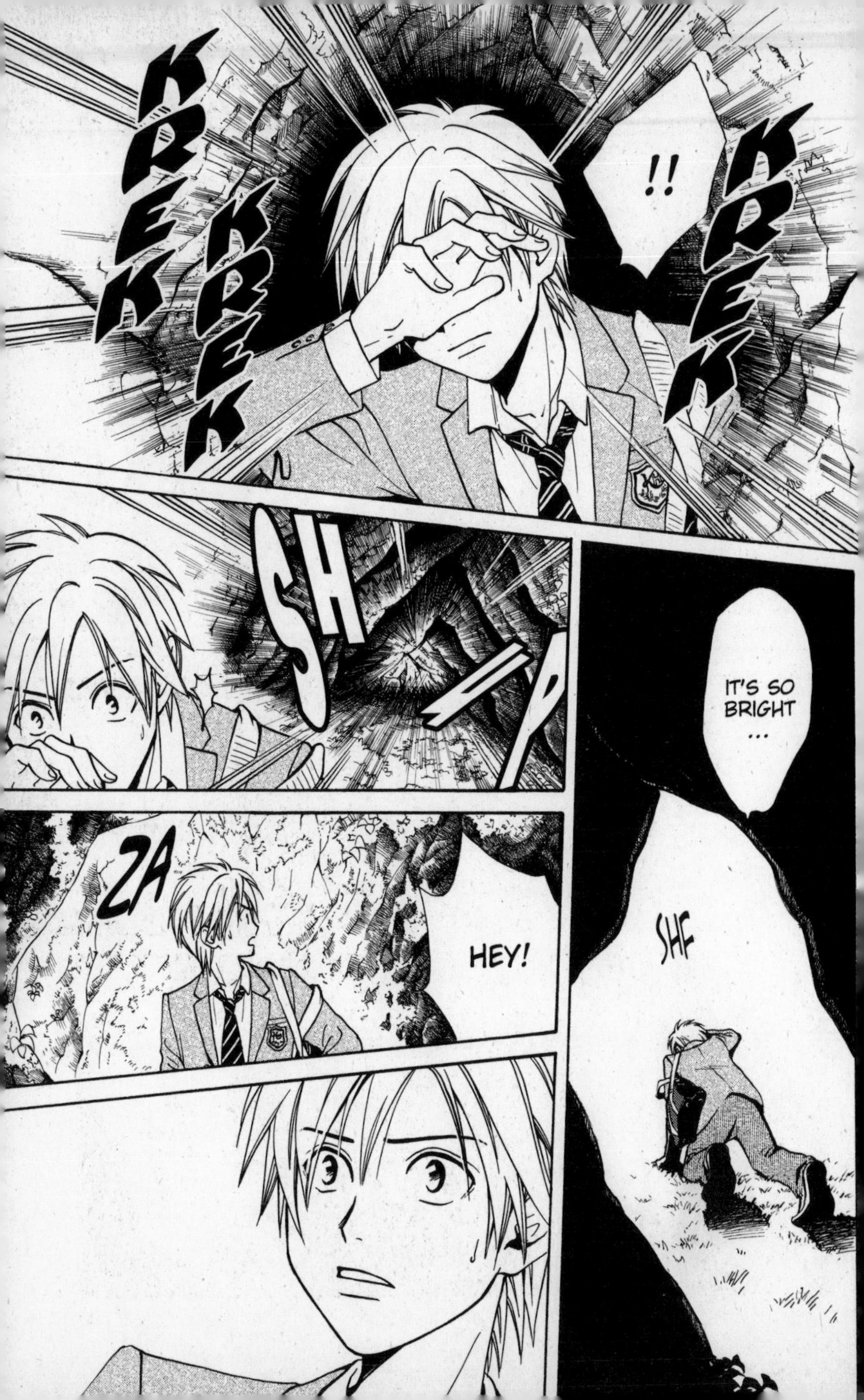
KREK
!!
KREK
KREK
IT'S SO BRIGHT ...
SHF
SHIP
ZA
HEY!

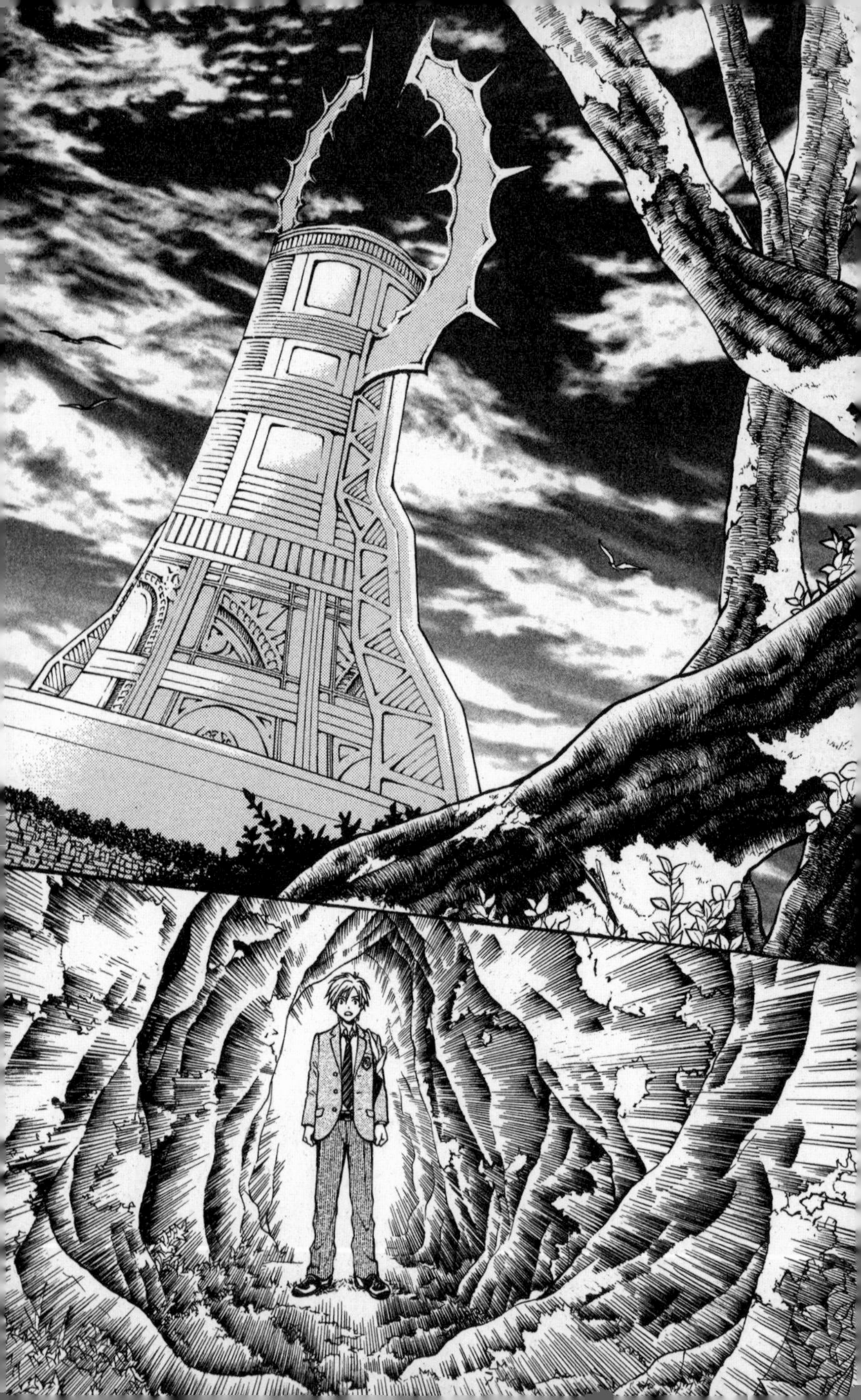

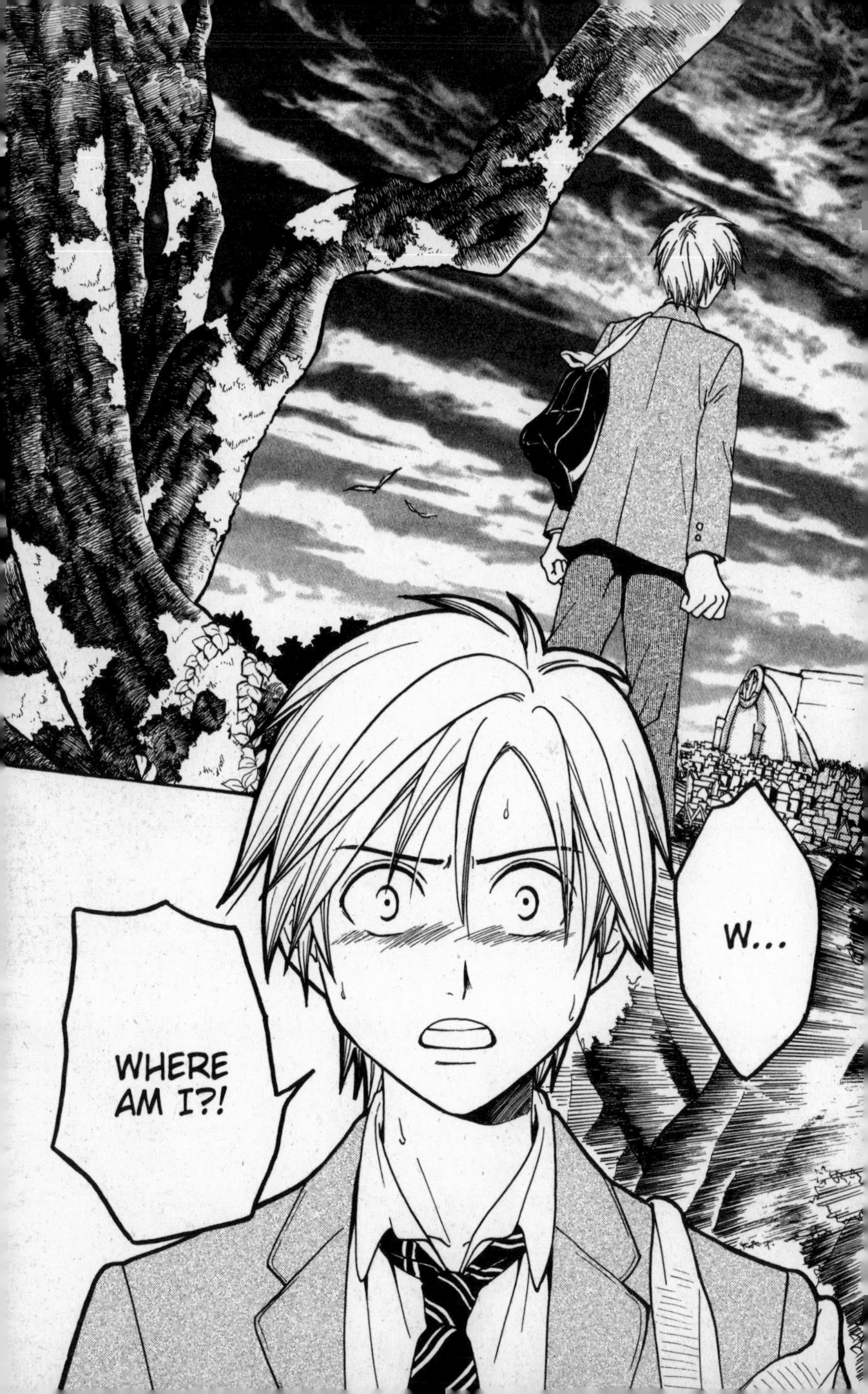
W...
WHERE AM I?!

Arata
THE LEGEND

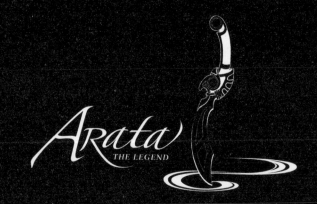

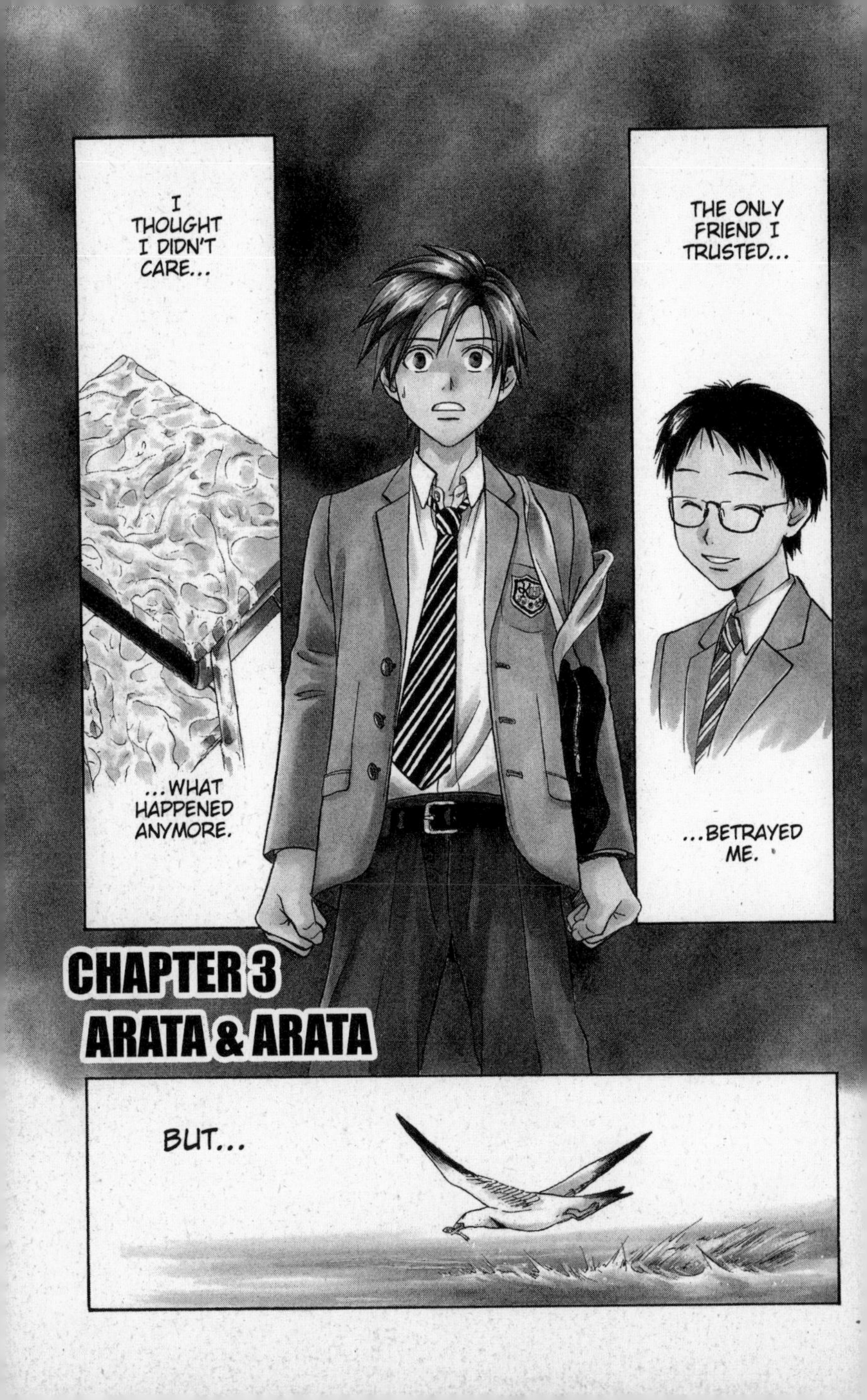
THE ONLY FRIEND I TRUSTED...
...BETRAYED ME.
I THOUGHT I DIDN'T CARE...
...WHAT HAPPENED ANYMORE.
CHAPTER 3
ARATA & ARATA
BUT...

CHAPTER 3
ARATA & ARATA

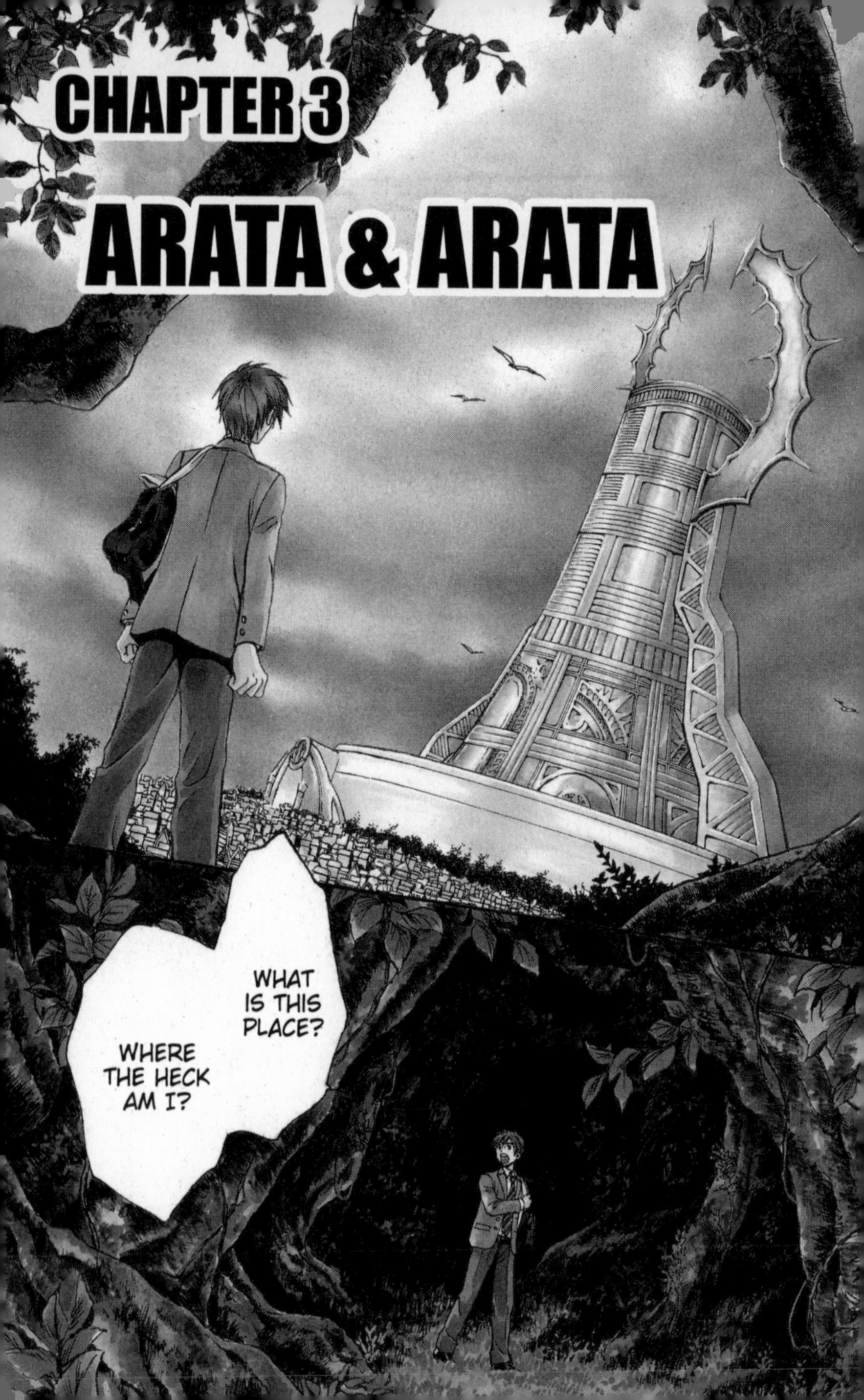
WHAT IS THIS PLACE?
WHERE THE HECK AM I?

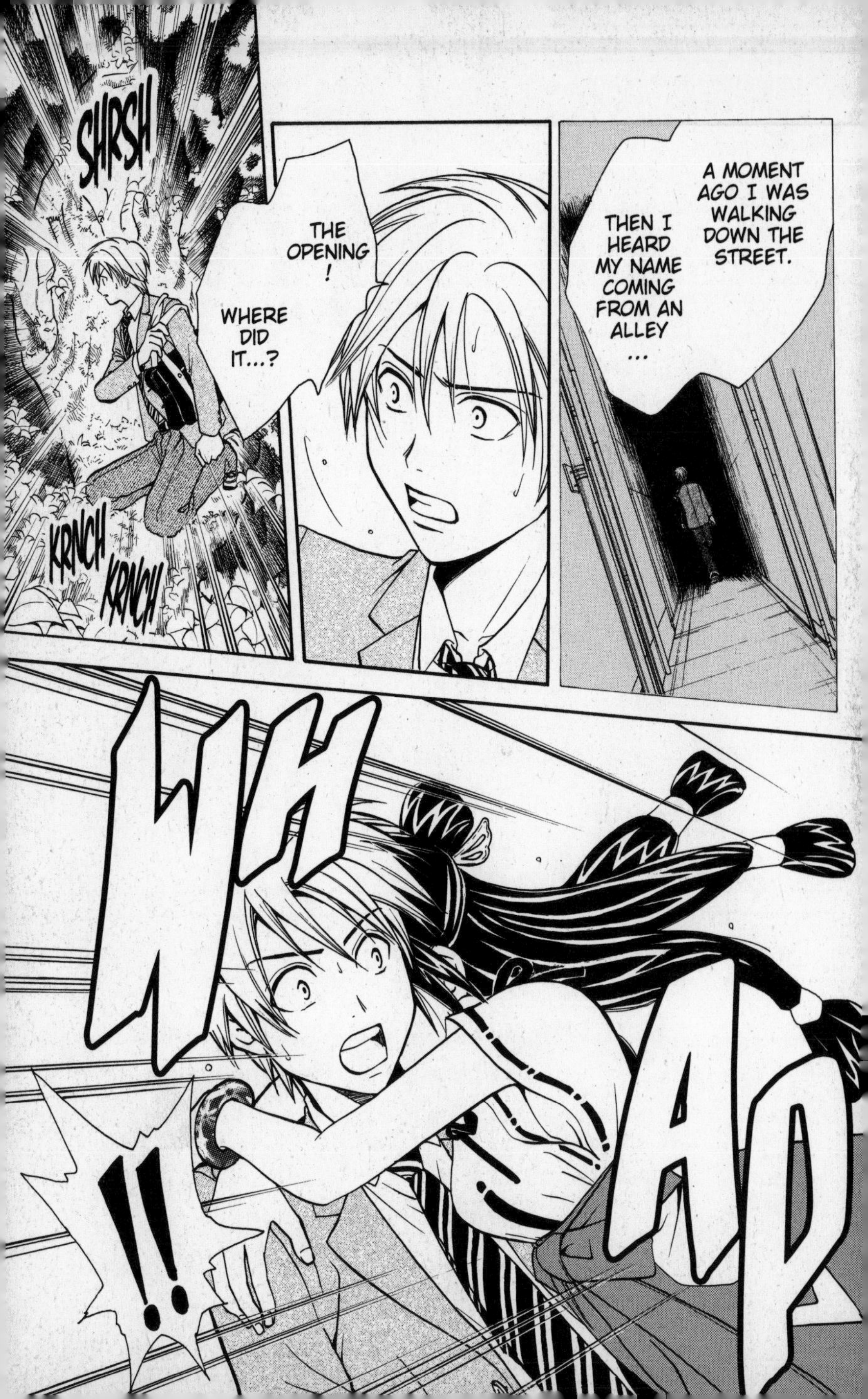
A MOMENT AGO I WAS WALKING DOWN THE STREET.
THEN I HEARD MY NAME COMING FROM AN ALLEY ...
THE OPENING!
WHERE DID IT...?
SHRSH
KRNCH KRNCH
WHAP
!!

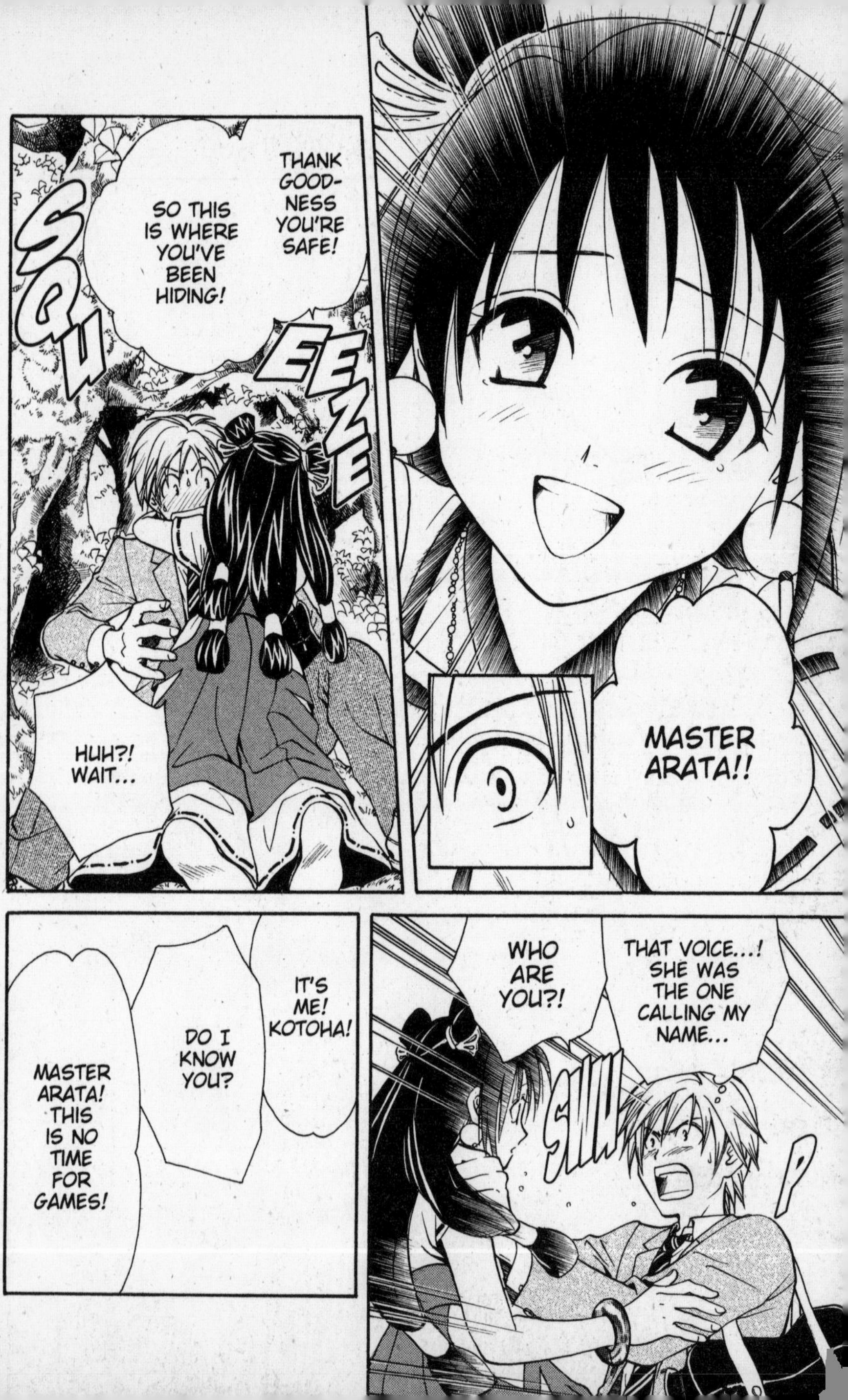
MASTER ARATA!!
THANK GOODNESS YOU'RE SAFE!
SO THIS IS WHERE YOU'VE BEEN HIDING!
SQUEEZE
HUH?! WAIT...
THAT VOICE...! SHE WAS THE ONE CALLING MY NAME...
WHO ARE YOU?!
IT'S ME! KOTOHA!
DO I KNOW YOU?
MASTER ARATA! THIS IS NO TIME FOR GAMES!

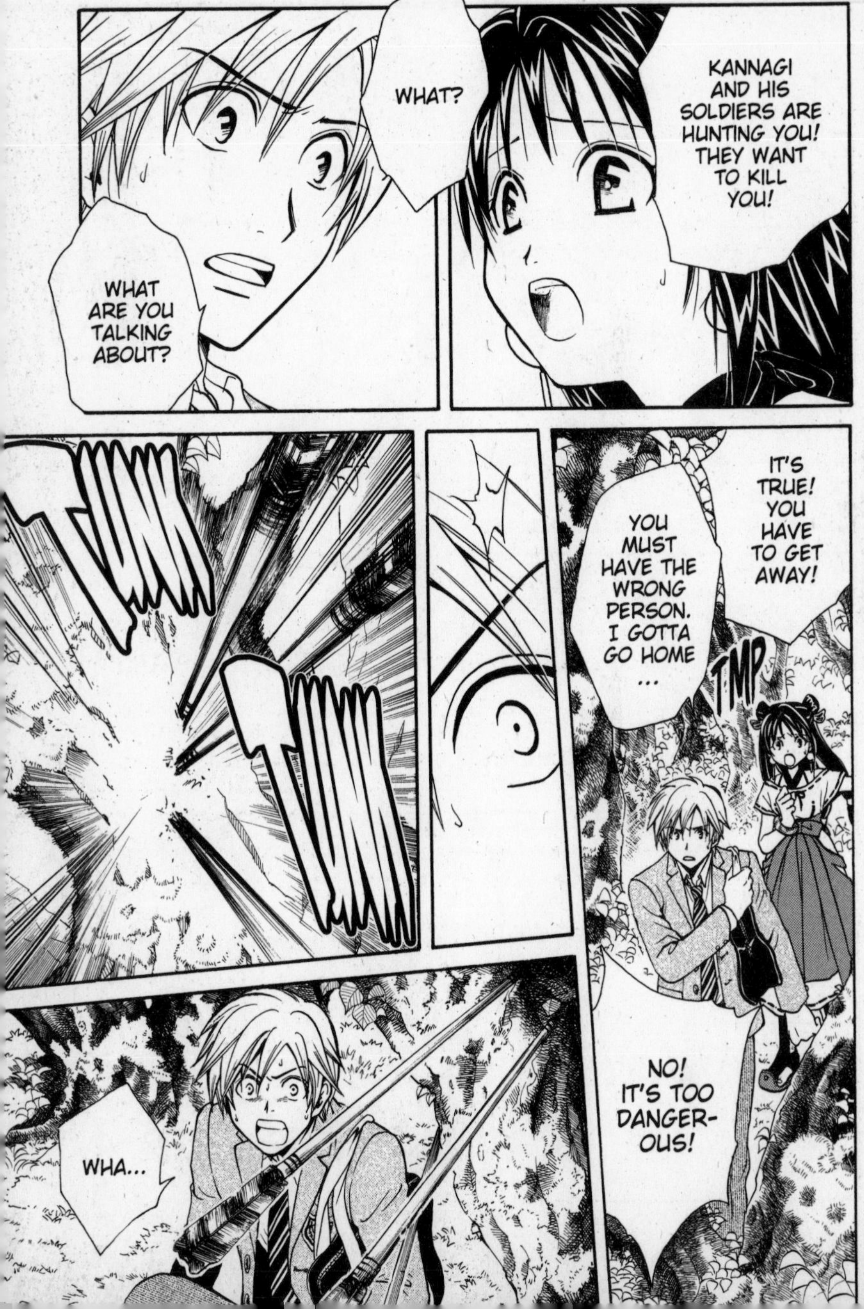
KANNAGI AND HIS SOLDIERS ARE HUNTING YOU! THEY WANT TO KILL YOU!
WHAT?
WHAT ARE YOU TALKING ABOUT?
IT'S TRUE! YOU HAVE TO GET AWAY!
YOU MUST HAVE THE WRONG PERSON. I GOTTA GO HOME ...
TMP
NO! IT'S TOO DANGER-OUS!
JUNK
JUNK
WHA...

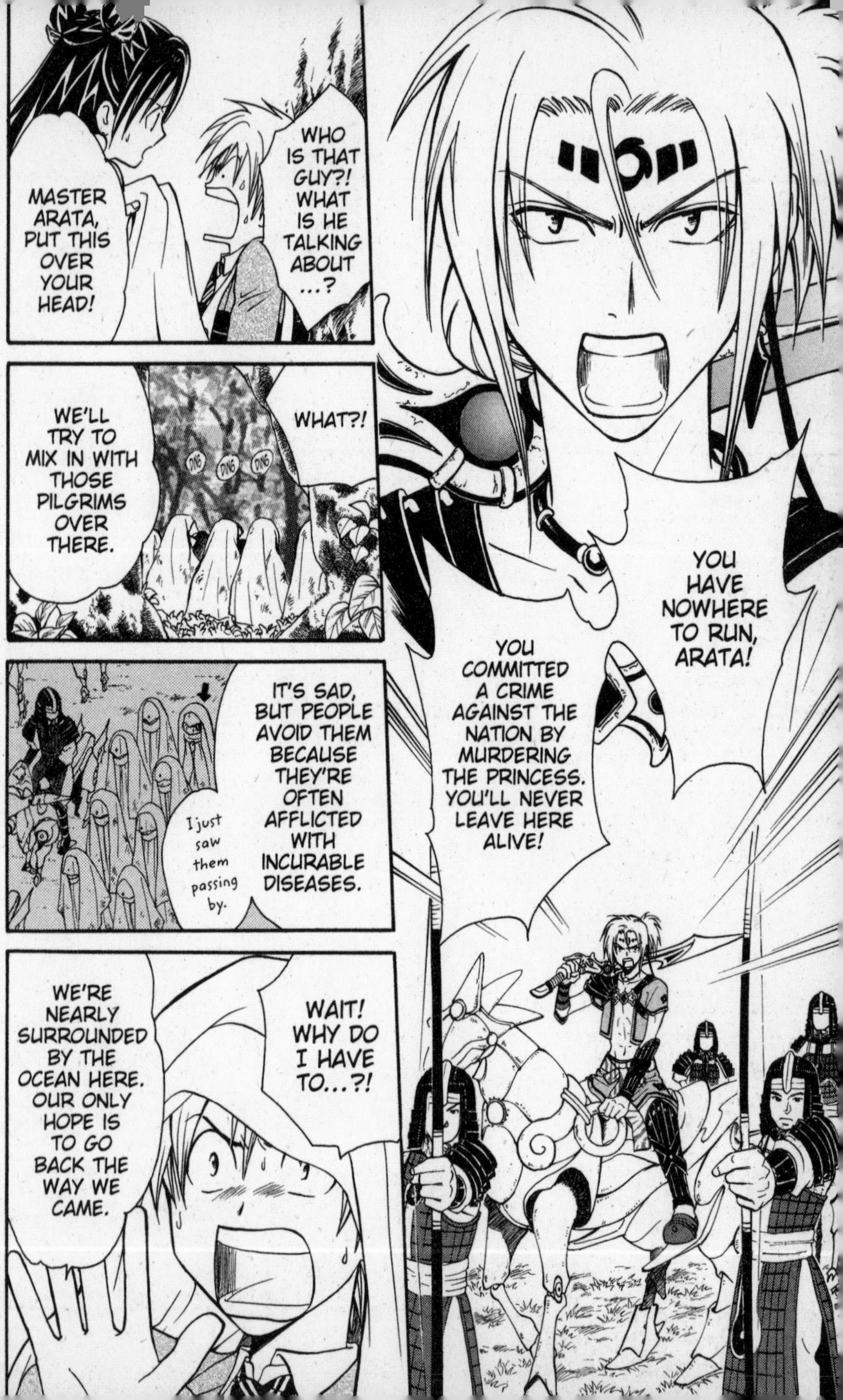
YOU HAVE NOWHERE TO RUN, ARATA!
YOU COMMITTED A CRIME AGAINST THE NATION BY MURDERING THE PRINCESS. YOU'LL NEVER LEAVE HERE ALIVE!
WHO IS THAT GUY?! WHAT IS HE TALKING ABOUT ...?
MASTER ARATA, PUT THIS OVER YOUR HEAD!
WHAT?!
DING DING DING
WE'LL TRY TO MIX IN WITH THOSE PILGRIMS OVER THERE.
IT'S SAD, BUT PEOPLE AVOID THEM BECAUSE THEY'RE OFTEN AFFLICTED WITH INCURABLE DISEASES.
I just saw them passing by.
WAIT! WHY DO I HAVE TO...?!
WE'RE NEARLY SURROUNDED BY THE OCEAN HERE. OUR ONLY HOPE IS TO GO BACK THE WAY WE CAME.

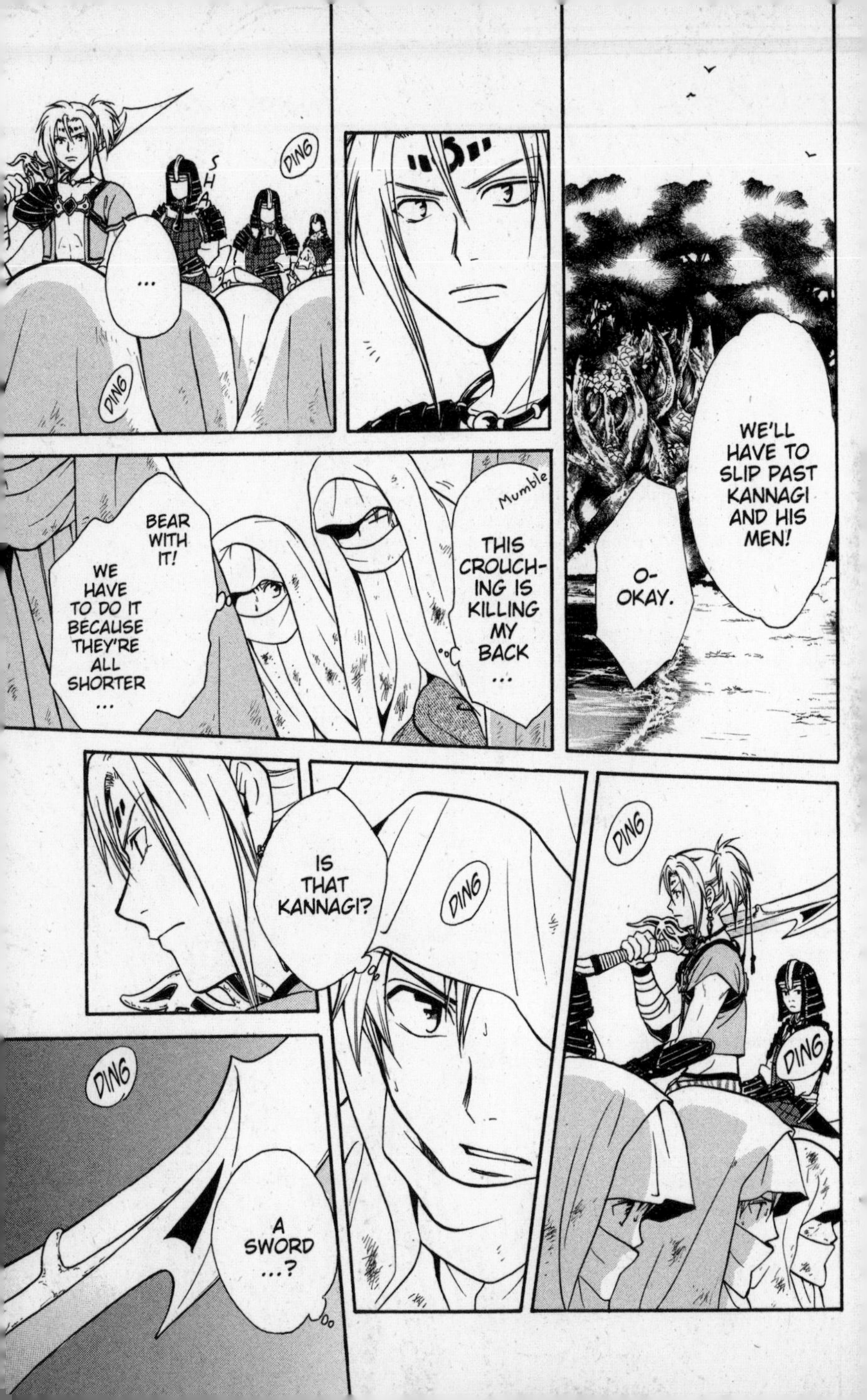

WE'LL HAVE TO SLIP PAST KANNAGI AND HIS MEN!
O-OKAY.
DING
SHA
...
DING
Mumble
THIS CROUCHING IS KILLING MY BACK...
BEAR WITH IT!
WE HAVE TO DO IT BECAUSE THEY'RE ALL SHORTER...
DING
DING
IS THAT KANNAGI?
DING
DING
A SWORD...?

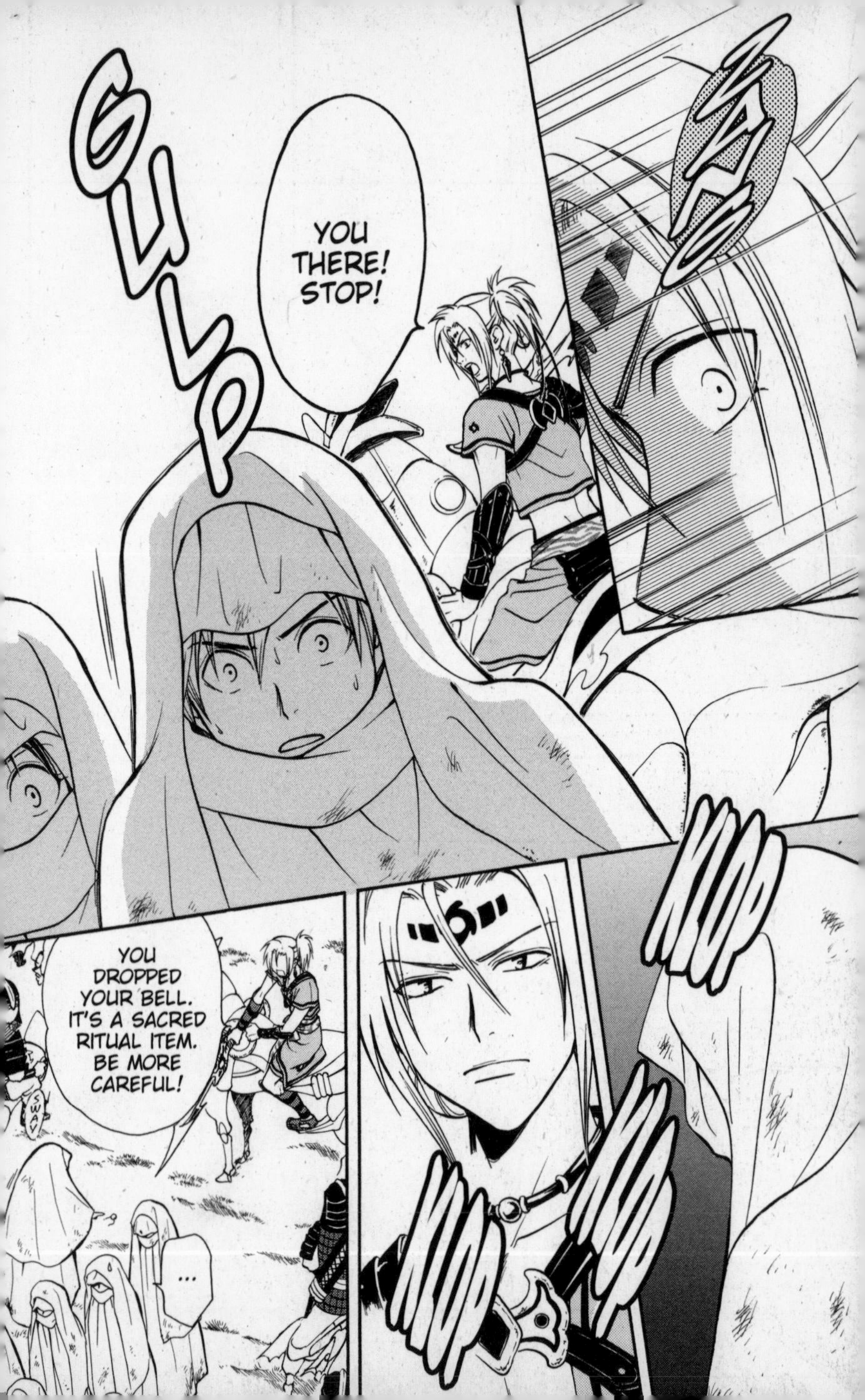
YOU THERE! STOP!
GULP
NOD
NOD
NOD
YOU DROPPED YOUR BELL. IT'S A SACRED RITUAL ITEM. BE MORE CAREFUL!
SWAY
...

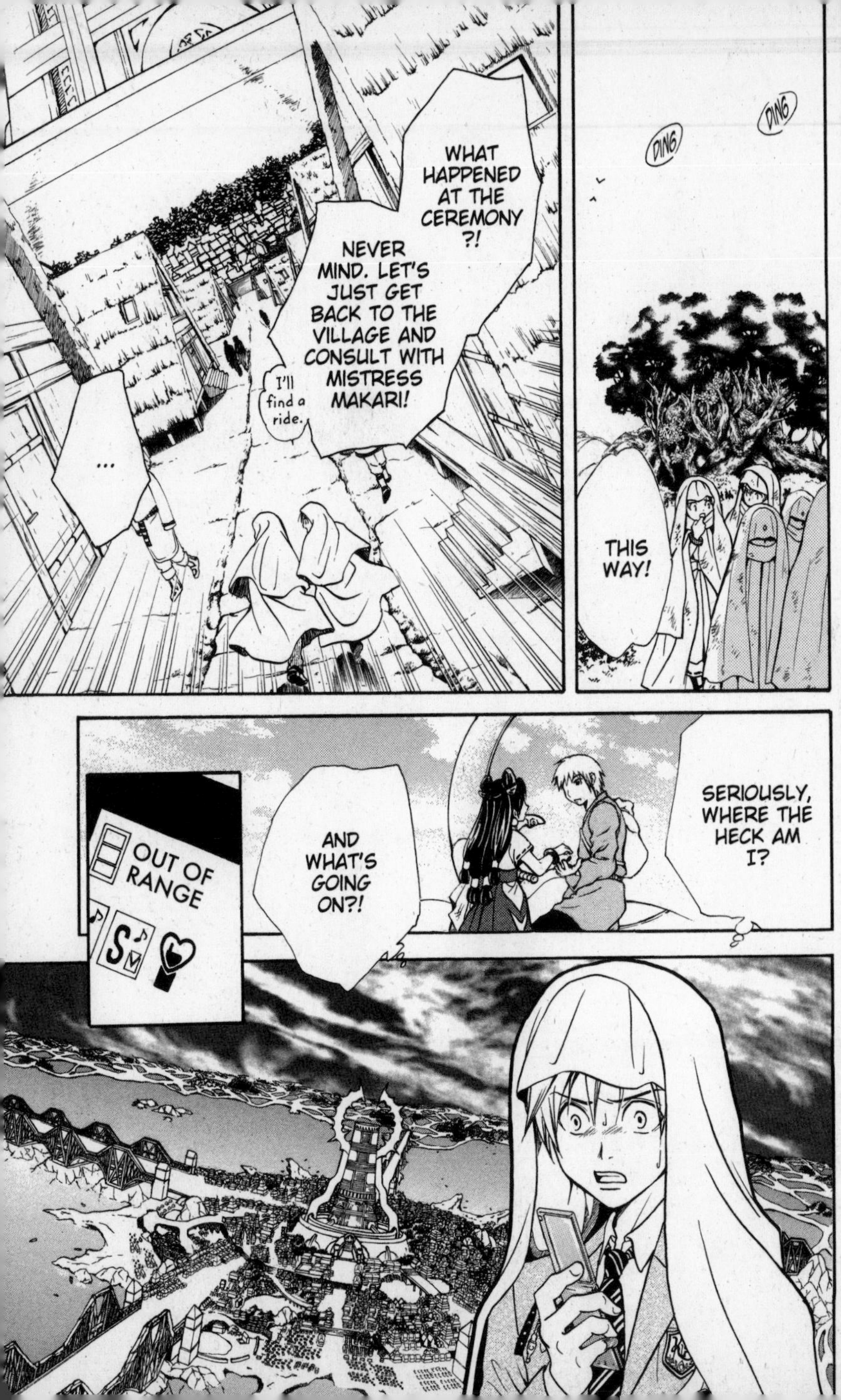
DING
DING
THIS WAY!
WHAT HAPPENED AT THE CEREMONY?!
NEVER MIND. LET'S JUST GET BACK TO THE VILLAGE AND CONSULT WITH MISTRESS MAKARI!
I'll find a ride.
...
SERIOUSLY, WHERE THE HECK AM I?
AND WHAT'S GOING ON?!
OUT OF RANGE
S

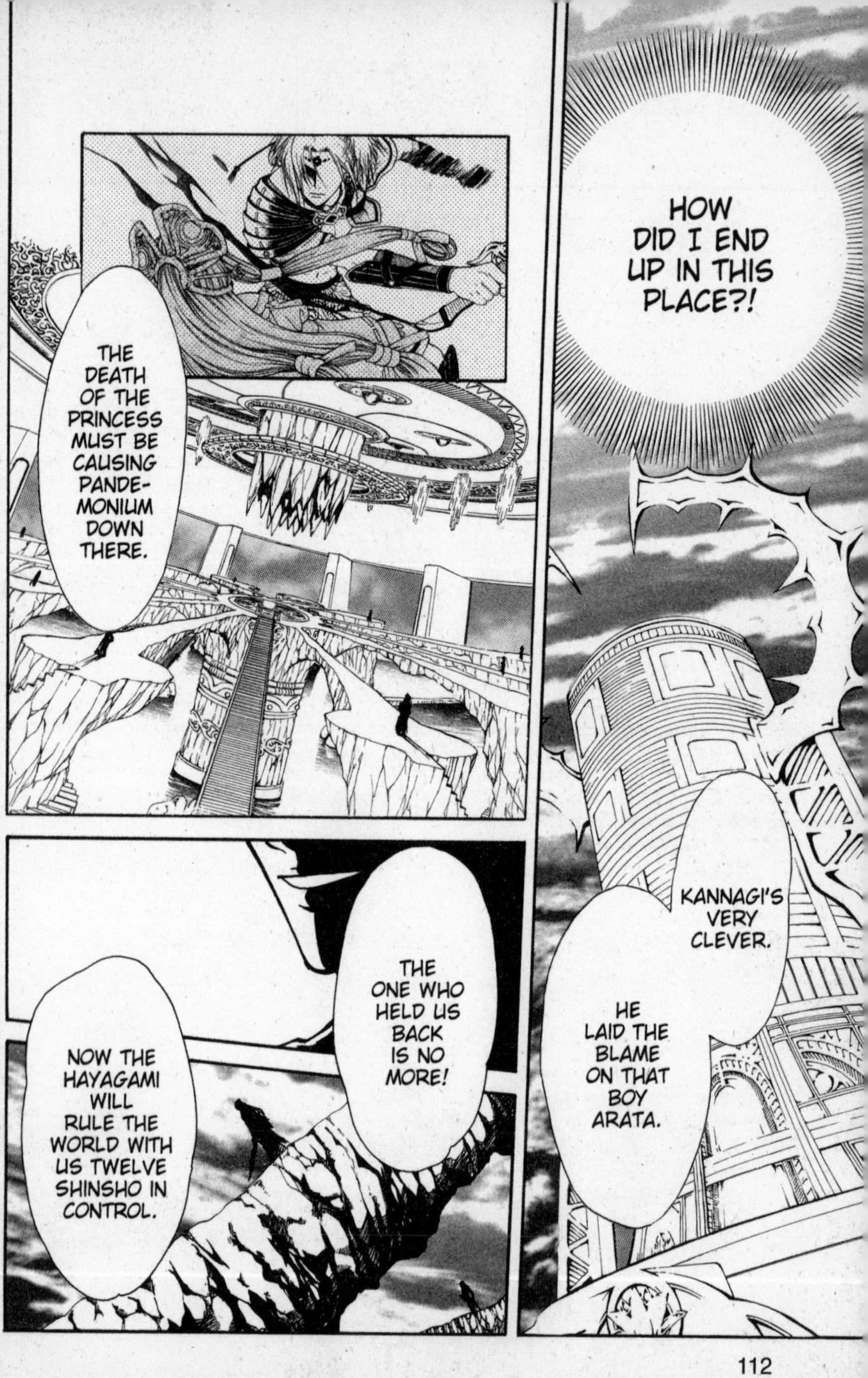
HOW DID I END UP IN THIS PLACE?!
KANNAGI'S VERY CLEVER.
HE LAID THE BLAME ON THAT BOY ARATA.
THE DEATH OF THE PRINCESS MUST BE CAUSING PANDE-MONIUM DOWN THERE.
THE ONE WHO HELD US BACK IS NO MORE!
NOW THE HAYAGAMI WILL RULE THE WORLD WITH US TWELVE SHINSHO IN CONTROL.

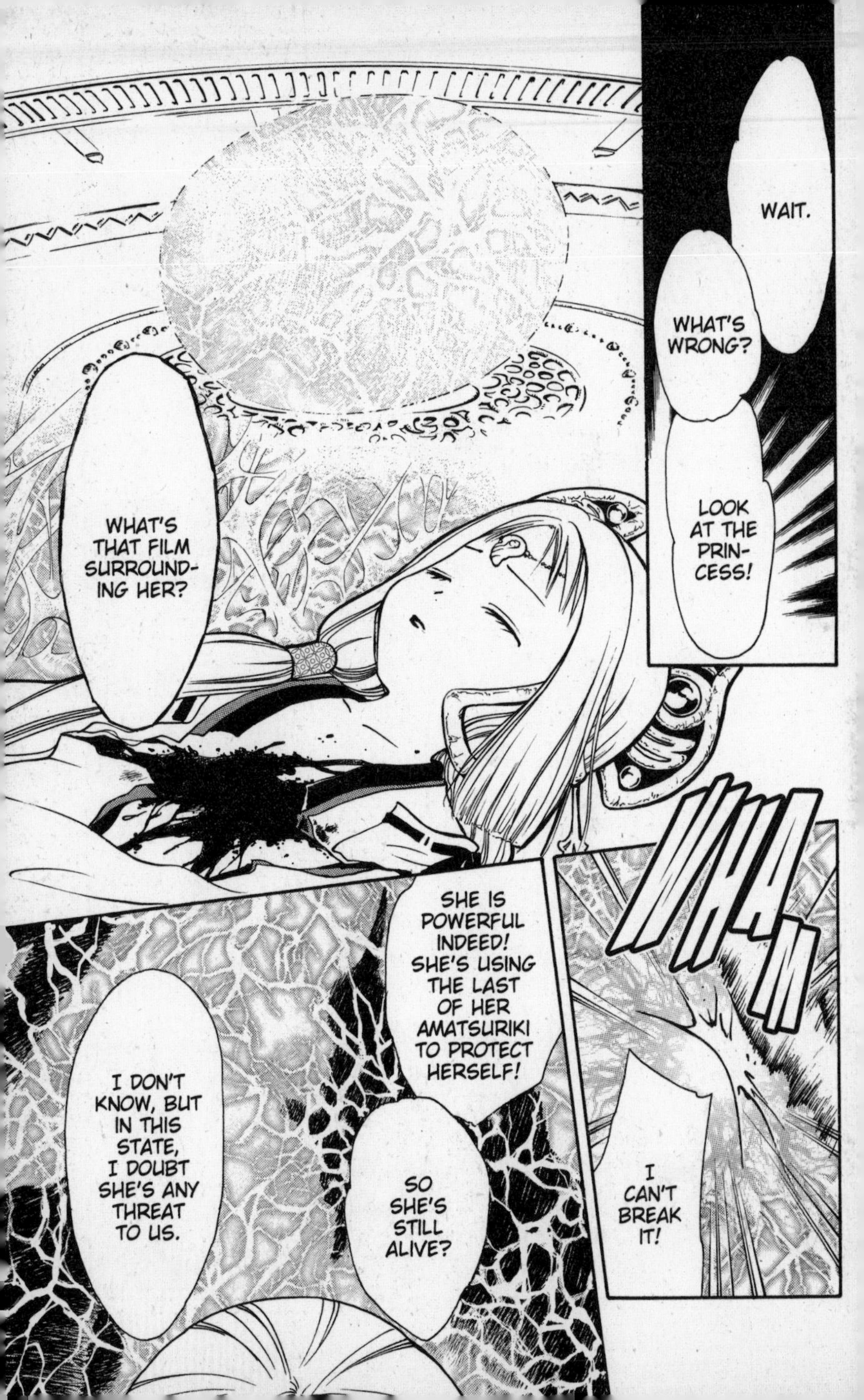
WAIT.
WHAT'S WRONG?
LOOK AT THE PRIN-CESS!
WHAT'S THAT FILM SURROUND-ING HER?
WHAM
I CAN'T BREAK IT!
SHE IS POWERFUL INDEED! SHE'S USING THE LAST OF HER AMATSURIKI TO PROTECT HERSELF!
SO SHE'S STILL ALIVE?
I DON'T KNOW, BUT IN THIS STATE, I DOUBT SHE'S ANY THREAT TO US.

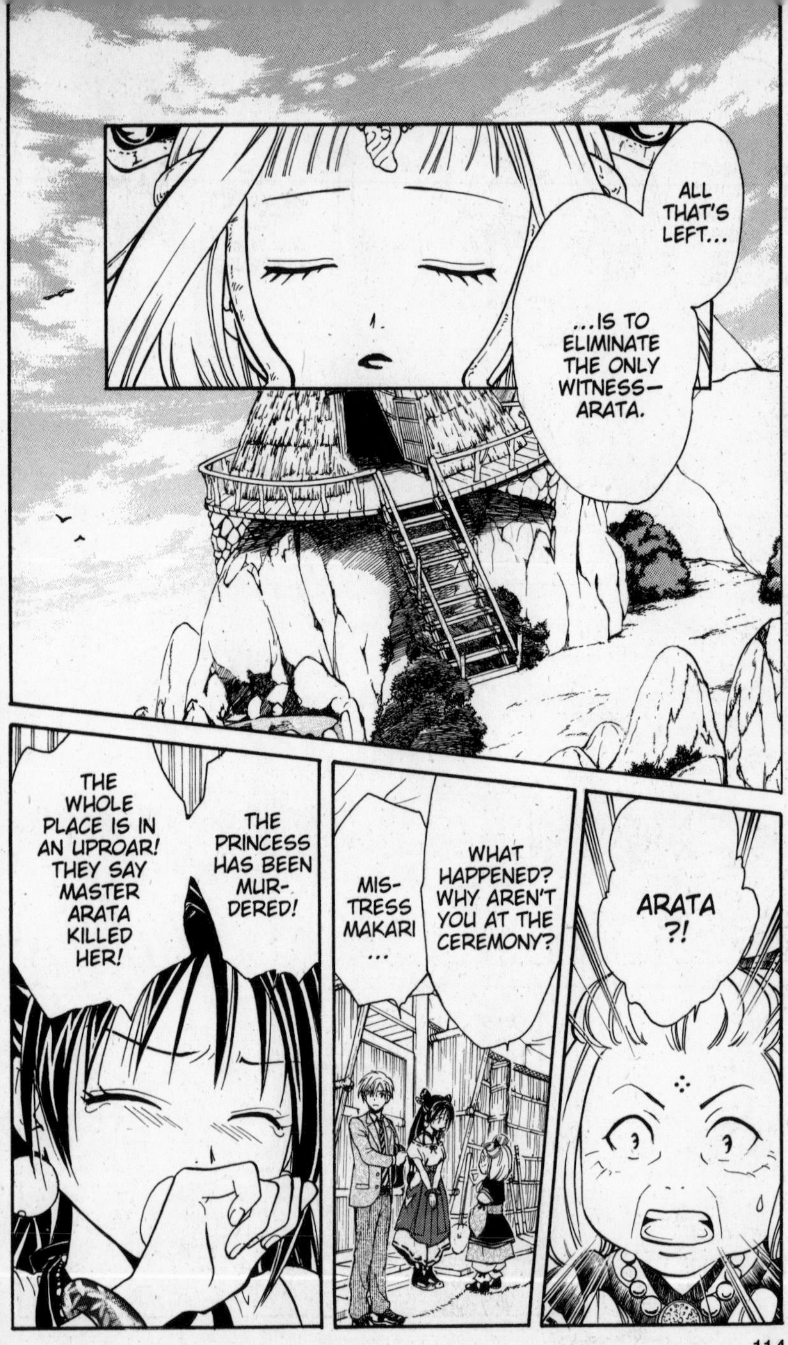
ALL THAT'S LEFT...
...IS TO ELIMINATE THE ONLY WITNESS—ARATA.
ARATA ?!
WHAT HAPPENED? WHY AREN'T YOU AT THE CEREMONY?
MISTRESS MAKARI ...
THE PRINCESS HAS BEEN MURDERED!
THE WHOLE PLACE IS IN AN UPROAR! THEY SAY MASTER ARATA KILLED HER!

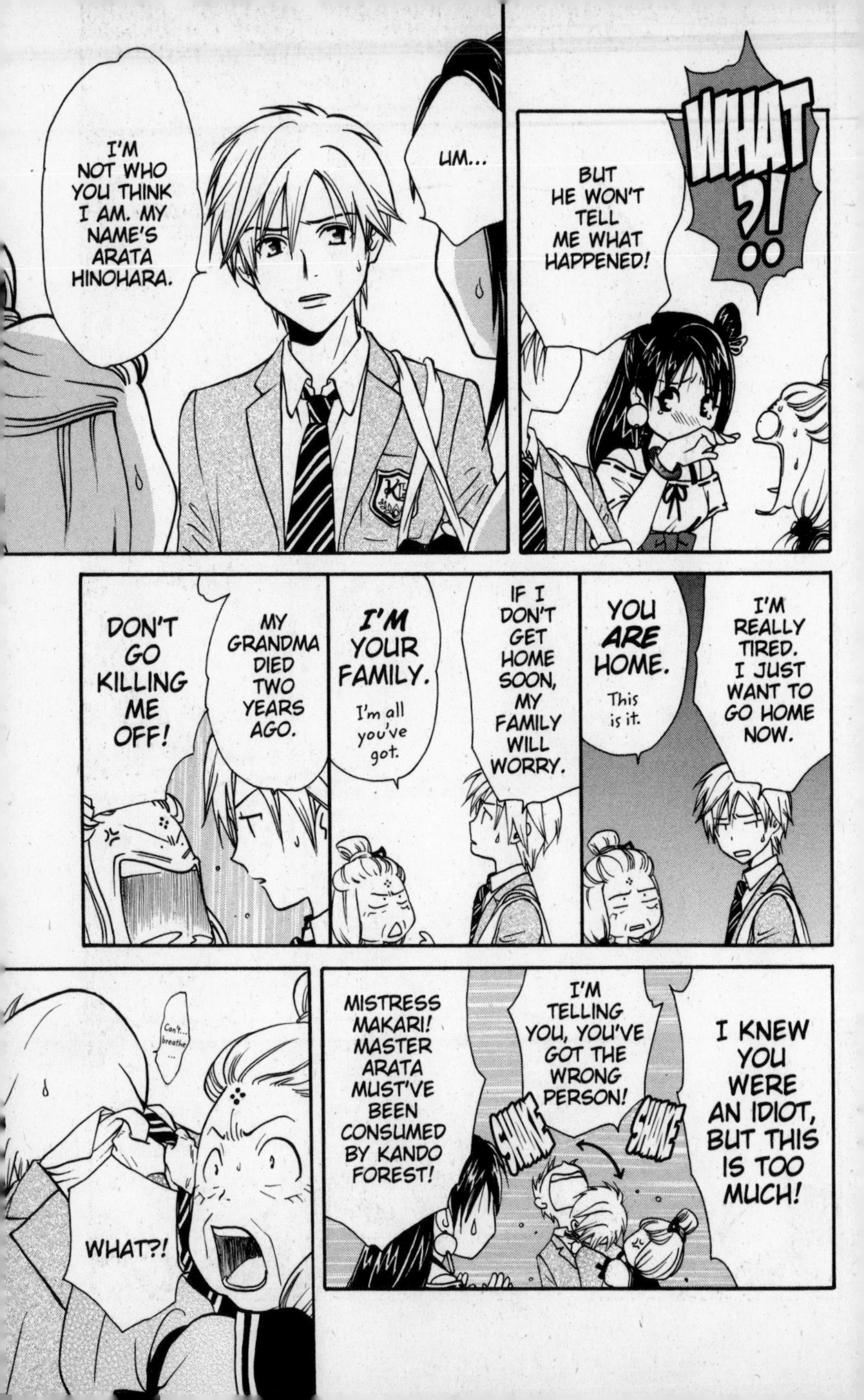

WHAT?!
BUT HE WON'T TELL ME WHAT HAPPENED!
UM...
I'M NOT WHO YOU THINK I AM. MY NAME'S ARATA HINOHARA.
I'M REALLY TIRED. I JUST WANT TO GO HOME NOW.
YOU *ARE* HOME.
This is it.
IF I DON'T GET HOME SOON, MY FAMILY WILL WORRY.
I'M YOUR FAMILY.
I'm all you've got.
MY GRANDMA DIED TWO YEARS AGO.
DON'T GO KILLING ME OFF!
I KNEW YOU WERE AN IDIOT, BUT THIS IS TOO MUCH!
SHAKE
SHAKE
I'M TELLING YOU, YOU'VE GOT THE WRONG PERSON!
MISTRESS MAKARI! MASTER ARATA MUST'VE BEEN CONSUMED BY KANDO FOREST!
Can't... breathe...
WHAT?!

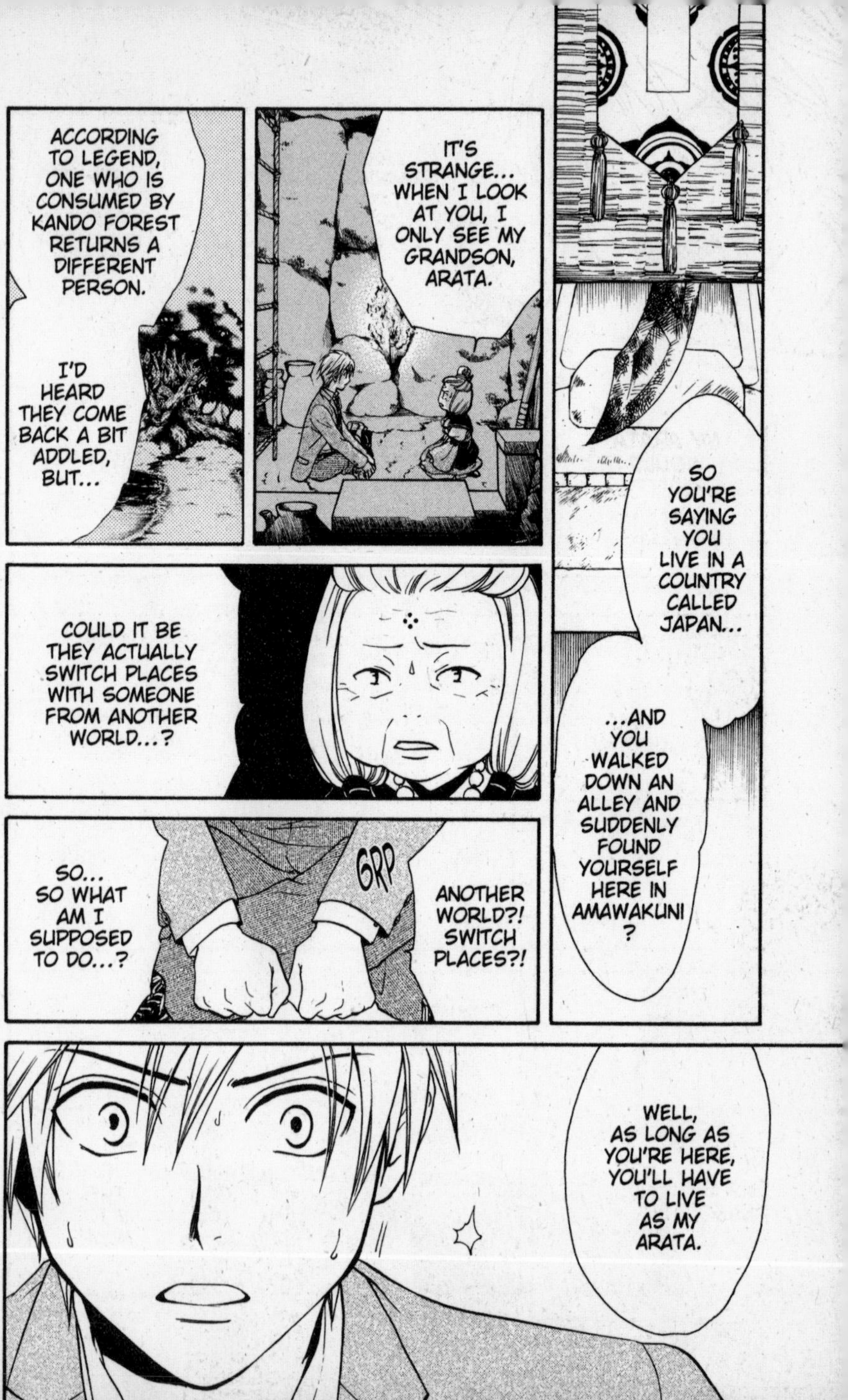
SO YOU'RE SAYING YOU LIVE IN A COUNTRY CALLED JAPAN...
...AND YOU WALKED DOWN AN ALLEY AND SUDDENLY FOUND YOURSELF HERE IN AMAWAKUNI?
IT'S STRANGE... WHEN I LOOK AT YOU, I ONLY SEE MY GRANDSON, ARATA.
ACCORDING TO LEGEND, ONE WHO IS CONSUMED BY KANDO FOREST RETURNS A DIFFERENT PERSON.
I'D HEARD THEY COME BACK A BIT ADDLED, BUT...
COULD IT BE THEY ACTUALLY SWITCH PLACES WITH SOMEONE FROM ANOTHER WORLD...?
ANOTHER WORLD?! SWITCH PLACES?!
GRP
SO... SO WHAT AM I SUPPOSED TO DO...?
WELL, AS LONG AS YOU'RE HERE, YOU'LL HAVE TO LIVE AS MY ARATA.

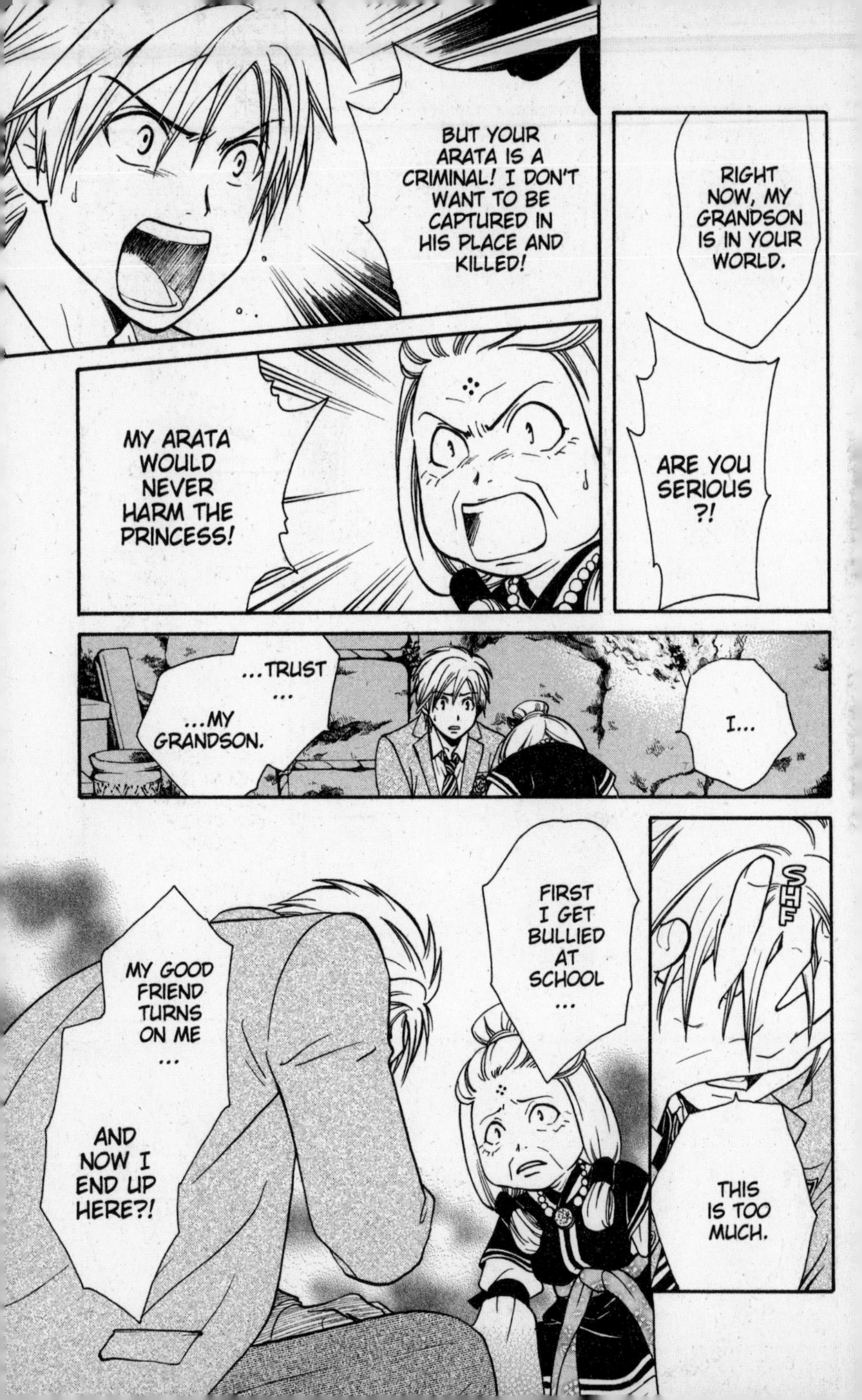
RIGHT NOW, MY GRANDSON IS IN YOUR WORLD.
ARE YOU SERIOUS?!
BUT YOUR ARATA IS A CRIMINAL! I DON'T WANT TO BE CAPTURED IN HIS PLACE AND KILLED!
MY ARATA WOULD NEVER HARM THE PRINCESS!
I...
...TRUST ...
...MY GRANDSON.
SHF
THIS IS TOO MUCH.
FIRST I GET BULLIED AT SCHOOL ...
MY GOOD FRIEND TURNS ON ME ...
AND NOW I END UP HERE?!

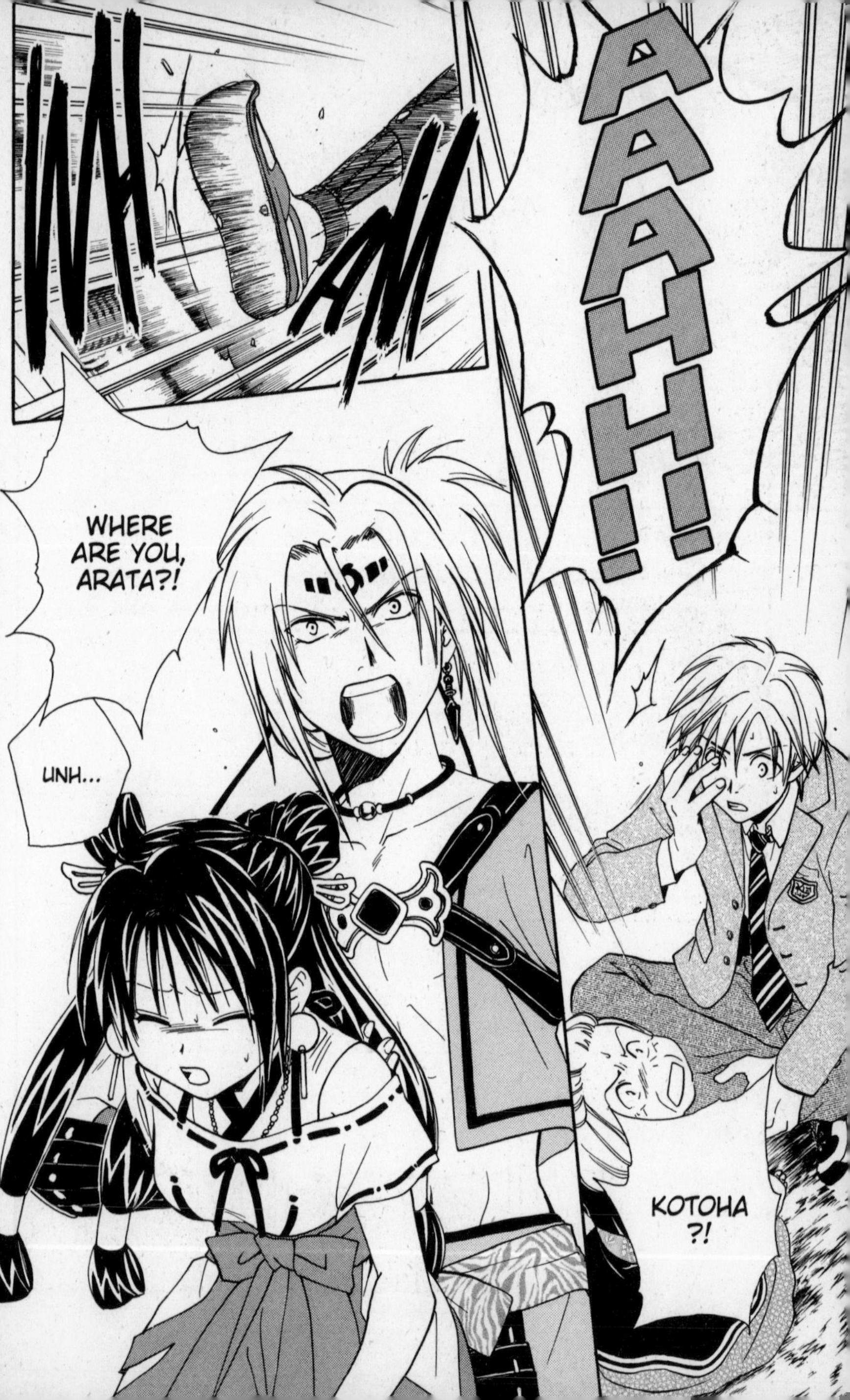
AAAHH!!
KOTOHA ?!
WHAM
WHERE ARE YOU, ARATA?!
UNH...

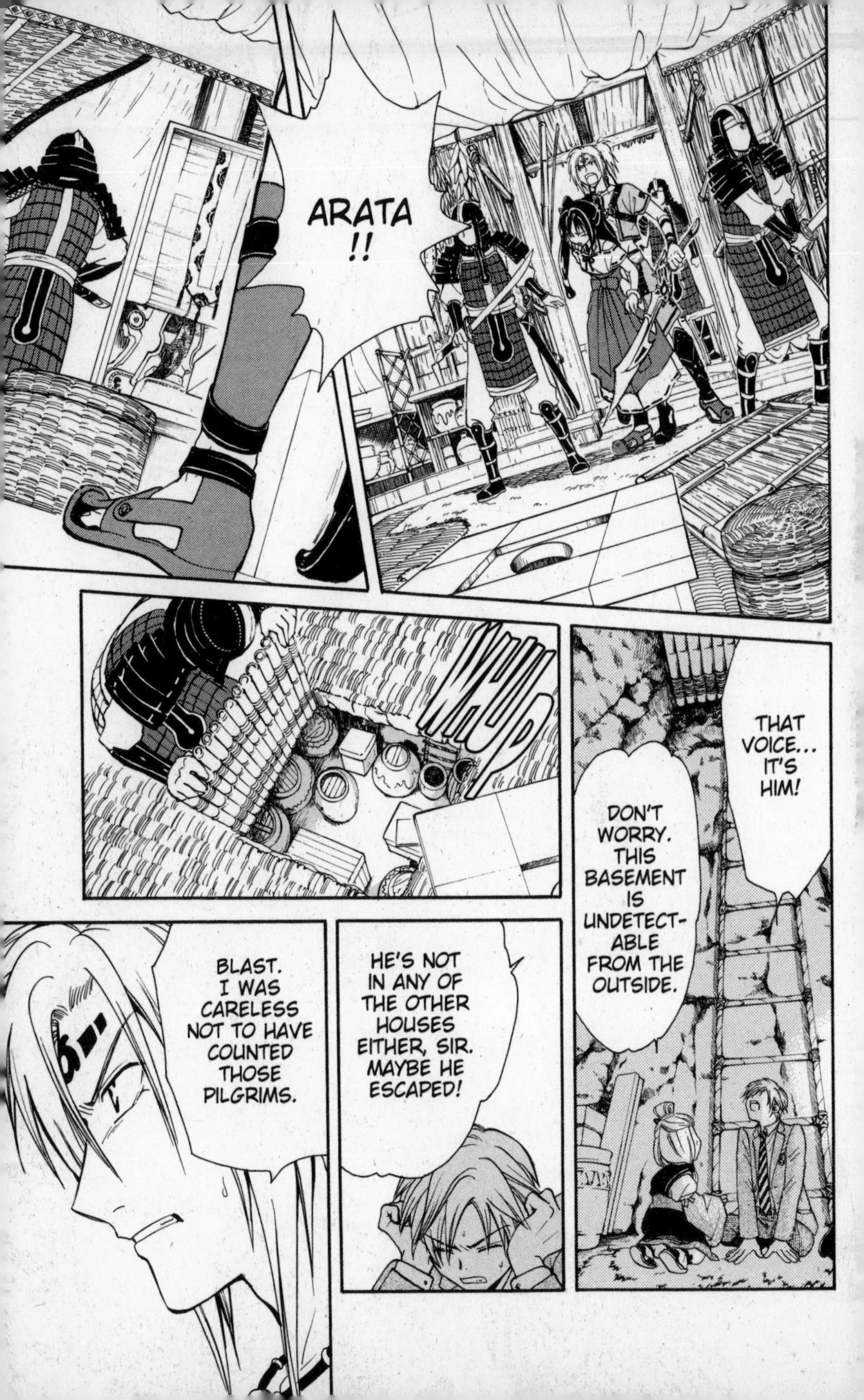
ARATA !!
THAT VOICE... IT'S HIM!
DON'T WORRY. THIS BASEMENT IS UNDETECT-ABLE FROM THE OUTSIDE.
HE'S NOT IN ANY OF THE OTHER HOUSES EITHER, SIR. MAYBE HE ESCAPED!
BLAST. I WAS CARELESS NOT TO HAVE COUNTED THOSE PILGRIMS.

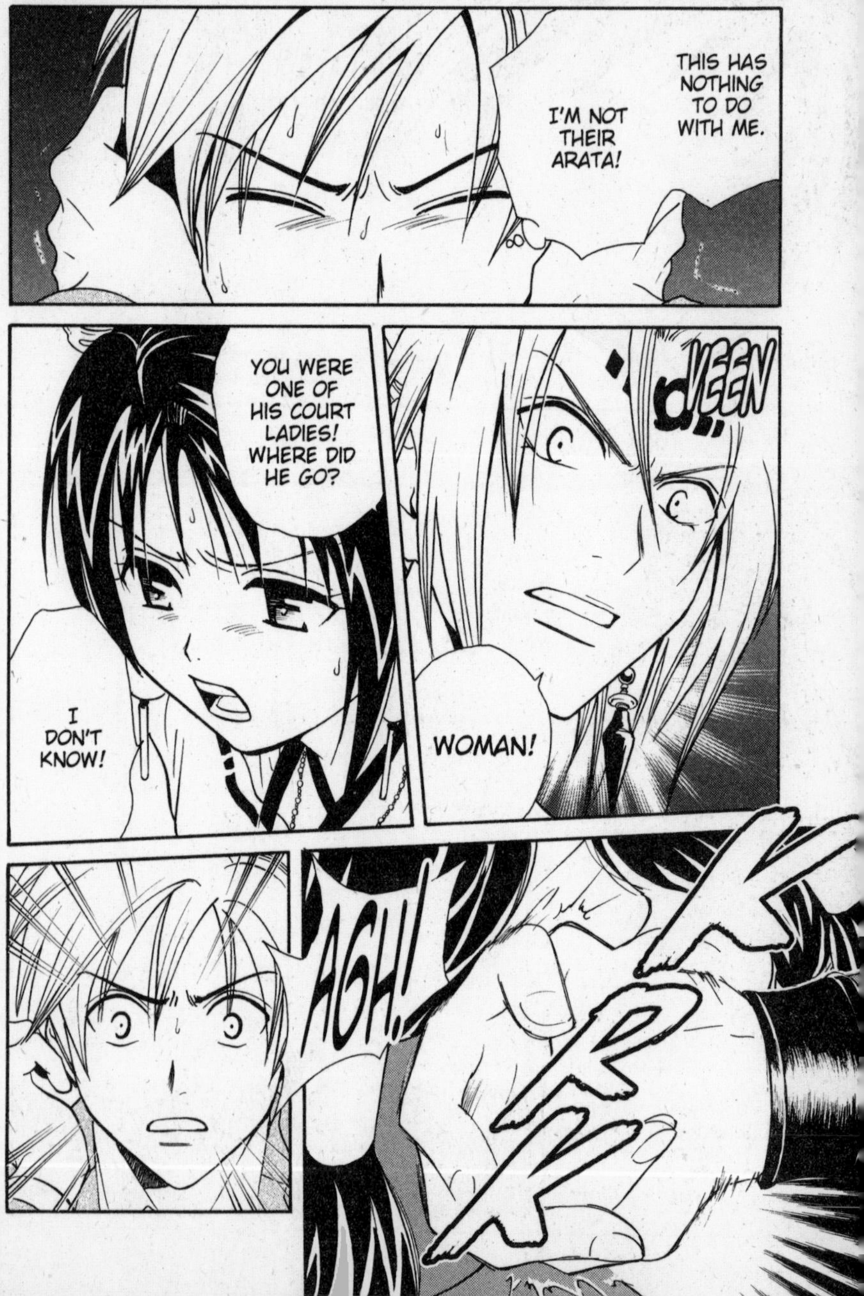
THIS HAS NOTHING TO DO WITH ME.
I'M NOT THEIR ARATA!
WOMAN!
YOU WERE ONE OF HIS COURT LADIES! WHERE DID HE GO?
I DON'T KNOW!
AGH!

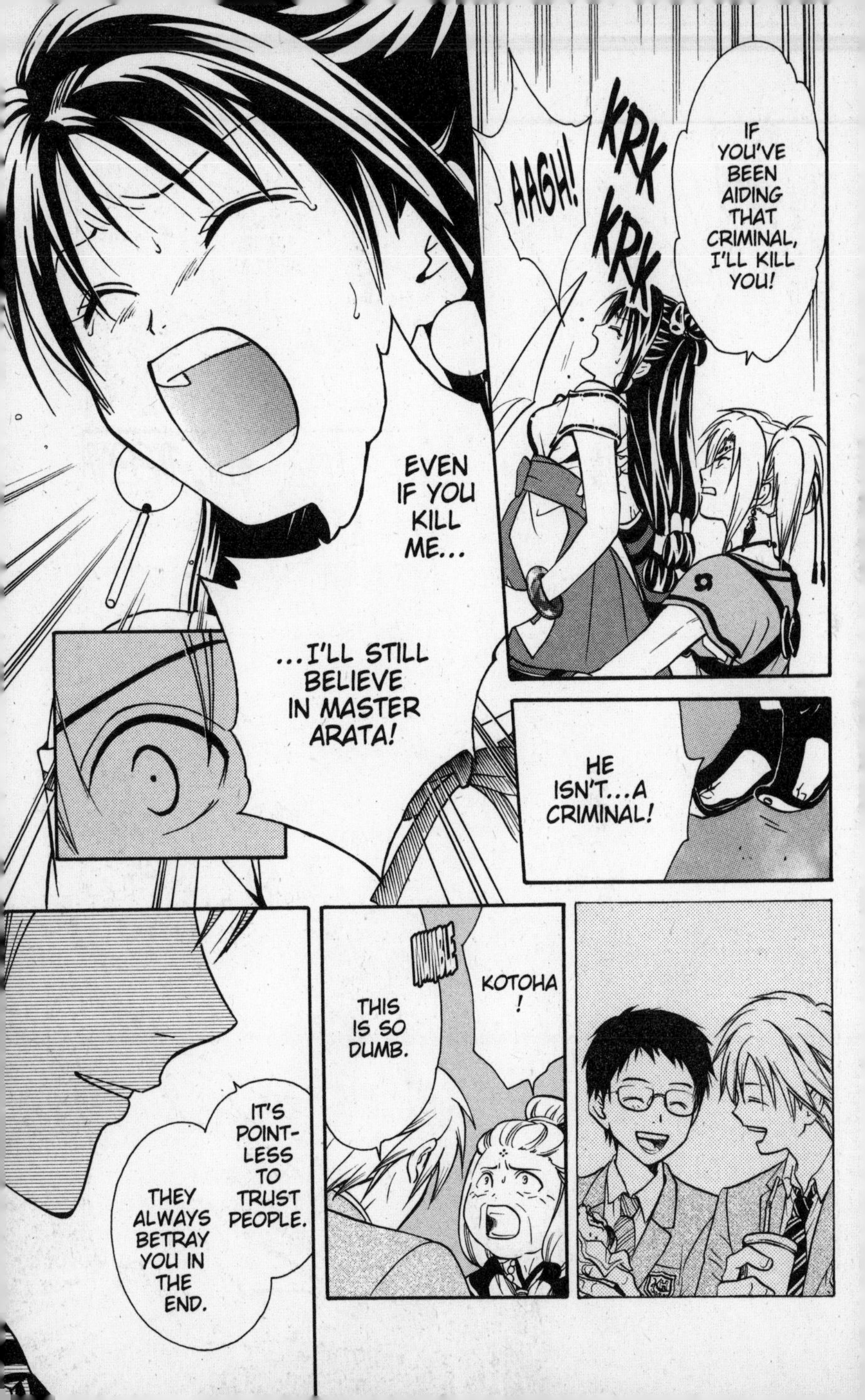
IF YOU'VE BEEN AIDING THAT CRIMINAL, I'LL KILL YOU!
KRK KRK
AAGH!
HE ISN'T...A CRIMINAL!
EVEN IF YOU KILL ME...
...I'LL STILL BELIEVE IN MASTER ARATA!
KOTOHA!
THIS IS SO DUMB.
IT'S POINTLESS TO TRUST PEOPLE.
THEY ALWAYS BETRAY YOU IN THE END.

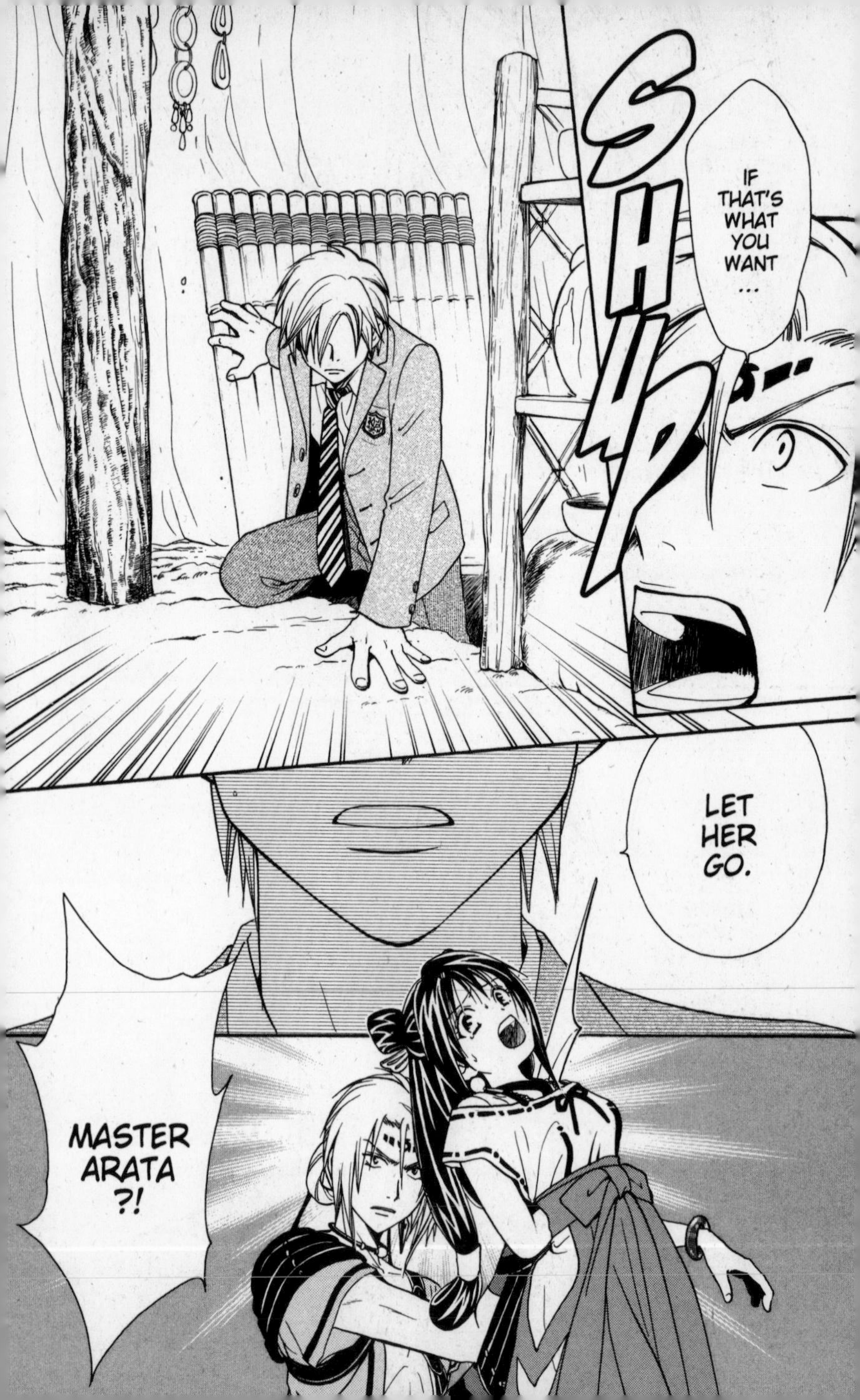
IF THAT'S WHAT YOU WANT...
SHUP
LET HER GO.
MASTER ARATA ?!

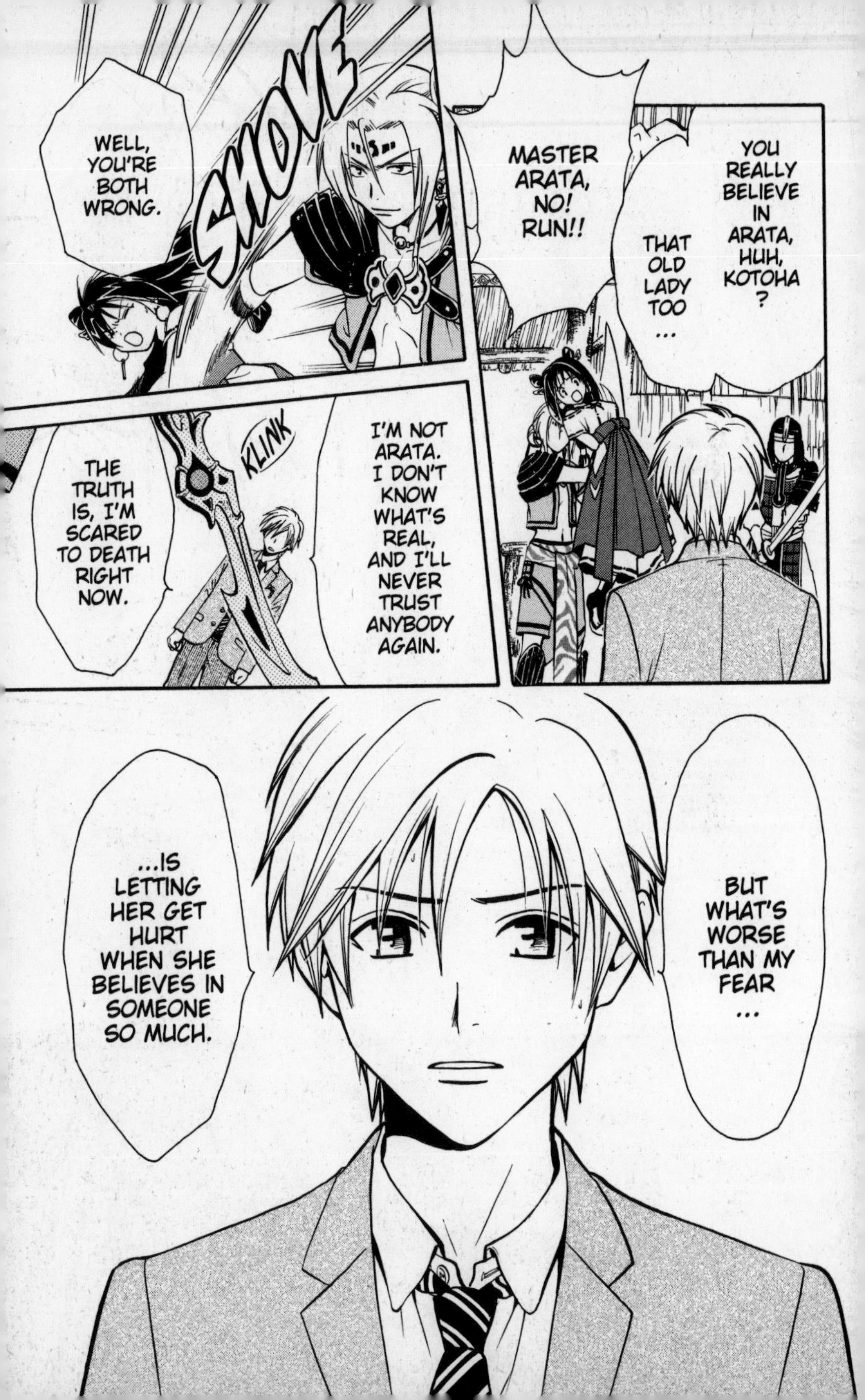
YOU REALLY BELIEVE IN ARATA, HUH, KOTOHA?
THAT OLD LADY TOO...
MASTER ARATA, NO! RUN!!
SHOVE
WELL, YOU'RE BOTH WRONG.
I'M NOT ARATA. I DON'T KNOW WHAT'S REAL, AND I'LL NEVER TRUST ANYBODY AGAIN.
KLINK
THE TRUTH IS, I'M SCARED TO DEATH RIGHT NOW.
BUT WHAT'S WORSE THAN MY FEAR...
...IS LETTING HER GET HURT WHEN SHE BELIEVES IN SOMEONE SO MUCH.

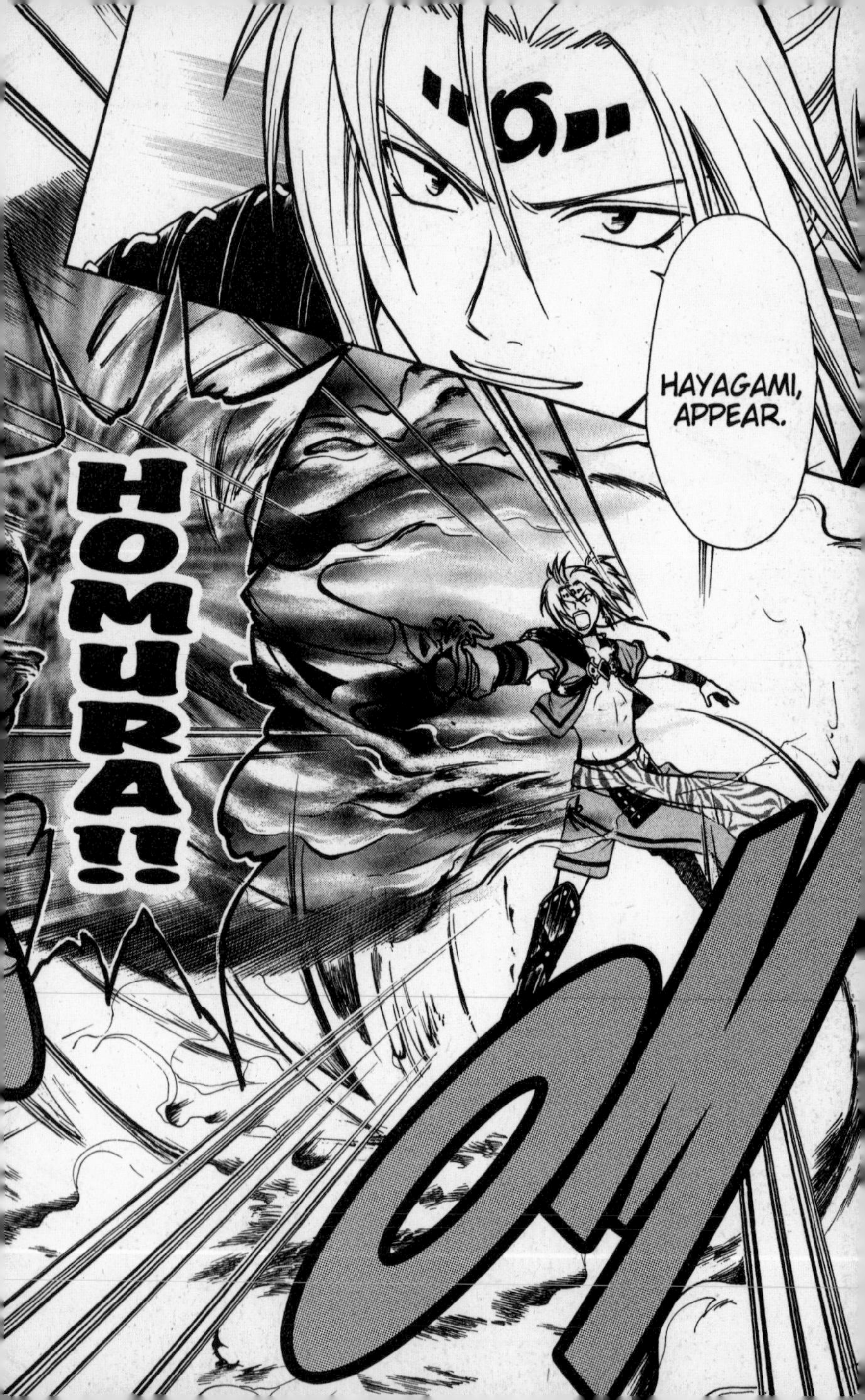
HAYAGAMI, APPEAR.
HOMURA!!

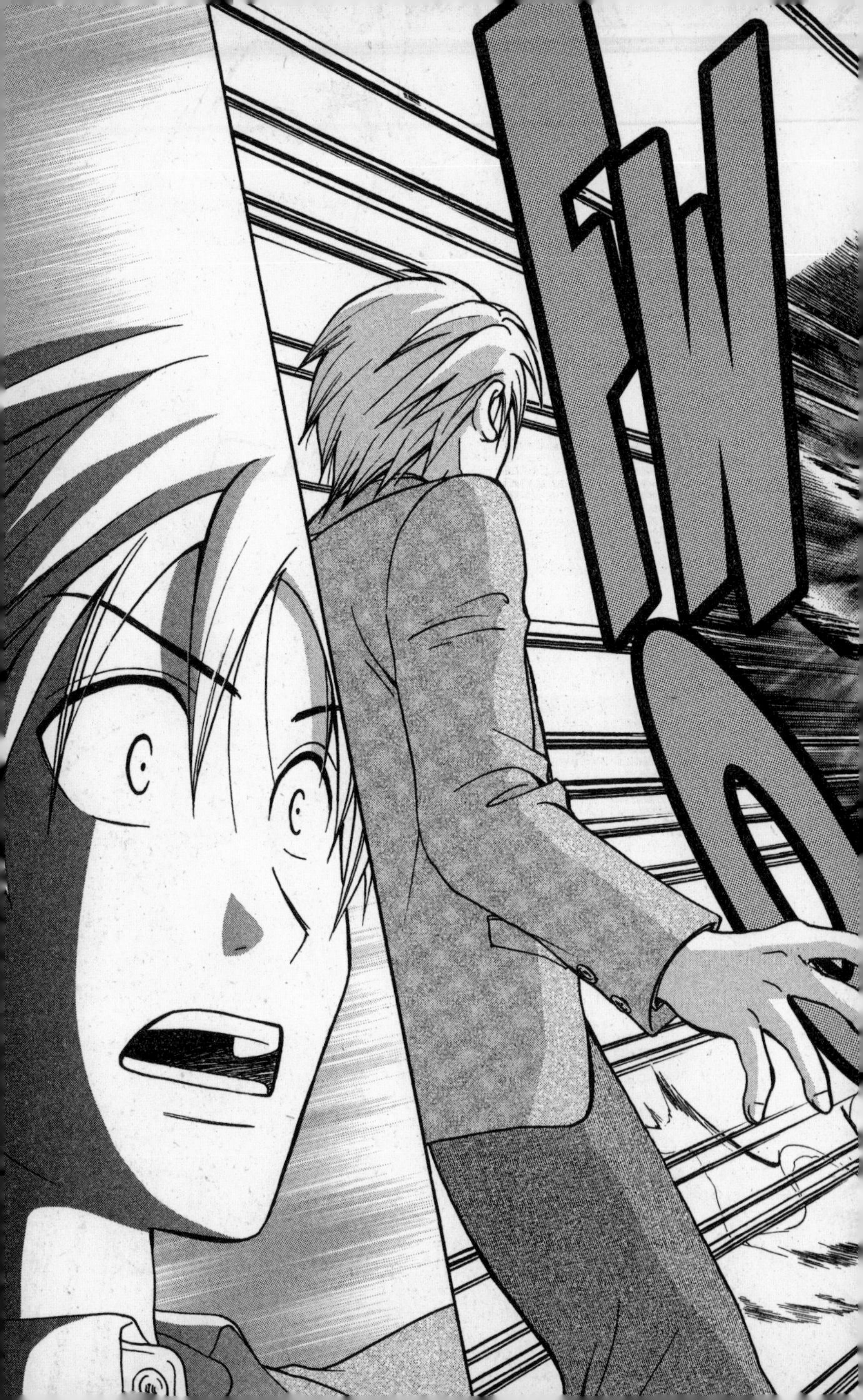

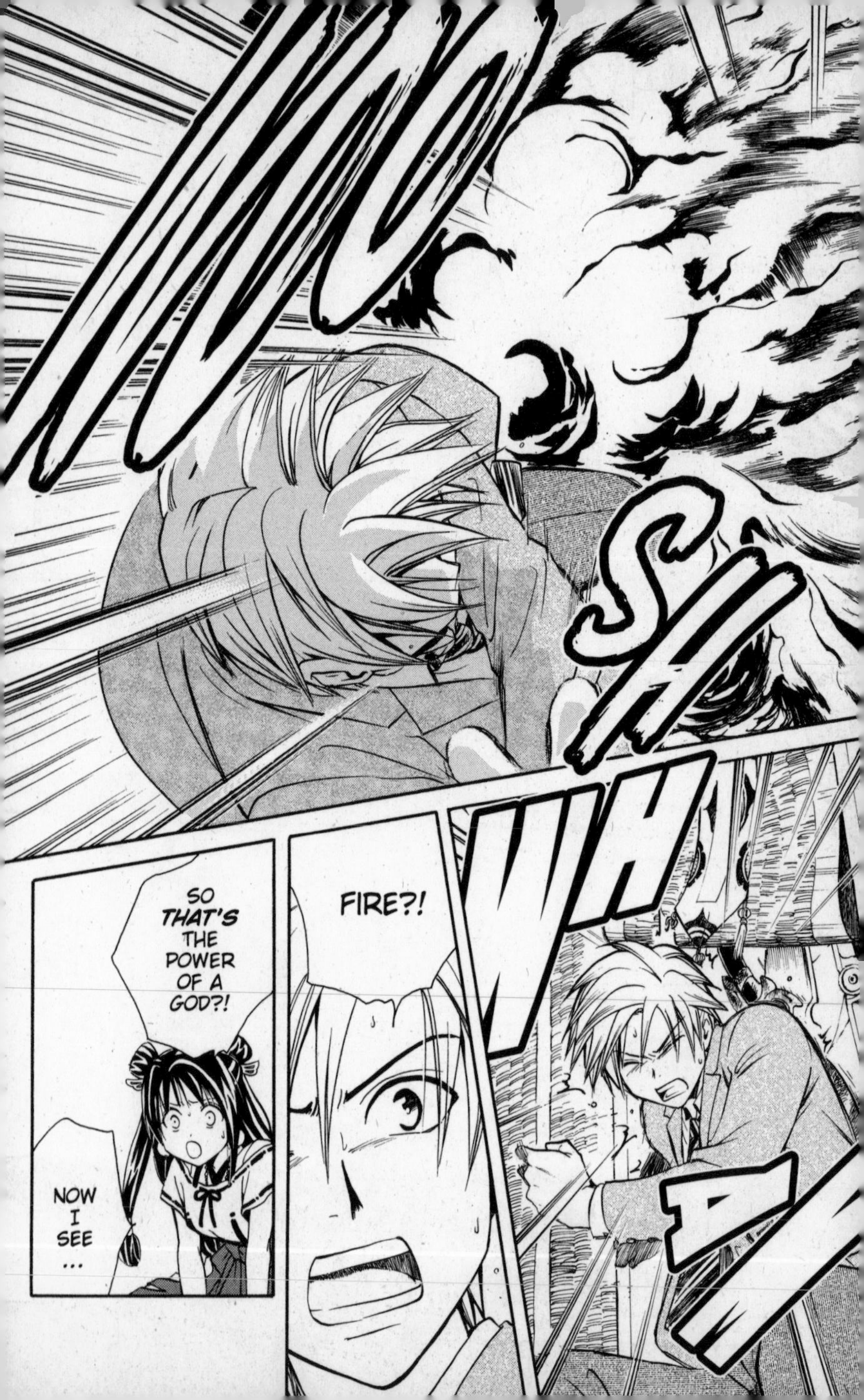
FIRE?!
SO THAT'S THE POWER OF A GOD?!
NOW I SEE ...

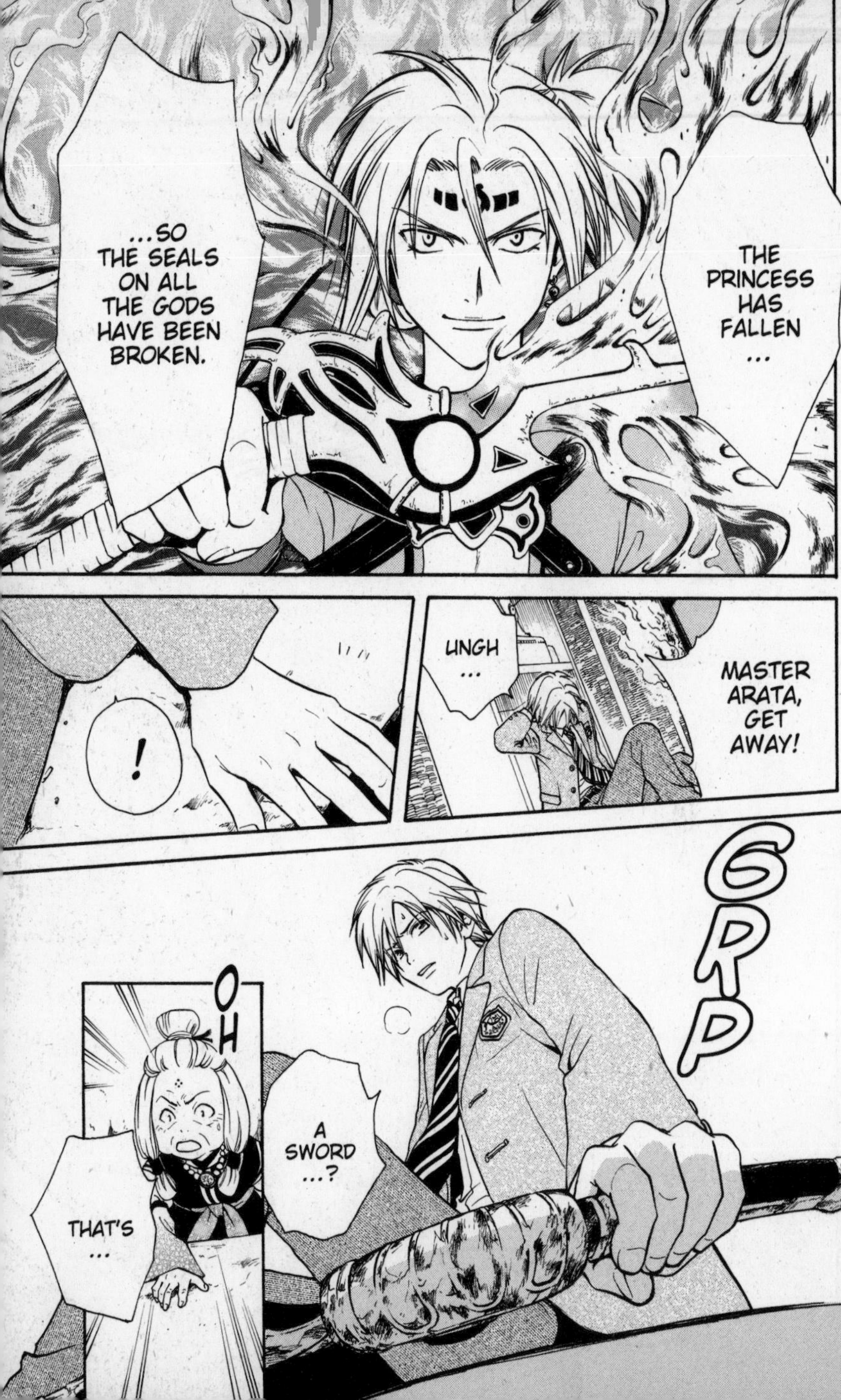
THE PRINCESS HAS FALLEN ...
...SO THE SEALS ON ALL THE GODS HAVE BEEN BROKEN.
MASTER ARATA, GET AWAY!
UNGH ...
!
GRP
A SWORD ...?
OH
THAT'S ...

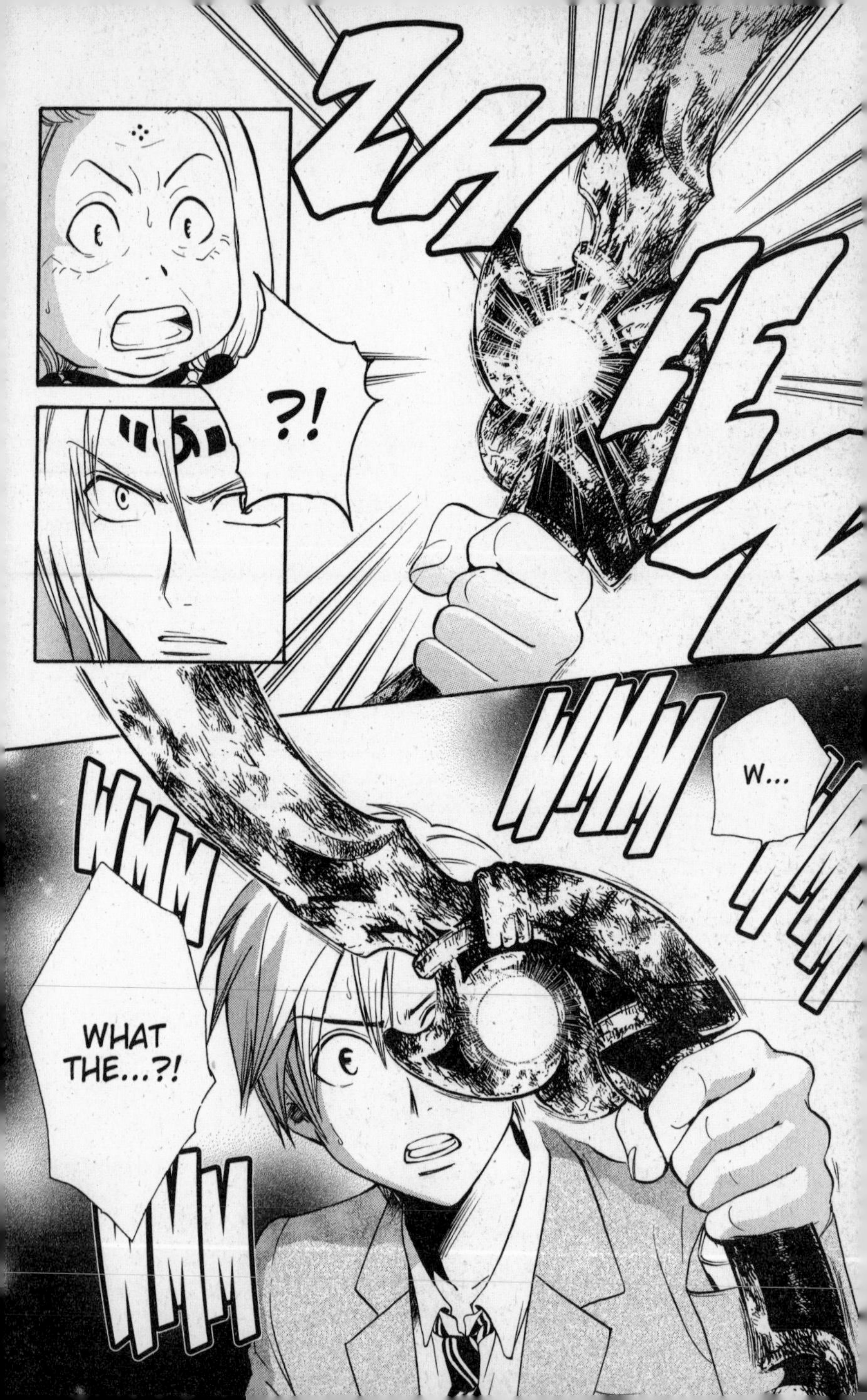
?!
W...
WMM
WMM
WHAT THE...?!
WMM

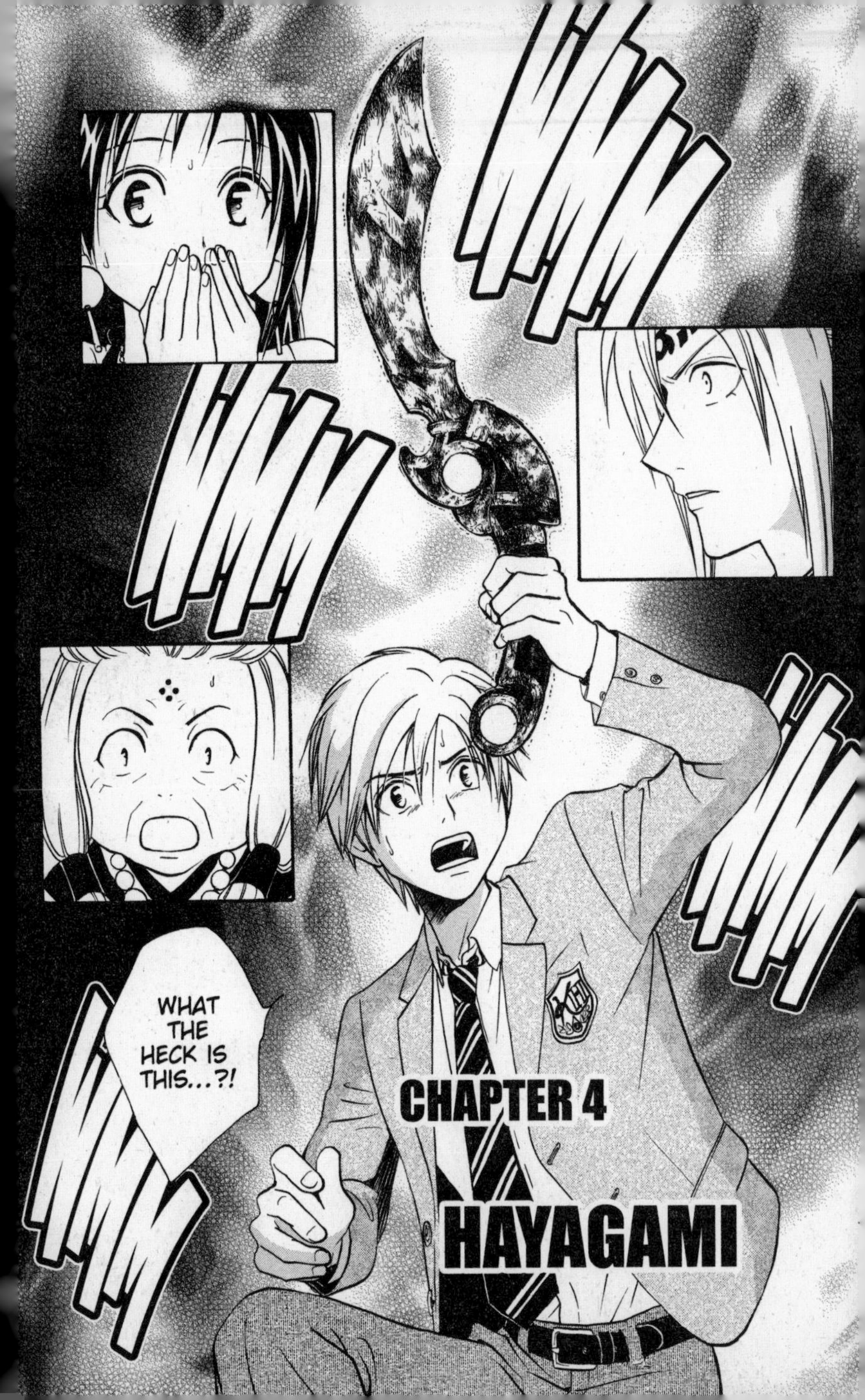
WHAT THE HECK IS THIS...?!
CHAPTER 4
HAYAGAMI

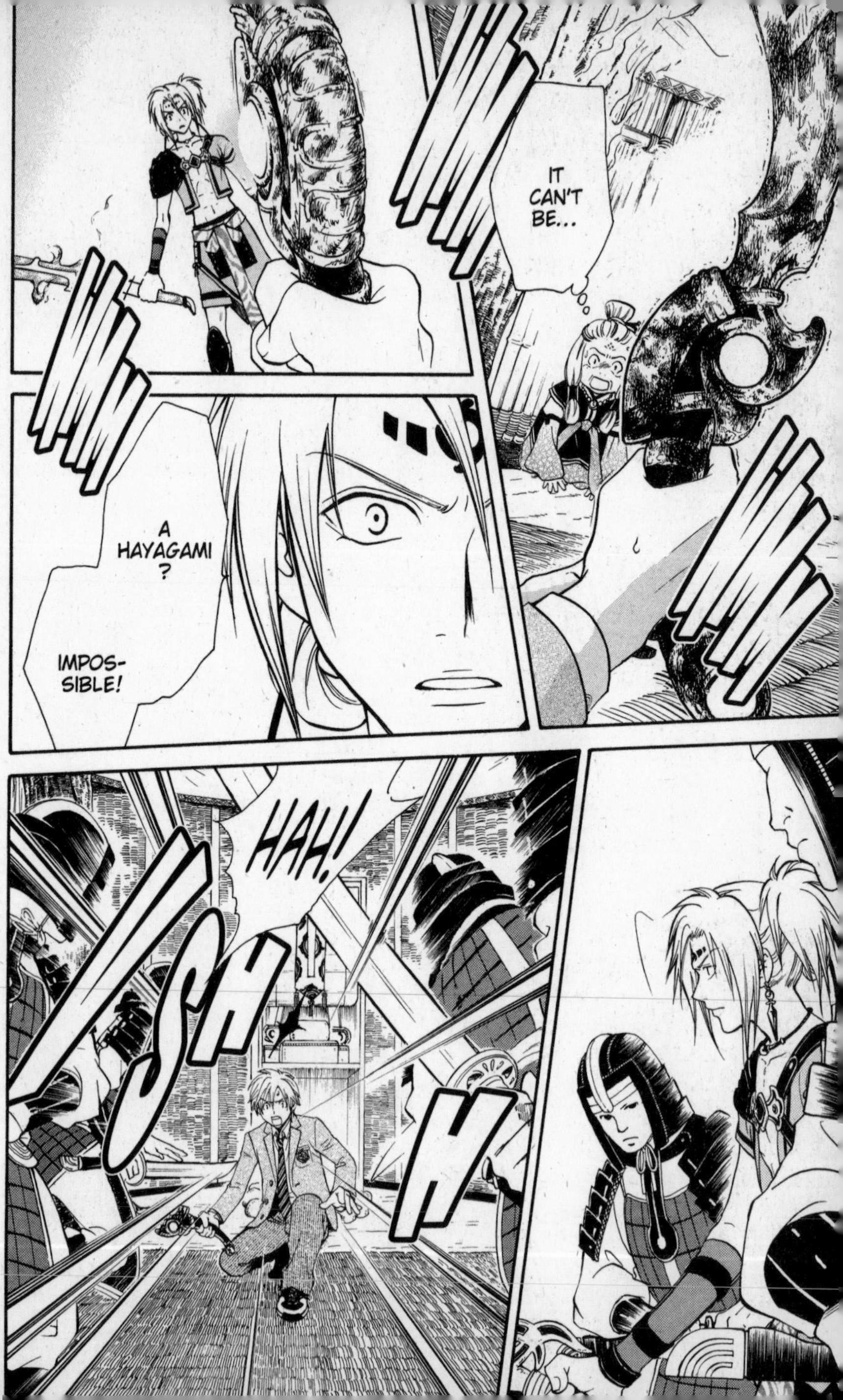
IT CAN'T BE...
A HAYAGAMI?
IMPOSSIBLE!
HAH!

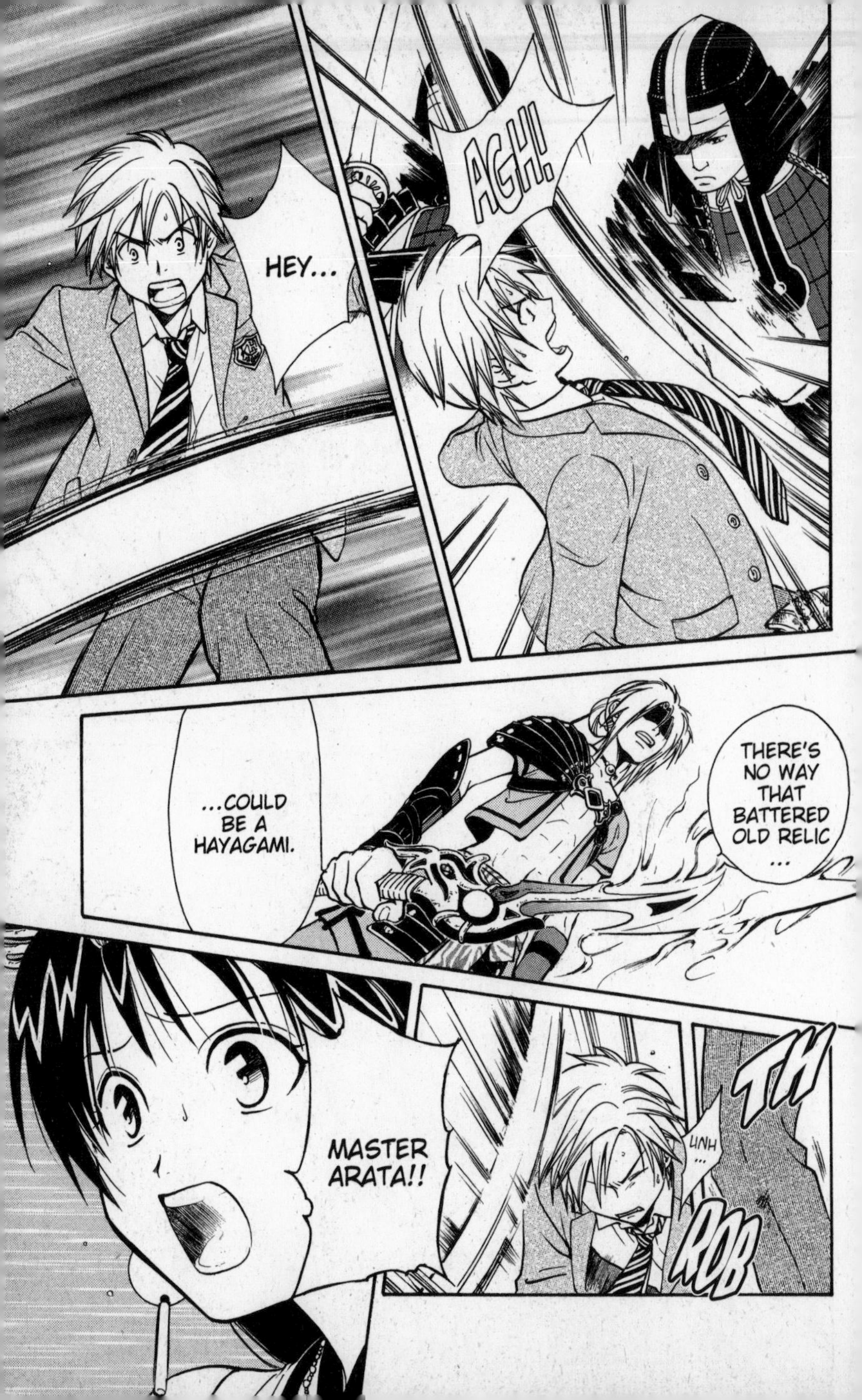
AGH!
HEY...
THERE'S NO WAY THAT BATTERED OLD RELIC ...
...COULD BE A HAYAGAMI.
TH
UNH ...
ROB
MASTER ARATA!!

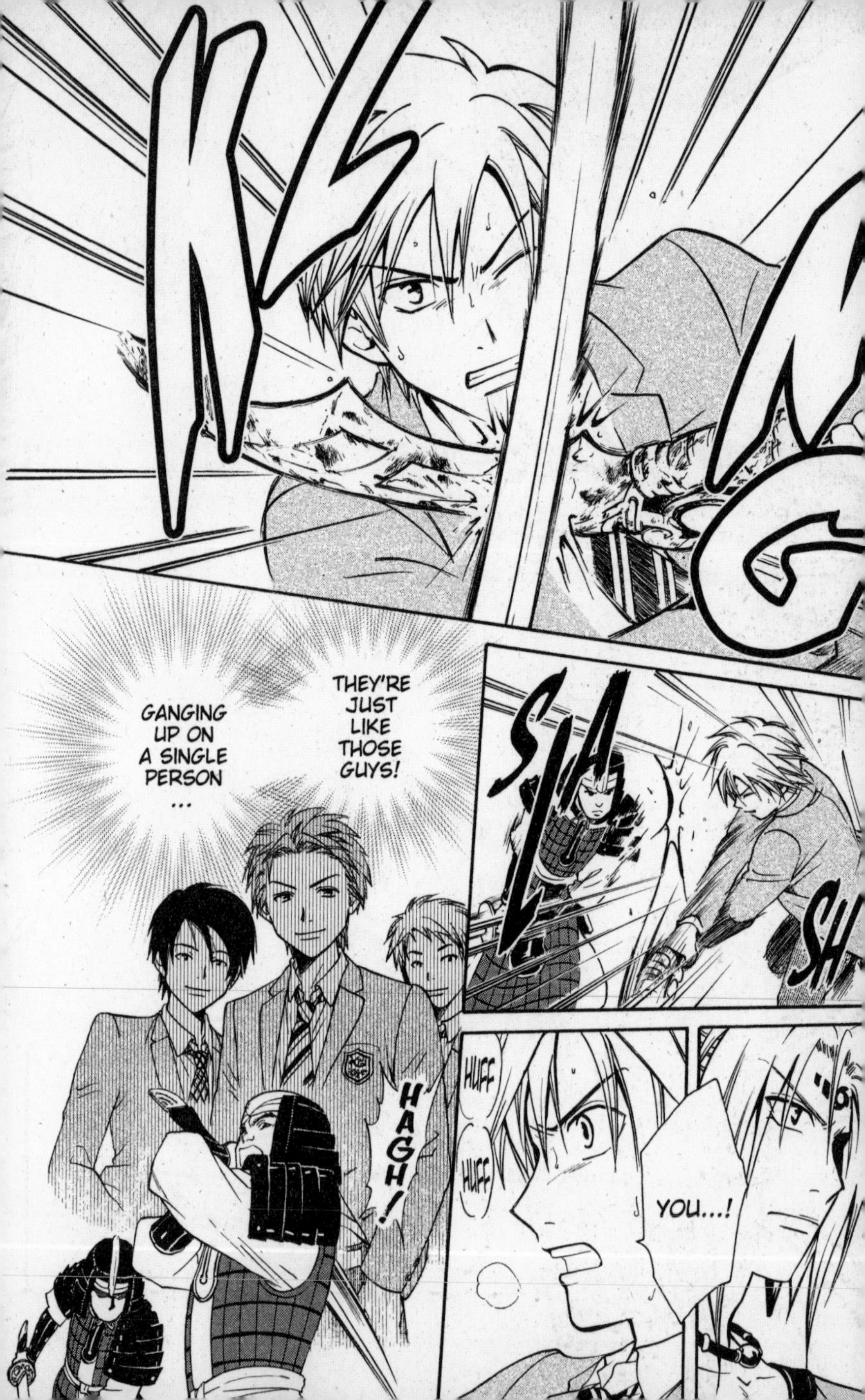

SHA
SH
HUFF
HUFF
YOU...!
THEY'RE JUST LIKE THOSE GUYS!
GANGING UP ON A SINGLE PERSON ...
HAGH!

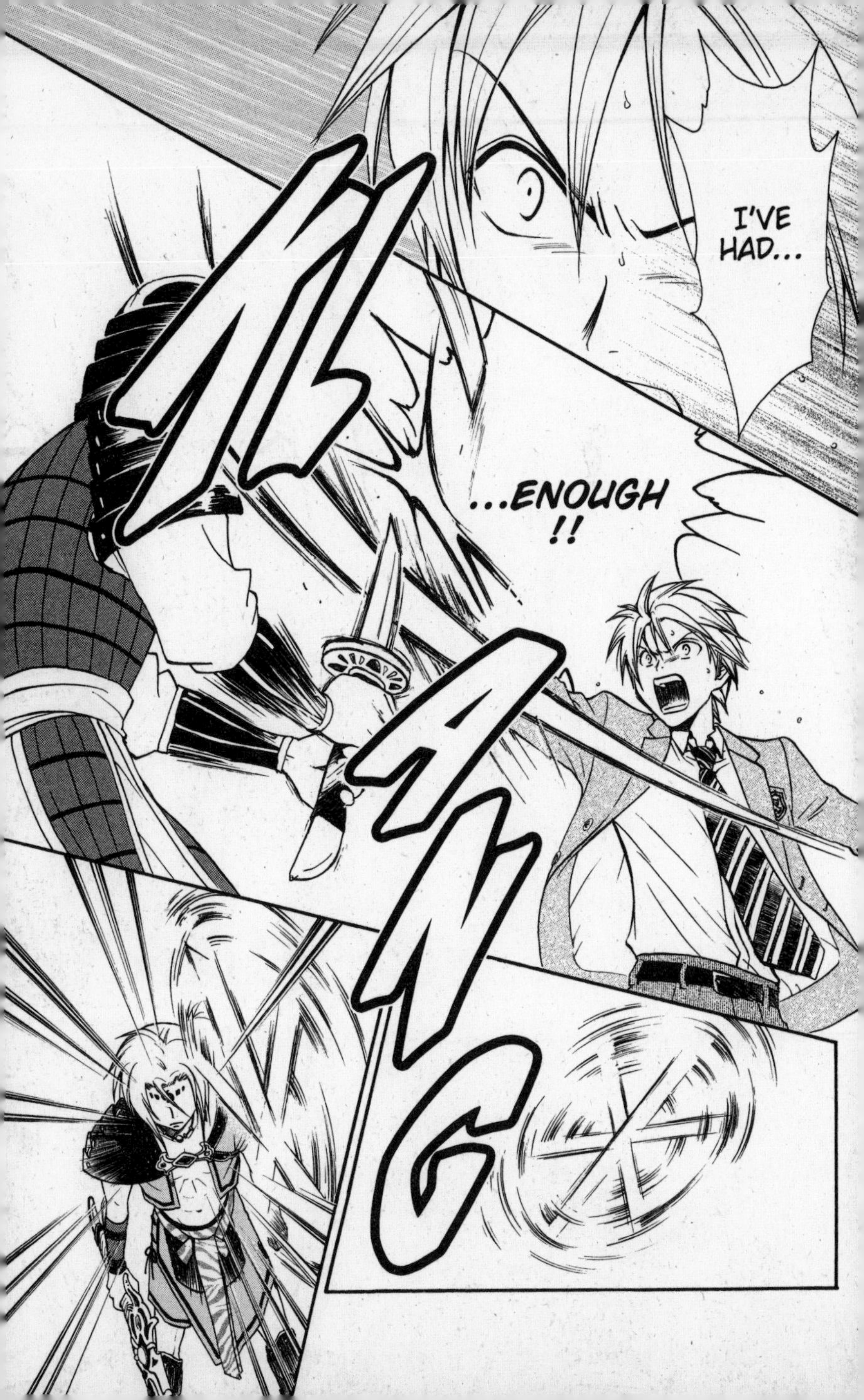
I'VE HAD...
...ENOUGH !!

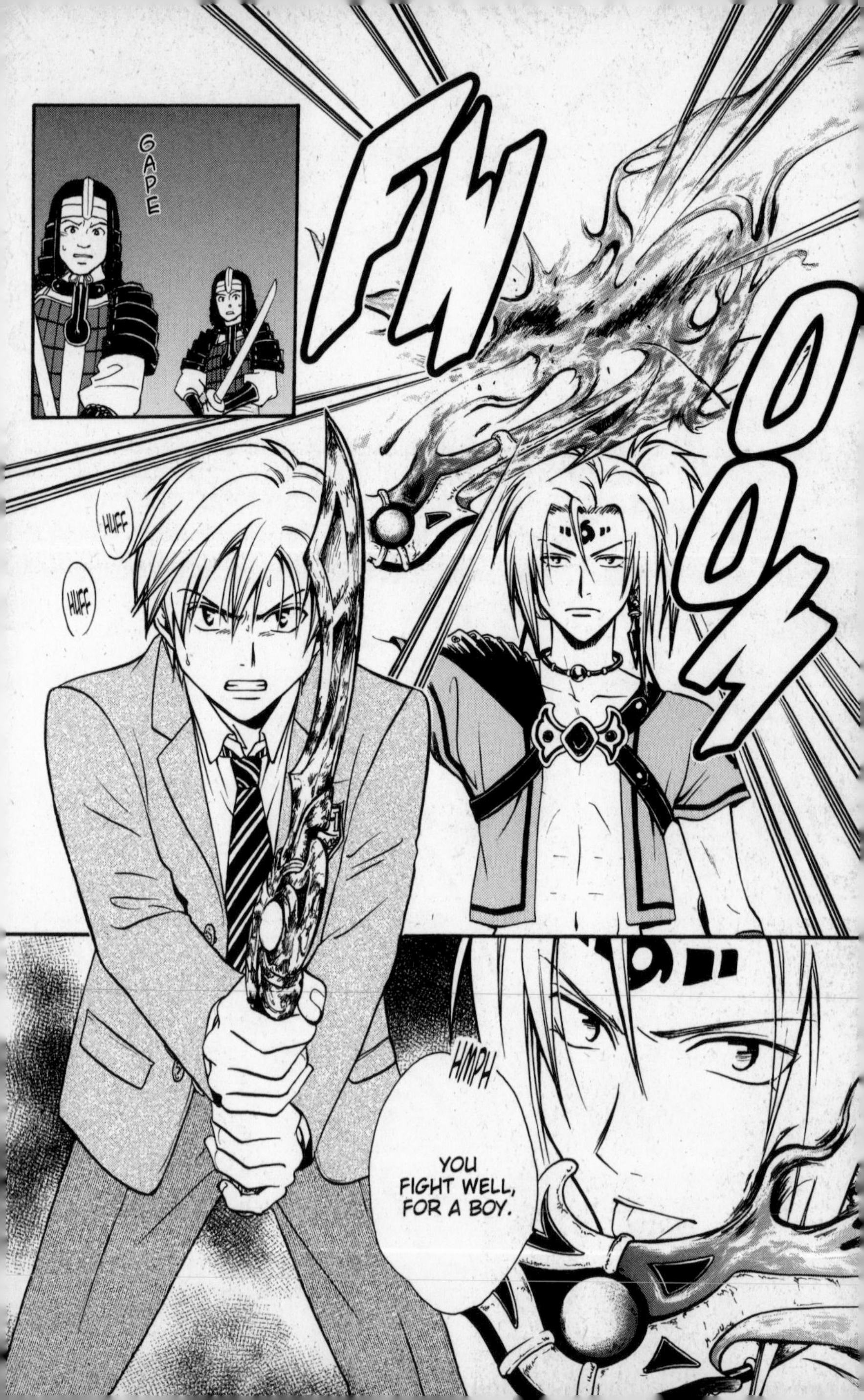
FWOOOM
GAPE
HUFF
HUFF
HMPH
YOU FIGHT WELL, FOR A BOY.

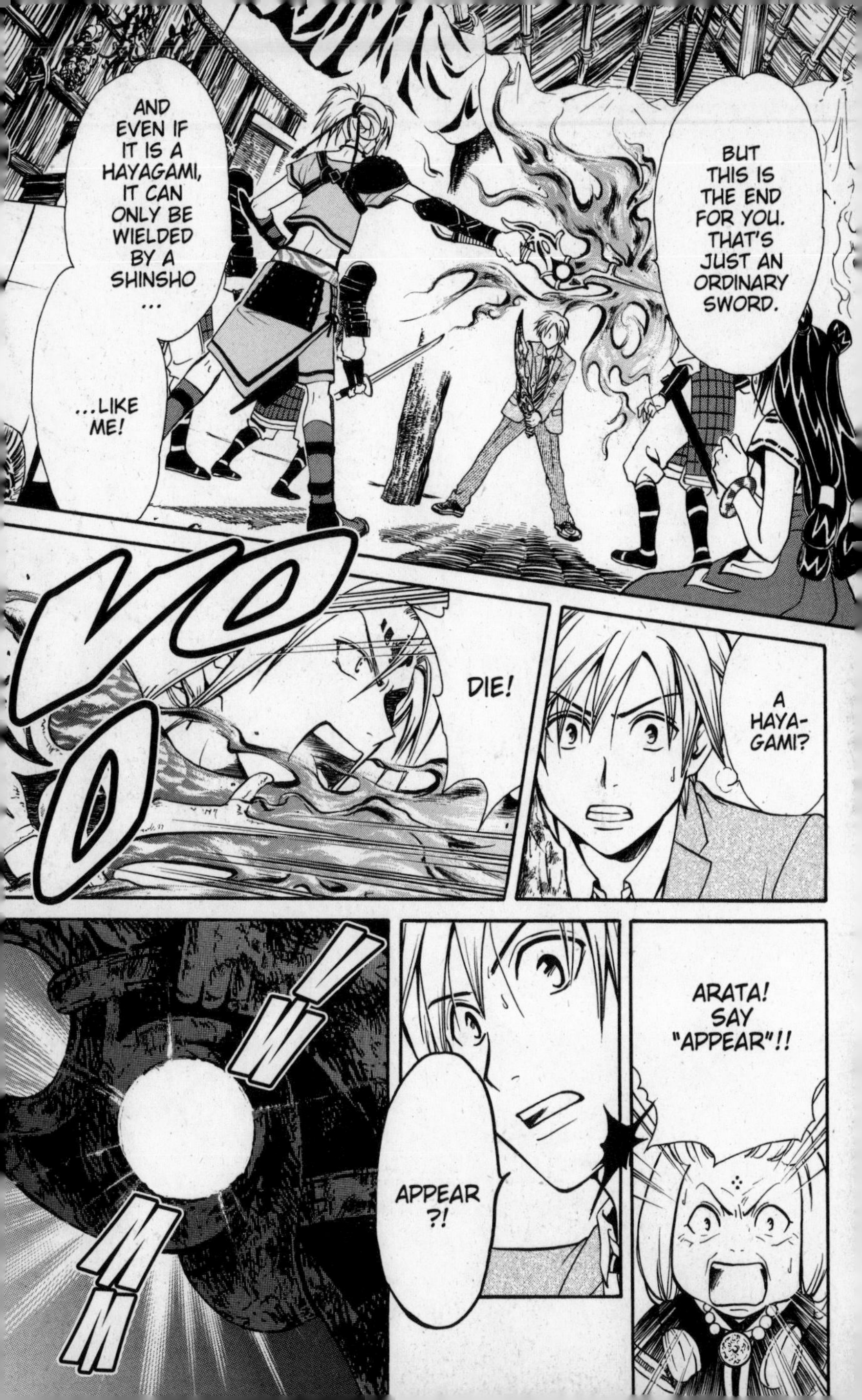
BUT THIS IS THE END FOR YOU. THAT'S JUST AN ORDINARY SWORD.
AND EVEN IF IT IS A HAYAGAMI, IT CAN ONLY BE WIELDED BY A SHINSHO...
...LIKE ME!
A HAYA-GAMI?
DIE!
VOO
ARATA! SAY "APPEAR"!!
APPEAR?!

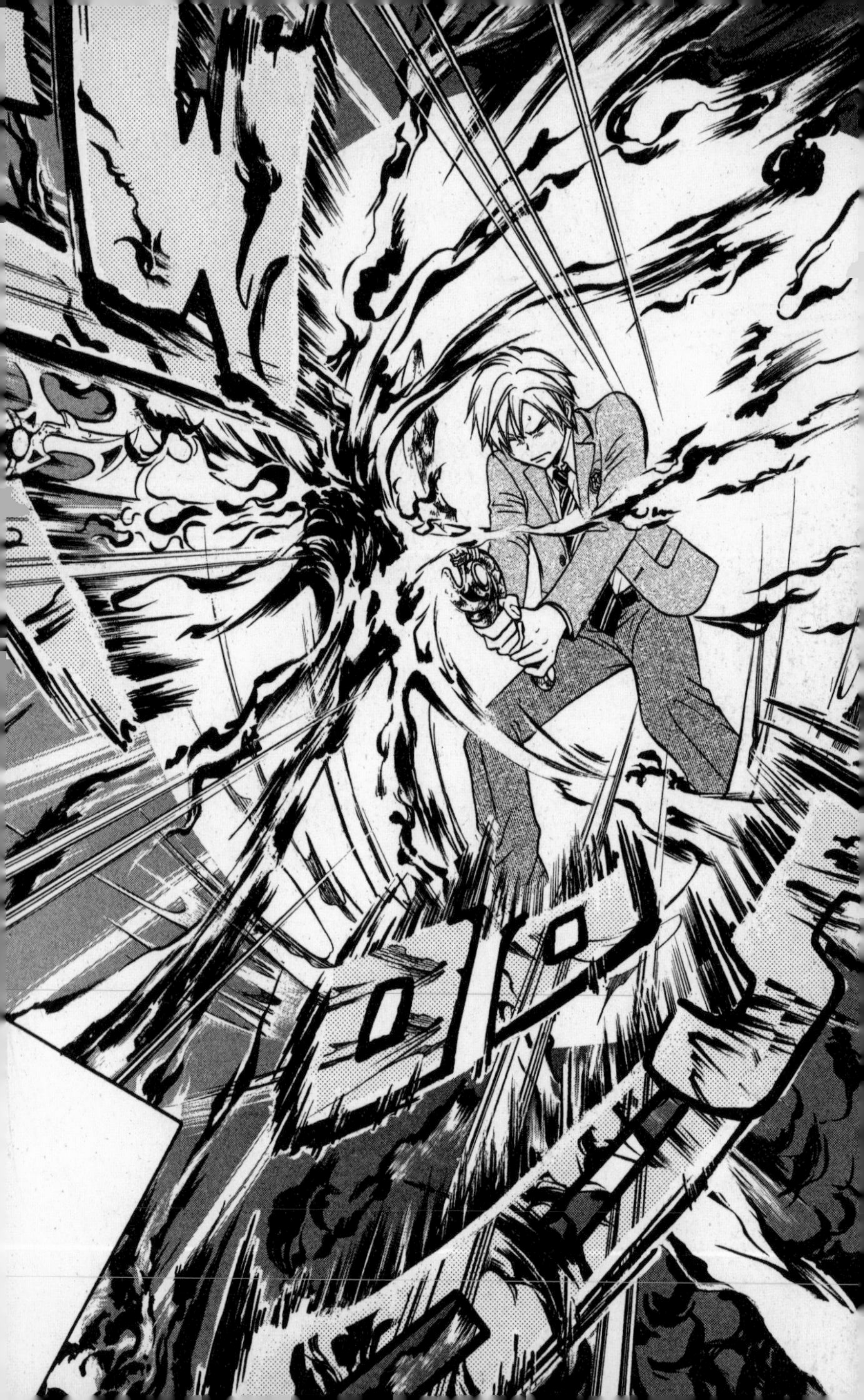

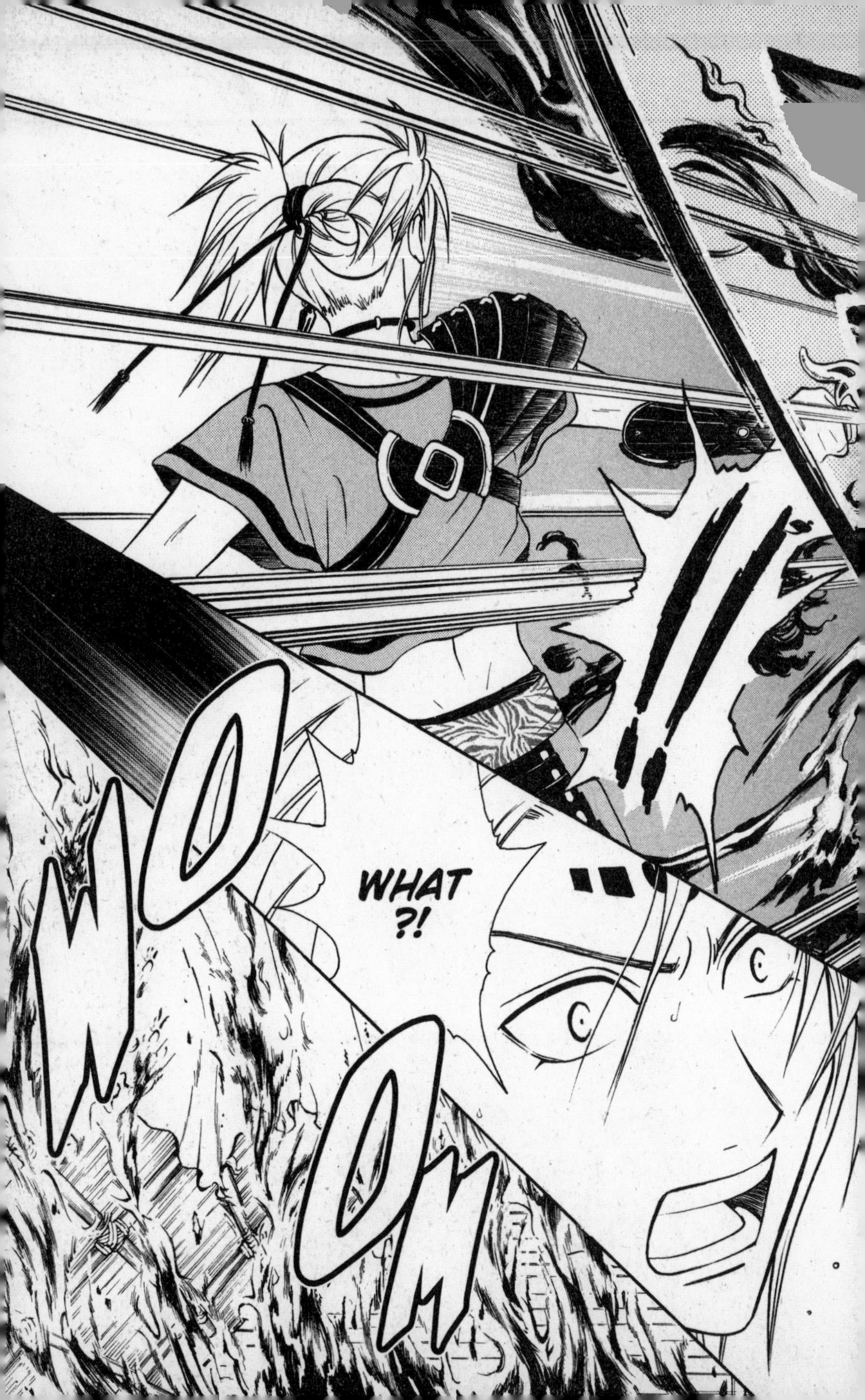
WHAT ?!
WOOOM

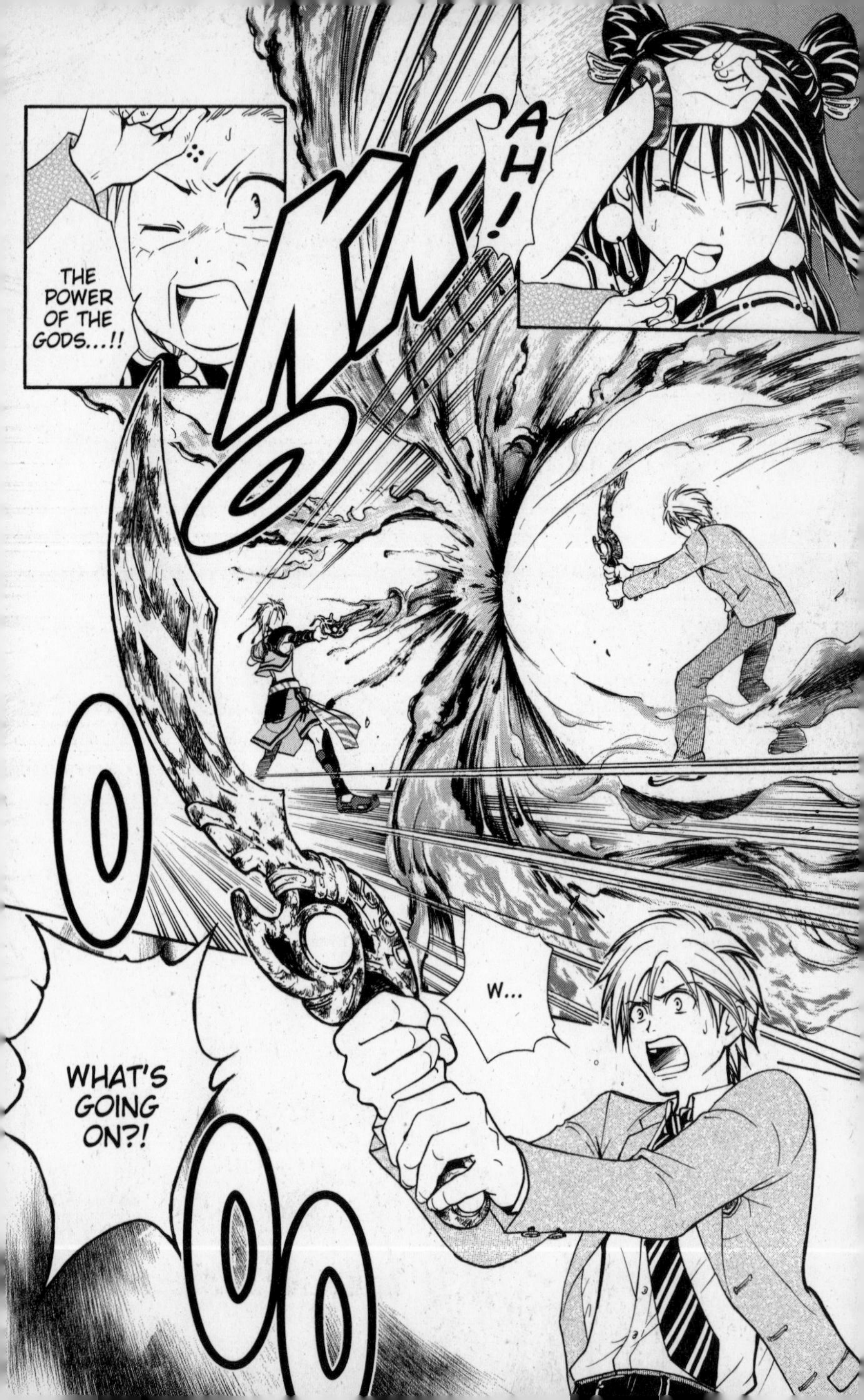
AH!
THE POWER OF THE GODS...!!
W...
WHAT'S GOING ON?!

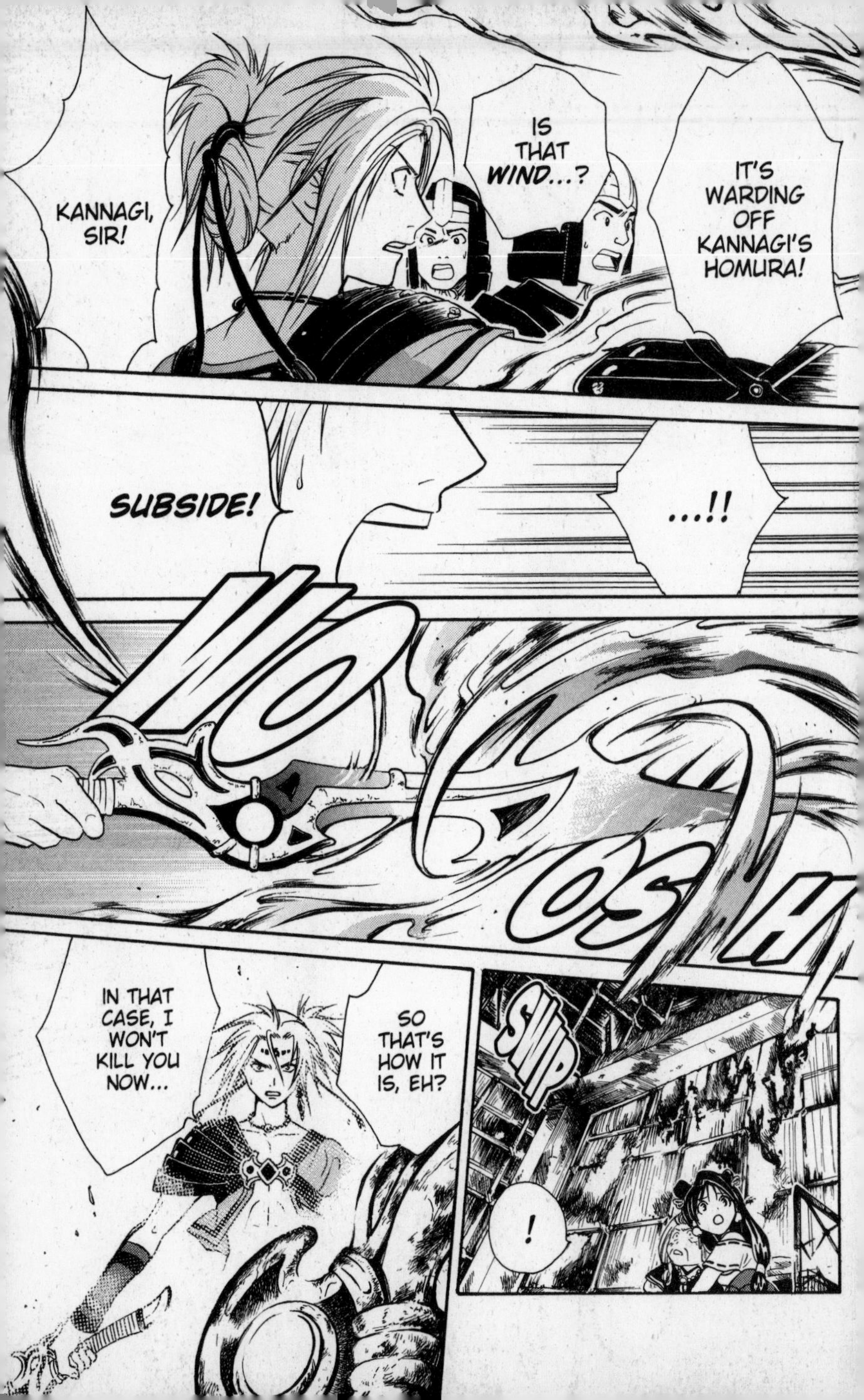
IT'S WARDING OFF KANNAGI'S HOMURA!
IS THAT *WIND*...?
KANNAGI, SIR!
...!!
SUBSIDE!
WHOOSH
SWIP
!
SO THAT'S HOW IT IS, EH?
IN THAT CASE, I WON'T KILL YOU NOW...

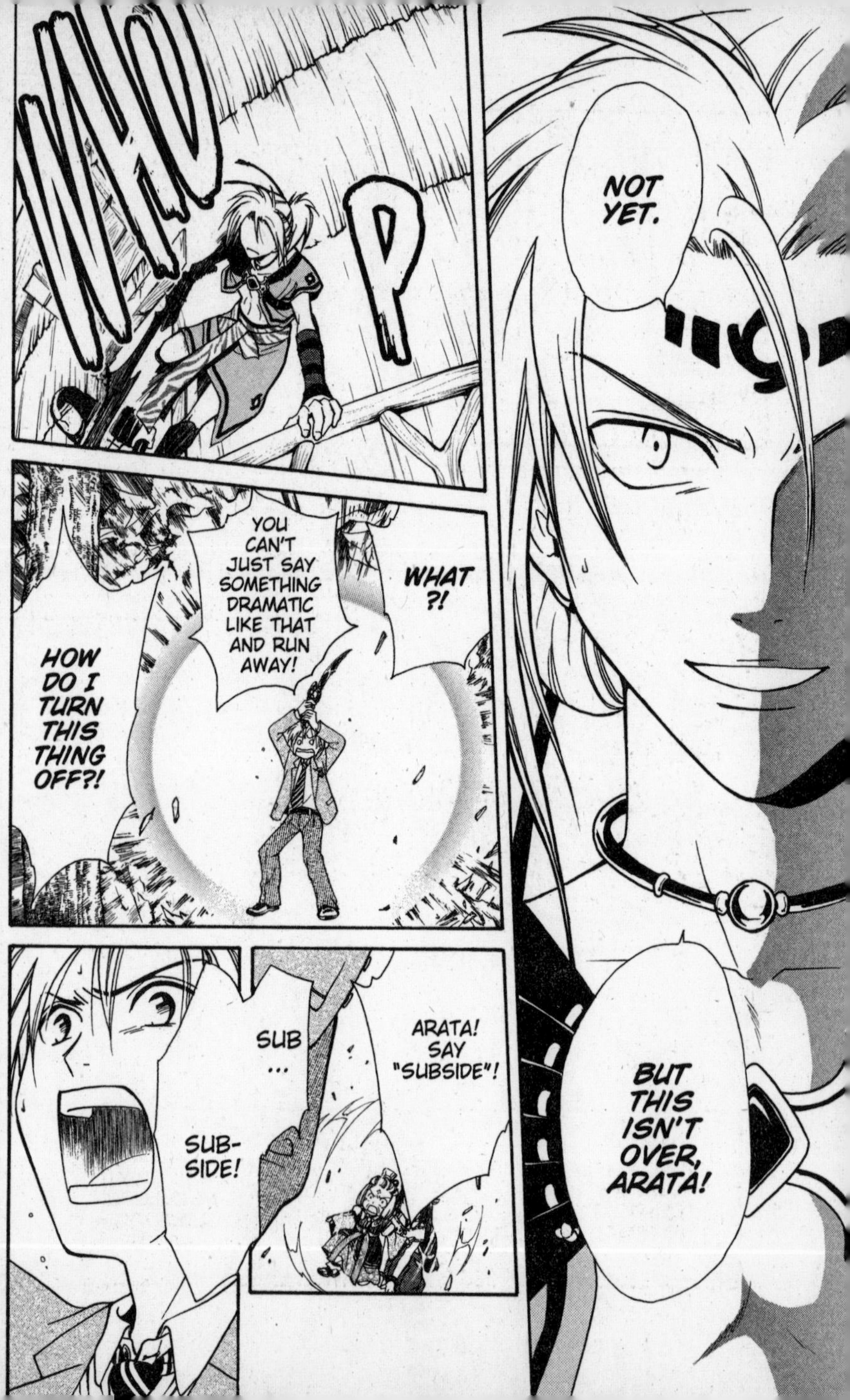
NOT YET.
BUT THIS ISN'T OVER, ARATA!
WHAT?!
YOU CAN'T JUST SAY SOMETHING DRAMATIC LIKE THAT AND RUN AWAY!
HOW DO I TURN THIS THING OFF?!
ARATA! SAY "SUBSIDE"!
SUB...
SUB-SIDE!

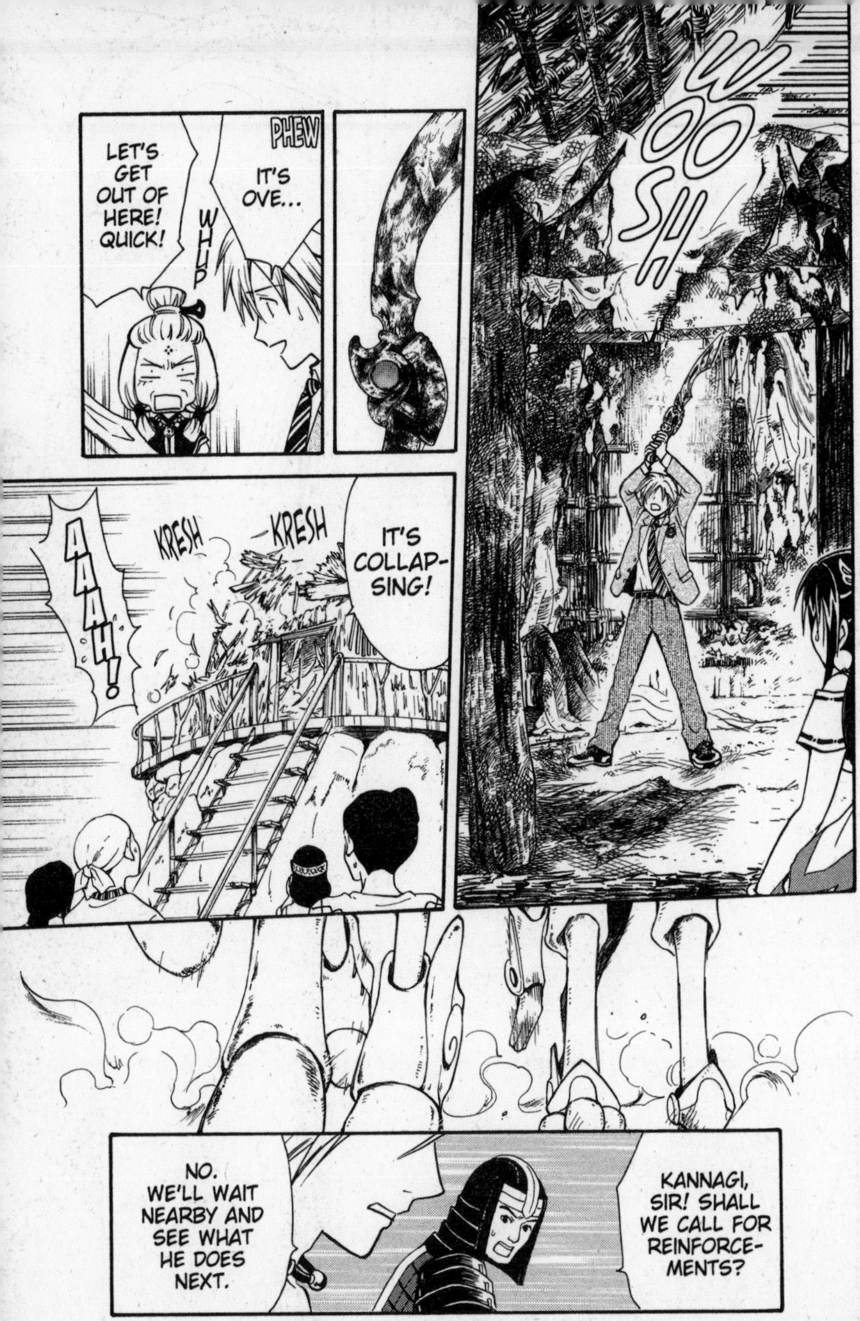
WOOOSH
PHEW
IT'S OVE...
WHUP
LET'S GET OUT OF HERE! QUICK!
IT'S COLLAP-SING!
KRESH
-KRESH
AAAAH!
KANNAGI, SIR! SHALL WE CALL FOR REINFORCE-MENTS?
NO. WE'LL WAIT NEARBY AND SEE WHAT HE DOES NEXT.

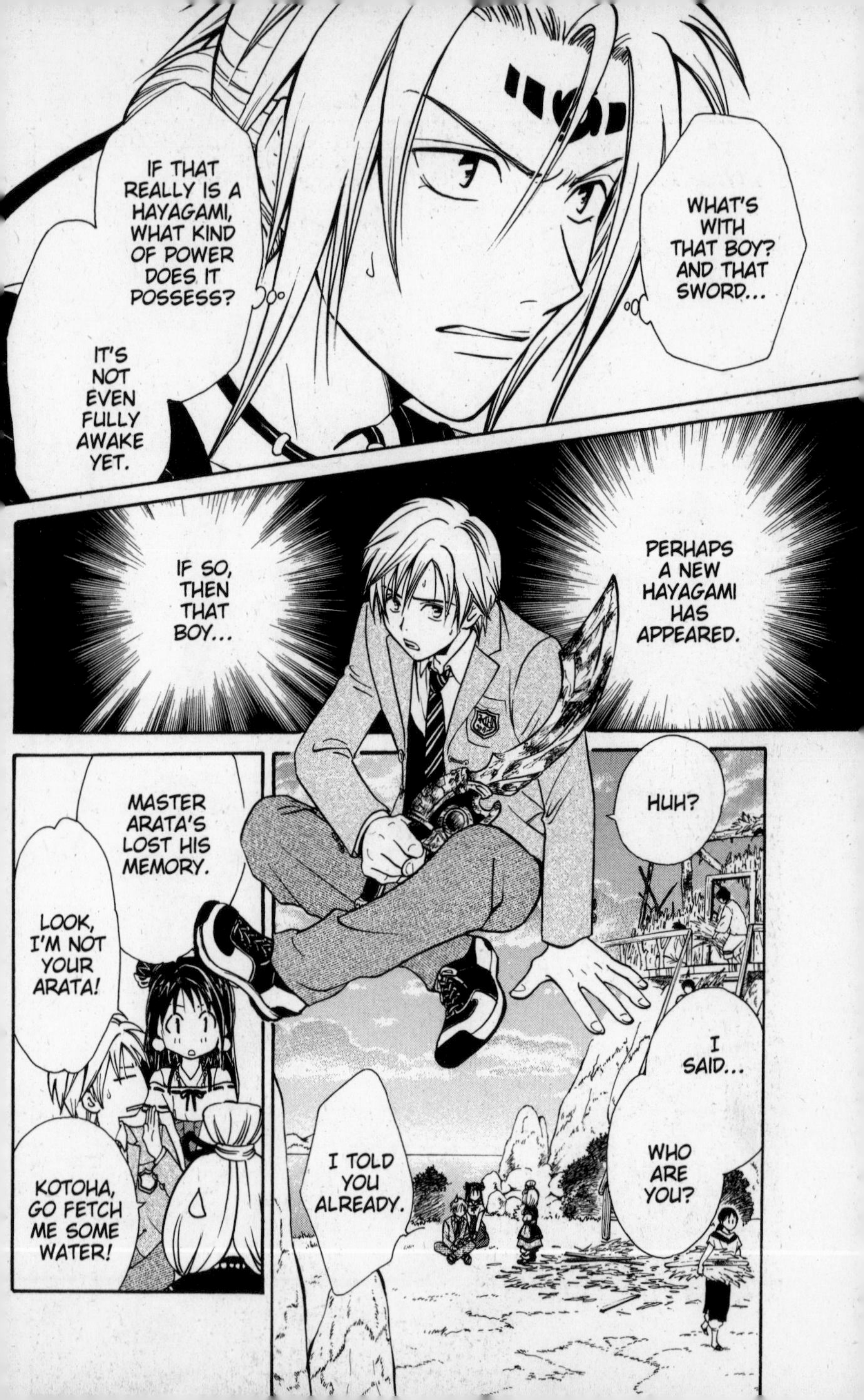
WHAT'S WITH THAT BOY? AND THAT SWORD...
IF THAT REALLY IS A HAYAGAMI, WHAT KIND OF POWER DOES IT POSSESS?
IT'S NOT EVEN FULLY AWAKE YET.
PERHAPS A NEW HAYAGAMI HAS APPEARED.
IF SO, THEN THAT BOY...
HUH?
I SAID...
WHO ARE YOU?
I TOLD YOU ALREADY.
MASTER ARATA'S LOST HIS MEMORY.
LOOK, I'M NOT YOUR ARATA!
KOTOHA, GO FETCH ME SOME WATER!

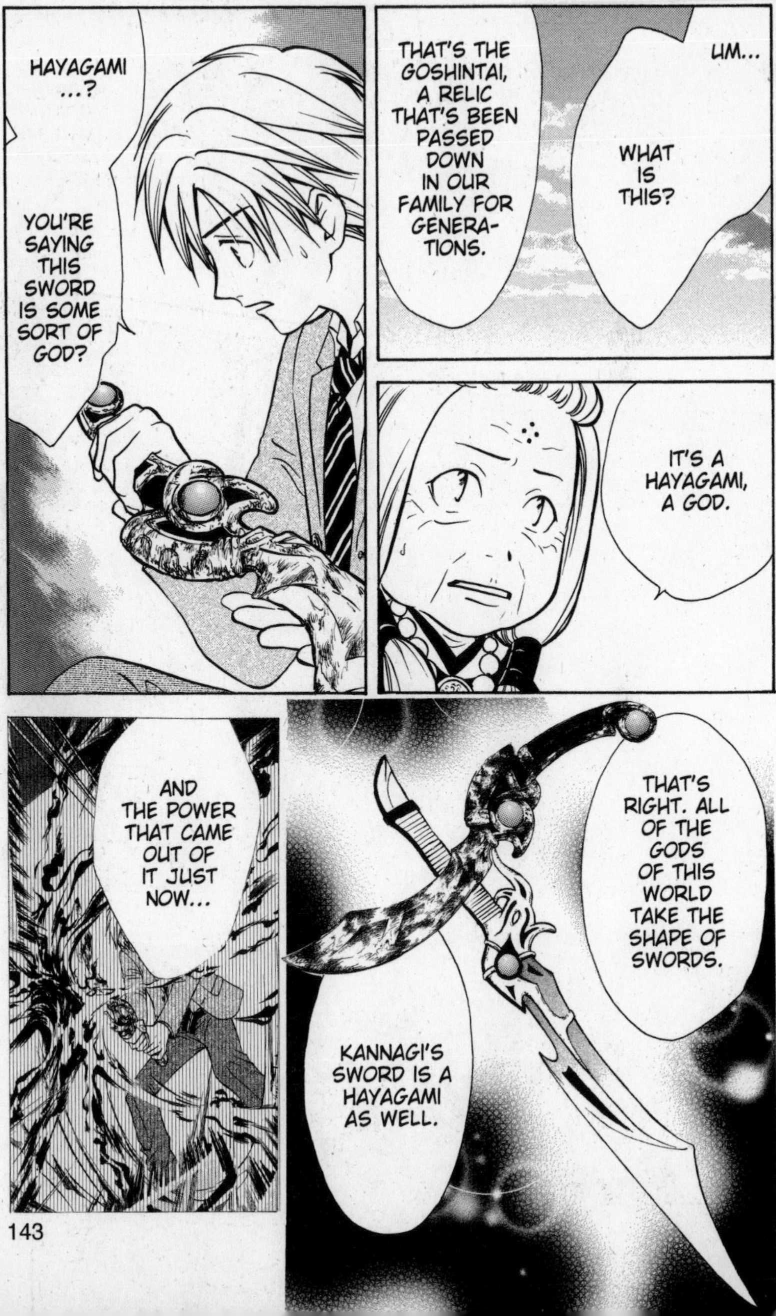
UM...
WHAT IS THIS?
THAT'S THE GOSHINTAI, A RELIC THAT'S BEEN PASSED DOWN IN OUR FAMILY FOR GENERATIONS.
IT'S A HAYAGAMI, A GOD.
HAYAGAMI ...?
YOU'RE SAYING THIS SWORD IS SOME SORT OF GOD?
THAT'S RIGHT. ALL OF THE GODS OF THIS WORLD TAKE THE SHAPE OF SWORDS.
KANNAGI'S SWORD IS A HAYAGAMI AS WELL.
AND THE POWER THAT CAME OUT OF IT JUST NOW...

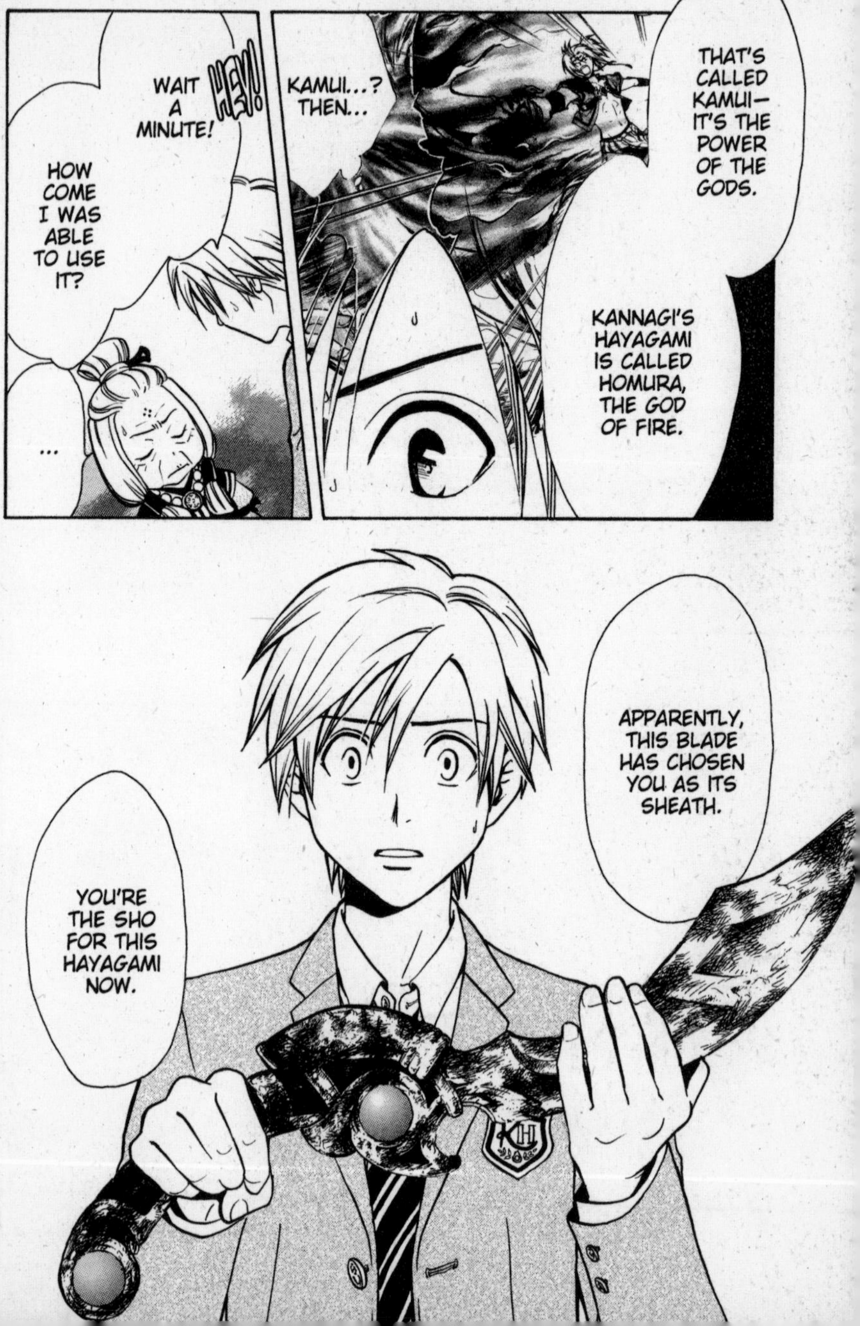
THAT'S CALLED KAMUI— IT'S THE POWER OF THE GODS.
KAMUI...? THEN...
KANNAGI'S HAYAGAMI IS CALLED HOMURA, THE GOD OF FIRE.
HEY!!
WAIT A MINUTE!
HOW COME I WAS ABLE TO USE IT?
...
APPARENTLY, THIS BLADE HAS CHOSEN YOU AS ITS SHEATH.
YOU'RE THE SHO FOR THIS HAYAGAMI NOW.

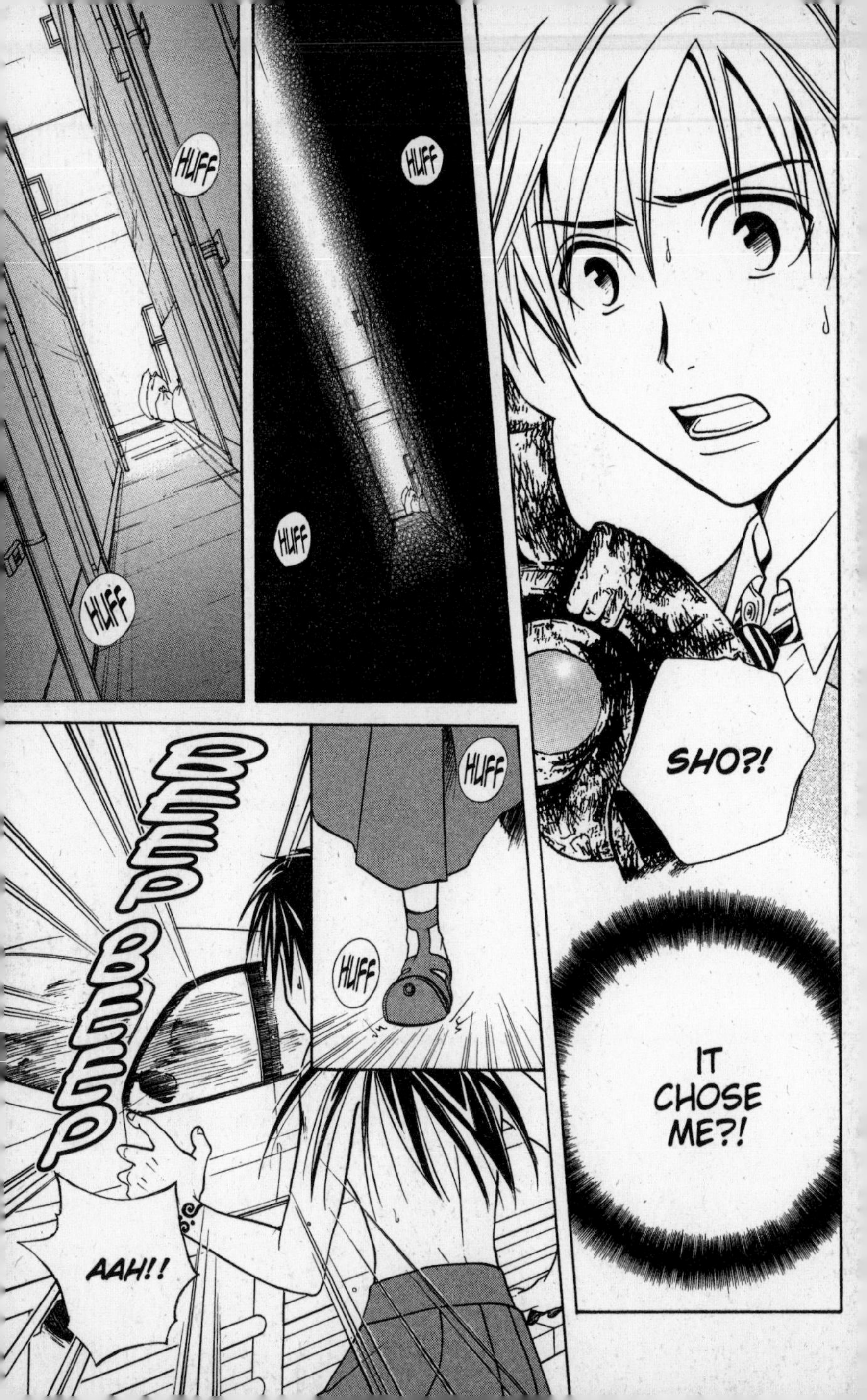
SHO?!
IT CHOSE ME?!
HUFF
HUFF
HUFF
HUFF
HUFF
HUFF
BEEP BEEP
AAH!!

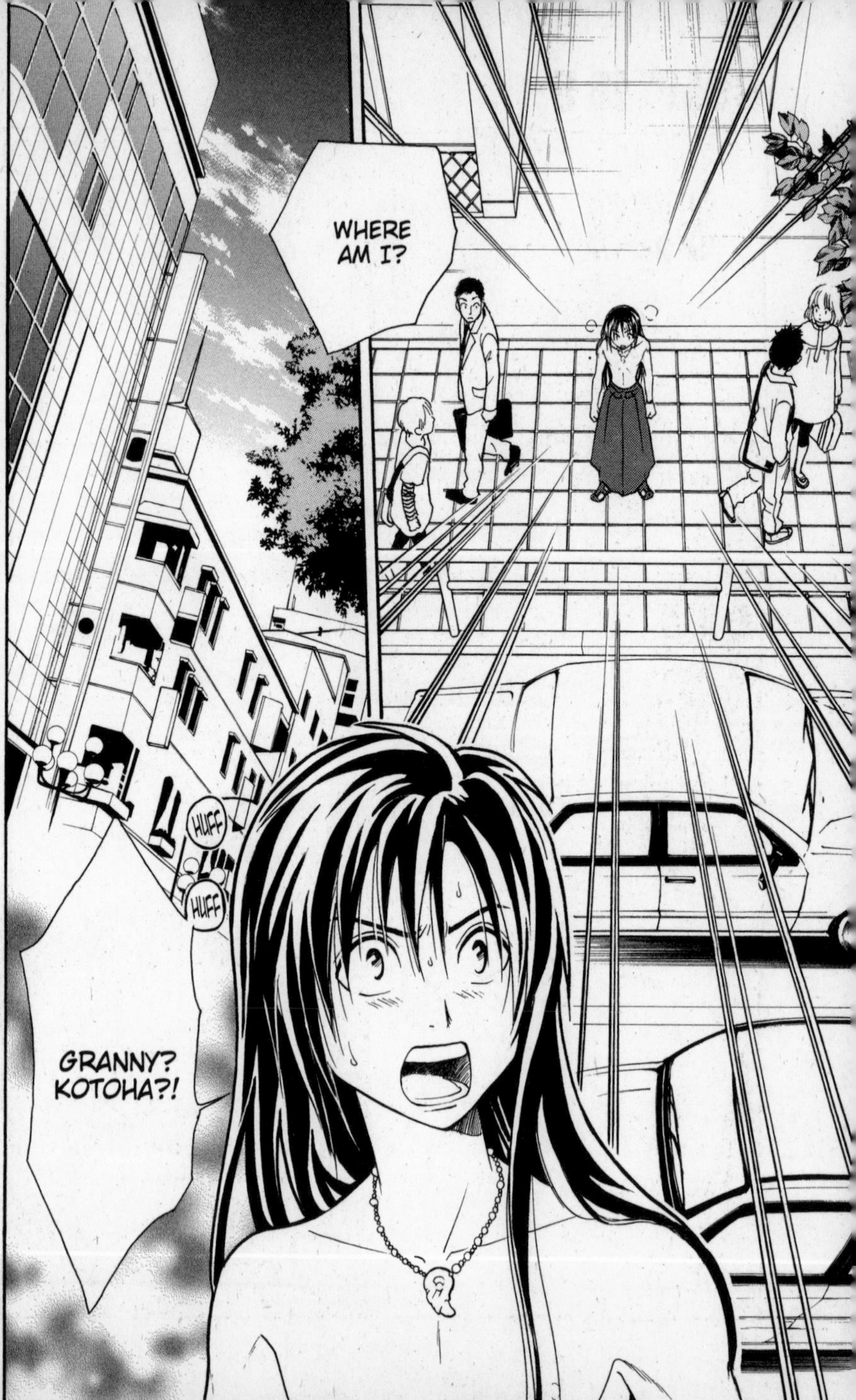
WHERE AM I?
HUFF
HUFF
GRANNY? KOTOHA?!

CHAPTER 5

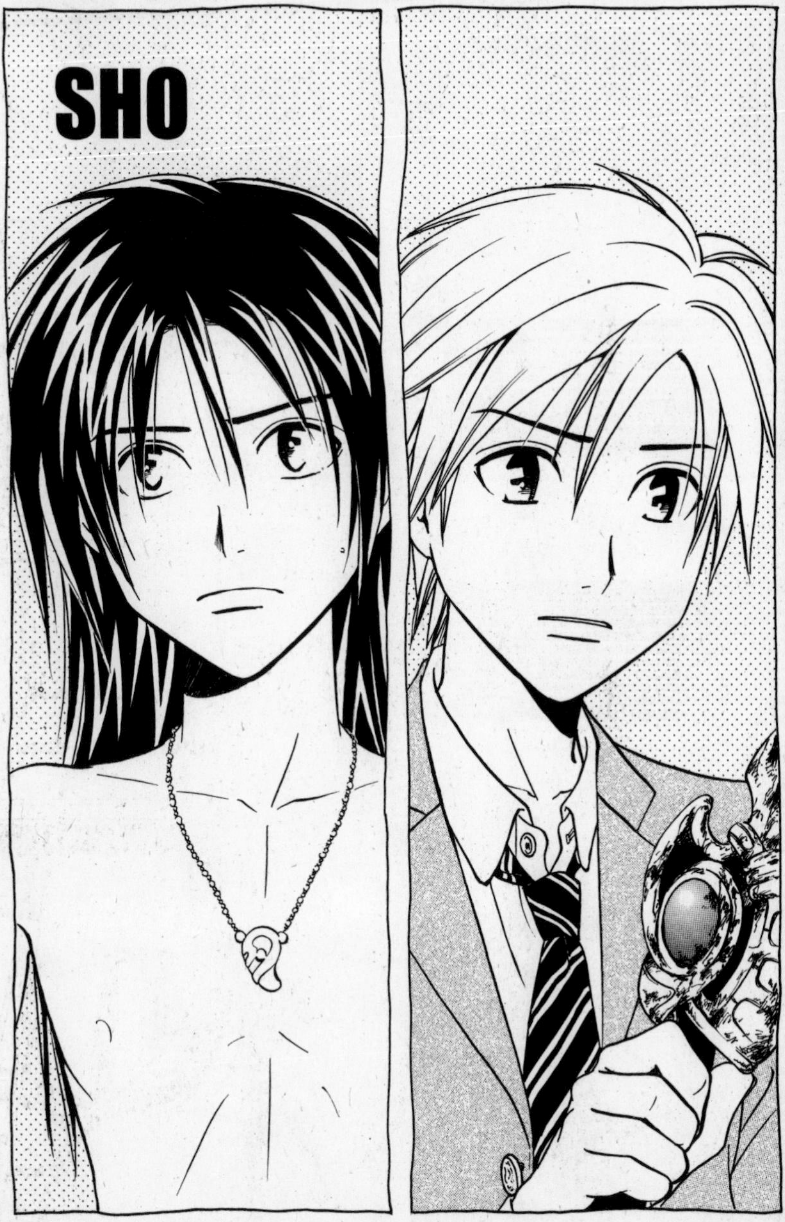

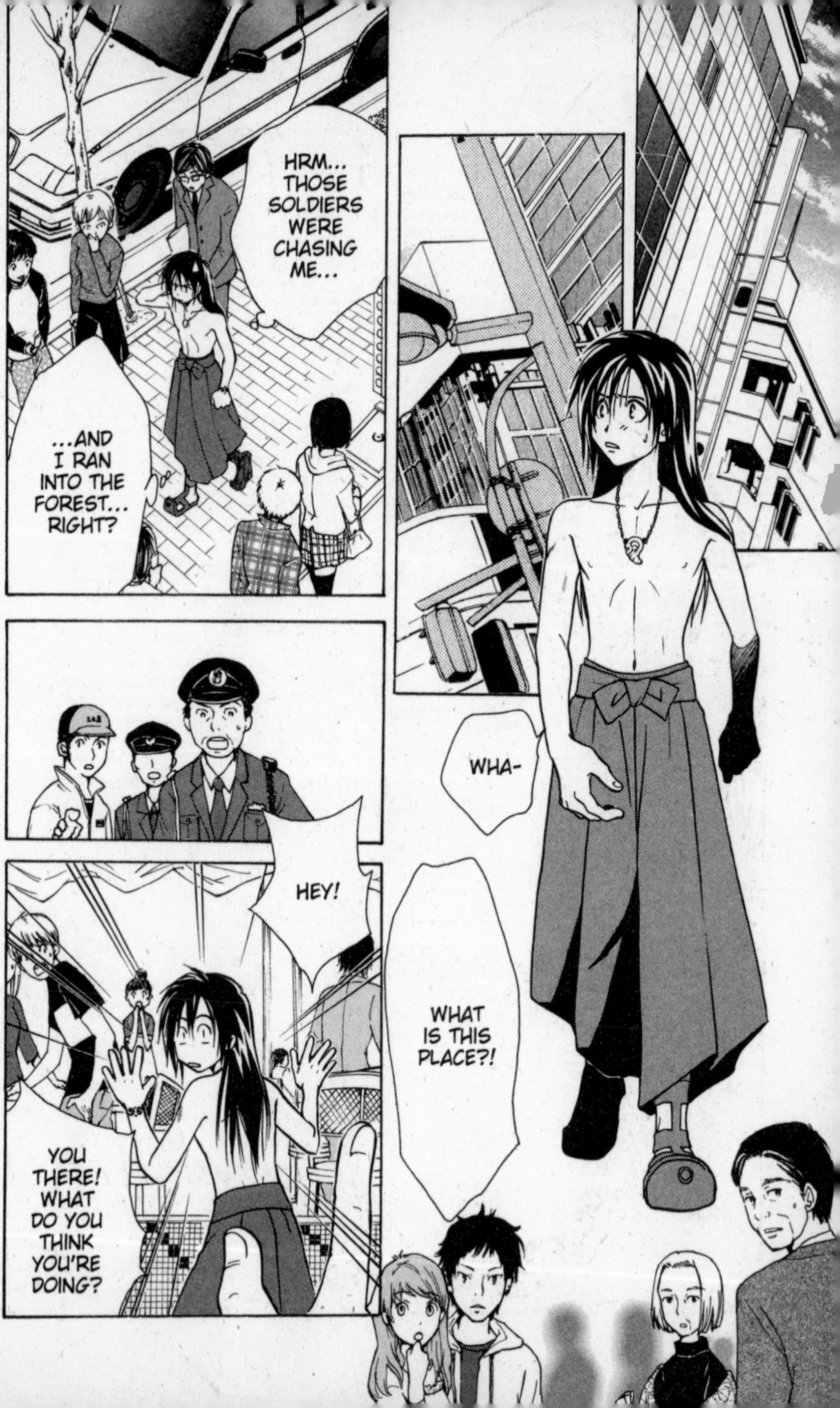
WHA-
WHAT IS THIS PLACE?!
HRM... THOSE SOLDIERS WERE CHASING ME...
...AND I RAN INTO THE FOREST... RIGHT?
HEY!
YOU THERE! WHAT DO YOU THINK YOU'RE DOING?

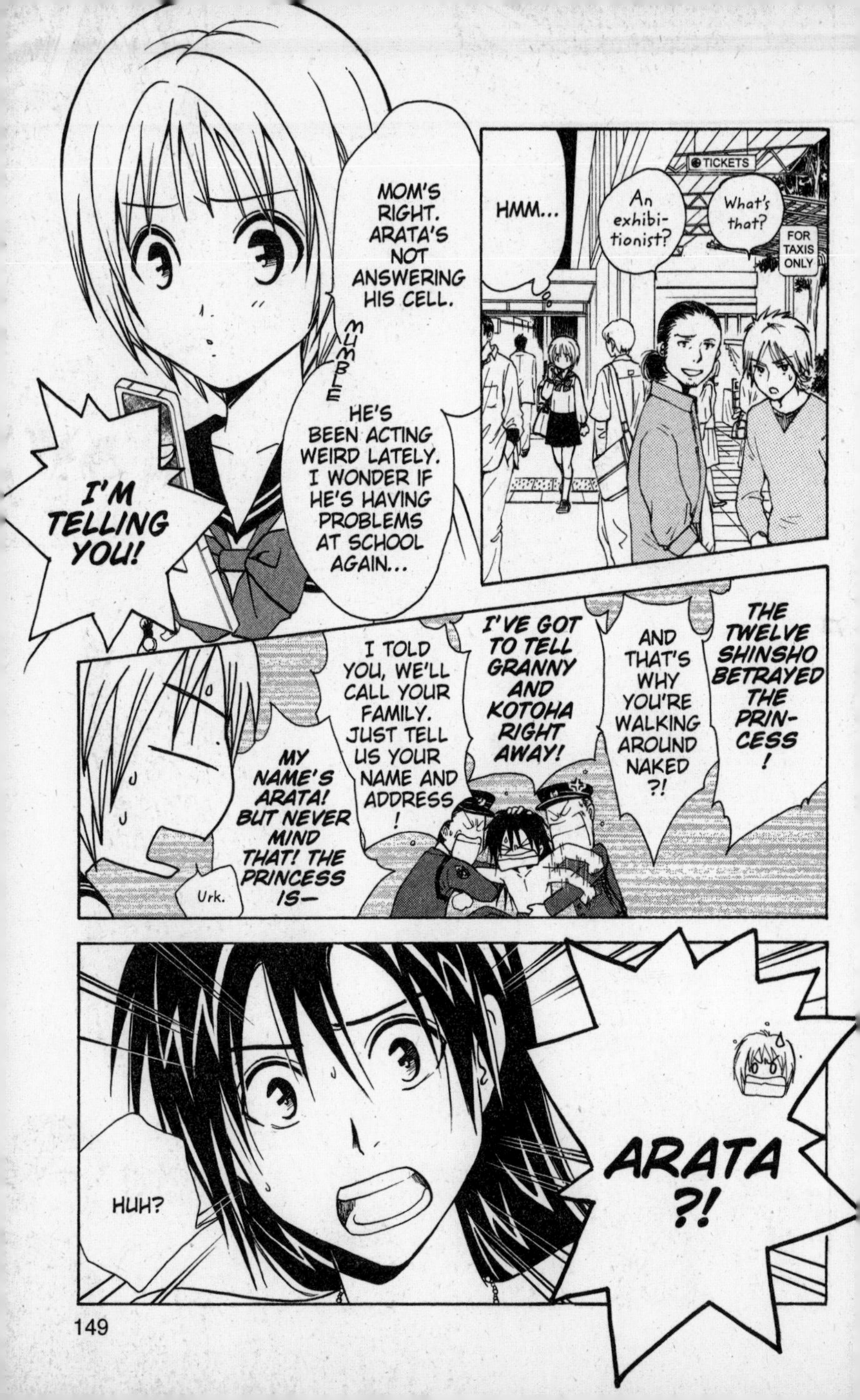
What's that?
An exhibitionist?
HMM...
MOM'S RIGHT. ARATA'S NOT ANSWERING HIS CELL.
MUMBLE
HE'S BEEN ACTING WEIRD LATELY. I WONDER IF HE'S HAVING PROBLEMS AT SCHOOL AGAIN...
I'M TELLING YOU!
TICKETS
FOR TAXIS ONLY
THE TWELVE SHINSHO BETRAYED THE PRINCESS!
AND THAT'S WHY YOU'RE WALKING AROUND NAKED?!
I'VE GOT TO TELL GRANNY AND KOTOHA RIGHT AWAY!
I TOLD YOU, WE'LL CALL YOUR FAMILY. JUST TELL US YOUR NAME AND ADDRESS!
MY NAME'S ARATA! BUT NEVER MIND THAT! THE PRINCESS IS—
Urk.
ARATA?!
HUH?

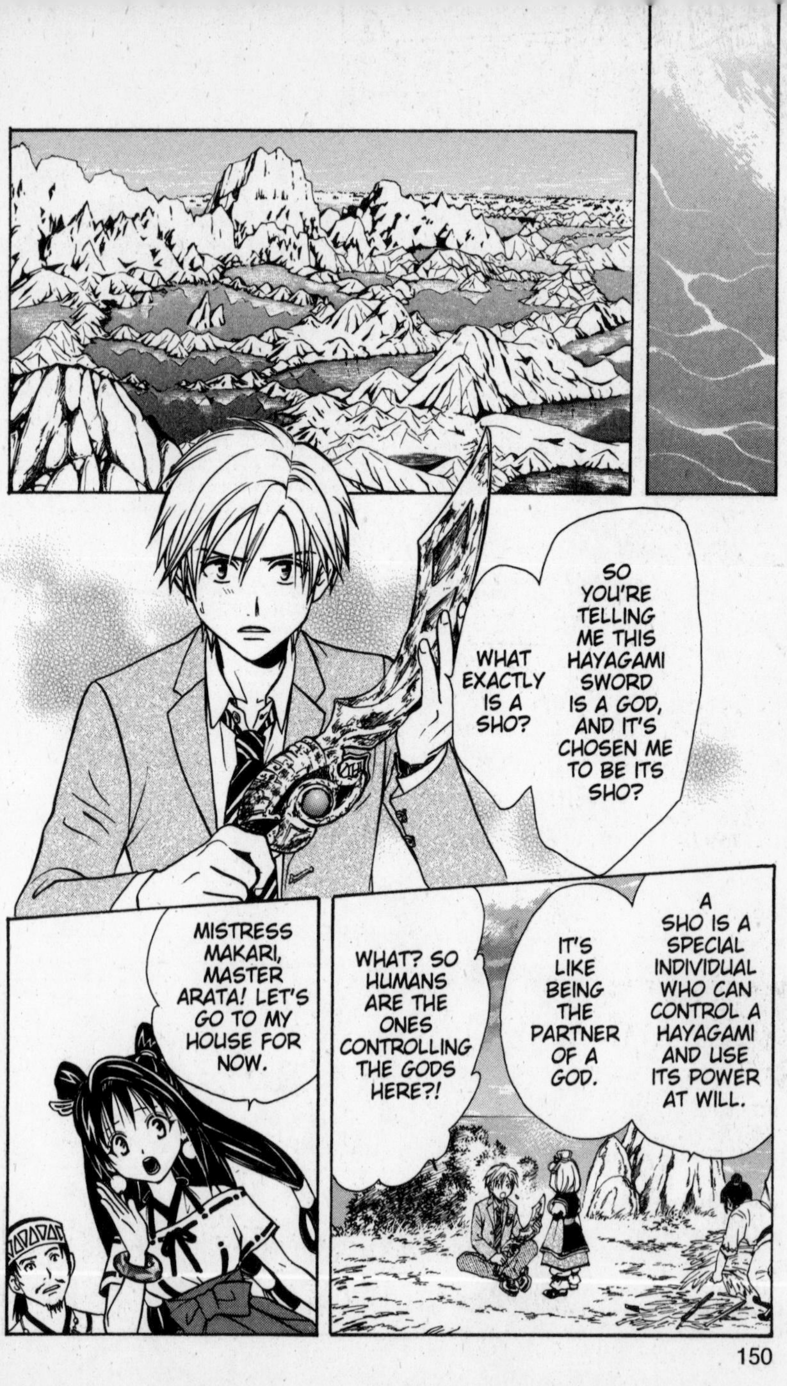
SO YOU'RE TELLING ME THIS HAYAGAMI SWORD IS A GOD, AND IT'S CHOSEN ME TO BE ITS SHO?
WHAT EXACTLY IS A SHO?
A SHO IS A SPECIAL INDIVIDUAL WHO CAN CONTROL A HAYAGAMI AND USE ITS POWER AT WILL.
IT'S LIKE BEING THE PARTNER OF A GOD.
WHAT? SO HUMANS ARE THE ONES CONTROLLING THE GODS HERE?!
MISTRESS MAKARI, MASTER ARATA! LET'S GO TO MY HOUSE FOR NOW.

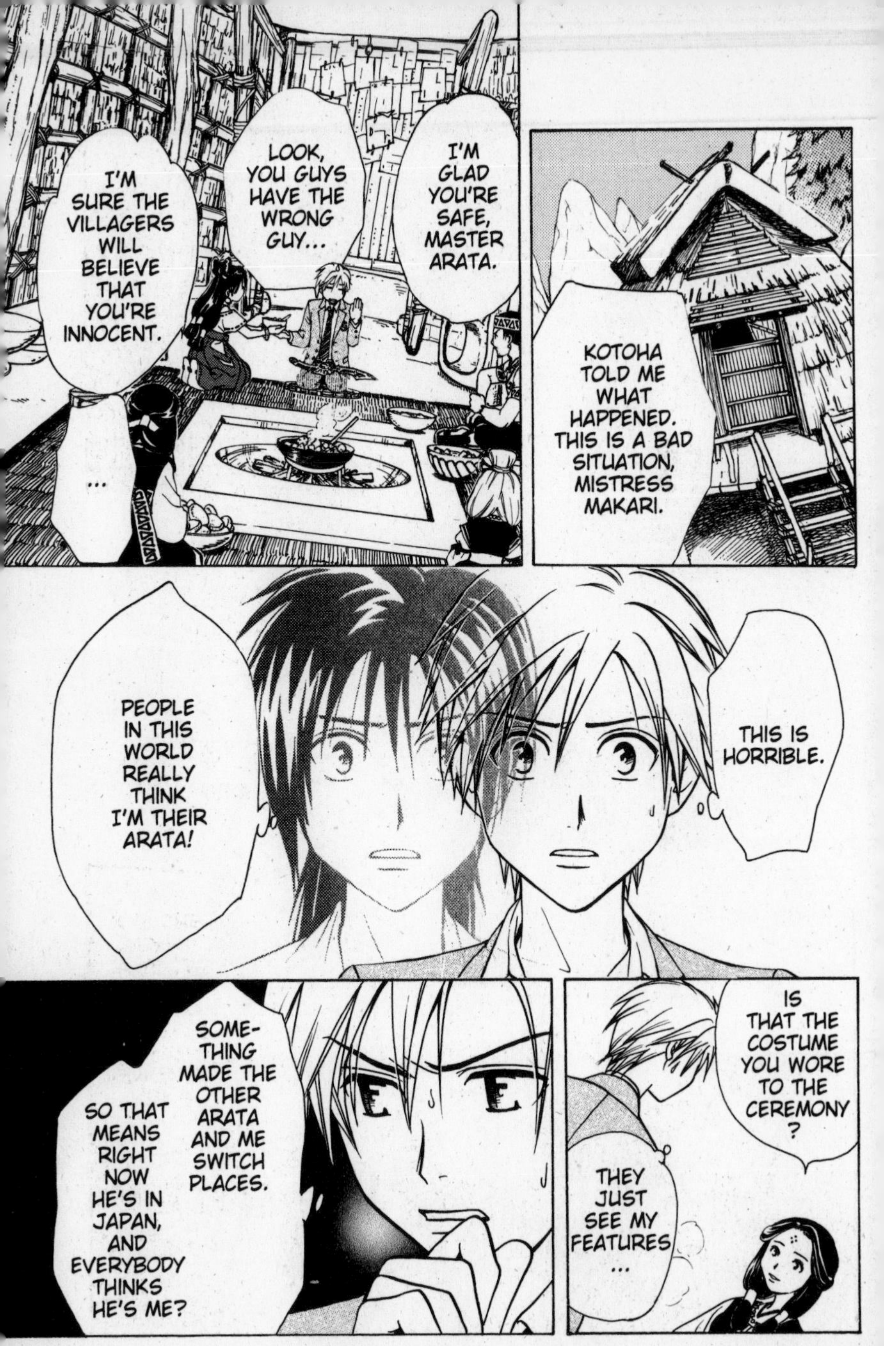
KOTOHA TOLD ME WHAT HAPPENED. THIS IS A BAD SITUATION, MISTRESS MAKARI.
I'M GLAD YOU'RE SAFE, MASTER ARATA.
LOOK, YOU GUYS HAVE THE WRONG GUY...
I'M SURE THE VILLAGERS WILL BELIEVE THAT YOU'RE INNOCENT.
...
THIS IS HORRIBLE.
PEOPLE IN THIS WORLD REALLY THINK I'M THEIR ARATA!
IS THAT THE COSTUME YOU WORE TO THE CEREMONY?
THEY JUST SEE MY FEATURES...
SOME-THING MADE THE OTHER ARATA AND ME SWITCH PLACES.
SO THAT MEANS RIGHT NOW HE'S IN JAPAN, AND EVERYBODY THINKS HE'S ME?

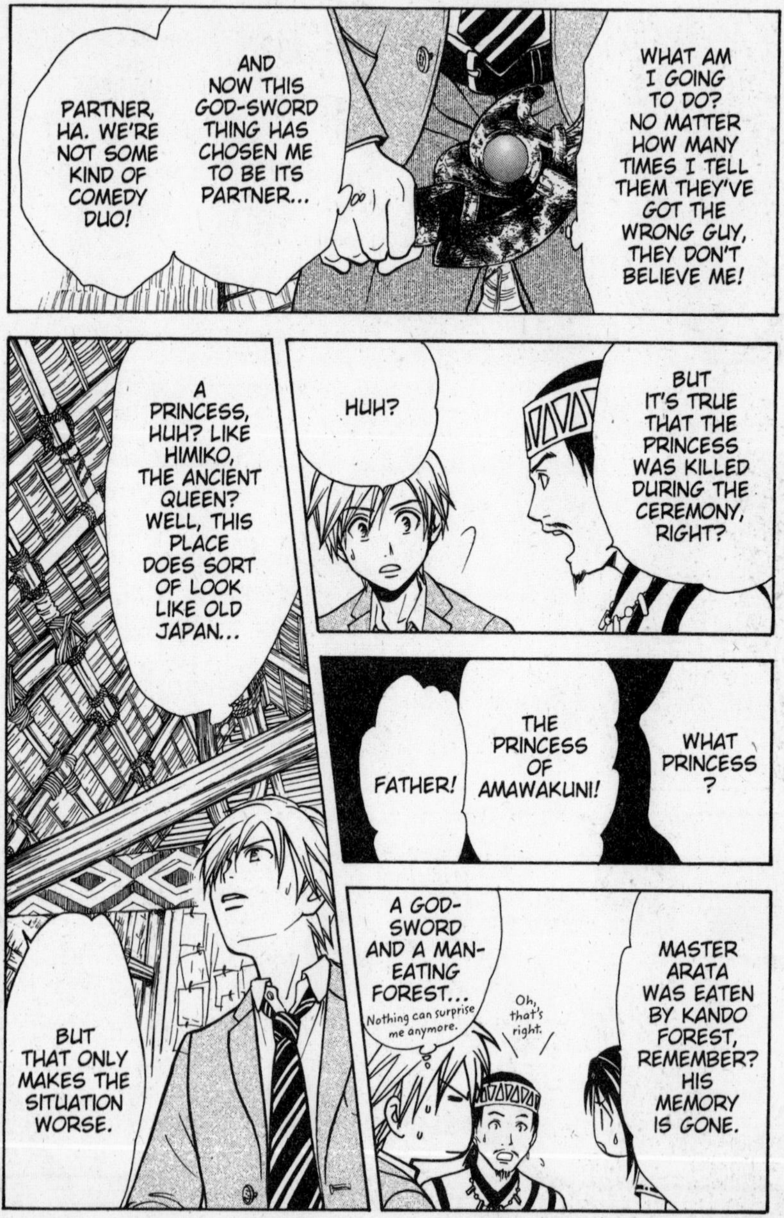
WHAT AM I GOING TO DO? NO MATTER HOW MANY TIMES I TELL THEM THEY'VE GOT THE WRONG GUY, THEY DON'T BELIEVE ME!
AND NOW THIS GOD-SWORD THING HAS CHOSEN ME TO BE ITS PARTNER...
PARTNER, HA. WE'RE NOT SOME KIND OF COMEDY DUO!
BUT IT'S TRUE THAT THE PRINCESS WAS KILLED DURING THE CEREMONY, RIGHT?
HUH?
WHAT PRINCESS?
THE PRINCESS OF AMAWAKUNI!
FATHER!
MASTER ARATA WAS EATEN BY KANDO FOREST, REMEMBER? HIS MEMORY IS GONE.
Oh, that's right.
A GOD-SWORD AND A MAN-EATING FOREST...
Nothing can surprise me anymore.
A PRINCESS, HUH? LIKE HIMIKO, THE ANCIENT QUEEN? WELL, THIS PLACE DOES SORT OF LOOK LIKE OLD JAPAN...
BUT THAT ONLY MAKES THE SITUATION WORSE.

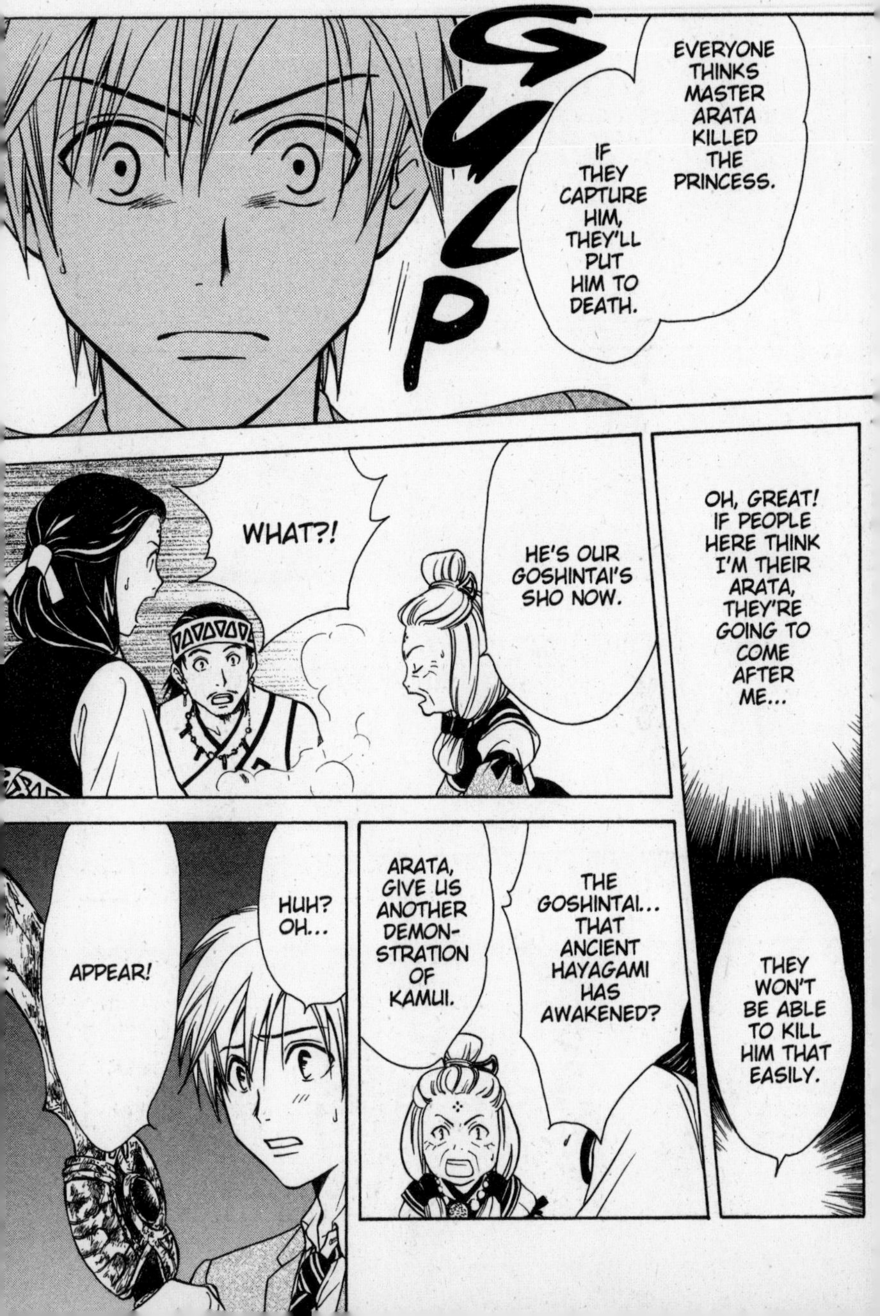
EVERYONE THINKS MASTER ARATA KILLED THE PRINCESS.
IF THEY CAPTURE HIM, THEY'LL PUT HIM TO DEATH.
GULP
OH, GREAT! IF PEOPLE HERE THINK I'M THEIR ARATA, THEY'RE GOING TO COME AFTER ME...
HE'S OUR GOSHINTAI'S SHO NOW.
WHAT?!
THEY WON'T BE ABLE TO KILL HIM THAT EASILY.
THE GOSHINTAI... THAT ANCIENT HAYAGAMI HAS AWAKENED?
ARATA, GIVE US ANOTHER DEMONSTRATION OF KAMUI.
HUH? OH...
APPEAR!

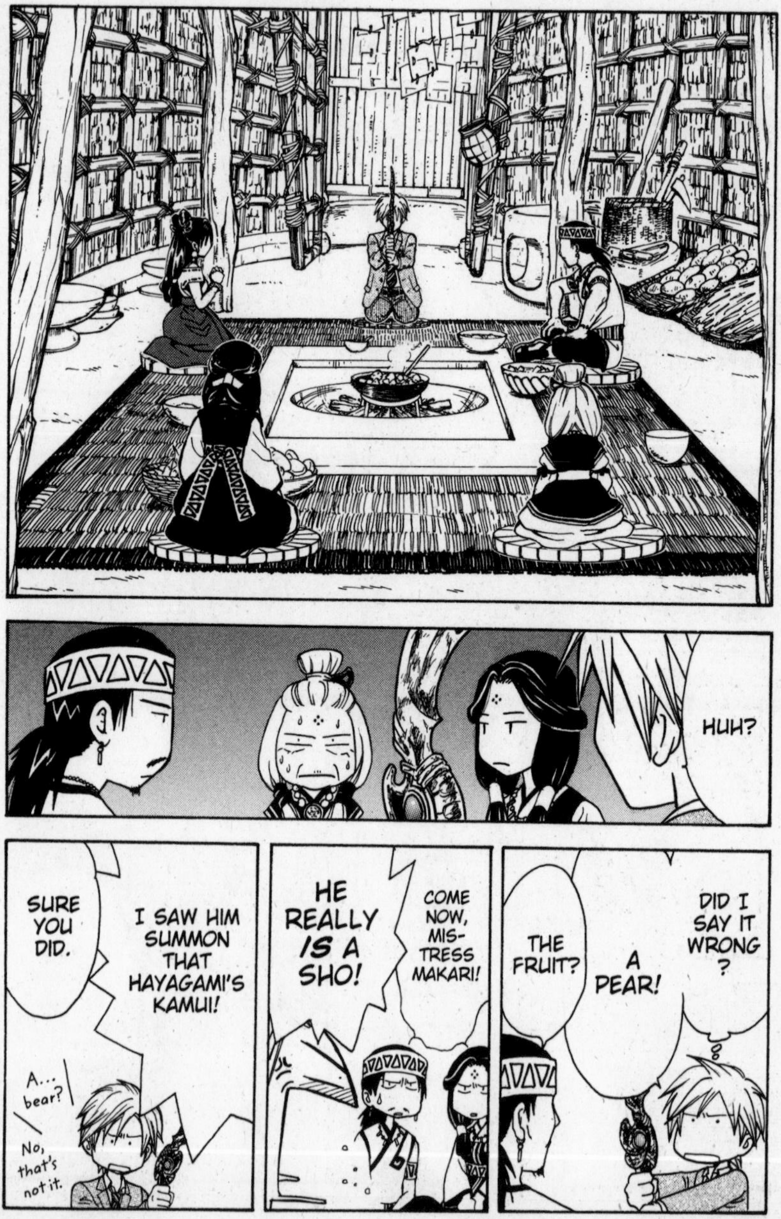
HUH?
DID I SAY IT WRONG?
A PEAR!
THE FRUIT?
COME NOW, MIS-TRESS MAKARI!
HE REALLY *IS* A SHO!
I SAW HIM SUMMON THAT HAYAGAMI'S KAMUI!
SURE YOU DID.
A... bear?
No, that's not it.

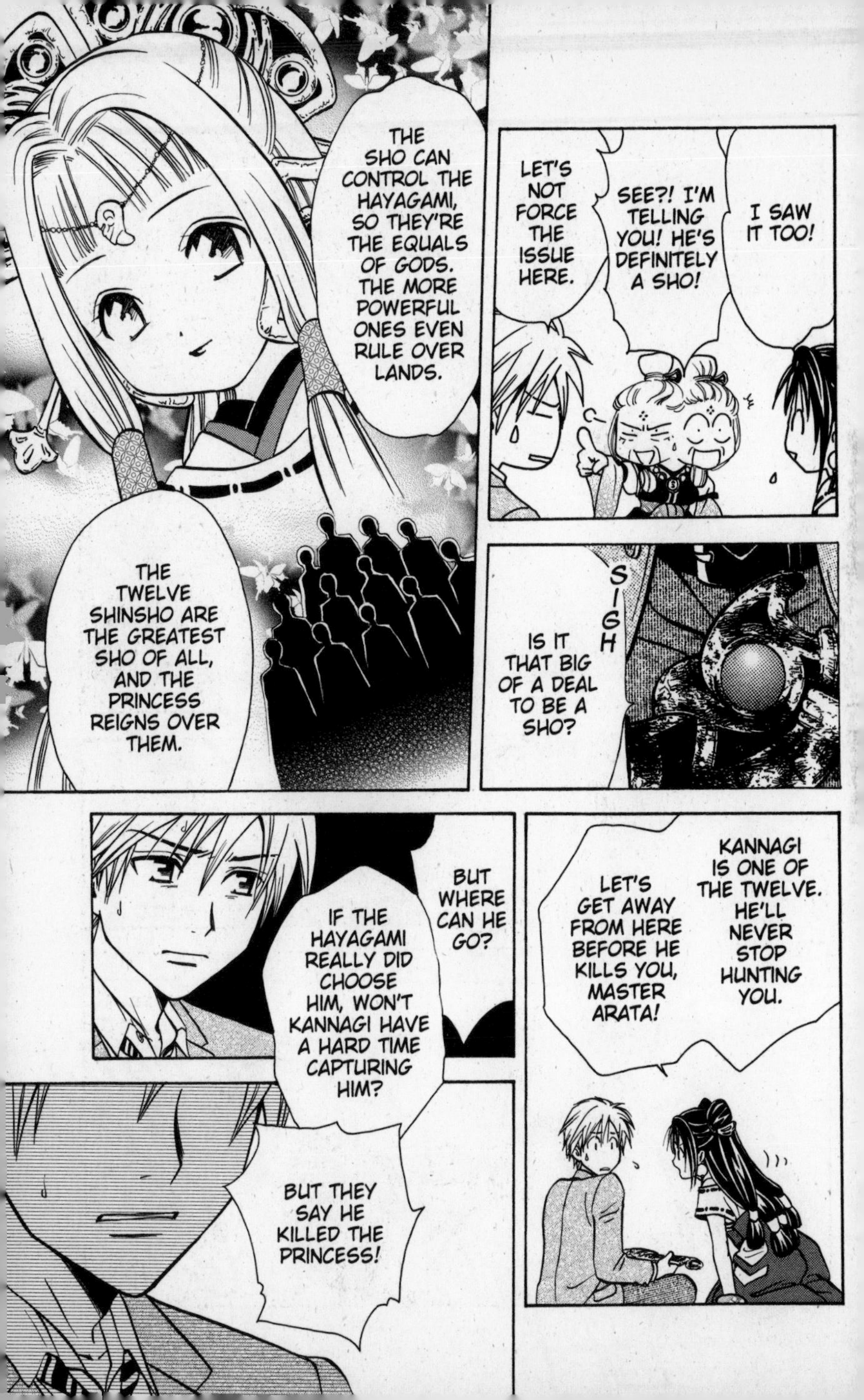
I SAW IT TOO!
SEE?! I'M TELLING YOU! HE'S DEFINITELY A SHO!
LET'S NOT FORCE THE ISSUE HERE.
SIGH
IS IT THAT BIG OF A DEAL TO BE A SHO?
THE SHO CAN CONTROL THE HAYAGAMI, SO THEY'RE THE EQUALS OF GODS. THE MORE POWERFUL ONES EVEN RULE OVER LANDS.
THE TWELVE SHINSHO ARE THE GREATEST SHO OF ALL, AND THE PRINCESS REIGNS OVER THEM.
KANNAGI IS ONE OF THE TWELVE. HE'LL NEVER STOP HUNTING YOU.
LET'S GET AWAY FROM HERE BEFORE HE KILLS YOU, MASTER ARATA!
BUT WHERE CAN HE GO?
IF THE HAYAGAMI REALLY DID CHOOSE HIM, WON'T KANNAGI HAVE A HARD TIME CAPTURING HIM?
BUT THEY SAY HE KILLED THE PRINCESS!

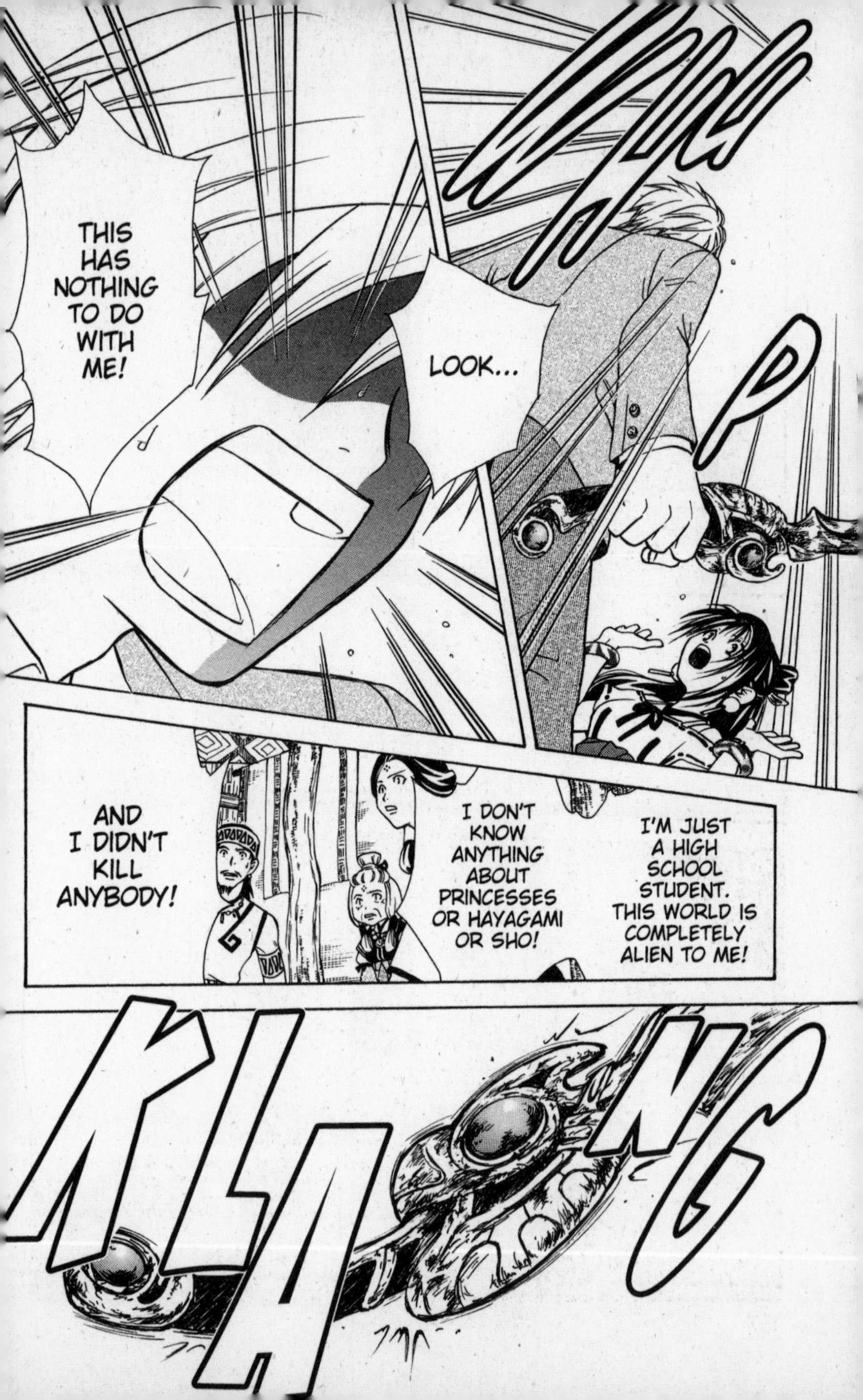

LOOK...
THIS HAS NOTHING TO DO WITH ME!
I'M JUST A HIGH SCHOOL STUDENT. THIS WORLD IS COMPLETELY ALIEN TO ME!
I DON'T KNOW ANYTHING ABOUT PRINCESSES OR HAYAGAMI OR SHO!
AND I DIDN'T KILL ANYBODY!
KLANG

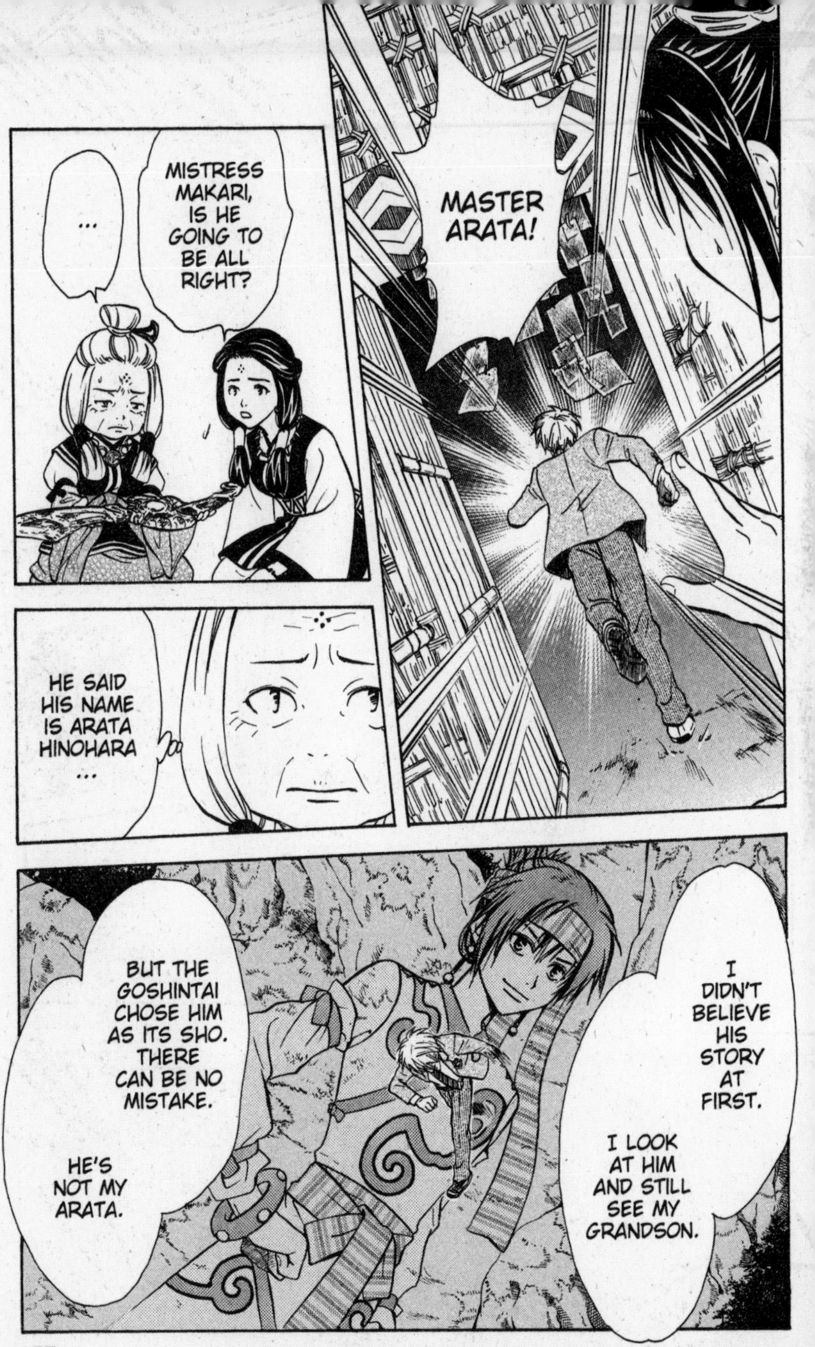
MASTER ARATA!
MISTRESS MAKARI, IS HE GOING TO BE ALL RIGHT?
...
HE SAID HIS NAME IS ARATA HINOHARA ...
I DIDN'T BELIEVE HIS STORY AT FIRST.
I LOOK AT HIM AND STILL SEE MY GRANDSON.
BUT THE GOSHINTAI CHOSE HIM AS ITS SHO. THERE CAN BE NO MISTAKE.
HE'S NOT MY ARATA.

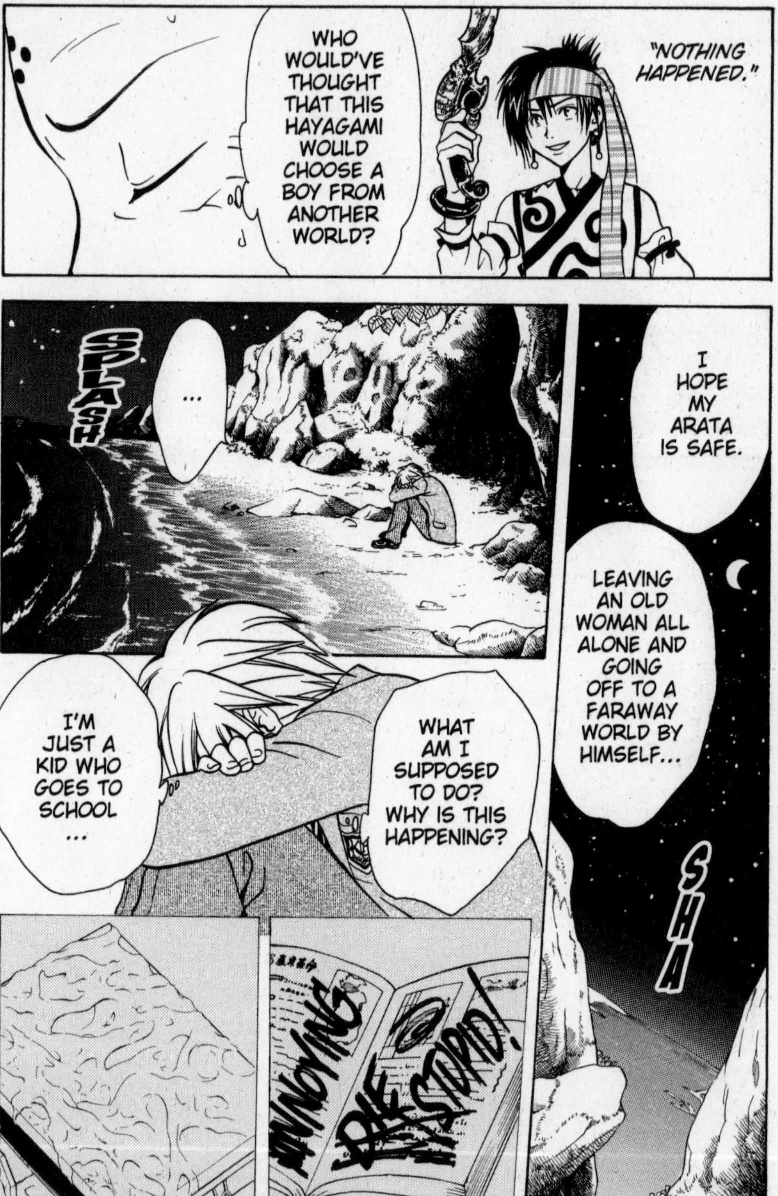
"NOTHING HAPPENED."
WHO WOULD'VE THOUGHT THAT THIS HAYAGAMI WOULD CHOOSE A BOY FROM ANOTHER WORLD?
I HOPE MY ARATA IS SAFE.
LEAVING AN OLD WOMAN ALL ALONE AND GOING OFF TO A FARAWAY WORLD BY HIMSELF...
SHA
SPLASH
...
WHAT AM I SUPPOSED TO DO? WHY IS THIS HAPPENING?
I'M JUST A KID WHO GOES TO SCHOOL ...
ANNOYING

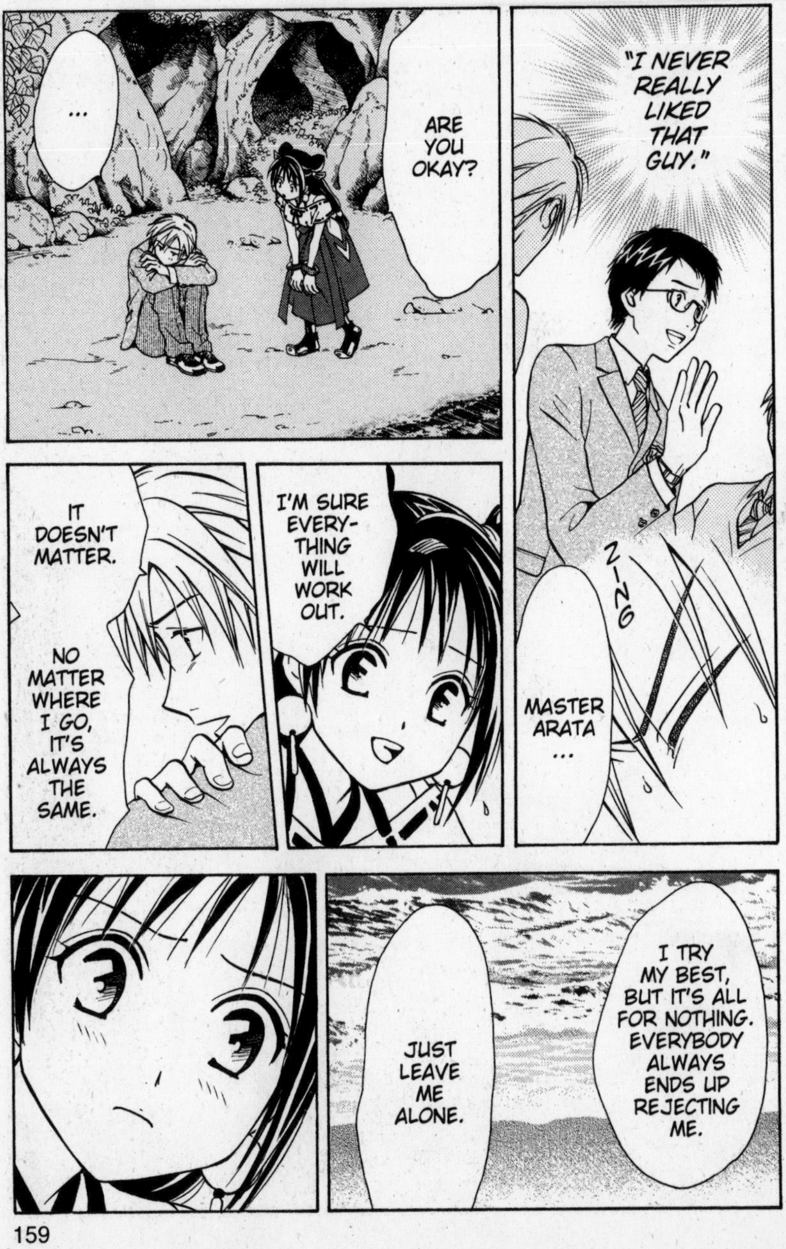
"I NEVER REALLY LIKED THAT GUY."
ZING
MASTER ARATA ...
ARE YOU OKAY?
...
I'M SURE EVERY-THING WILL WORK OUT.
IT DOESN'T MATTER.
NO MATTER WHERE I GO, IT'S ALWAYS THE SAME.
I TRY MY BEST, BUT IT'S ALL FOR NOTHING. EVERYBODY ALWAYS ENDS UP REJECTING ME.
JUST LEAVE ME ALONE.

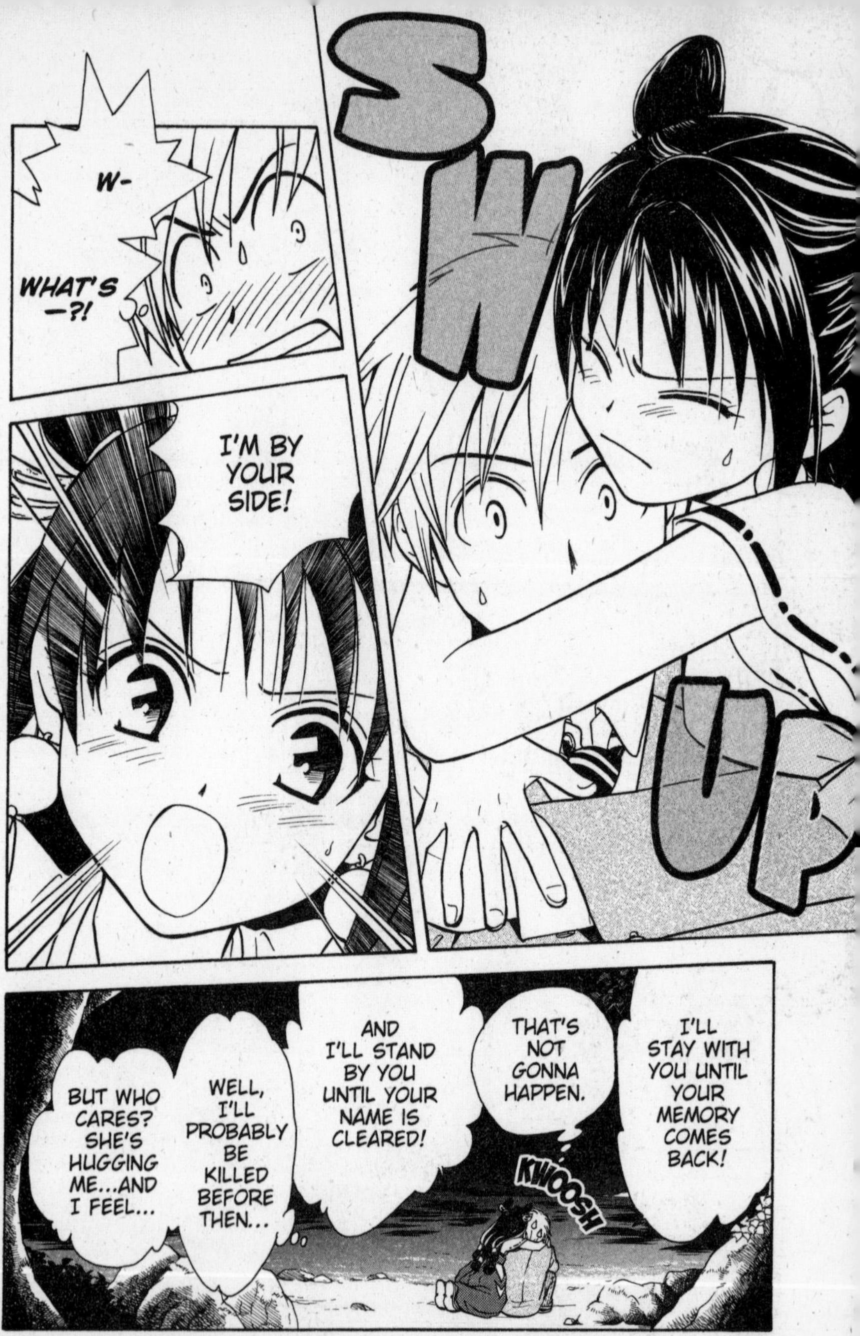
SHWUP
W-
WHAT'S —?!
I'M BY YOUR SIDE!
I'LL STAY WITH YOU UNTIL YOUR MEMORY COMES BACK!
THAT'S NOT GONNA HAPPEN.
KWOOSH
AND I'LL STAND BY YOU UNTIL YOUR NAME IS CLEARED!
WELL, I'LL PROBABLY BE KILLED BEFORE THEN...
BUT WHO CARES? SHE'S HUGGING ME...AND I FEEL...

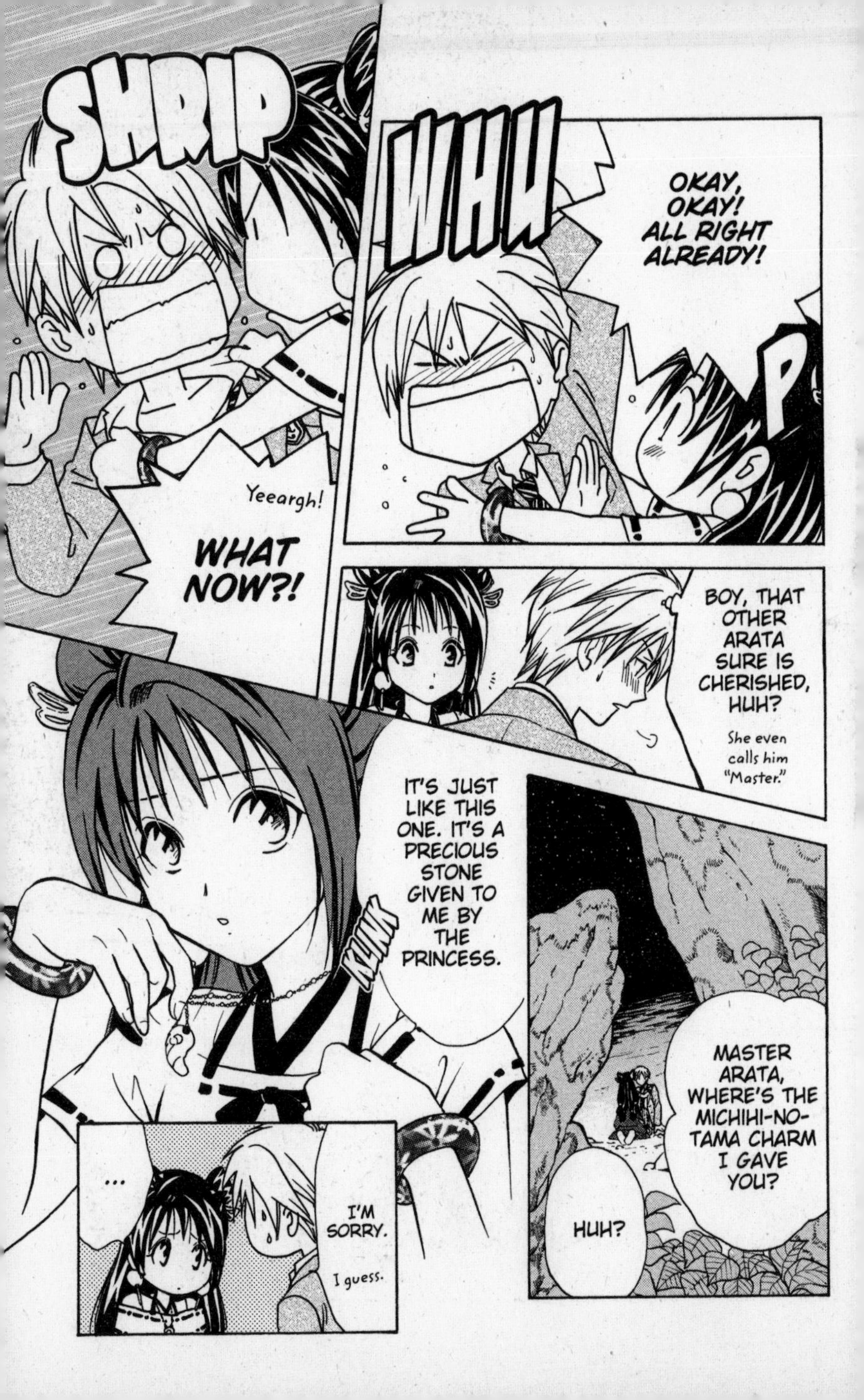
WHU
OKAY, OKAY! ALL RIGHT ALREADY!
P
BOY, THAT OTHER ARATA SURE IS CHERISHED, HUH?
She even calls him "Master."
SHRIP
Yeeargh!
WHAT NOW?!
MASTER ARATA, WHERE'S THE MICHIHI-NO-TAMA CHARM I GAVE YOU?
HUH?
IT'S JUST LIKE THIS ONE. IT'S A PRECIOUS STONE GIVEN TO ME BY THE PRINCESS.
KLINK
...
I'M SORRY.
I guess.

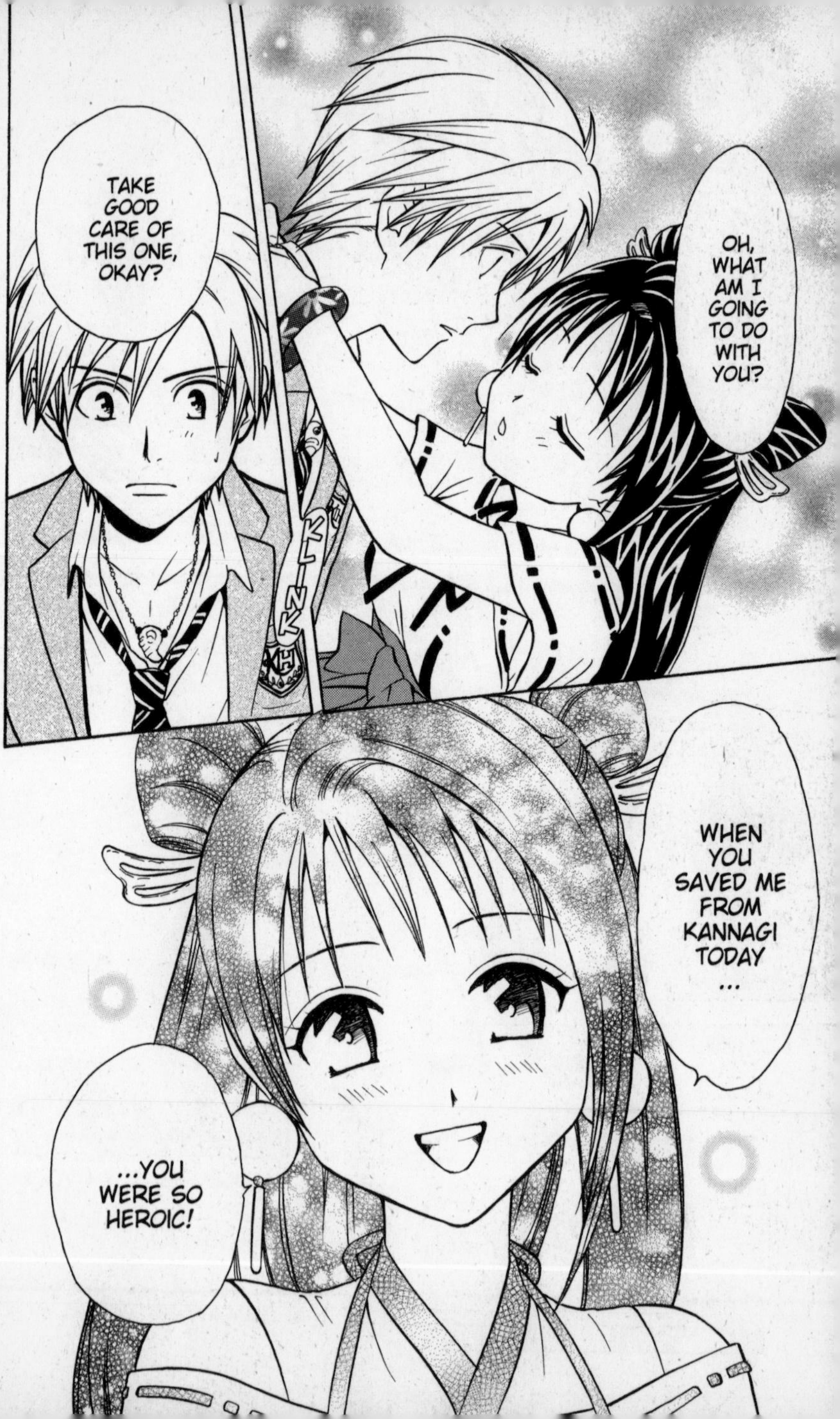
OH, WHAT AM I GOING TO DO WITH YOU?
KLINK
TAKE GOOD CARE OF THIS ONE, OKAY?
WHEN YOU SAVED ME FROM KANNAGI TODAY...
...YOU WERE SO HEROIC!

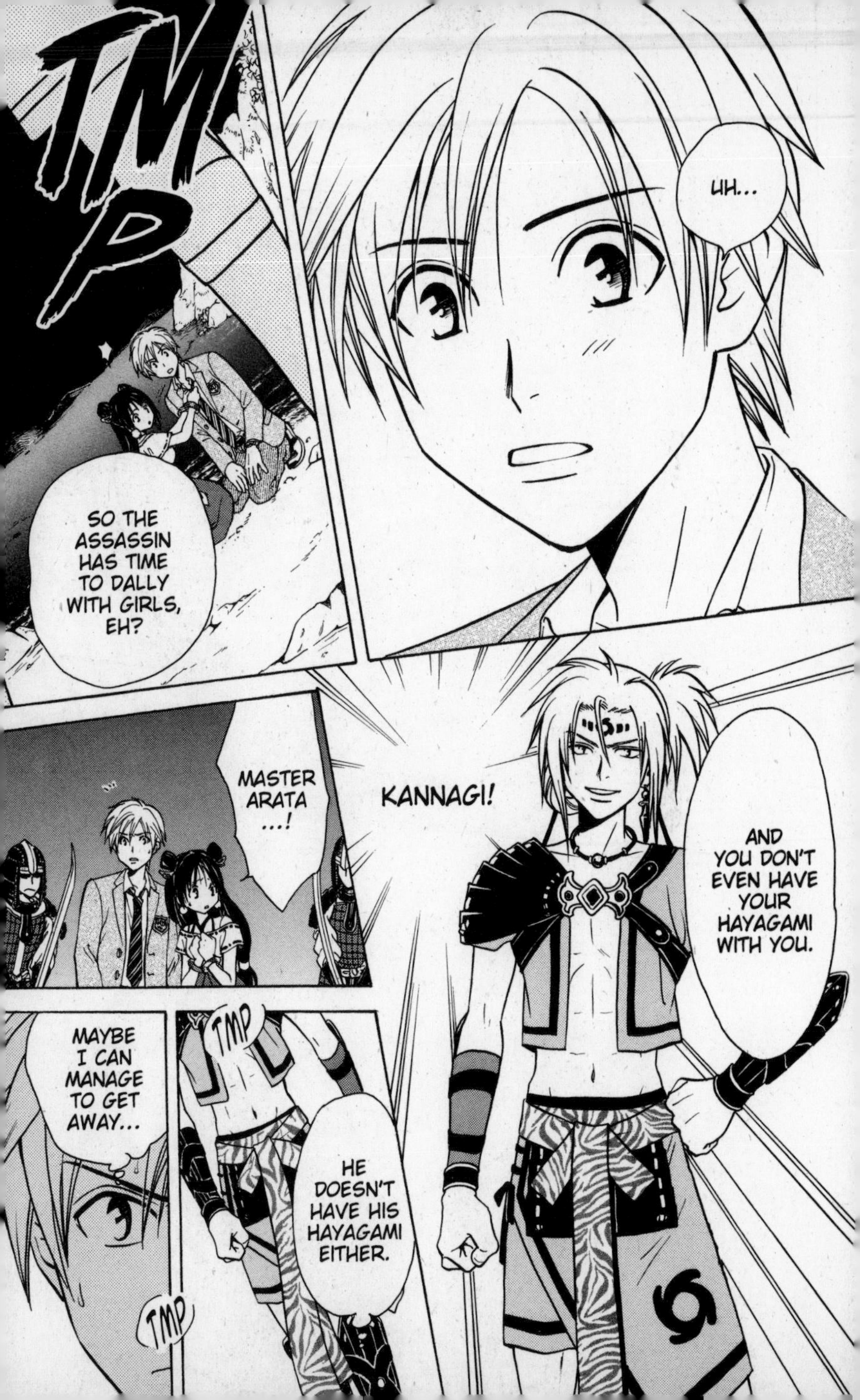
UH...
TMP
SO THE ASSASSIN HAS TIME TO DALLY WITH GIRLS, EH?
AND YOU DON'T EVEN HAVE YOUR HAYAGAMI WITH YOU.
KANNAGI!
MASTER ARATA ...!
TMP
HE DOESN'T HAVE HIS HAYAGAMI EITHER.
MAYBE I CAN MANAGE TO GET AWAY...
TMP

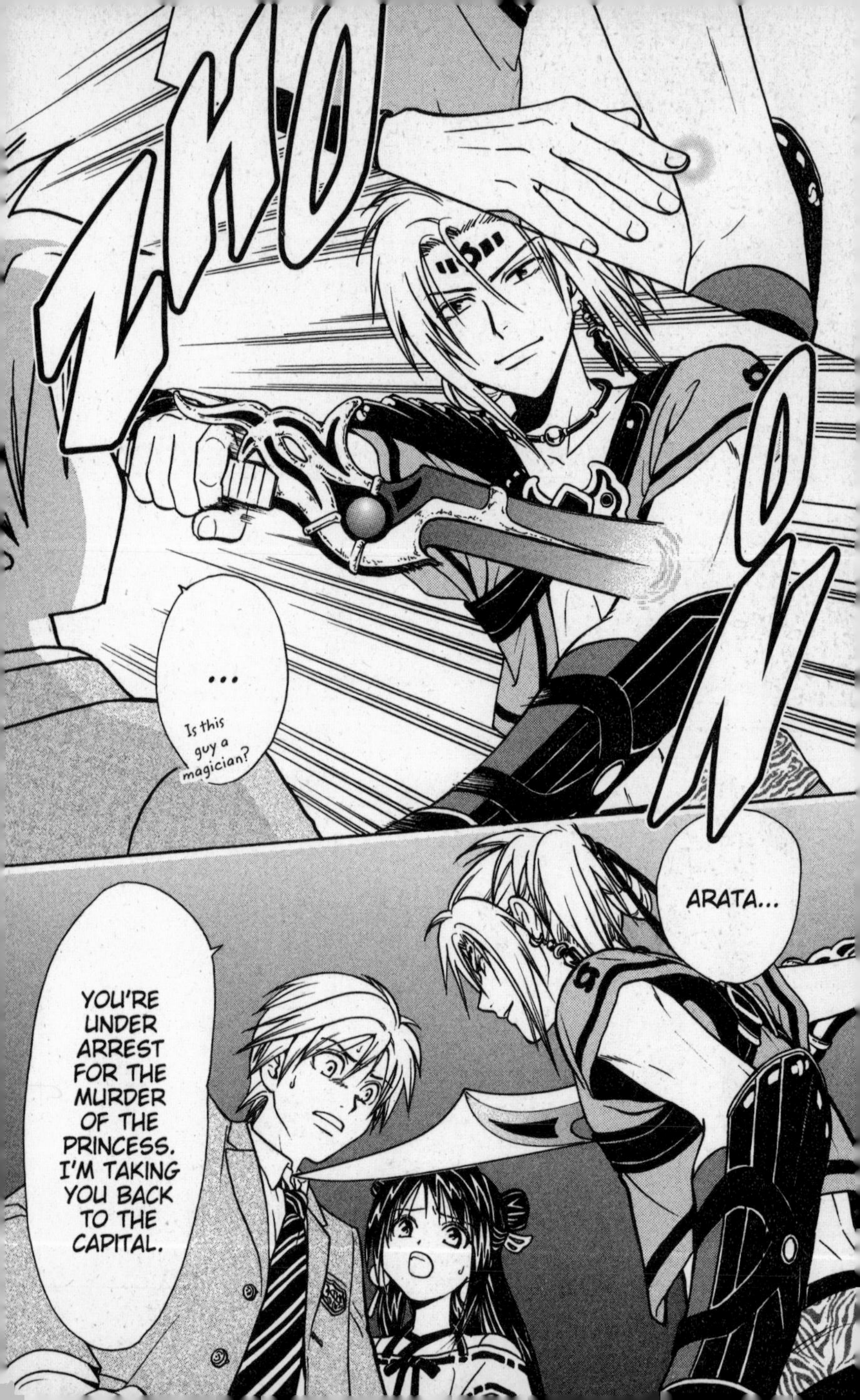
ZHOON
...
Is this guy a magician?
ARATA...
YOU'RE UNDER ARREST FOR THE MURDER OF THE PRINCESS. I'M TAKING YOU BACK TO THE CAPITAL.

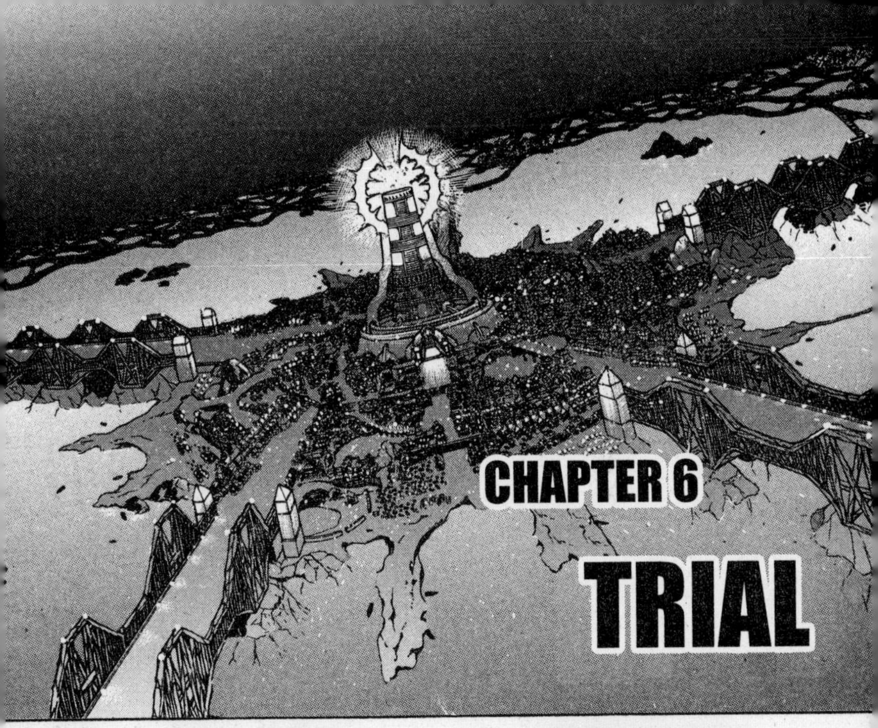
CHAPTER 6
TRIAL

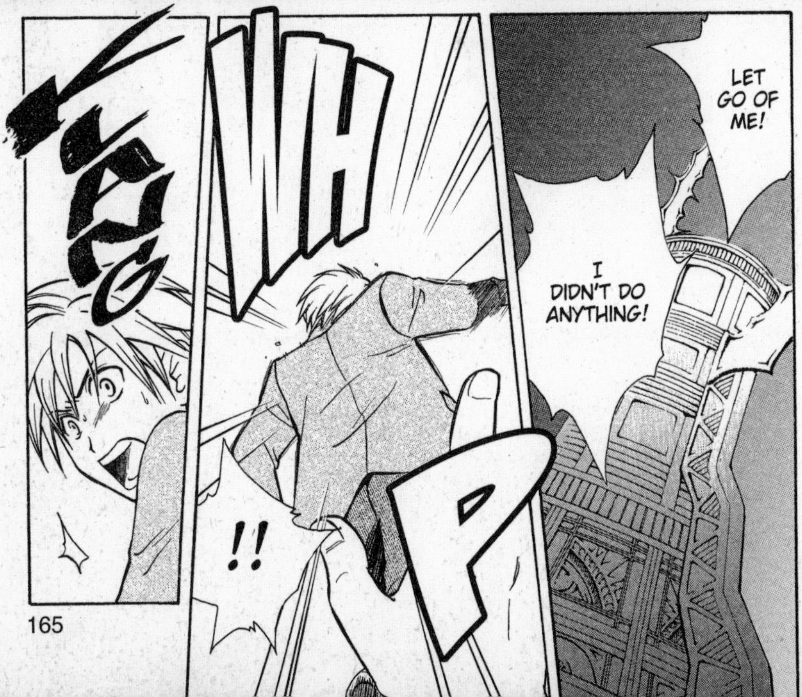
LET GO OF ME!
I DIDN'T DO ANYTHING!
WH
!!
P

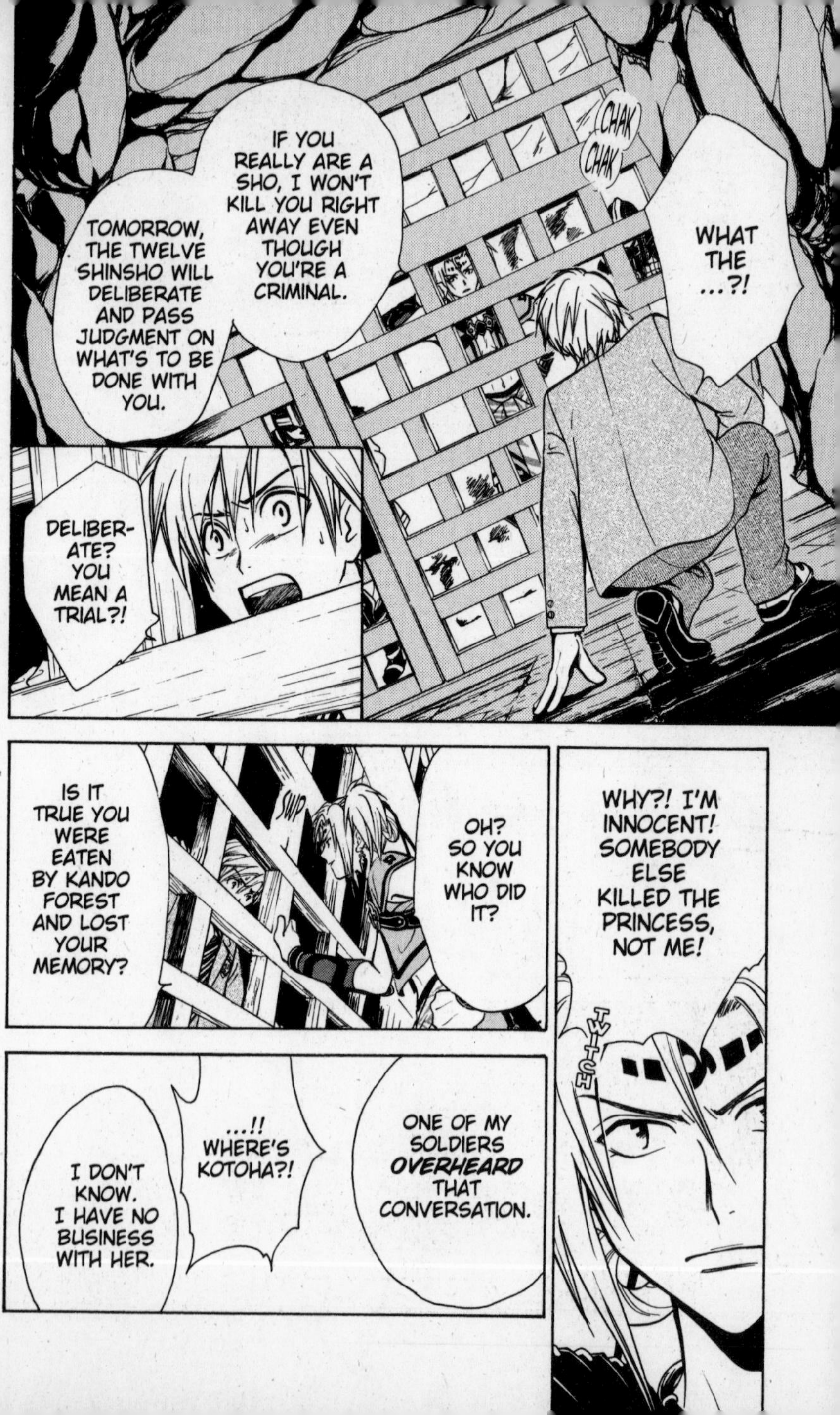
WHAT THE...?!
CHAK
CHAK
IF YOU REALLY ARE A SHO, I WON'T KILL YOU RIGHT AWAY EVEN THOUGH YOU'RE A CRIMINAL.
TOMORROW, THE TWELVE SHINSHO WILL DELIBERATE AND PASS JUDGMENT ON WHAT'S TO BE DONE WITH YOU.
DELIBER-ATE? YOU MEAN A TRIAL?!
WHY?! I'M INNOCENT! SOMEBODY ELSE KILLED THE PRINCESS, NOT ME!
TWITCH
OH? SO YOU KNOW WHO DID IT?
SLIP
IS IT TRUE YOU WERE EATEN BY KANDO FOREST AND LOST YOUR MEMORY?
ONE OF MY SOLDIERS *OVERHEARD* THAT CONVERSATION.
...!! WHERE'S KOTOHA?!
I DON'T KNOW. I HAVE NO BUSINESS WITH HER.

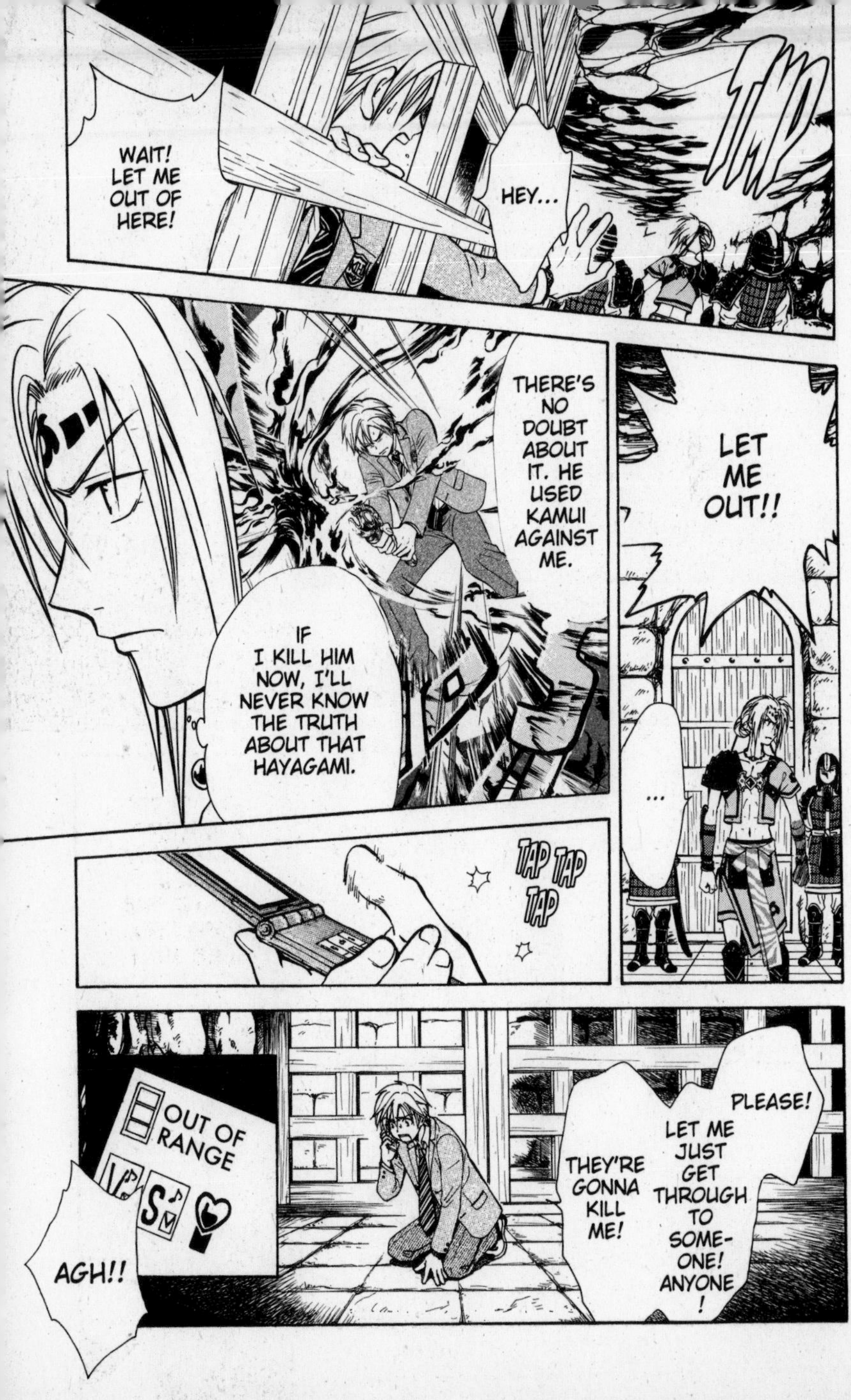
TAP
HEY...
WAIT! LET ME OUT OF HERE!
LET ME OUT!!
...
THERE'S NO DOUBT ABOUT IT. HE USED KAMUI AGAINST ME.
IF I KILL HIM NOW, I'LL NEVER KNOW THE TRUTH ABOUT THAT HAYAGAMI.
TAP TAP TAP
PLEASE!
LET ME JUST GET THROUGH TO SOME-ONE! ANYONE!
THEY'RE GONNA KILL ME!
OUT OF RANGE
AGH!!

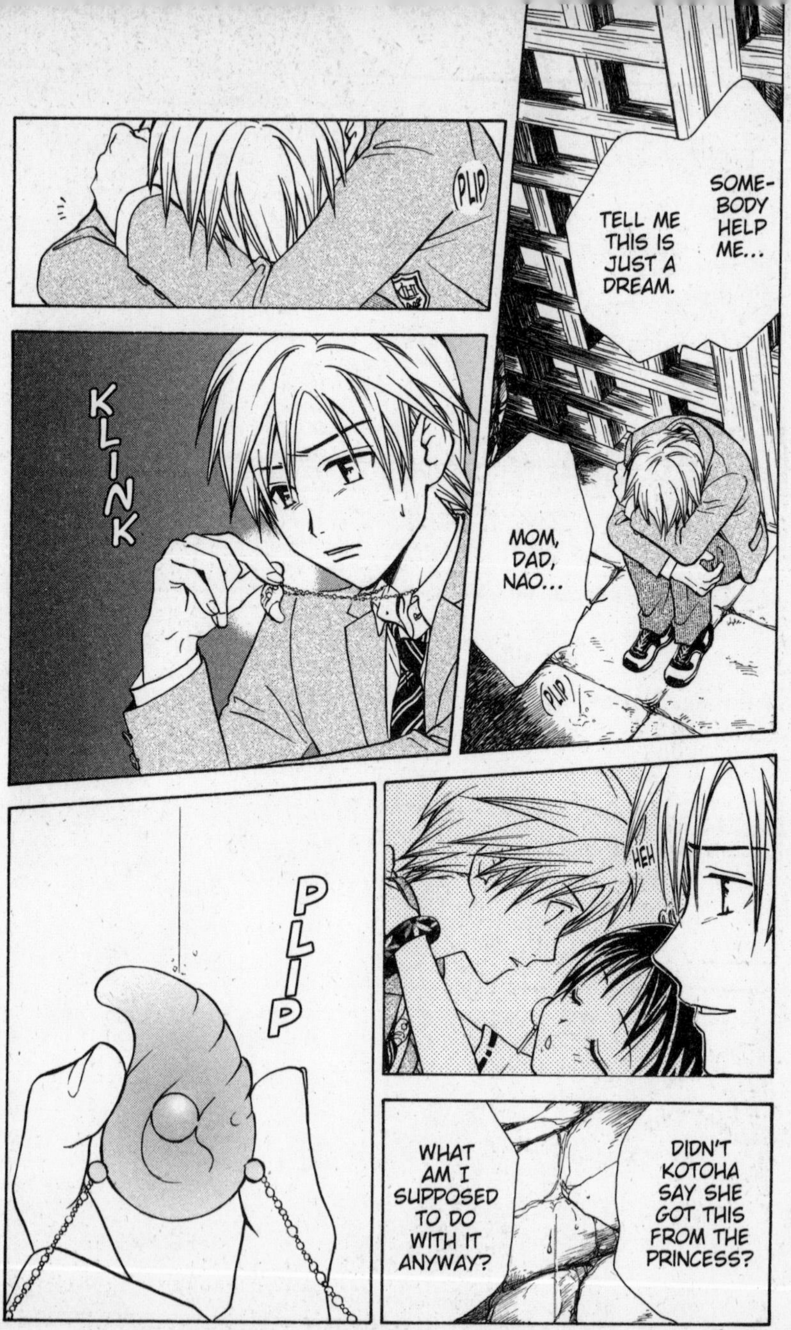
SOMEBODY HELP ME...
TELL ME THIS IS JUST A DREAM.
MOM, DAD, NAO...
PLIP
PLIP
KLINK
HEH
DIDN'T KOTOHA SAY SHE GOT THIS FROM THE PRINCESS?
WHAT AM I SUPPOSED TO DO WITH IT ANYWAY?
PLIP

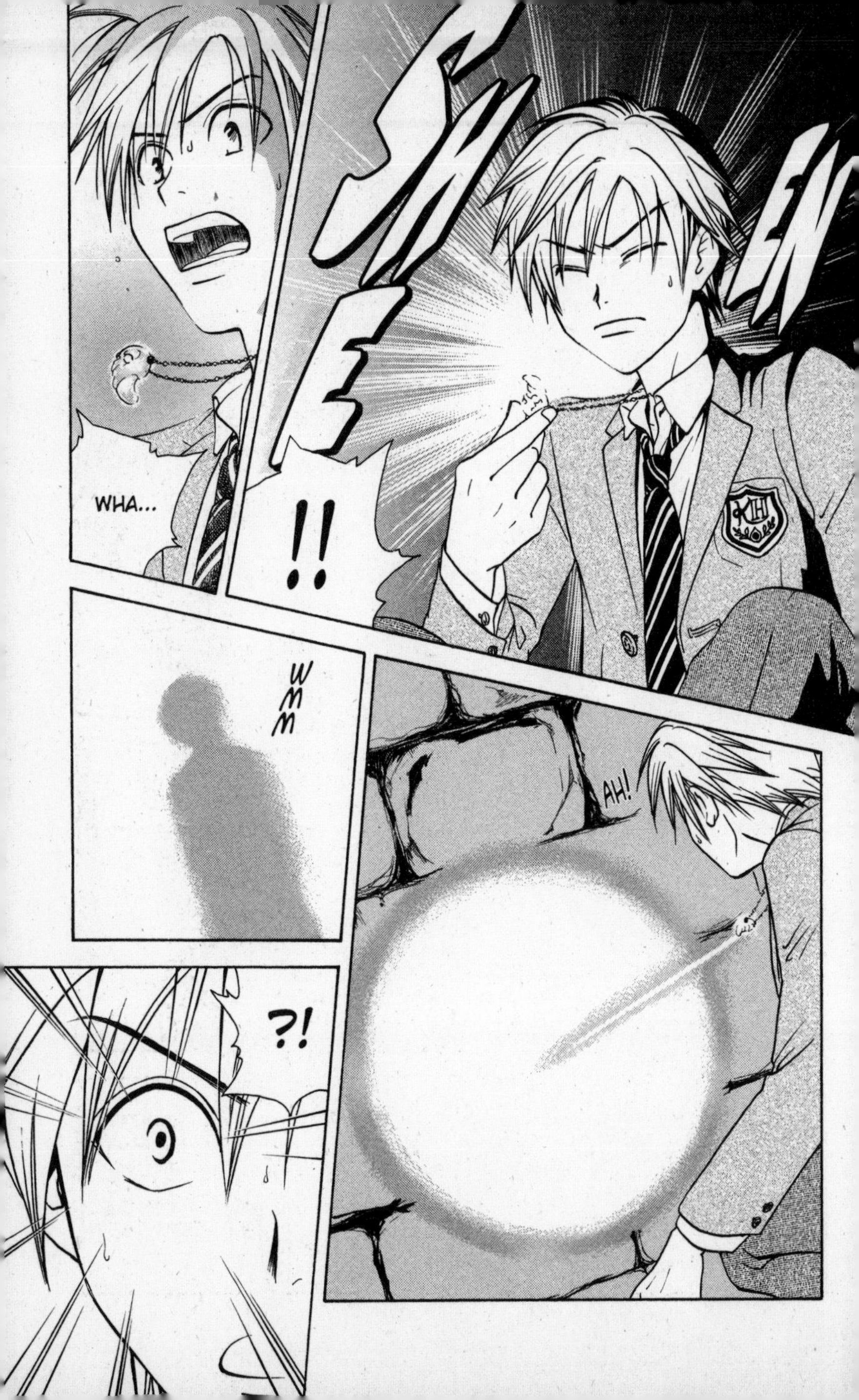
!!
WHA...
AH!
WMM
?!

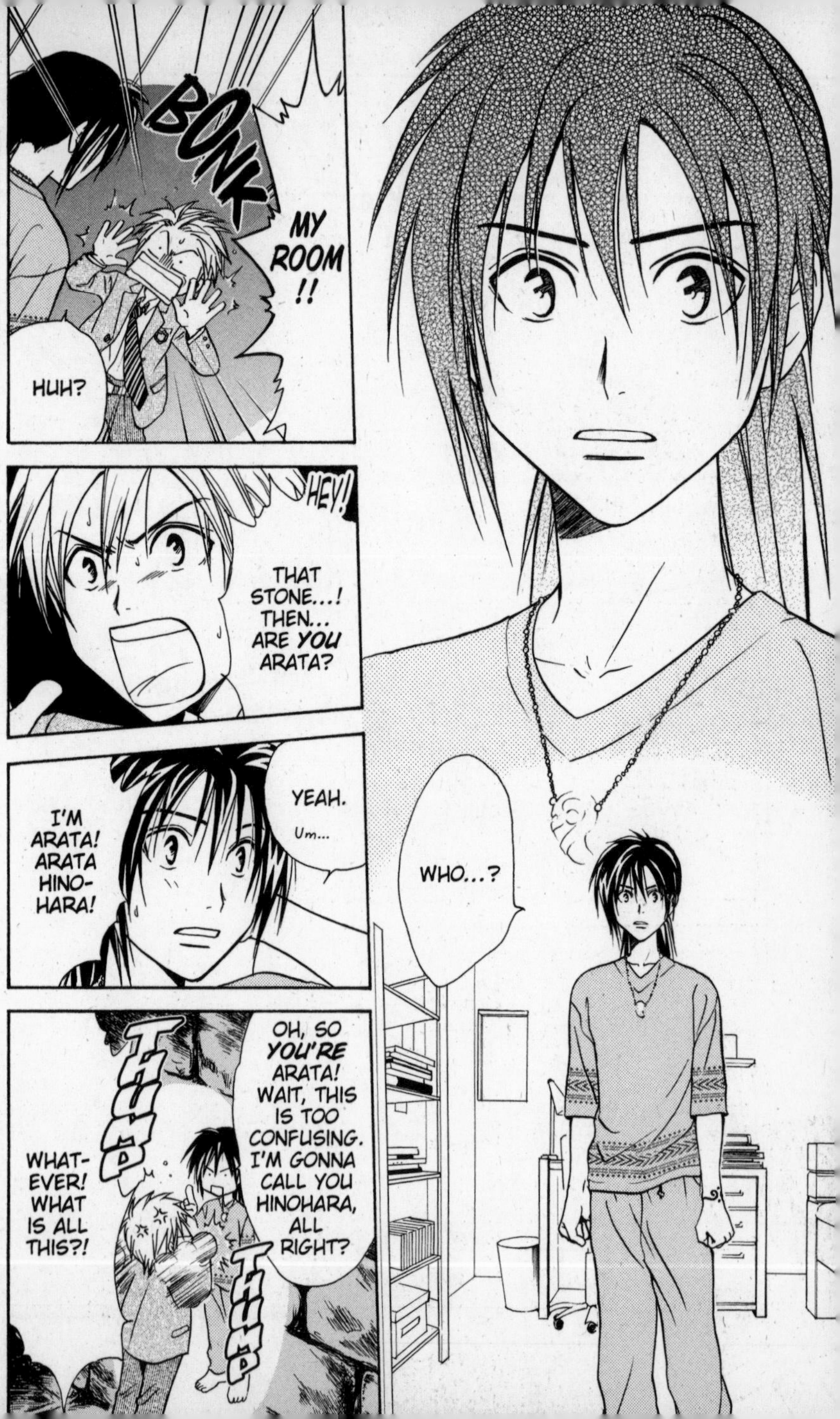
WHO...?
BONK
MY ROOM!!
HUH?
HEY!
THAT STONE...! THEN... ARE *YOU* ARATA?
YEAH.
Um...
I'M ARATA! ARATA HINOHARA!
OH, SO *YOU'RE* ARATA! WAIT, THIS IS TOO CONFUSING. I'M GONNA CALL YOU HINOHARA, ALL RIGHT?
THUMP
WHAT-EVER! WHAT IS ALL THIS?!
THUMP

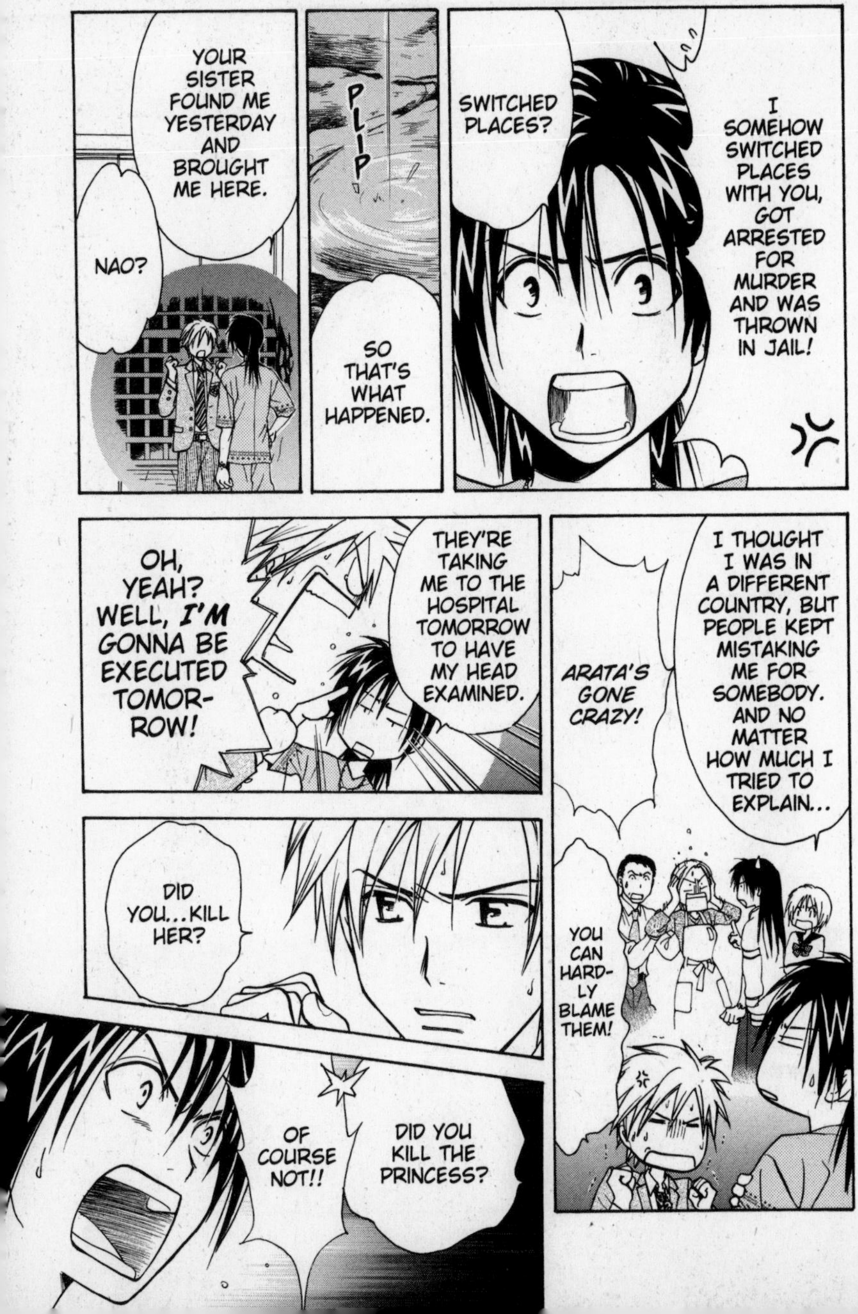
I SOMEHOW SWITCHED PLACES WITH YOU, GOT ARRESTED FOR MURDER AND WAS THROWN IN JAIL!
SWITCHED PLACES?
PLIP
SO THAT'S WHAT HAPPENED.
YOUR SISTER FOUND ME YESTERDAY AND BROUGHT ME HERE.
NAO?
I THOUGHT I WAS IN A DIFFERENT COUNTRY, BUT PEOPLE KEPT MISTAKING ME FOR SOMEBODY. AND NO MATTER HOW MUCH I TRIED TO EXPLAIN...
ARATA'S GONE CRAZY!
YOU CAN HARDLY BLAME THEM!
THEY'RE TAKING ME TO THE HOSPITAL TOMORROW TO HAVE MY HEAD EXAMINED.
OH, YEAH? WELL, I'M GONNA BE EXECUTED TOMORROW!
DID YOU...KILL HER?
DID YOU KILL THE PRINCESS?
OF COURSE NOT!!

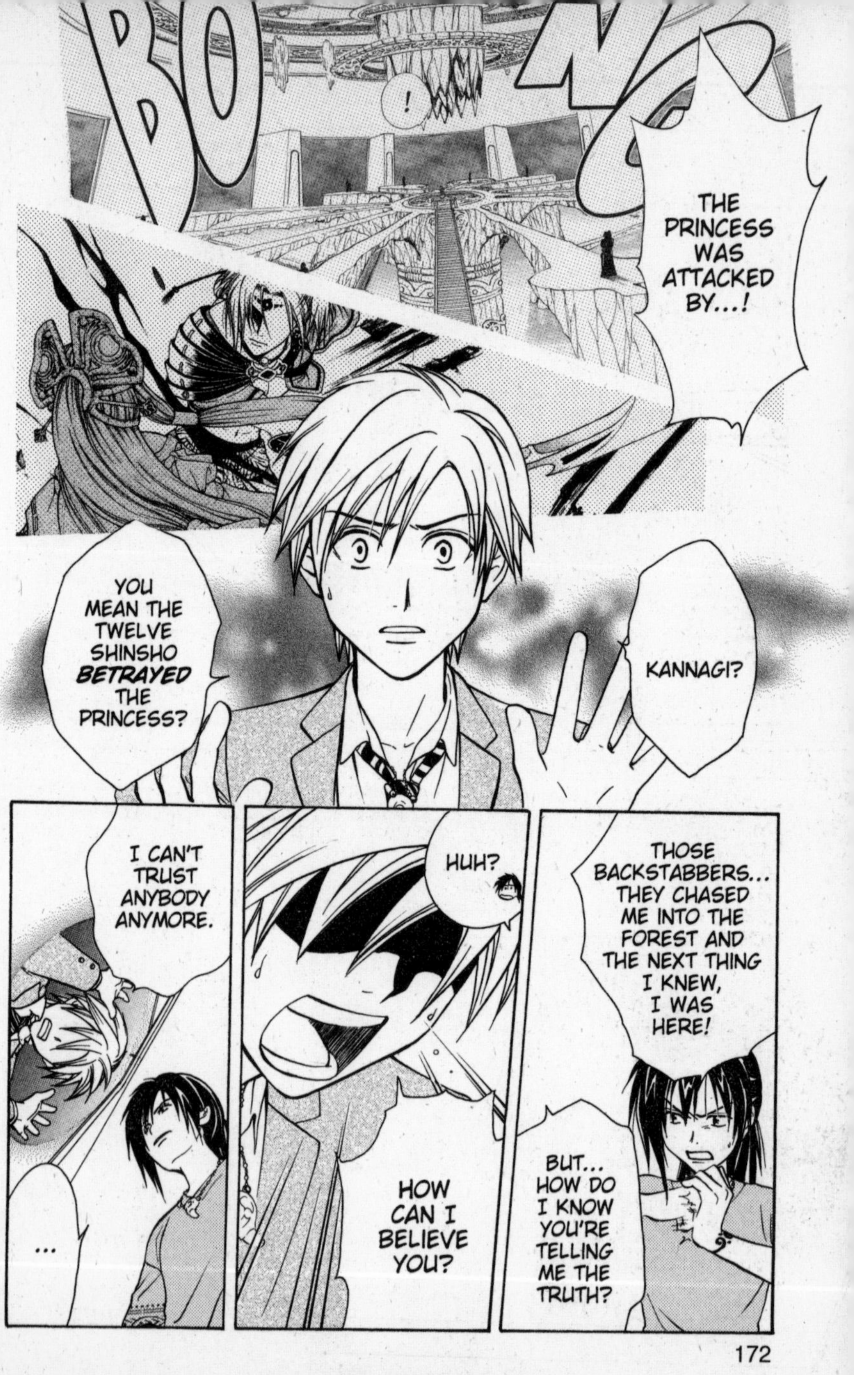
!
THE PRINCESS WAS ATTACKED BY...!
KANNAGI?
YOU MEAN THE TWELVE SHINSHO ***BETRAYED*** THE PRINCESS?
THOSE BACKSTABBERS... THEY CHASED ME INTO THE FOREST AND THE NEXT THING I KNEW, I WAS HERE!
BUT... HOW DO I KNOW YOU'RE TELLING ME THE TRUTH?
HUH?
HOW CAN I BELIEVE YOU?
I CAN'T TRUST ANYBODY ANYMORE.
...

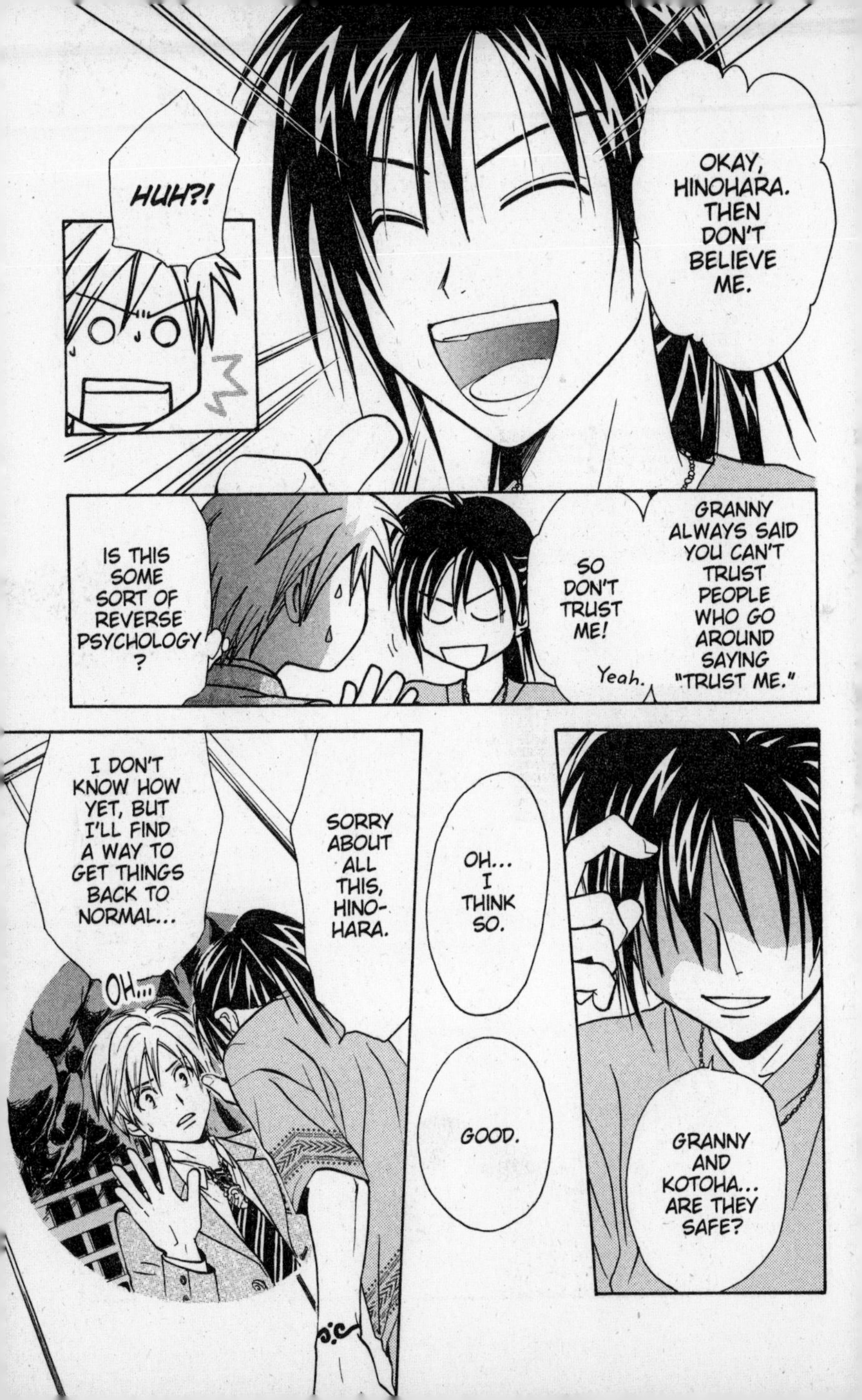
OKAY, HINOHARA. THEN DON'T BELIEVE ME.
HUH?!
GRANNY ALWAYS SAID YOU CAN'T TRUST PEOPLE WHO GO AROUND SAYING "TRUST ME."
Yeah.
SO DON'T TRUST ME!
IS THIS SOME SORT OF REVERSE PSYCHOLOGY?
GRANNY AND KOTOHA... ARE THEY SAFE?
OH... I THINK SO.
GOOD.
SORRY ABOUT ALL THIS, HINO-HARA.
I DON'T KNOW HOW YET, BUT I'LL FIND A WAY TO GET THINGS BACK TO NORMAL...
OH...

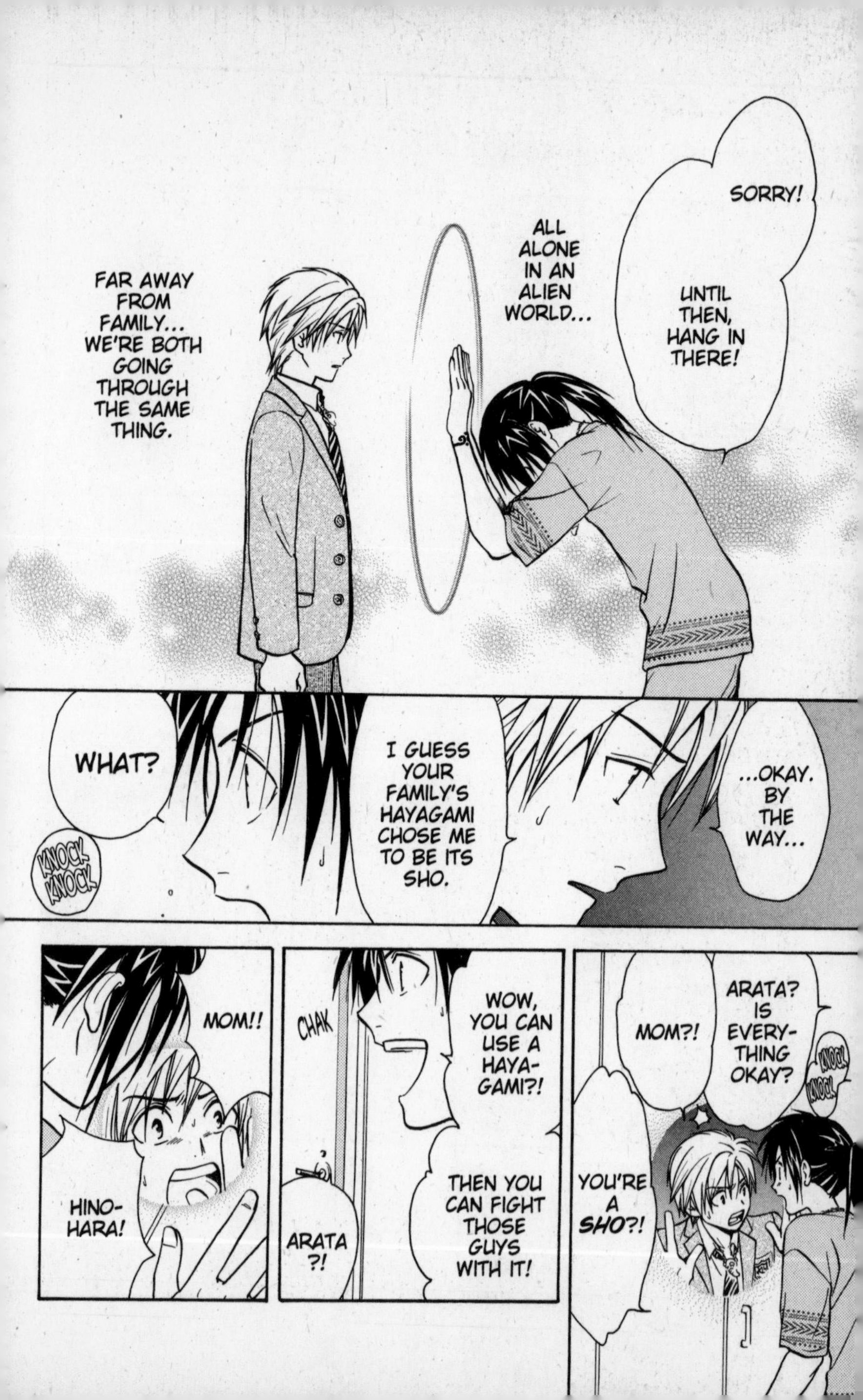
SORRY!
UNTIL THEN, HANG IN THERE!
ALL ALONE IN AN ALIEN WORLD...
FAR AWAY FROM FAMILY... WE'RE BOTH GOING THROUGH THE SAME THING.
...OKAY. BY THE WAY...
I GUESS YOUR FAMILY'S HAYAGAMI CHOSE ME TO BE ITS SHO.
WHAT?
KNOCK KNOCK
ARATA? IS EVERY-THING OKAY?
KNOCK KNOCK
MOM?!
YOU'RE A SHO?!
WOW, YOU CAN USE A HAYA-GAMI?!
CHAK
THEN YOU CAN FIGHT THOSE GUYS WITH IT!
ARATA?!
MOM!!
HINO-HARA!

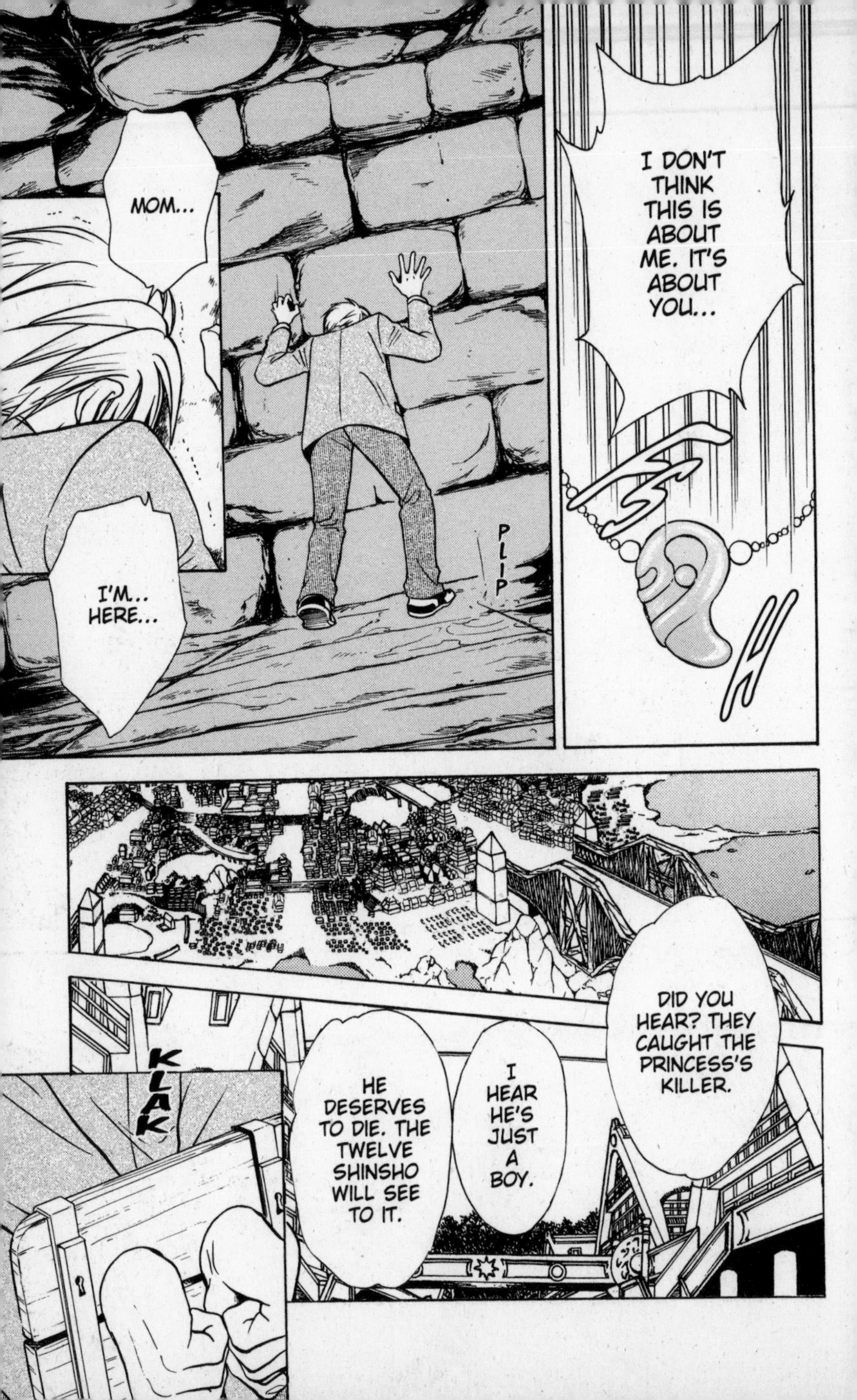
I DON'T THINK THIS IS ABOUT ME. IT'S ABOUT YOU...
MOM...
PLIP
I'M... HERE...
DID YOU HEAR? THEY CAUGHT THE PRINCESS'S KILLER.
I HEAR HE'S JUST A BOY.
HE DESERVES TO DIE. THE TWELVE SHINSHO WILL SEE TO IT.
KLAK

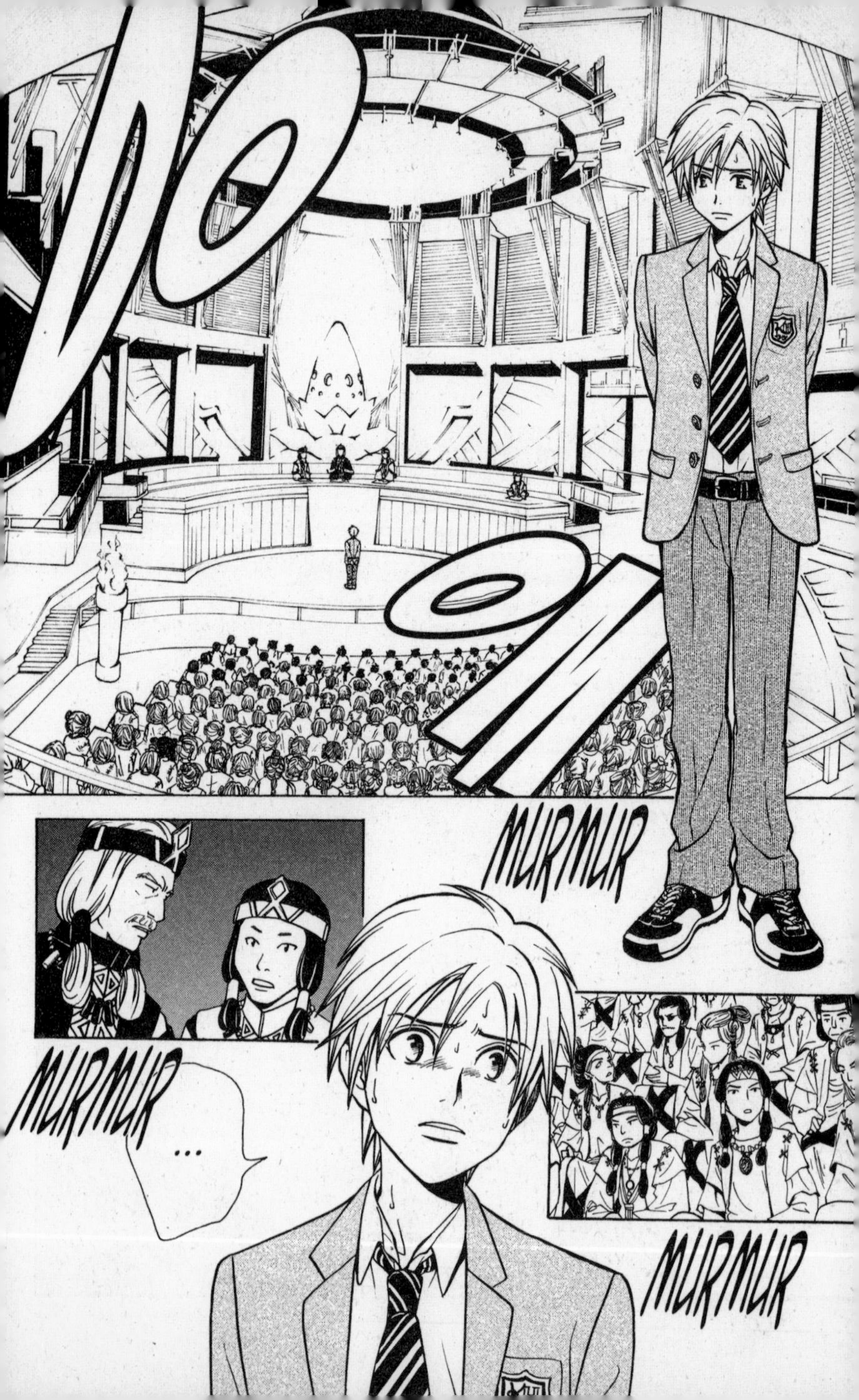
DO
O
MURMUR
MURMUR
...
MURMUR

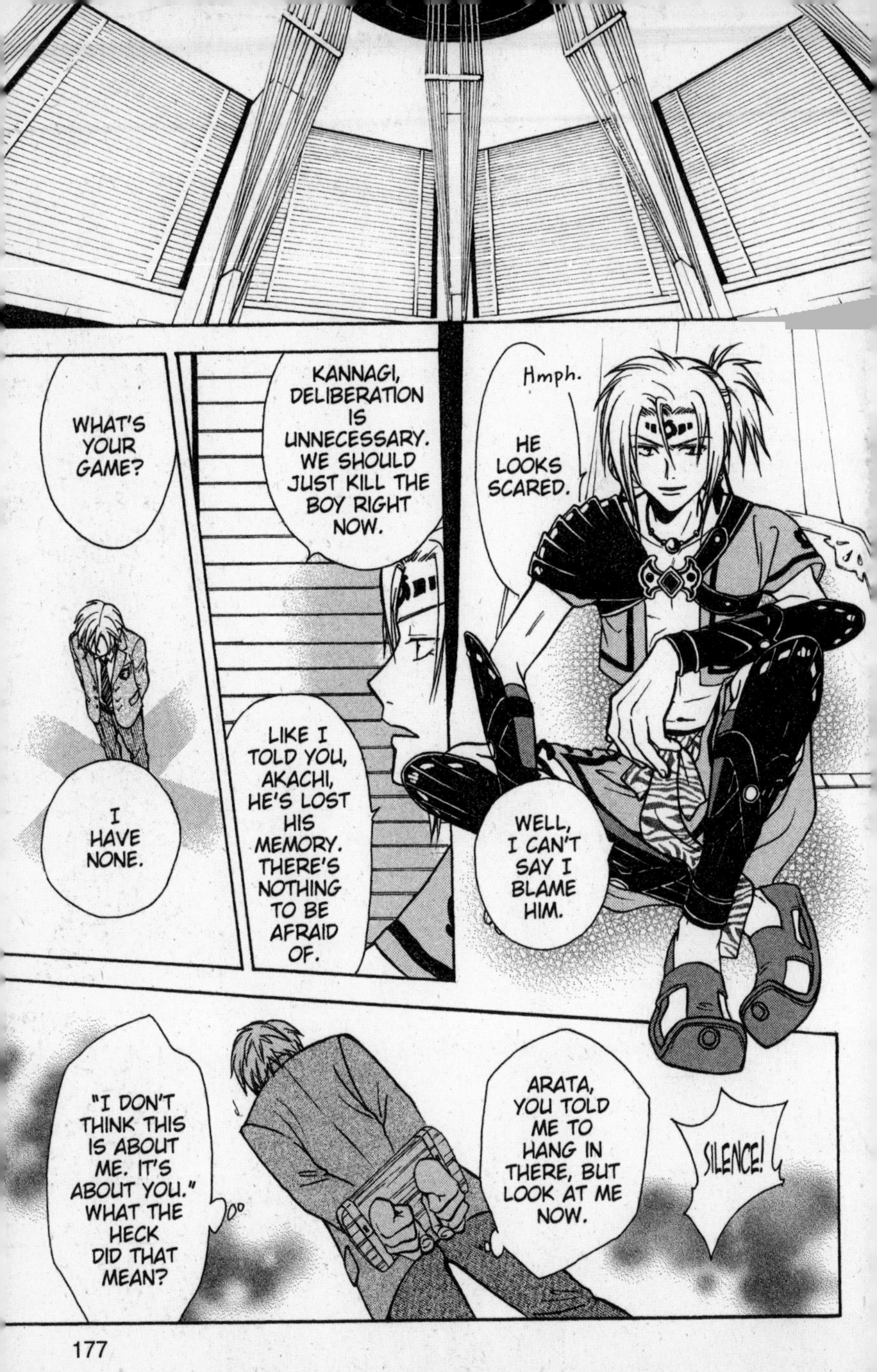
Hmph.
HE LOOKS SCARED.
WELL, I CAN'T SAY I BLAME HIM.
KANNAGI, DELIBERATION IS UNNECESSARY. WE SHOULD JUST KILL THE BOY RIGHT NOW.
LIKE I TOLD YOU, AKACHI, HE'S LOST HIS MEMORY. THERE'S NOTHING TO BE AFRAID OF.
WHAT'S YOUR GAME?
I HAVE NONE.
SILENCE!
ARATA, YOU TOLD ME TO HANG IN THERE, BUT LOOK AT ME NOW.
"I DON'T THINK THIS IS ABOUT ME. IT'S ABOUT YOU." WHAT THE HECK DID THAT MEAN?

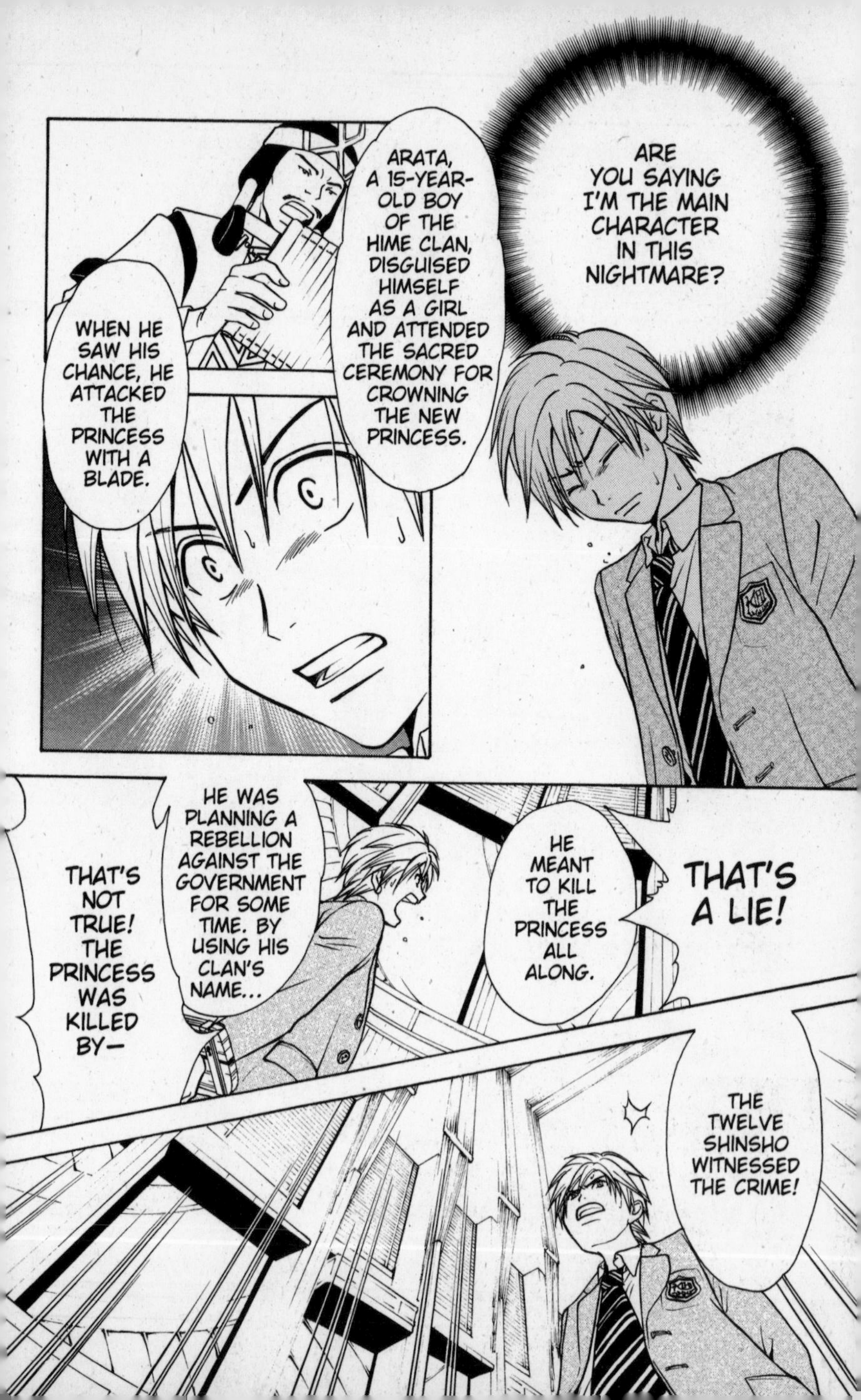
ARE YOU SAYING I'M THE MAIN CHARACTER IN THIS NIGHTMARE?
ARATA, A 15-YEAR-OLD BOY OF THE HIME CLAN, DISGUISED HIMSELF AS A GIRL AND ATTENDED THE SACRED CEREMONY FOR CROWNING THE NEW PRINCESS.
WHEN HE SAW HIS CHANCE, HE ATTACKED THE PRINCESS WITH A BLADE.
THAT'S A LIE!
HE MEANT TO KILL THE PRINCESS ALL ALONG.
HE WAS PLANNING A REBELLION AGAINST THE GOVERNMENT FOR SOME TIME. BY USING HIS CLAN'S NAME...
THAT'S NOT TRUE! THE PRINCESS WAS KILLED BY—
THE TWELVE SHINSHO WITNESSED THE CRIME!

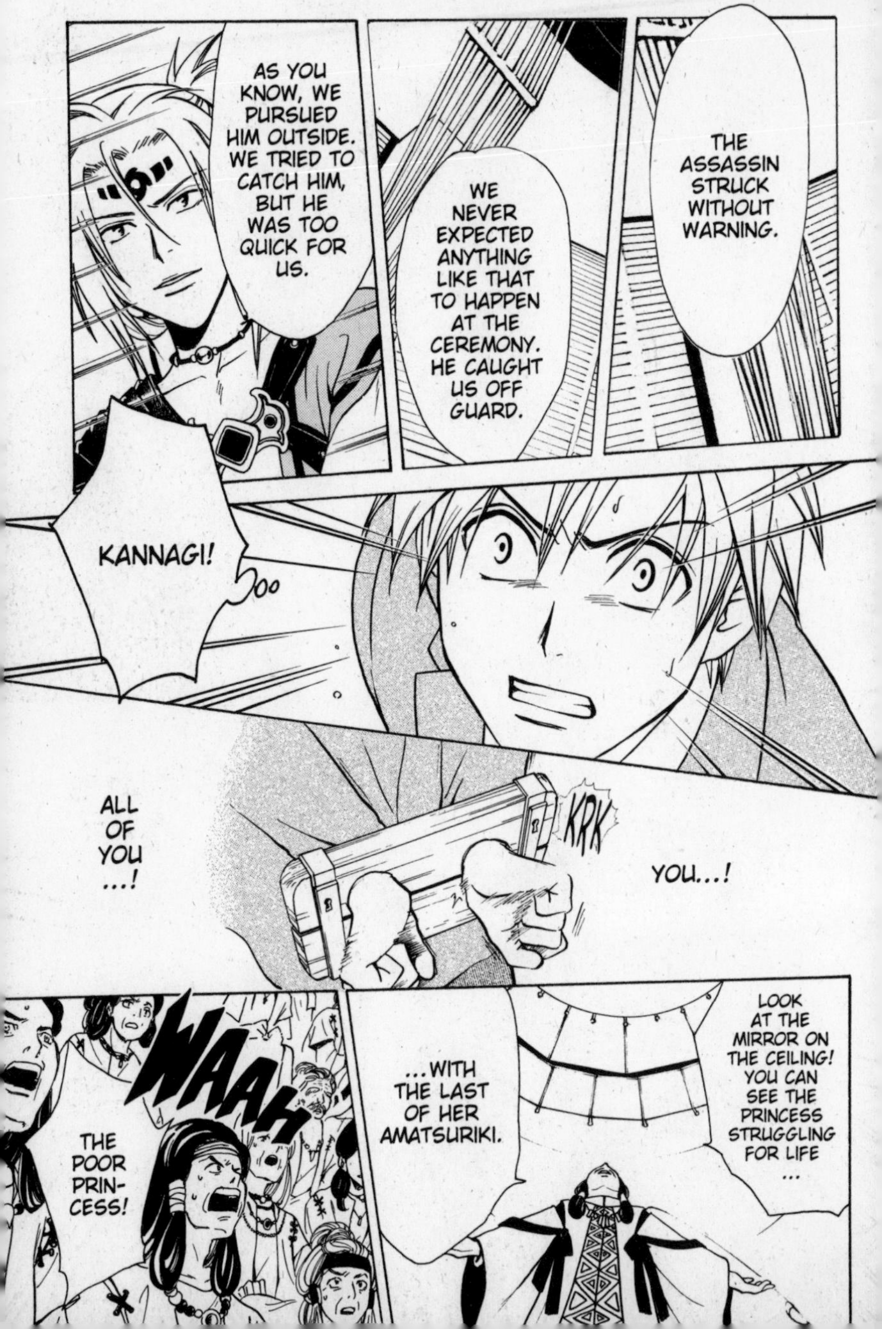
THE ASSASSIN STRUCK WITHOUT WARNING.
WE NEVER EXPECTED ANYTHING LIKE THAT TO HAPPEN AT THE CEREMONY. HE CAUGHT US OFF GUARD.
AS YOU KNOW, WE PURSUED HIM OUTSIDE. WE TRIED TO CATCH HIM, BUT HE WAS TOO QUICK FOR US.
KANNAGI!
YOU...!
KRK
ALL OF YOU ...!
LOOK AT THE MIRROR ON THE CEILING! YOU CAN SEE THE PRINCESS STRUGGLING FOR LIFE ...
...WITH THE LAST OF HER AMATSURIKI.
WAAAH
THE POOR PRIN-CESS!

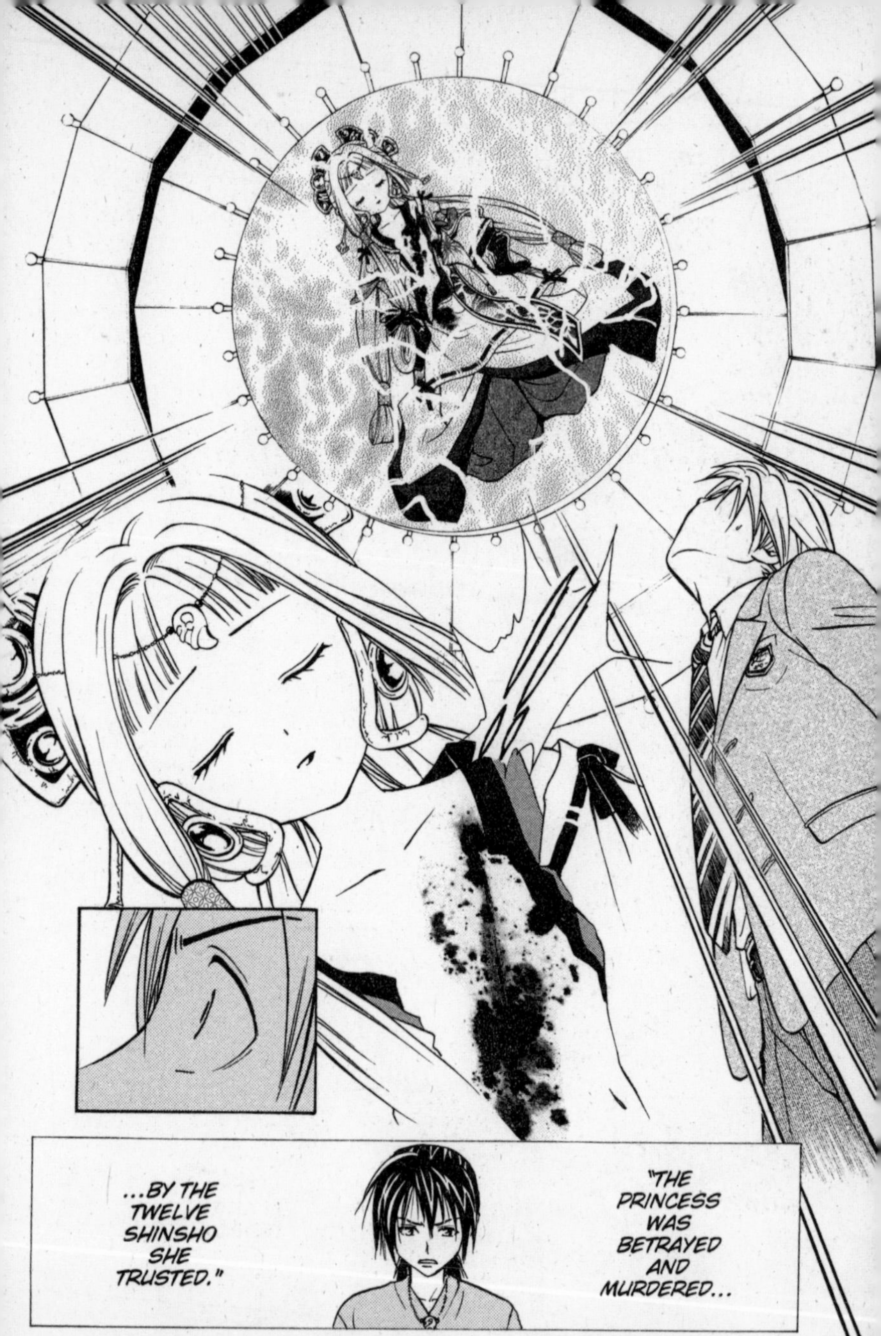
"THE PRINCESS WAS BETRAYED AND MURDERED...
...BY THE TWELVE SHINSHO SHE TRUSTED."

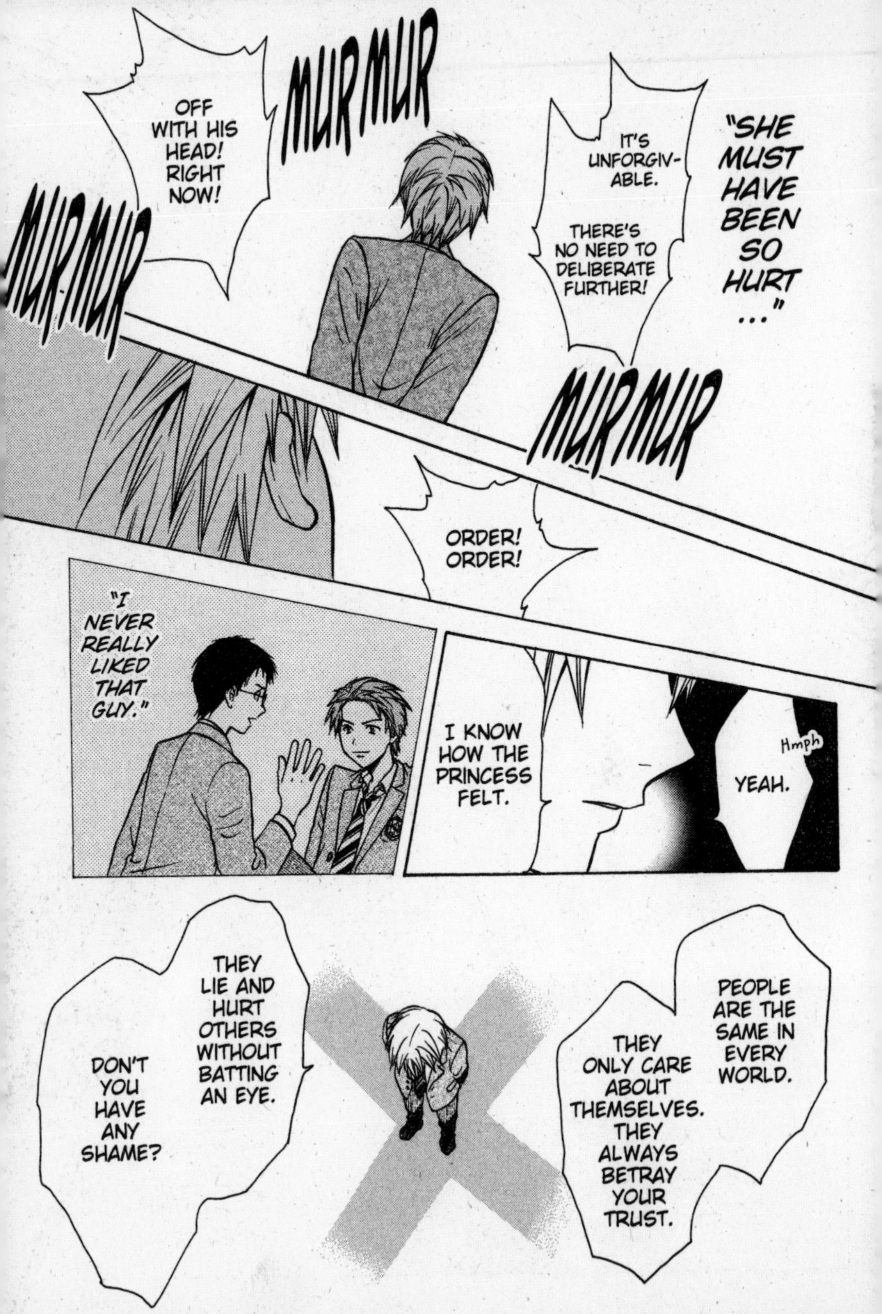
"SHE MUST HAVE BEEN SO HURT..."
IT'S UNFORGIV-ABLE.
THERE'S NO NEED TO DELIBERATE FURTHER!
MURMUR
OFF WITH HIS HEAD! RIGHT NOW!
MURMUR
MURMUR
ORDER! ORDER!
Hmph
YEAH.
I KNOW HOW THE PRINCESS FELT.
"I NEVER REALLY LIKED THAT GUY."
PEOPLE ARE THE SAME IN EVERY WORLD.
THEY ONLY CARE ABOUT THEMSELVES. THEY ALWAYS BETRAY YOUR TRUST.
THEY LIE AND HURT OTHERS WITHOUT BATTING AN EYE.
DON'T YOU HAVE ANY SHAME?

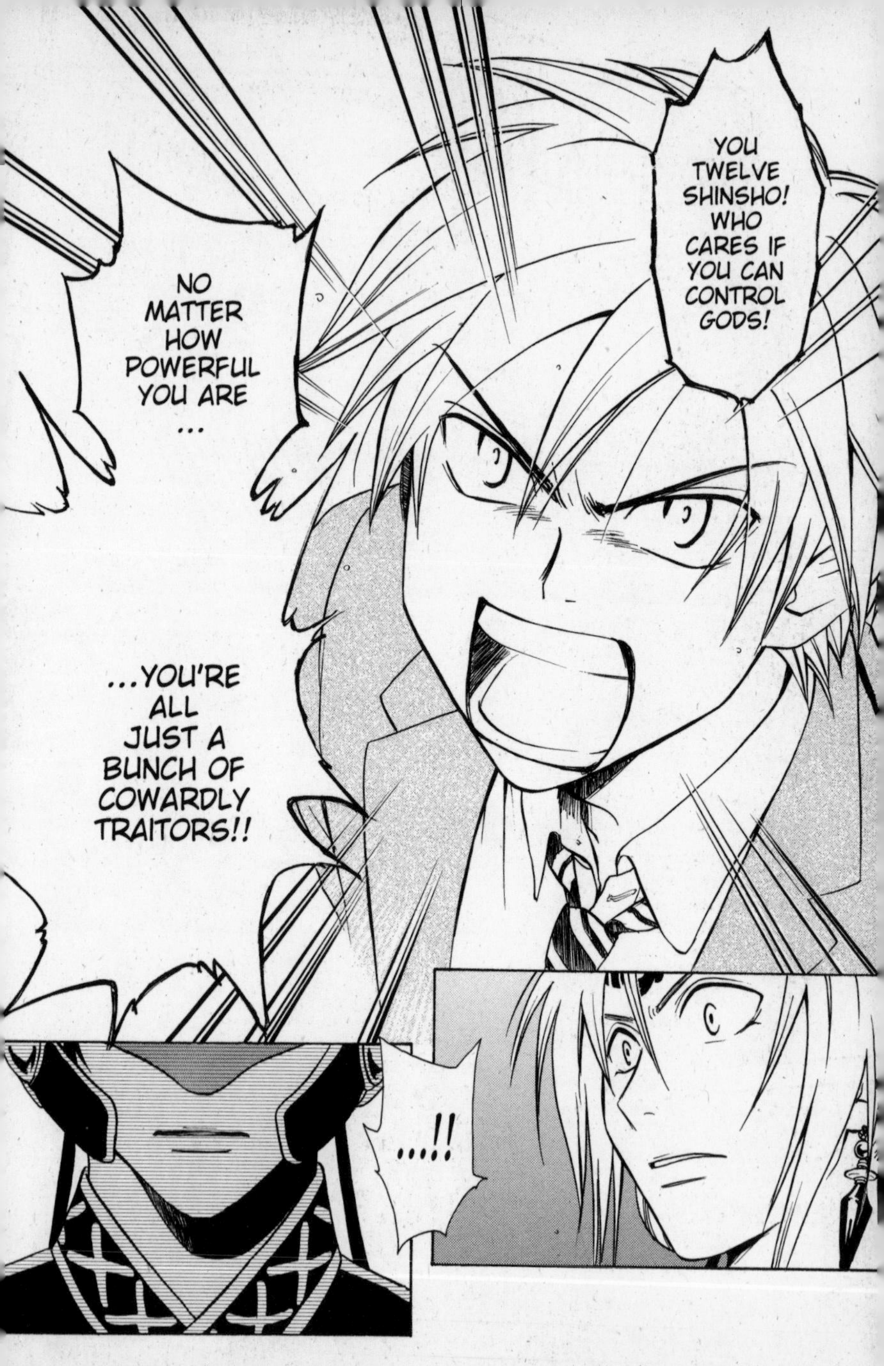
YOU TWELVE SHINSHO! WHO CARES IF YOU CAN CONTROL GODS!
NO MATTER HOW POWERFUL YOU ARE ...
...YOU'RE ALL JUST A BUNCH OF COWARDLY TRAITORS!!
...!!

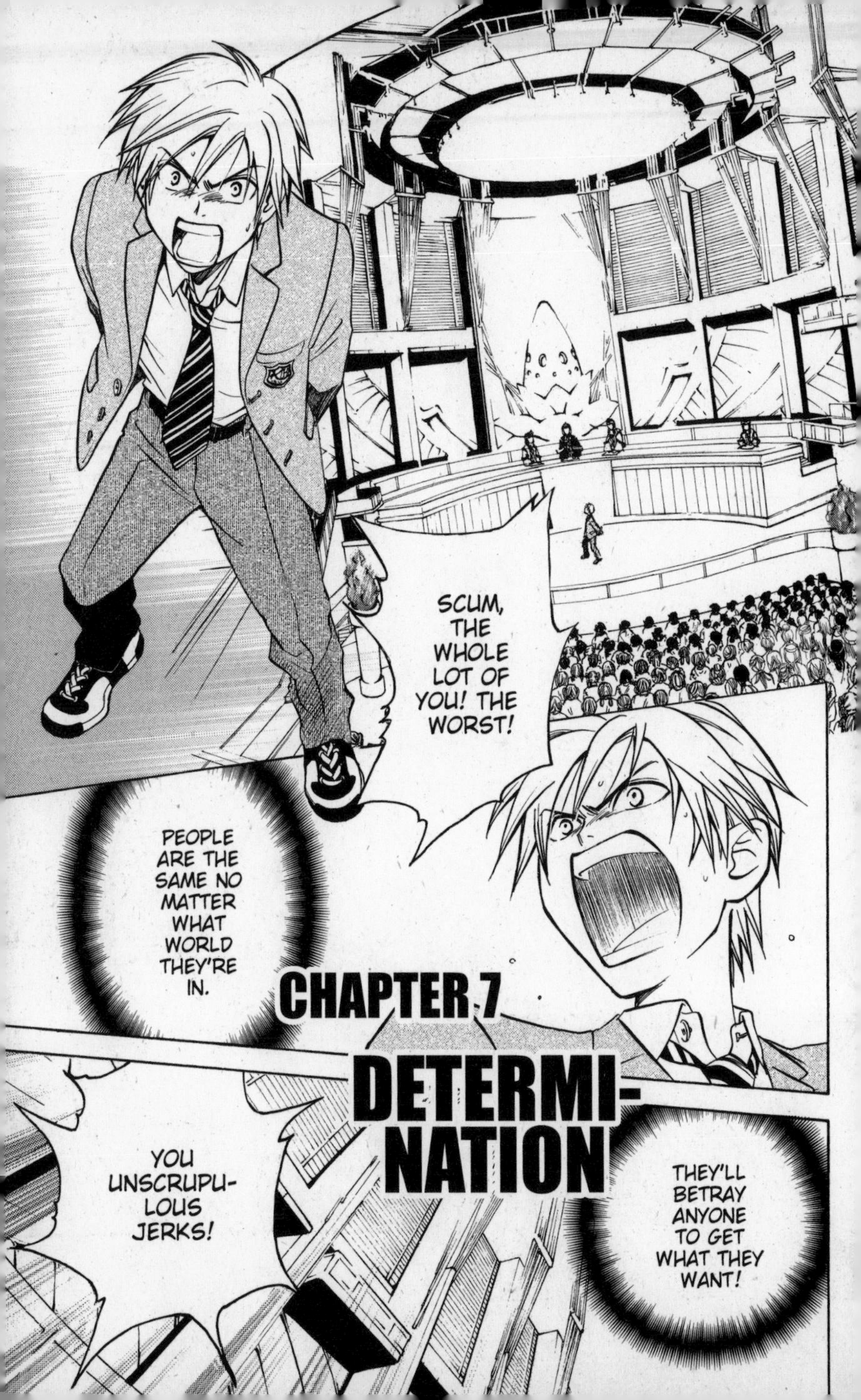
SCUM, THE WHOLE LOT OF YOU! THE WORST!
PEOPLE ARE THE SAME NO MATTER WHAT WORLD THEY'RE IN.
CHAPTER 7
DETERMI-NATION
THEY'LL BETRAY ANYONE TO GET WHAT THEY WANT!
YOU UNSCRUPULOUS JERKS!

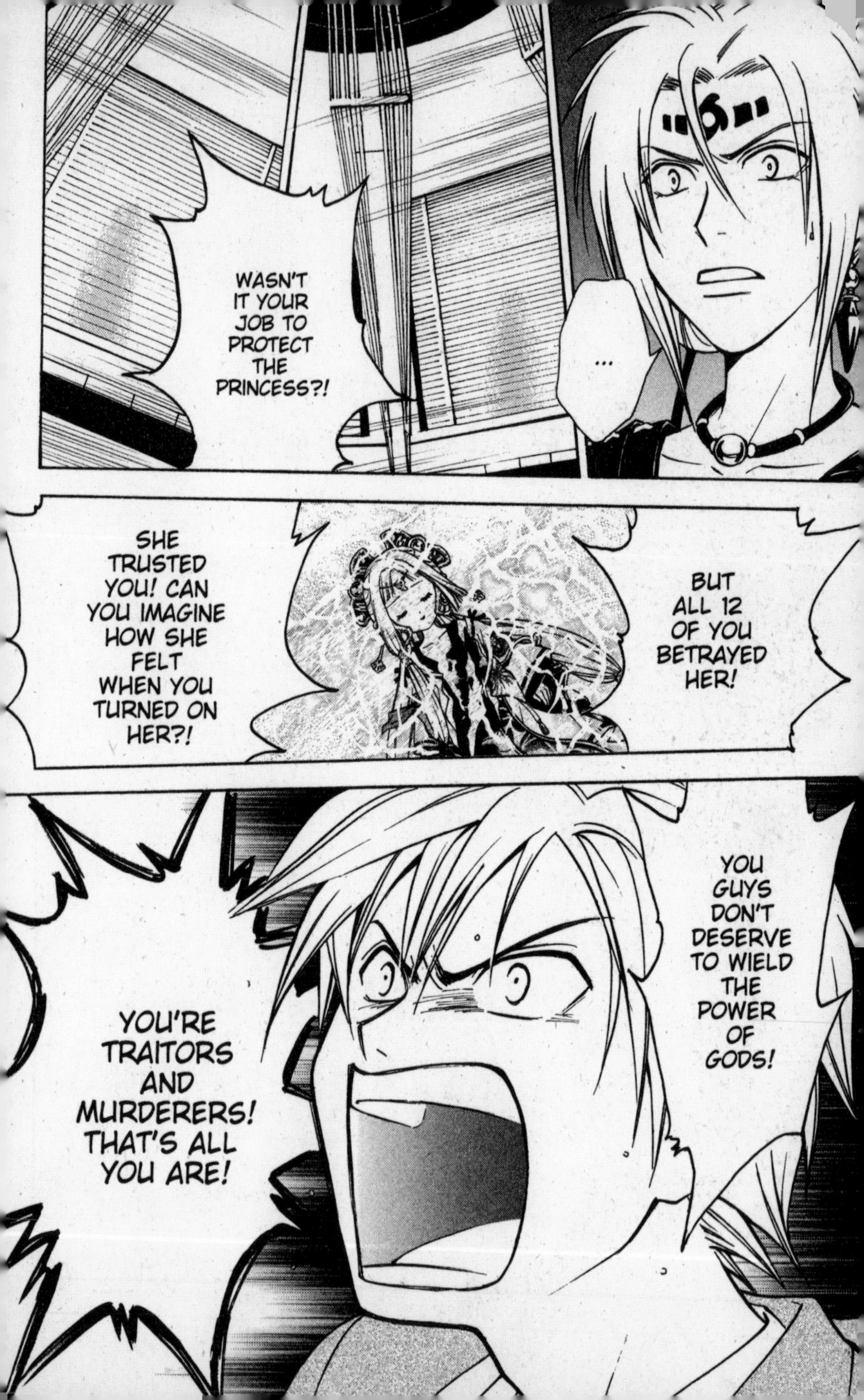
WASN'T IT YOUR JOB TO PROTECT THE PRINCESS?!
...
SHE TRUSTED YOU! CAN YOU IMAGINE HOW SHE FELT WHEN YOU TURNED ON HER?!
BUT ALL 12 OF YOU BETRAYED HER!
YOU GUYS DON'T DESERVE TO WIELD THE POWER OF GODS!
YOU'RE TRAITORS AND MURDERERS! THAT'S ALL YOU ARE!

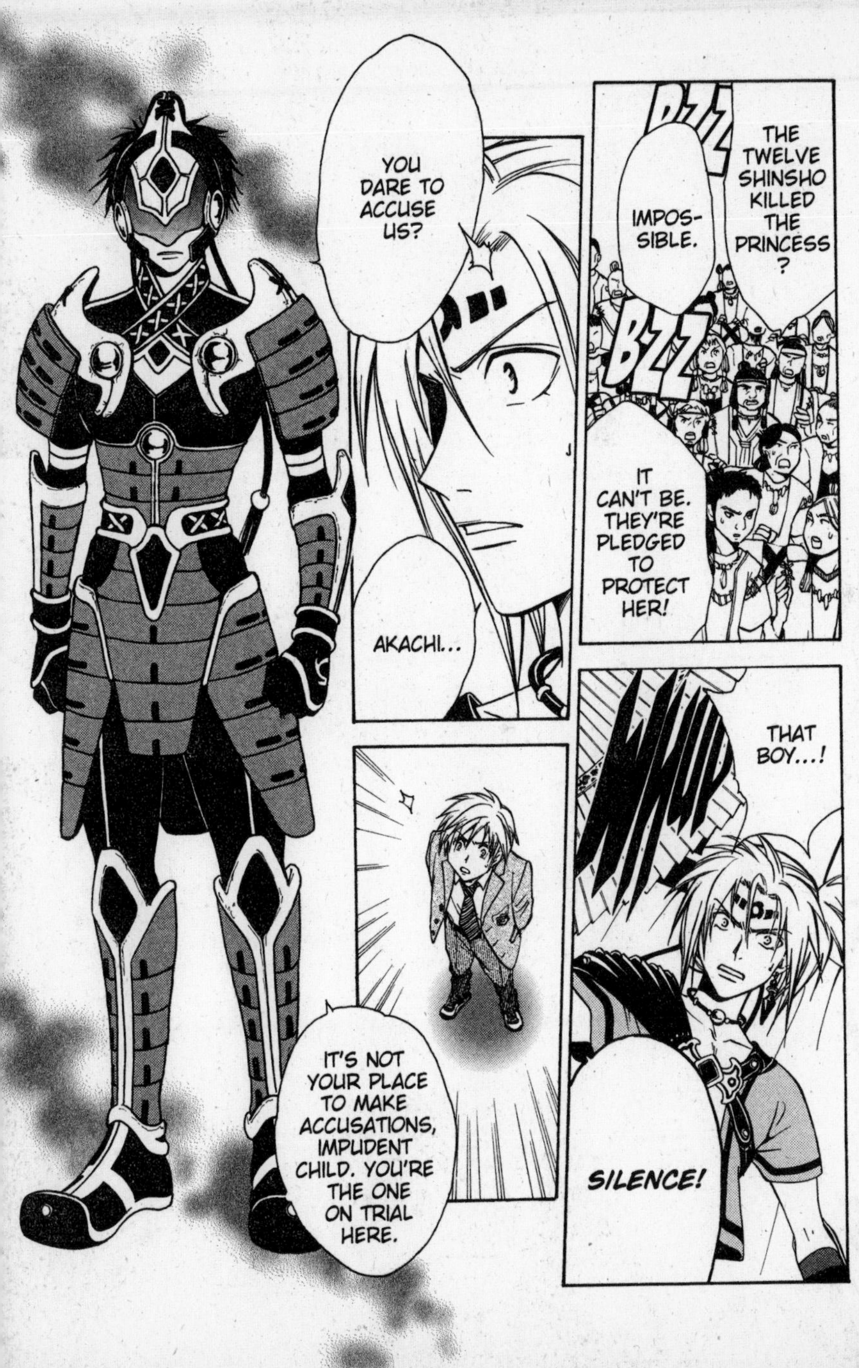
BZZ
THE TWELVE SHINSHO KILLED THE PRINCESS?
IMPOS-SIBLE.
BZZ
IT CAN'T BE. THEY'RE PLEDGED TO PROTECT HER!
THAT BOY...!
SILENCE!
IT'S NOT YOUR PLACE TO MAKE ACCUSATIONS, IMPUDENT CHILD. YOU'RE THE ONE ON TRIAL HERE.
YOU DARE TO ACCUSE US?
AKACHI...

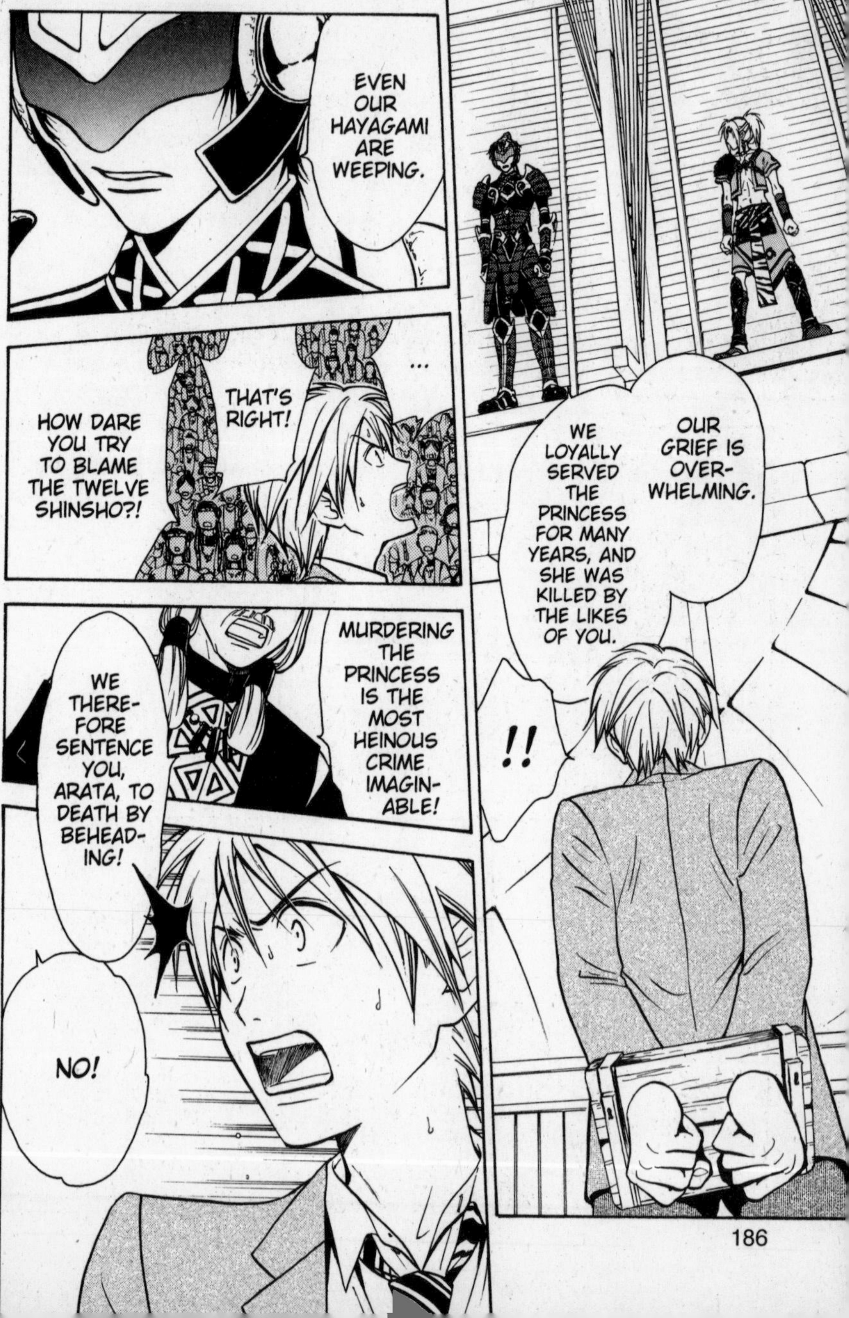
OUR GRIEF IS OVER-WHELMING.
WE LOYALLY SERVED THE PRINCESS FOR MANY YEARS, AND SHE WAS KILLED BY THE LIKES OF YOU.
!!
EVEN OUR HAYAGAMI ARE WEEPING.
...
THAT'S RIGHT!
HOW DARE YOU TRY TO BLAME THE TWELVE SHINSHO?!
MURDERING THE PRINCESS IS THE MOST HEINOUS CRIME IMAGIN-ABLE!
WE THERE-FORE SENTENCE YOU, ARATA, TO DEATH BY BEHEAD-ING!
NO!

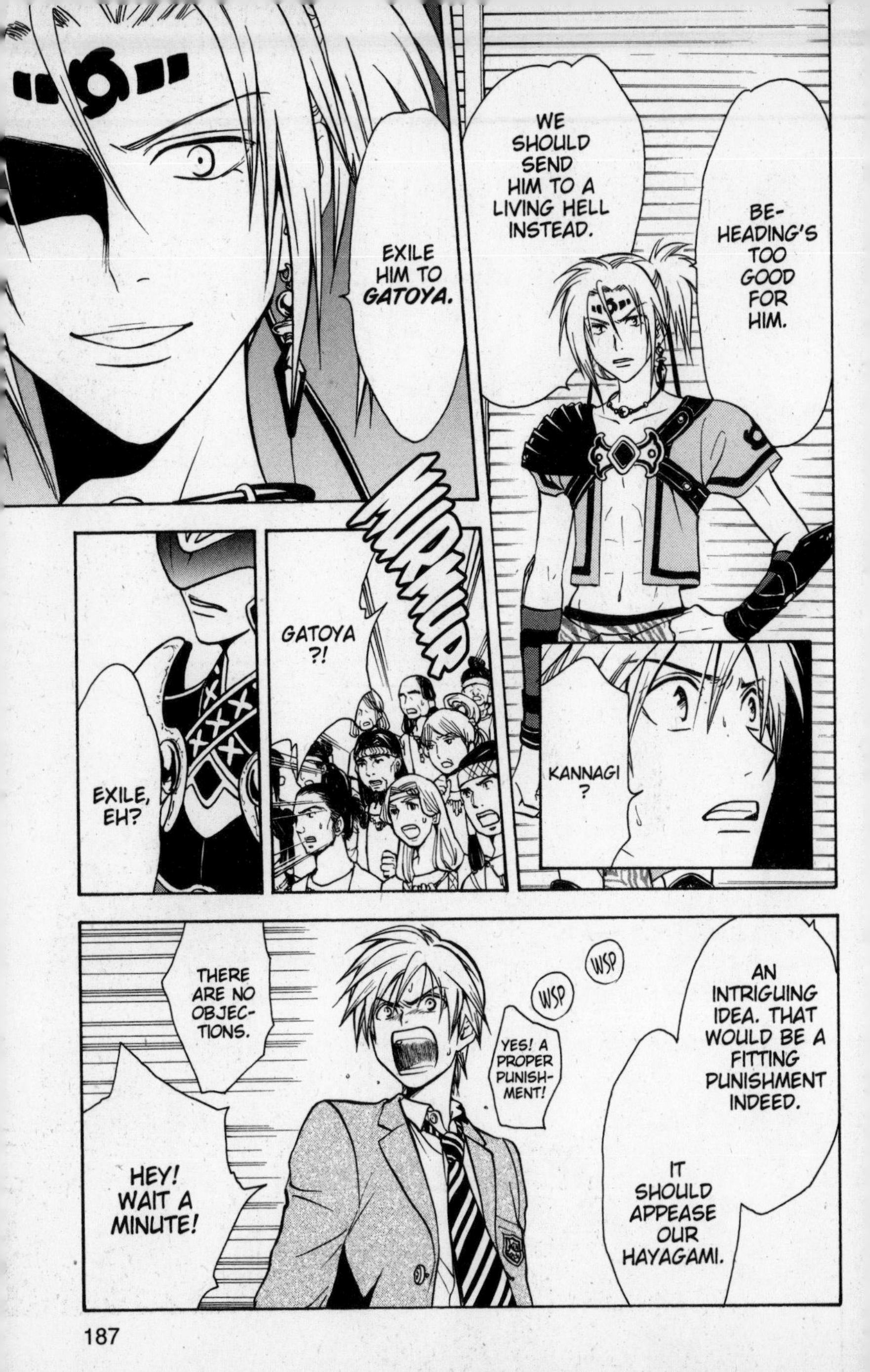
BE-HEADING'S TOO GOOD FOR HIM.
WE SHOULD SEND HIM TO A LIVING HELL INSTEAD.
EXILE HIM TO GATOYA.
KANNAGI?
MURMUR
GATOYA?!
EXILE, EH?
AN INTRIGUING IDEA. THAT WOULD BE A FITTING PUNISHMENT INDEED.
IT SHOULD APPEASE OUR HAYAGAMI.
WSP
WSP
YES! A PROPER PUNISHMENT!
THERE ARE NO OBJECTIONS.
HEY! WAIT A MINUTE!

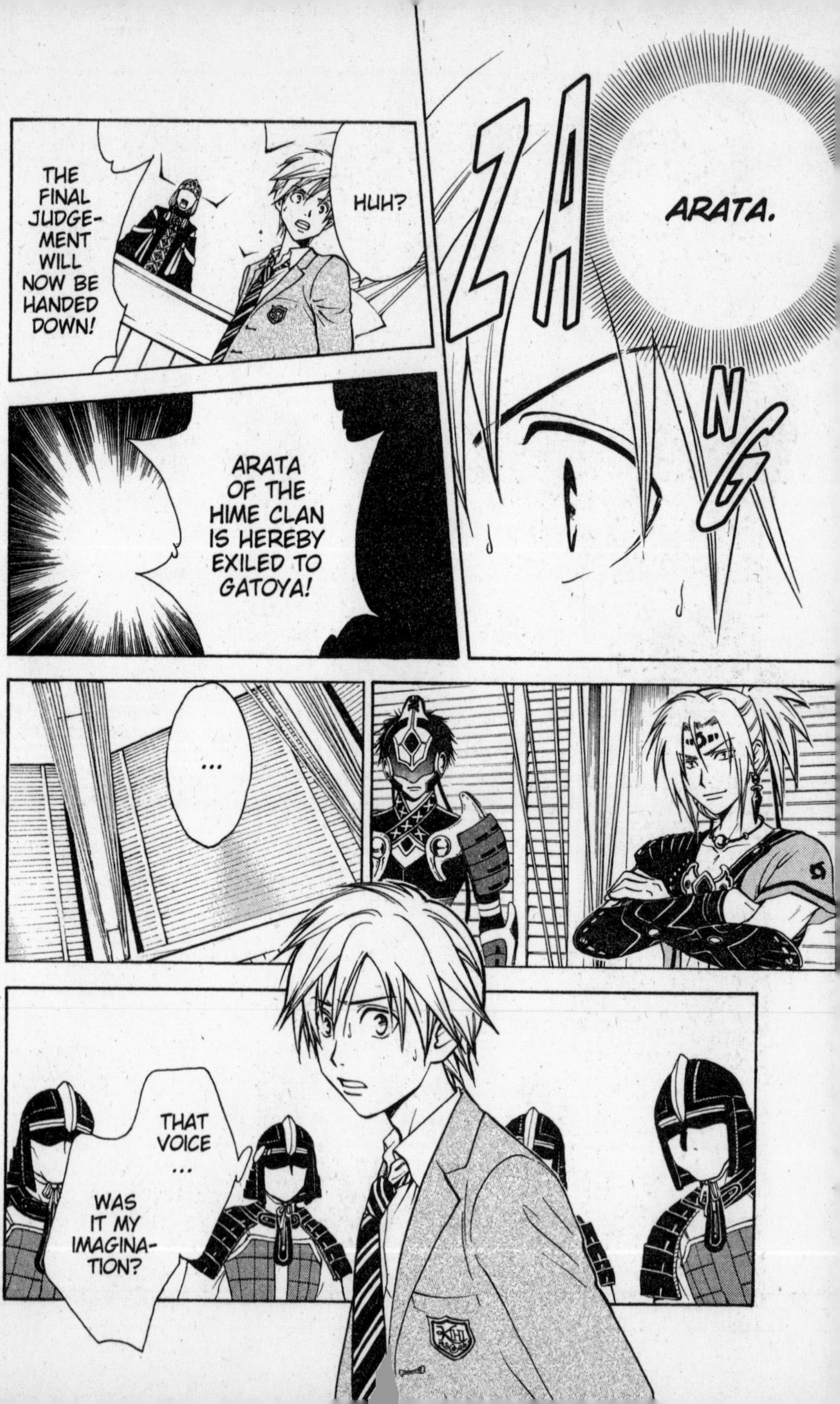
ARATA.
ZANG
THE FINAL JUDGEMENT WILL NOW BE HANDED DOWN!
HUH?
ARATA OF THE HIME CLAN IS HEREBY EXILED TO GATOYA!
...
THAT VOICE ... WAS IT MY IMAGINATION?

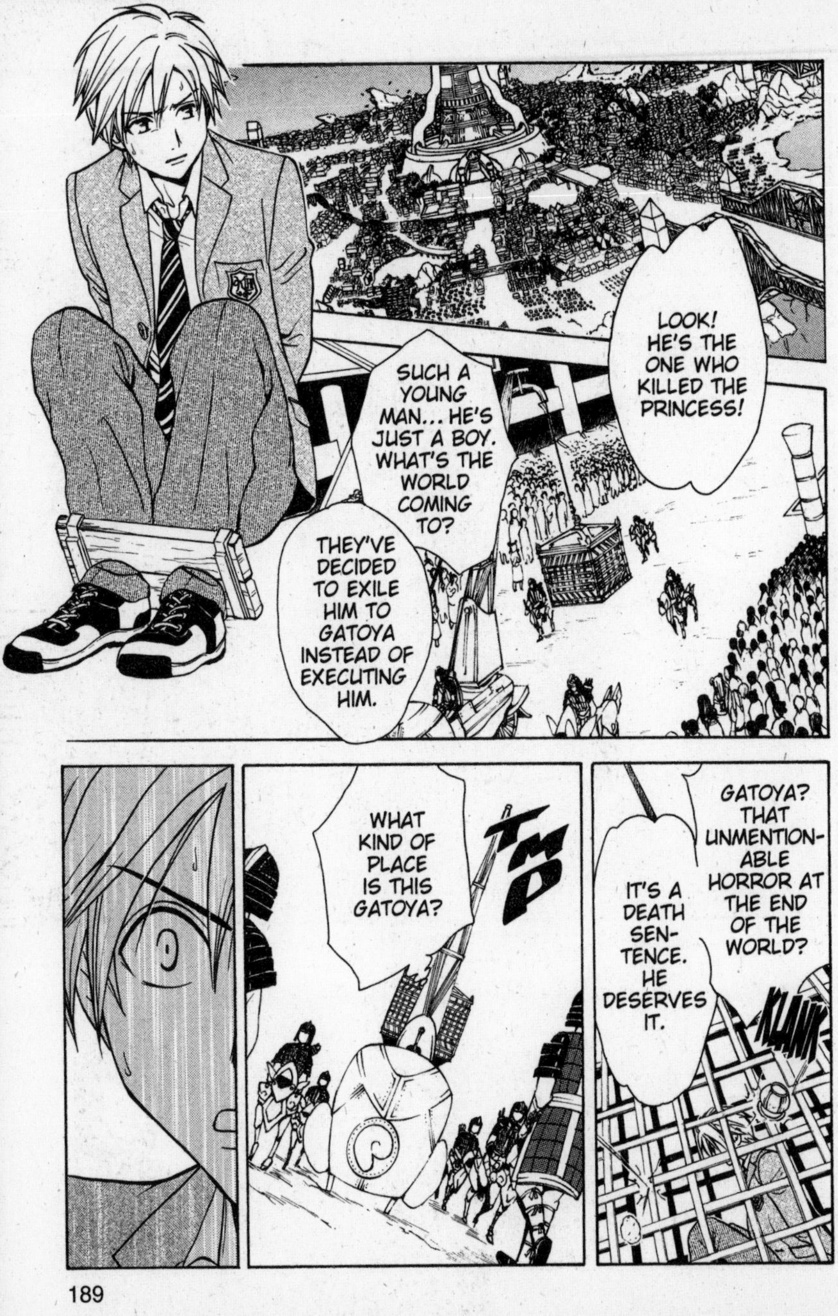
LOOK! HE'S THE ONE WHO KILLED THE PRINCESS!
SUCH A YOUNG MAN... HE'S JUST A BOY. WHAT'S THE WORLD COMING TO?
THEY'VE DECIDED TO EXILE HIM TO GATOYA INSTEAD OF EXECUTING HIM.
GATOYA? THAT UNMENTION-ABLE HORROR AT THE END OF THE WORLD?
IT'S A DEATH SEN-TENCE. HE DESERVES IT.
KLANK
WHAT KIND OF PLACE IS THIS GATOYA?
TMP

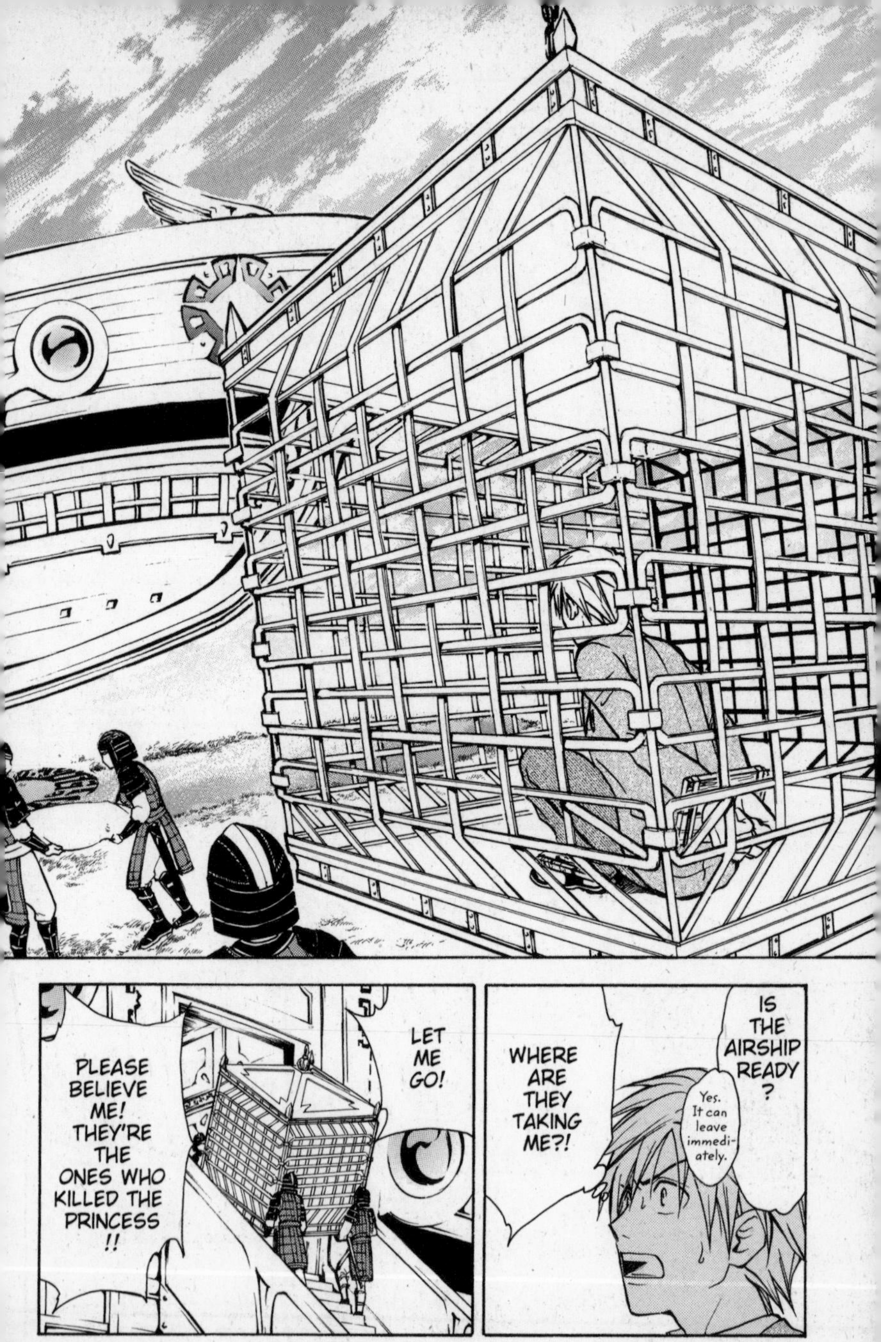
IS THE AIRSHIP READY?
Yes. It can leave immediately.
WHERE ARE THEY TAKING ME?!
LET ME GO!
PLEASE BELIEVE ME! THEY'RE THE ONES WHO KILLED THE PRINCESS!!

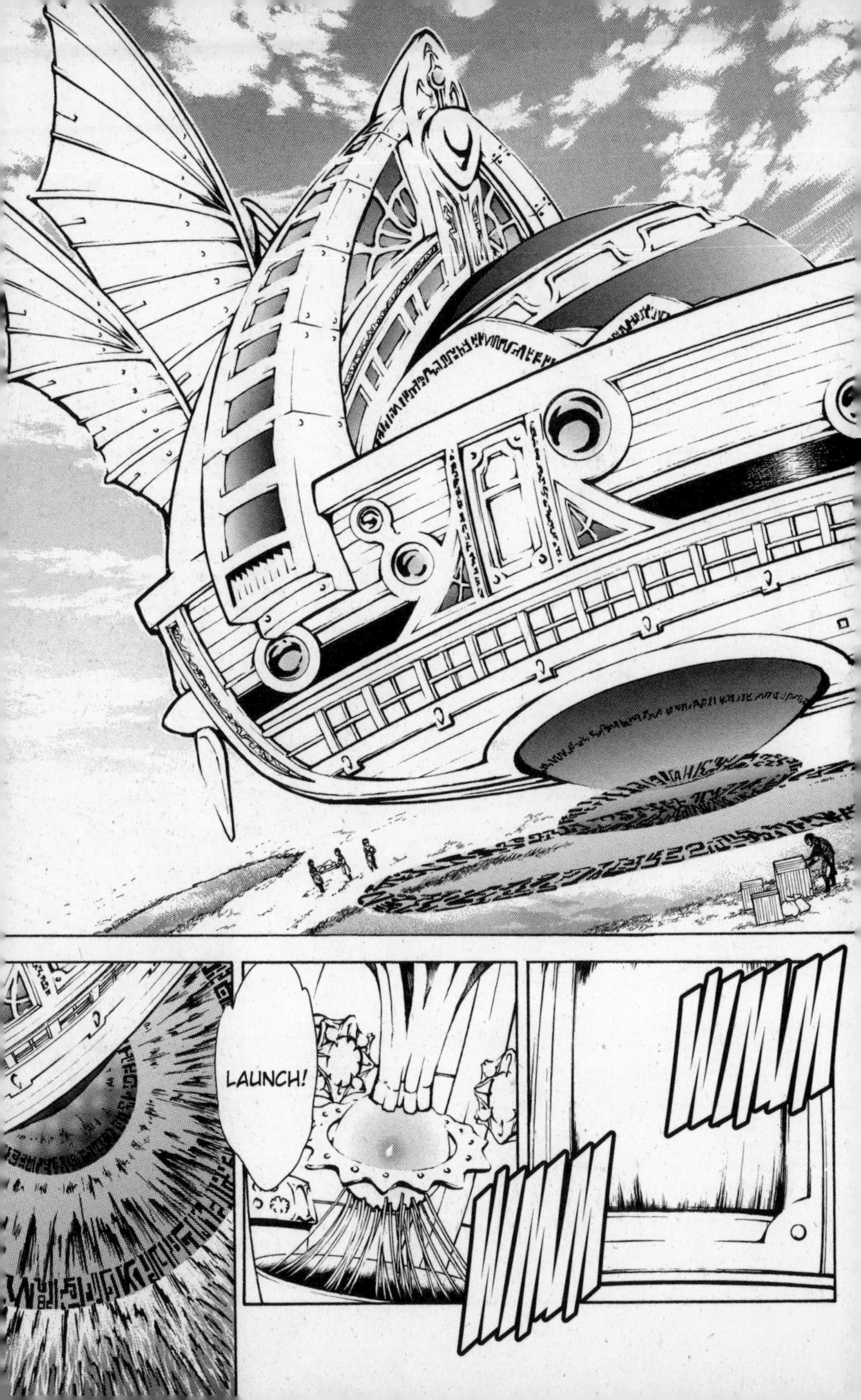
LAUNCH!
WMMM
WMMM

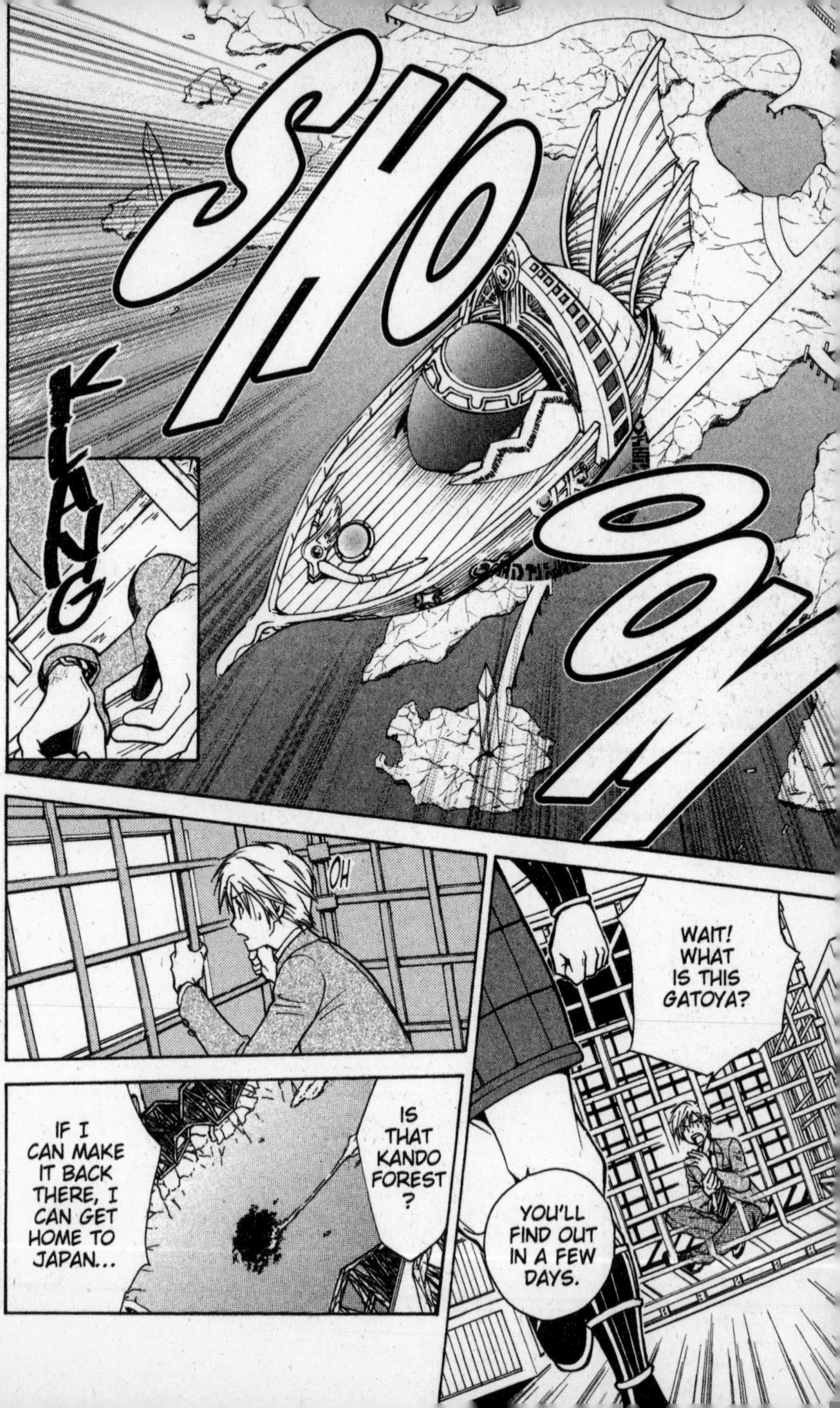
SHOOOM
KLANG
WAIT! WHAT IS THIS GATOYA?
YOU'LL FIND OUT IN A FEW DAYS.
OH
IS THAT KANDO FOREST?
IF I CAN MAKE IT BACK THERE, I CAN GET HOME TO JAPAN...

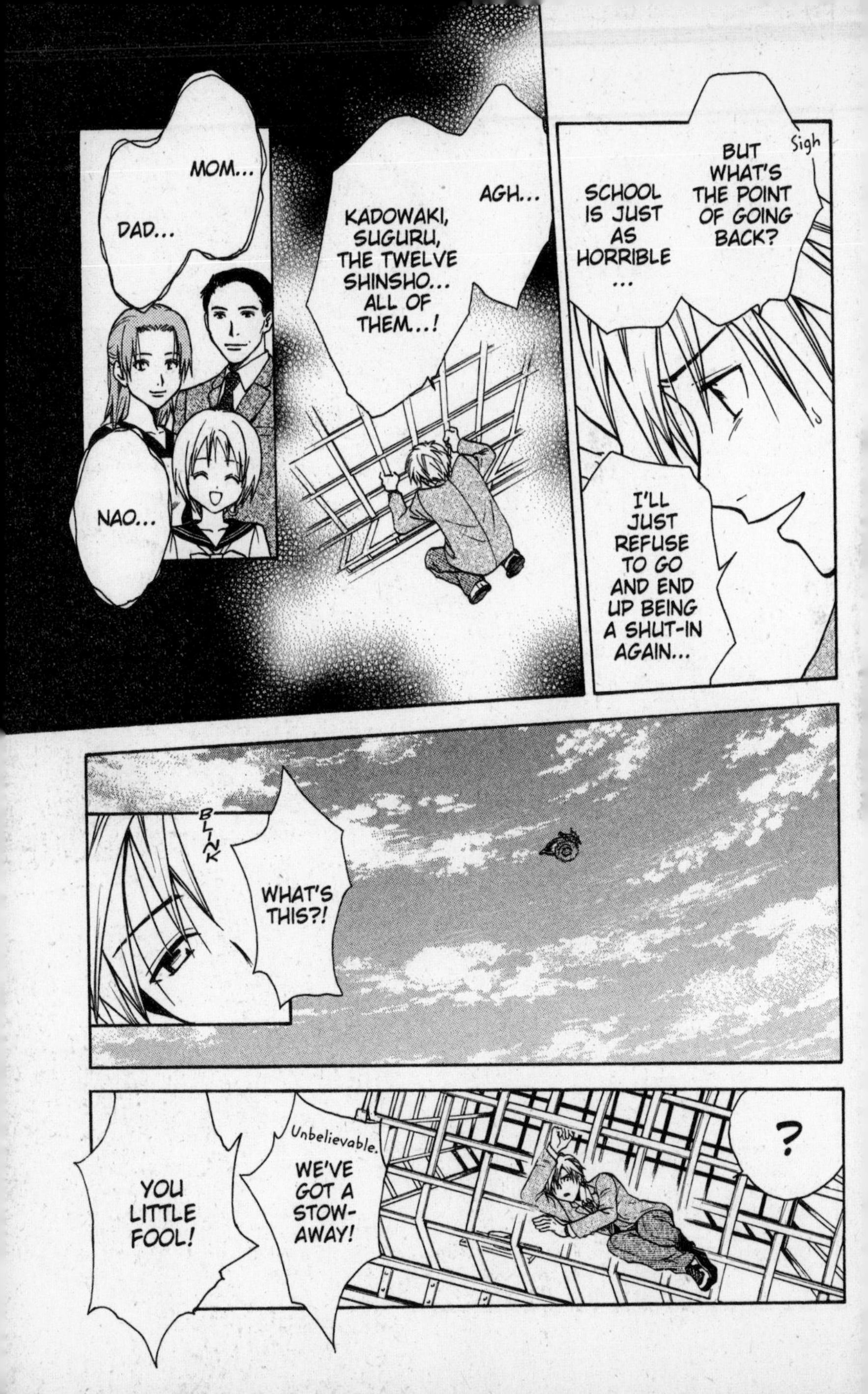
Sigh
BUT WHAT'S THE POINT OF GOING BACK?
SCHOOL IS JUST AS HORRIBLE...
I'LL JUST REFUSE TO GO AND END UP BEING A SHUT-IN AGAIN...
AGH...
KADOWAKI, SUGURU, THE TWELVE SHINSHO... ALL OF THEM...!
MOM...
DAD...
NAO...
BLINK
WHAT'S THIS?!
?
Unbelievable.
WE'VE GOT A STOW-AWAY!
YOU LITTLE FOOL!

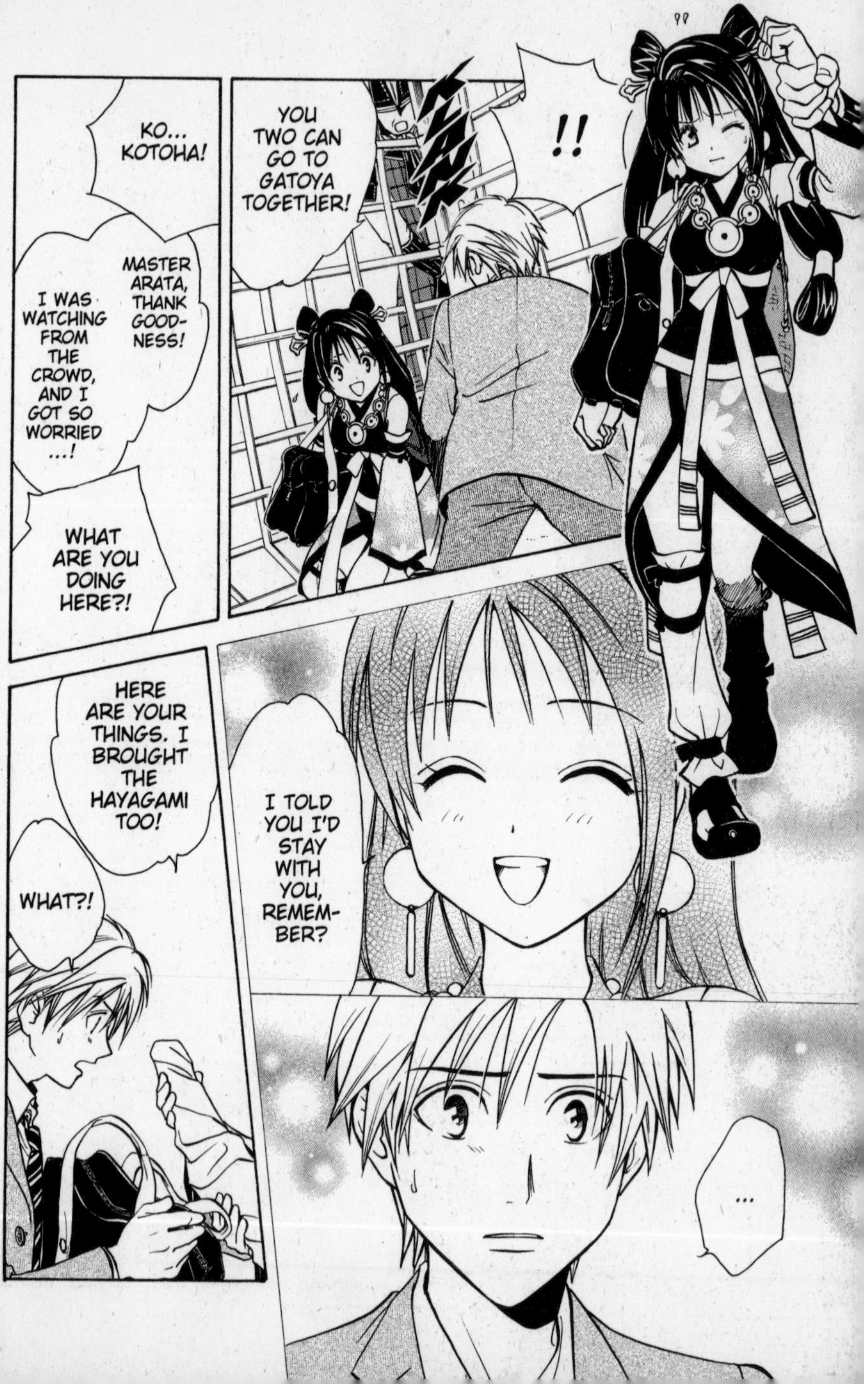

!!
YOU TWO CAN GO TO GATOYA TOGETHER!
KO... KOTOHA!
MASTER ARATA, THANK GOODNESS!
I WAS WATCHING FROM THE CROWD, AND I GOT SO WORRIED ...!
WHAT ARE YOU DOING HERE?!
I TOLD YOU I'D STAY WITH YOU, REMEMBER?
...
HERE ARE YOUR THINGS. I BROUGHT THE HAYAGAMI TOO!
WHAT?!

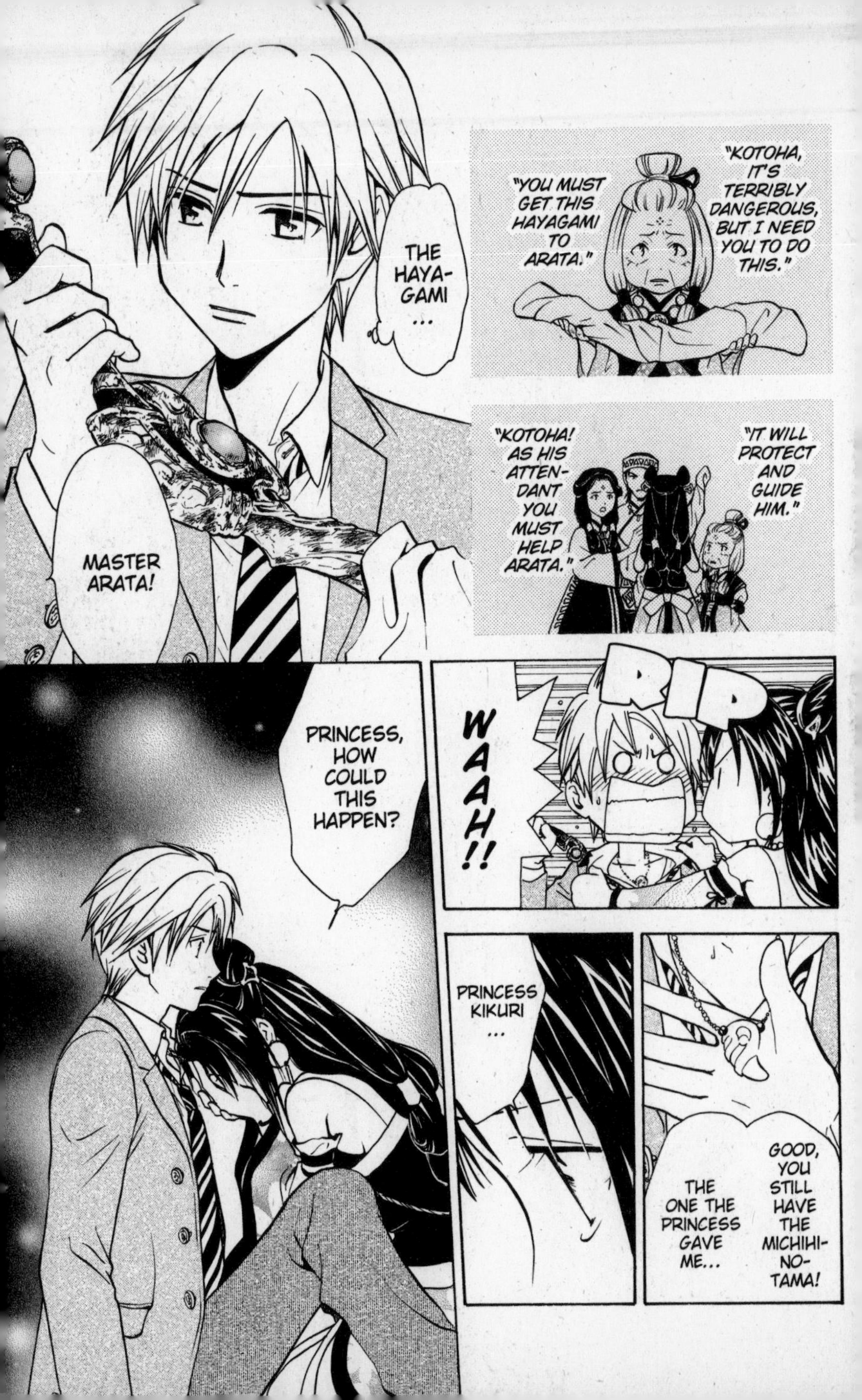
"KOTOHA, IT'S TERRIBLY DANGEROUS, BUT I NEED YOU TO DO THIS."
"YOU MUST GET THIS HAYAGAMI TO ARATA."
"IT WILL PROTECT AND GUIDE HIM."
"KOTOHA! AS HIS ATTENDANT YOU MUST HELP ARATA."
THE HAYAGAMI...
MASTER ARATA!
RIP
WAAAH!!
GOOD, YOU STILL HAVE THE MICHIHI-NO-TAMA!
THE ONE THE PRINCESS GAVE ME...
PRINCESS KIKURI...
PRINCESS, HOW COULD THIS HAPPEN?

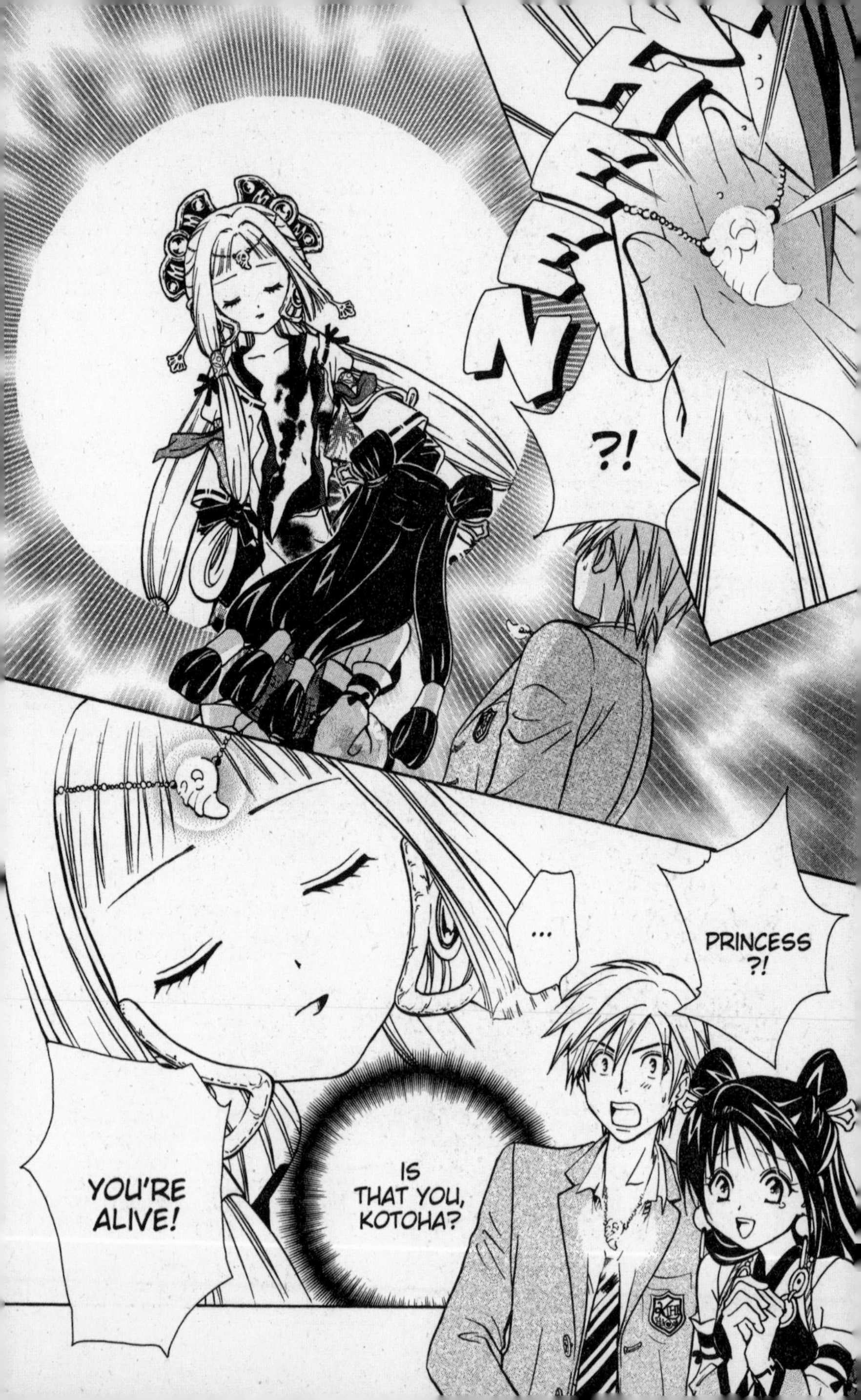
?!
PRINCESS ?!
...
IS THAT YOU, KOTOHA?
YOU'RE ALIVE!

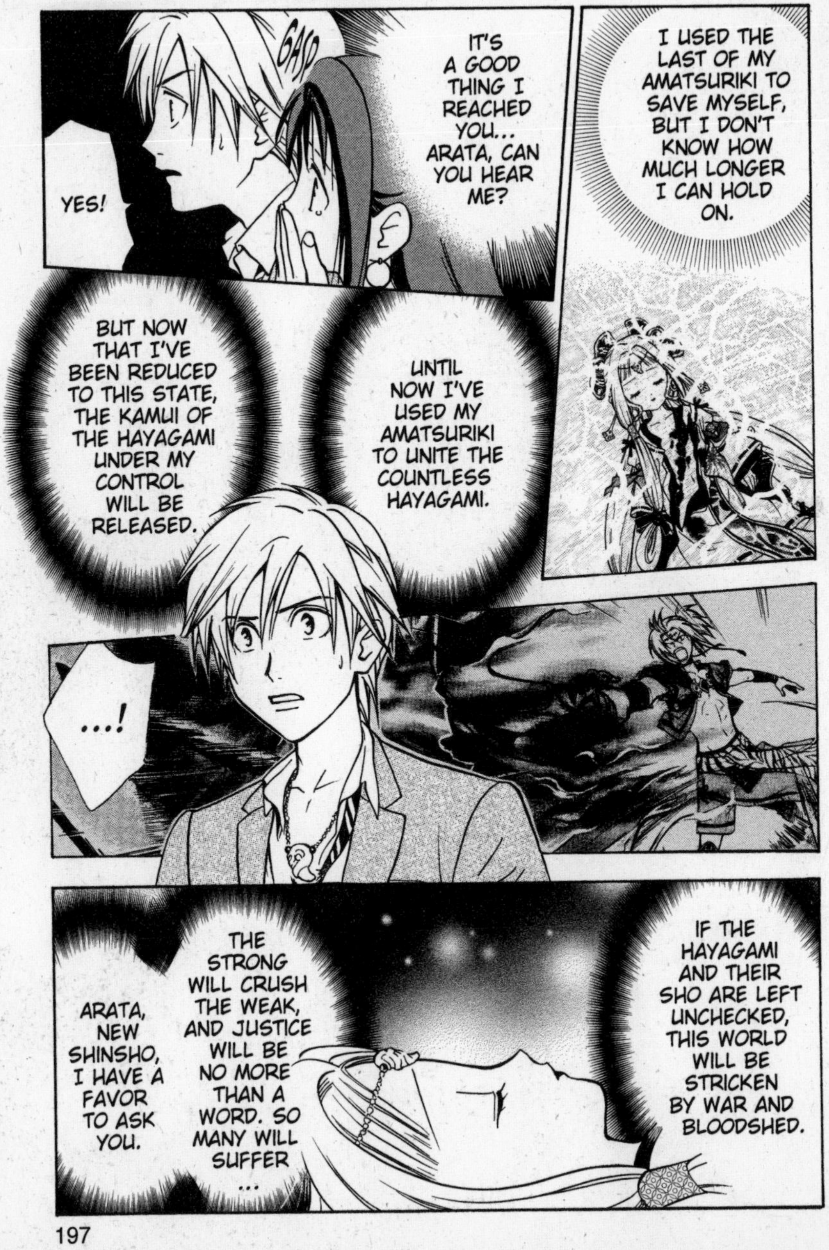
I USED THE LAST OF MY AMATSURIKI TO SAVE MYSELF, BUT I DON'T KNOW HOW MUCH LONGER I CAN HOLD ON.
IT'S A GOOD THING I REACHED YOU... ARATA, CAN YOU HEAR ME?
YES!
UNTIL NOW I'VE USED MY AMATSURIKI TO UNITE THE COUNTLESS HAYAGAMI.
BUT NOW THAT I'VE BEEN REDUCED TO THIS STATE, THE KAMUI OF THE HAYAGAMI UNDER MY CONTROL WILL BE RELEASED.
...!
IF THE HAYAGAMI AND THEIR SHO ARE LEFT UNCHECKED, THIS WORLD WILL BE STRICKEN BY WAR AND BLOODSHED.
THE STRONG WILL CRUSH THE WEAK, AND JUSTICE WILL BE NO MORE THAN A WORD. SO MANY WILL SUFFER ...
ARATA, NEW SHINSHO, I HAVE A FAVOR TO ASK YOU.

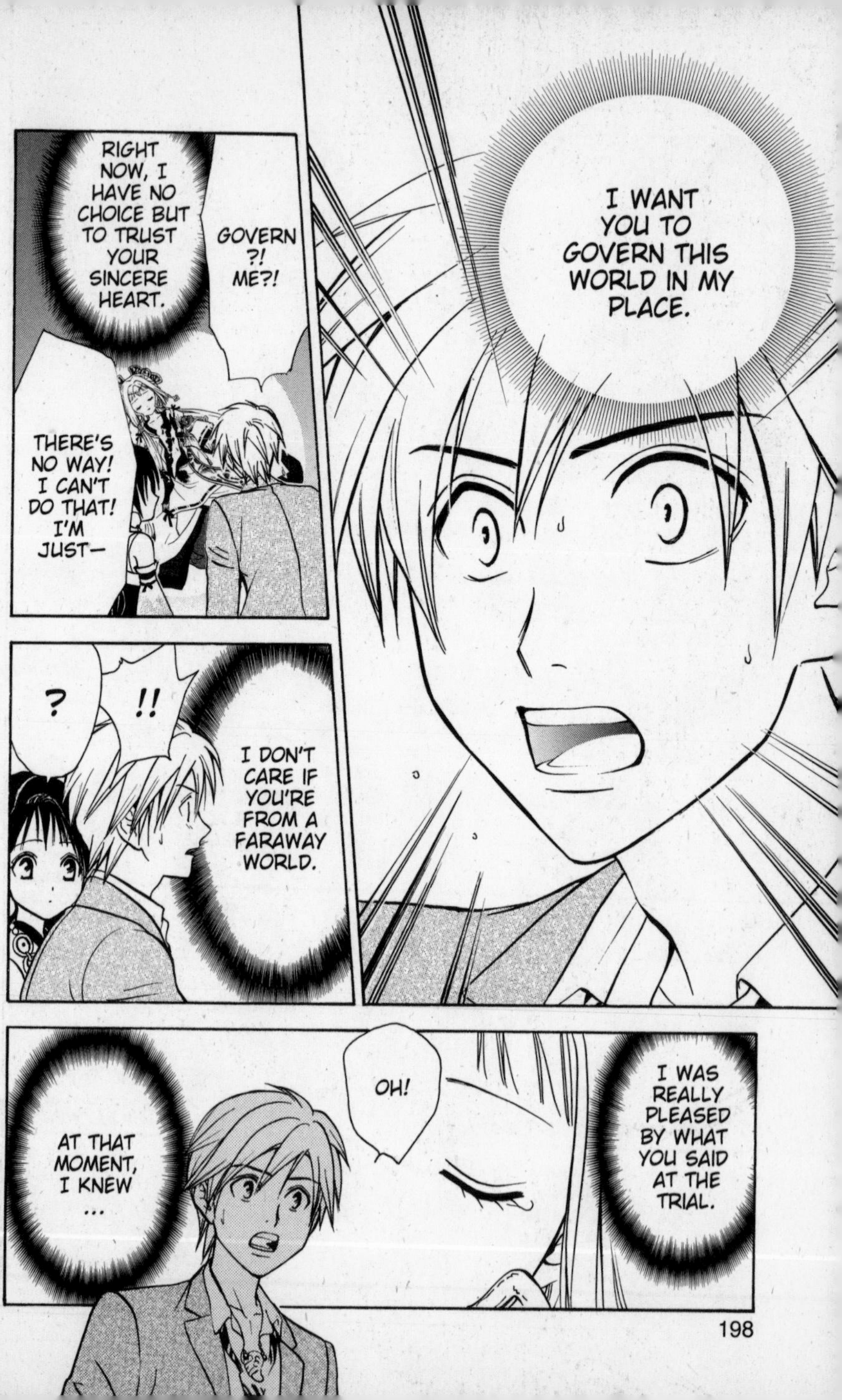
I WANT YOU TO GOVERN THIS WORLD IN MY PLACE.
GOVERN?! ME?!
RIGHT NOW, I HAVE NO CHOICE BUT TO TRUST YOUR SINCERE HEART.
THERE'S NO WAY! I CAN'T DO THAT! I'M JUST—
I DON'T CARE IF YOU'RE FROM A FARAWAY WORLD.
!!
?
I WAS REALLY PLEASED BY WHAT YOU SAID AT THE TRIAL.
OH!
AT THAT MOMENT, I KNEW ...

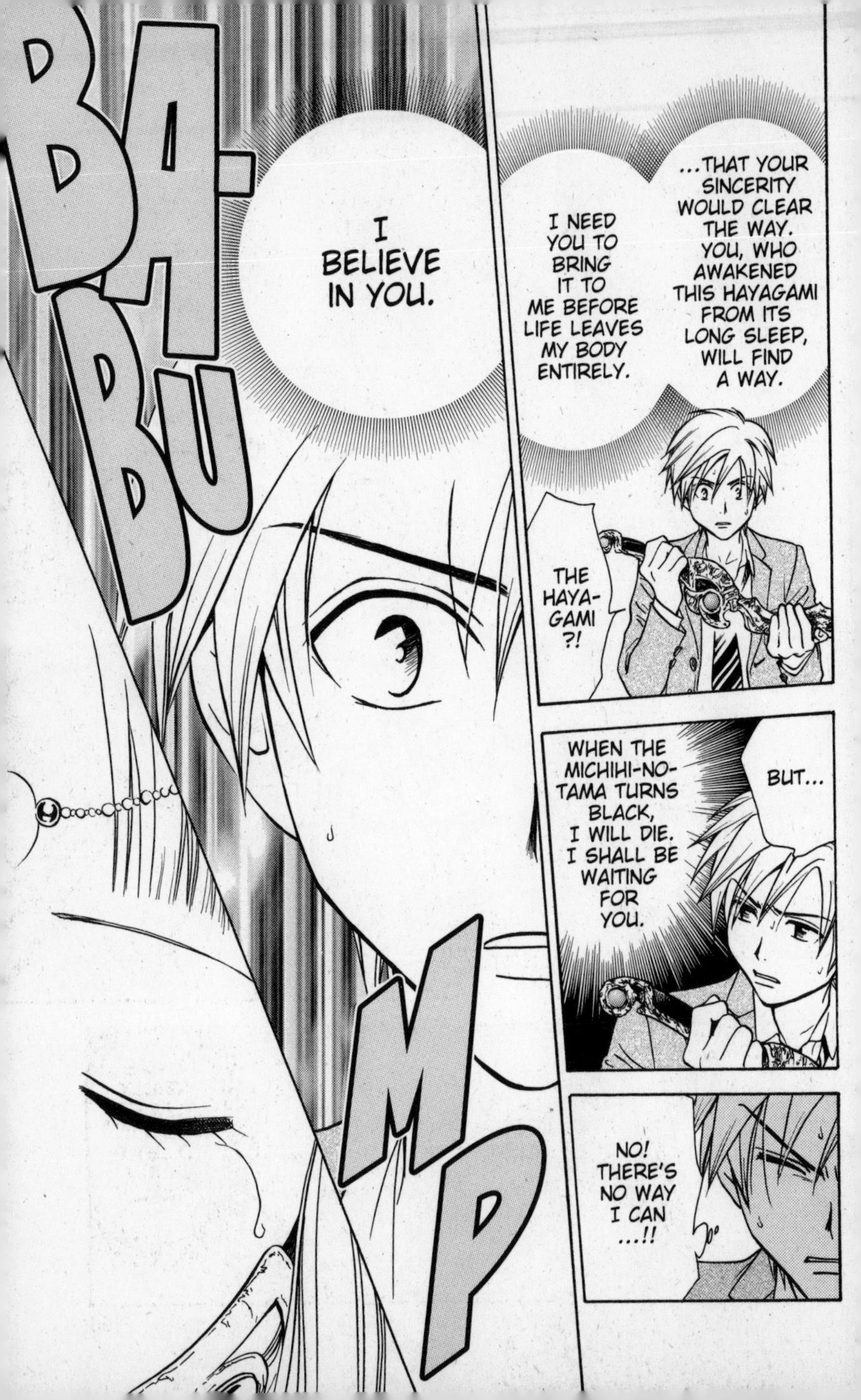
...THAT YOUR SINCERITY WOULD CLEAR THE WAY. YOU, WHO AWAKENED THIS HAYAGAMI FROM ITS LONG SLEEP, WILL FIND A WAY.
I NEED YOU TO BRING IT TO ME BEFORE LIFE LEAVES MY BODY ENTIRELY.
THE HAYA-GAMI ?!
BUT...
WHEN THE MICHIHI-NO-TAMA TURNS BLACK, I WILL DIE. I SHALL BE WAITING FOR YOU.
NO! THERE'S NO WAY I CAN ...!!
I BELIEVE IN YOU.
BA-BUMP

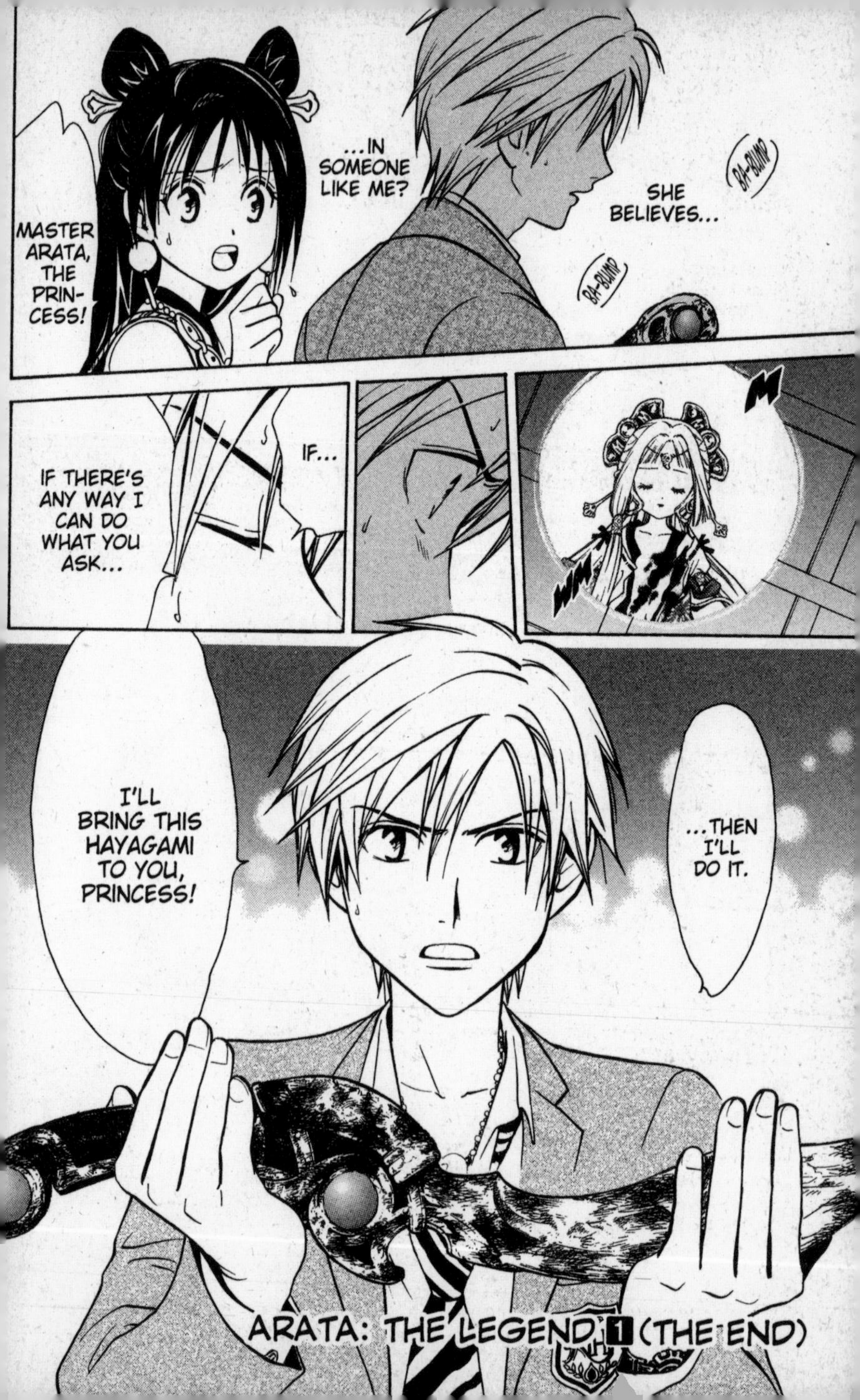
SHE BELIEVES...
BA-BUMP
BA-BUMP
...IN SOMEONE LIKE ME?
MASTER ARATA, THE PRIN-CESS!
M
WM
IF...
IF THERE'S ANY WAY I CAN DO WHAT YOU ASK...
...THEN I'LL DO IT.
I'LL BRING THIS HAYAGAMI TO YOU, PRINCESS!
ARATA: THE LEGEND 1 (THE END)

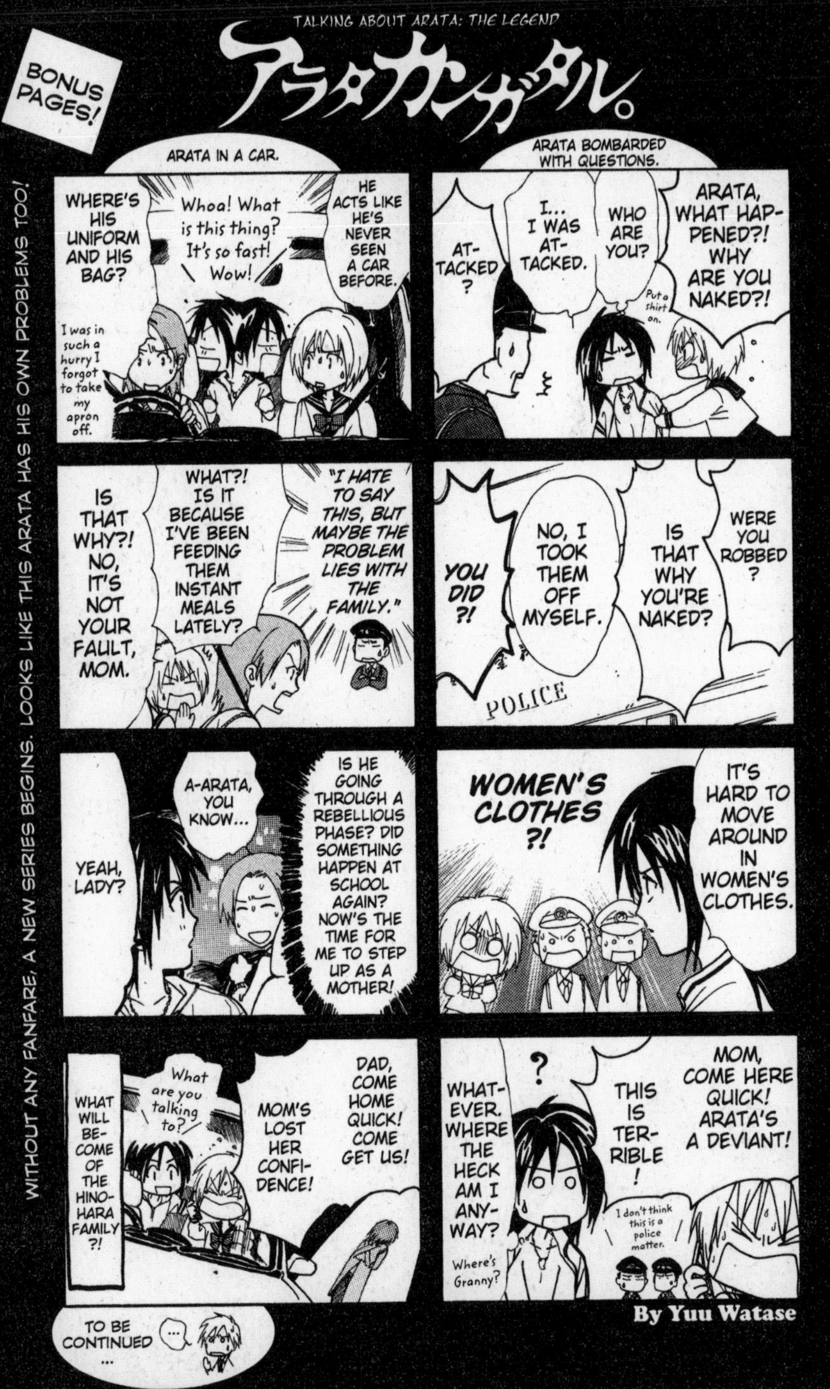
TALKING ABOUT ARATA: THE LEGEND
アラタカンガタル。
BONUS PAGES!
ARATA BOMBARDED WITH QUESTIONS.
ARATA, WHAT HAPPENED?! WHY ARE YOU NAKED?!
Put a shirt on.
WHO ARE YOU?
I... I WAS ATTACKED.
ATTACKED?
WERE YOU ROBBED?
IS THAT WHY YOU'RE NAKED?
NO, I TOOK THEM OFF MYSELF.
YOU DID?!
POLICE
IT'S HARD TO MOVE AROUND IN WOMEN'S CLOTHES.
WOMEN'S CLOTHES?!
MOM, COME HERE QUICK! ARATA'S A DEVIANT!
THIS IS TERRIBLE!
WHATEVER. WHERE THE HECK AM I ANYWAY?
?
I don't think this is a police matter.
Where's Granny?
ARATA IN A CAR.
HE ACTS LIKE HE'S NEVER SEEN A CAR BEFORE.
Whoa! What is this thing? It's so fast! Wow!
WHERE'S HIS UNIFORM AND HIS BAG?
I was in such a hurry I forgot to take my apron off.
"I HATE TO SAY THIS, BUT MAYBE THE PROBLEM LIES WITH THE FAMILY."
WHAT?! IS IT BECAUSE I'VE BEEN FEEDING THEM INSTANT MEALS LATELY?
IS THAT WHY?! NO, IT'S NOT YOUR FAULT, MOM.
IS HE GOING THROUGH A REBELLIOUS PHASE? DID SOMETHING HAPPEN AT SCHOOL AGAIN? NOW'S THE TIME FOR ME TO STEP UP AS A MOTHER!
A-ARATA, YOU KNOW...
YEAH, LADY?
DAD, COME HOME QUICK! COME GET US!
MOM'S LOST HER CONFIDENCE!
What are you talking to?
WHAT WILL BECOME OF THE HINOHARA FAMILY?!
TO BE CONTINUED...
...
WITHOUT ANY FANFARE, A NEW SERIES BEGINS. LOOKS LIKE THIS ARATA HAS HIS OWN PROBLEMS TOO!
By Yuu Watase

ARATA: THE LEGEND

アラタカンガタリ

CELEBRATING THE RELEASE OF VOLUME 1!

CONGRATULATIONS ON THE RELEASE OF VOLUME 1!

VOLUME 1 INCLUDES (Bonus!) THE ADVENTURES OF MY PERSONAL FAVORITE, THE BLACK-HAIRED ARATA. I HOPE YOU'LL ALL BUY IT AND READ IT. I'M GOING TO KEEP WORKING HARD ON ARATA!

By Mineri

Wow! It's Arata in a school uniform!
Actually, you may soon see him like that, so stay with us.
My assistants drew the following cartoons. Thanks, everyone!
Thank goodness I was able to fill all the pages!

I'm pooped...

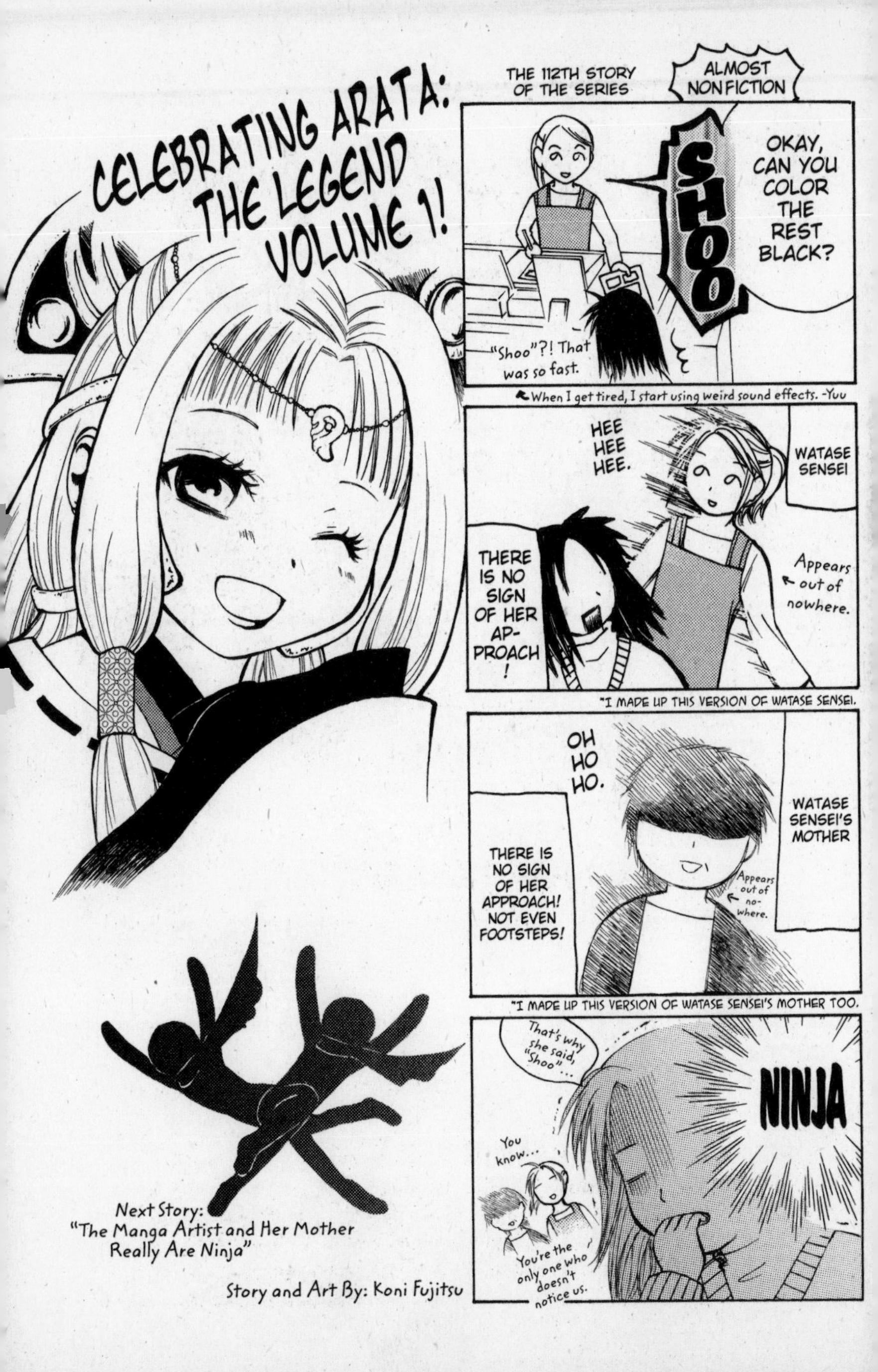

ALMOST NONFICTION
THE 112TH STORY OF THE SERIES
OKAY, CAN YOU COLOR THE REST BLACK?
SHOO
"Shoo"?! That was so fast.
When I get tired, I start using weird sound effects. -Yuu
WATASE SENSEI
Appears out of nowhere.
HEE HEE HEE.
THERE IS NO SIGN OF HER AP-PROACH!
*I MADE UP THIS VERSION OF WATASE SENSEI.
WATASE SENSEI'S MOTHER
Appears out of no-where.
OH HO HO.
THERE IS NO SIGN OF HER APPROACH! NOT EVEN FOOTSTEPS!
*I MADE UP THIS VERSION OF WATASE SENSEI'S MOTHER TOO.
NINJA
That's why she said, "Shoo"...
You know...
You're the only one who doesn't notice us.
CELEBRATING ARATA: THE LEGEND VOLUME 1!
Next Story:
"The Manga Artist and Her Mother Really Are Ninja"
Story and Art By: Koni Fujitsu

STORIES FROM THE ASSISTANTS OF *ARATA: THE LEGEND*

THE FEMALE CHARACTERS ARE POPULAR IN THE WORKPLACE.

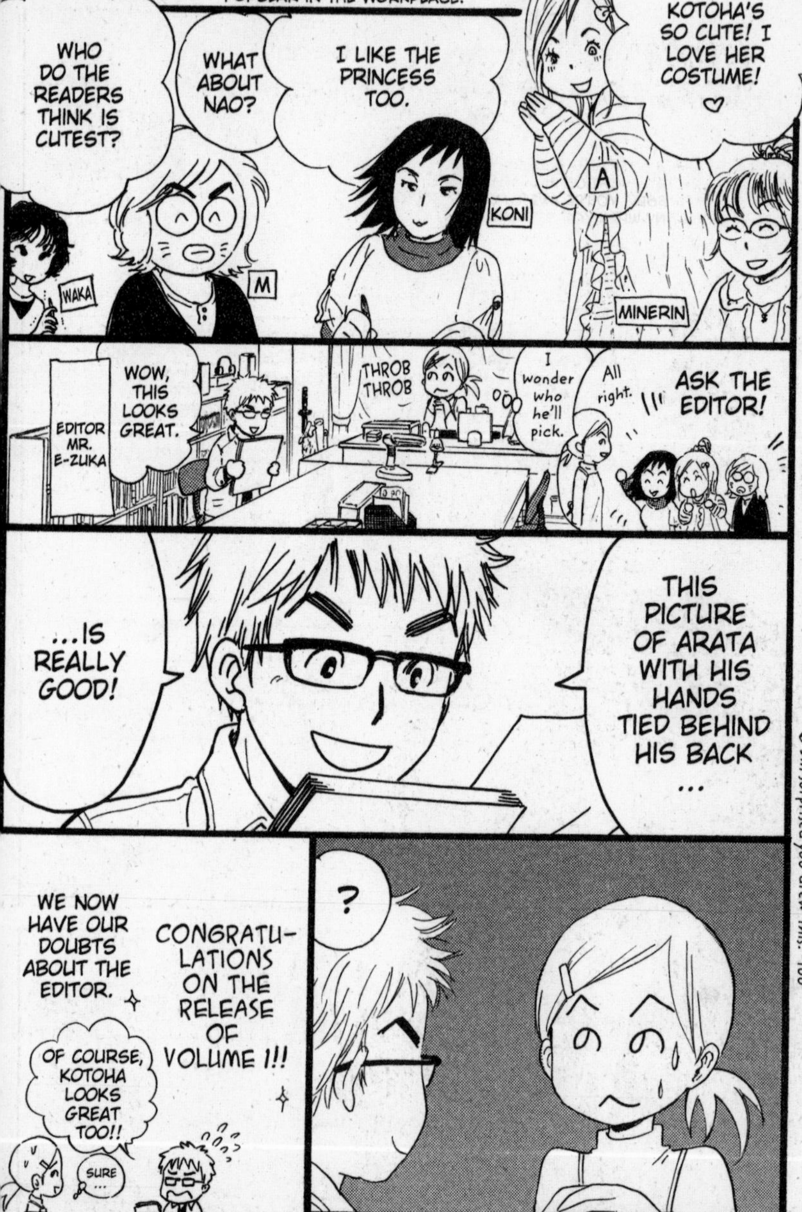
KOTOHA'S SO CUTE! I LOVE HER COSTUME! ♡
A
MINERIN
I LIKE THE PRINCESS TOO.
KONI
WHAT ABOUT NAO?
M
WHO DO THE READERS THINK IS CUTEST?
WAKA
ASK THE EDITOR!
All right.
I wonder who he'll pick.
THROB THROB
WOW, THIS LOOKS GREAT.
EDITOR MR. E-ZUKA
THIS PICTURE OF ARATA WITH HIS HANDS TIED BEHIND HIS BACK...
...IS REALLY GOOD!
?
CONGRATU-LATIONS ON THE RELEASE OF VOLUME 1!!
WE NOW HAVE OUR DOUBTS ABOUT THE EDITOR.
OF COURSE, KOTOHA LOOKS GREAT TOO!!
SURE...

← I'm surprised you drew this. -Yuu

WE'LL GO ALL OUT IN VOLUME 2 AS WELL!! (ALL THE ASSISTANTS)

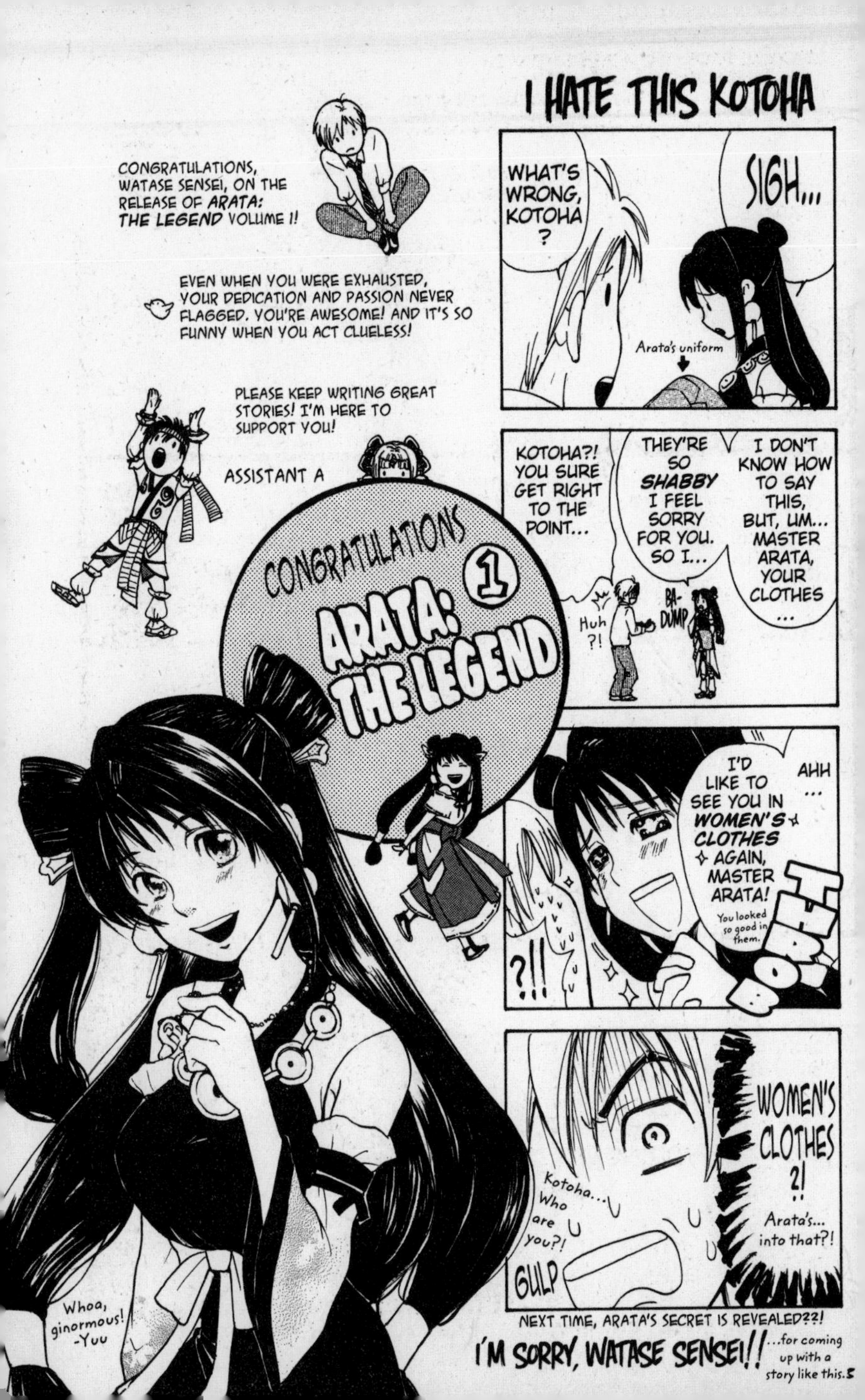
I HATE THIS KOTOHA
SIGH...
WHAT'S WRONG, KOTOHA?
Arata's uniform
I DON'T KNOW HOW TO SAY THIS, BUT, UM... MASTER ARATA, YOUR CLOTHES...
THEY'RE SO *SHABBY* I FEEL SORRY FOR YOU. SO I...
BA-DUMP
KOTOHA?! YOU SURE GET RIGHT TO THE POINT...
Huh?!
AHH...
THROB
I'D LIKE TO SEE YOU IN *WOMEN'S CLOTHES* AGAIN, MASTER ARATA!
You looked so good in them.
?!!
WOMEN'S CLOTHES?!
Arata's... into that?!
Kotoha... Who are you?!
GULP
NEXT TIME, ARATA'S SECRET IS REVEALED??!
I'M SORRY, WATASE SENSEI!! ...for coming up with a story like this.
5
CONGRATULATIONS, WATASE SENSEI, ON THE RELEASE OF *ARATA: THE LEGEND* VOLUME 1!
EVEN WHEN YOU WERE EXHAUSTED, YOUR DEDICATION AND PASSION NEVER FLAGGED. YOU'RE AWESOME! AND IT'S SO FUNNY WHEN YOU ACT CLUELESS!
PLEASE KEEP WRITING GREAT STORIES! I'M HERE TO SUPPORT YOU!
ASSISTANT A
CONGRATULATIONS 1
ARATA: THE LEGEND
Whoa, ginormous! -Yuu

This story began with me wanting to write about a boy's journey.
I'd worry about things like genre and setting later. I just wanted to
create a character that would feel natural for me to write about.
I didn't care where the story took place as long as he could grow
and change there. It ended up being a fantasy world. That made the
drawings a little more complicated than I'd have liked, but if the
people who read this story can follow the adventures of Arata and
empathize with him as he grows and changes, I will be very happy.
That is my wish as I write this. I hope you enjoy it.

–YUU WATASE

AUTHOR BIO

Born March 5 in Osaka, Yuu Watase debuted in the *Shôjo Comic* manga anthology
in 1989. She won the 43rd Shogakukan Manga Award with *Ceres: Celestial Legend*.
One of her most famous works is *Fushigi Yûgi*, a series that has inspired the prequel
Fushigi Yûgi: Genbu Kaiden. In 2008, *Arata: The Legend* started serialization in
Shonen Sunday.

ARATA: THE LEGEND

Volume 1

Shonen Sunday Edition

Story and Art by Yuu WATASE

© 2009 Yuu WATASE/Shogakukan
All rights reserved.
Original Japanese edition "ARATAKANGATARI"
published by SHOGAKUKAN Inc.

English Adaptation: Lance Caselman
Translation: JN Productions
Touch-up Art & Lettering: Rina Mapa
Design: Frances O. Liddell
Editor: Amy Yu

VP, Production: Alvin Lu
VP, Sales & Product Marketing: Gonzalo Ferreyra
VP, Creative: Linda Espinosa
Publisher: Hyoe Narita

Printed in the U.S.A.

Published by VIZ Media, LLC
P.O. Box 77010
San Francisco, CA 94107

10 9 8 7 6 5 4 3 2 1
First printing, March 2010

PARENTAL ADVISORY
ARATA: THE LEGEND is rated T for
Teen and is recommended for ages
13 and up. This volume contains
fantasy violence.
ratings.viz.com

www.viz.com

WWW.SHONENSUNDAY.COM

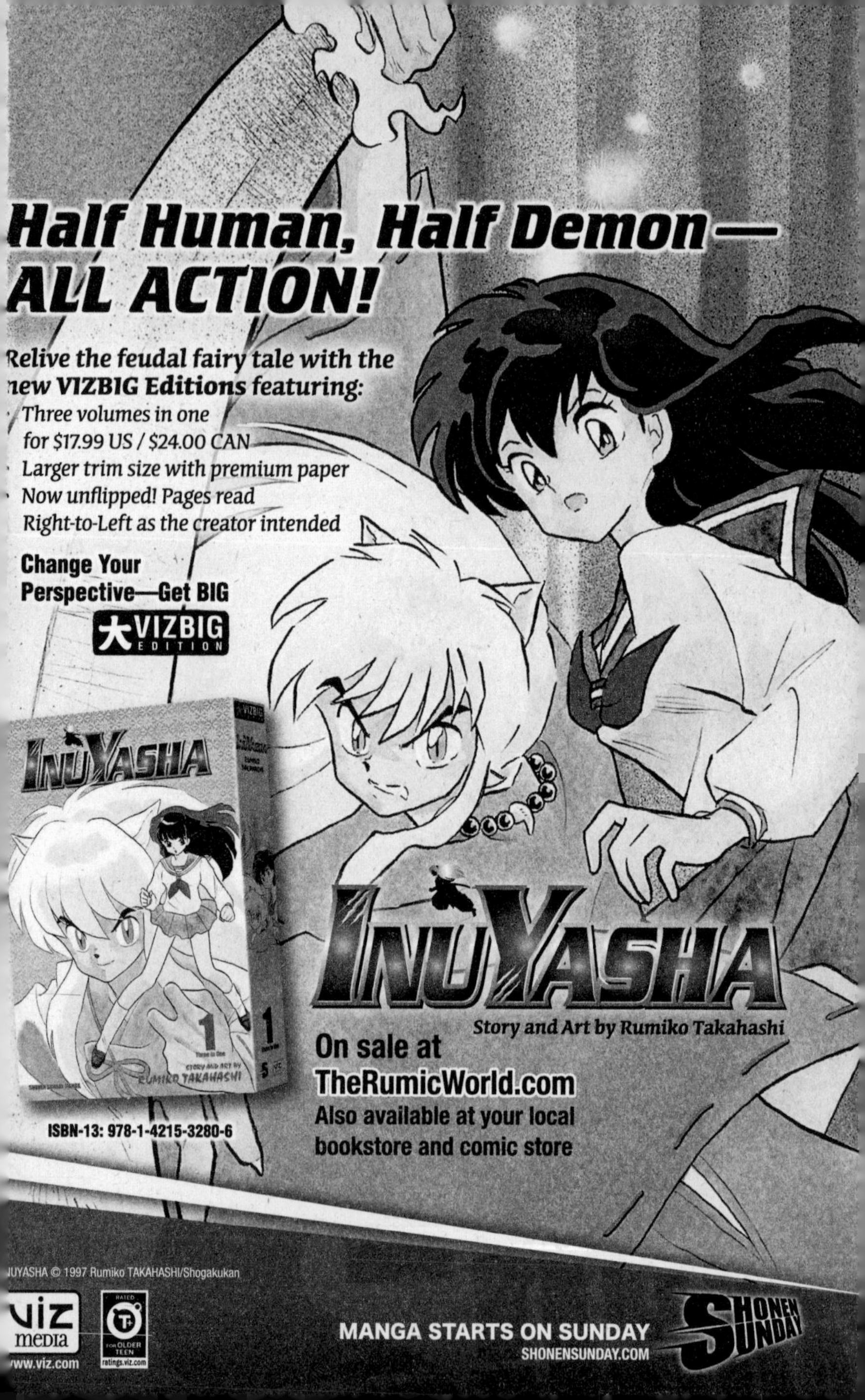

Half Human, Half Demon—
ALL ACTION!
Relive the feudal fairy tale with the new VIZBIG Editions featuring:
• Three volumes in one for $17.99 US / $24.00 CAN
• Larger trim size with premium paper
• Now unflipped! Pages read Right-to-Left as the creator intended
Change Your Perspective—Get BIG
大 VIZBIG EDITION
INUYASHA
ISBN-13: 978-1-4215-3280-6
INUYASHA
Story and Art by Rumiko Takahashi
On sale at TheRumicWorld.com
Also available at your local bookstore and comic store
INUYASHA © 1997 Rumiko TAKAHASHI/Shogakukan
viz media
www.viz.com
RATED T+ FOR OLDER TEEN
ratings.viz.com
MANGA STARTS ON SUNDAY
SHONENSUNDAY.COM
SHONEN SUNDAY